AMER

A Multicultu
for Developmental Writers

AMERICAS

A Multicultural Reader
for Developmental Writers

Neil Grill
Bronx Community College

Bernard Witlieb
Bronx Community College

McGraw-Hill, Inc.

New York   St. Louis   San Francisco   Auckland   Bogotá   Caracas
Lisbon   London   Madrid   Mexico   Milan   Montreal   New Delhi
Paris   San Juan   Singapore   Sydney   Tokyo   Toronto

This book was developed by STEVEN PENSINGER, Inc.

Americas
A Multicultural Reader for Developmental Writers

2 3 4 5 6 7 8 9 0 DOC DOC 9 0 9 8 7 6 5 4 3 2

ISBN 0-07-024820-6

This book was set in Times Roman by General Graphic Services, Inc.
The editors were Steve Pensinger and Tom Holton;
the designer was Caliber/Phoenix Color Corporation;
the production supervisor was Friederich W. Schulte.
The photo editor was Anne Manning;
the photo researcher was Rita Geffert.
R. R. Donnelly & Sons Company was printer and binder.

Library of Congress Cataloging-in-Publication Data

Grill, Neil, (date).
    Americas: a multicultural reader for developmental writers / Neil
Grill, Bernard Witlieb
        p.   cm.
    Includes index.
    ISBN 0-07-024820-6
    1. Readers—United States.   2. United States—Civilization—
Problems, exercises, etc.   3. English language—Grammar—1950-
4. English language—Rhetoric.   5. College readers.   I. Witlieb,
Bernard, (date).   II. Title.
PE1127.H5G75   1992   91-34486
428.6′4—dc20

PERMISSIONS/ ACKNOWLEDGMENTS

Arias Sanchez, Oscar. *Only Peace Can Write the New History.* Nobel lecture, December 11, 1987. © The Nobel Foundation 1987. Excerpted by permission.

Armstrong, Neil, Michael Collins, Edwin E. Aldrin, Jr., written with Gene Farmer and Dora Jean Hamblin. *First on the Moon.* Published by Little, Brown & Company, 1970. Copyright © 1970. Excerpted by permission.

Atwood, Margaret. "True North." First published in *Saturday Night,* January 1987. © 1987 by Margaret Atwood. Reprinted by permission of Margaret Atwood.

Borges, Jose Luis, with Margaret Guerrero. *The Book of Imaginary Beings,* rev. enl. and trans. Norman Thomas di Giovanni. Translation copyright © 1969 by Jorge Luis Borges and Norman Thomas di Giovanni. Excerpted by permission of the publisher, Dutton, an imprint of New American Library, a division of Penguin Books USA Inc.

Bowen, Catherine Drinker. *Miracle at Philadelphia: The Story of the Constitutional Convention, May to September 1787.* Copyright © 1966 by Catherine Drinker Bowen. Excerpted by permission of Little, Brown & Co.

Carson, Rachel. "A Fable for Tomorrow" from *Silent Spring.* Copyright © 1962 by Rachel L. Carson. Reprinted by permission of Houghton Mifflin Co.

Chen, Jack. *The Chinese of America: From the Beginnings to the Present.* Copyright © 1980 by Jack Chen. Reprinted by permission of HarperCollins Publisher.

Columbus, Christopher. *The Log of Christopher Columbus,* trans. Robert H. Fuson. Copyright © 1987 by Robert H. Fuson. Published by International Marine/TAB Books, a division of McGraw-Hill, Blue Ridge Summit, Pennsylvania.

Donnan, Elizabeth. *Documents Illustrative of the History of the Slave Trade to America: Vol I, 1441–1700.* Originally published 1930 by Carnegie Institute of Washington as publication no. 409, document no. 117. Excerpted by permission of Carnegie Institute of Washington.

Douglass, Frederick. "What, to the American Slave, is Your Fourth of July?" from *The Frederick Douglass Papers: Series One: Speeches, Debates, and Interviews,* ed. John W. Blassingame, vol. 2: 1847–1854. Excerpted by permission of Yale University Press.

Momaday, N. Scott. *The Way to Rainy Mountain*. © 1969 The University of New Mexico Press. Excerpted by permission of The University of New Mexico Press.

Moreno, Elsa M., Nestor Suarez Ojeda, and Ciro de Quadros. "Children of Latin America and the Caribbean" from *World Health,* October 1987. Excerpted by permission of the World Health Organization, Geneva.

O'Neill, Thomas P., Jr. with William Novak. *Man of the House: The Life and Political Memoirs of Speaker Tip O'Neill.* Copyright © 1987 by Thomas P. O'Neill, Jr. Excerpted by permission of Random House, Inc.

Robinson, Jackie, as told to Alfred Duckett. *I Never Had It Made.* Copyright © 1972 by Jackie Robinson and Alfred Duckett. Excerpted by permission.

Rogers, Will. Radio address of October 25, 1931, published in *Pardon Us, Mr. President!.* Excerpted by permission of the Will Rogers Memorial.

Roosevelt, Eleanor. *The Autobiography of Eleanor Roosevelt.* Copyright © 1961 by Anna Eleanor Roosevelt. Excerpted by permission of HarperCollins Publishers.

Torres, Luis Llorens. *The Cry of Lares,* first published by Editorial Cordillera, San Juan, Puerto Rico, 1967; reprinted in *Obras Completas* (Instituto de Cultura Puertorriqueña, San Juan, 1969) and in *Borinquén: An Anthology of Puerto Rican Literature* ed. Maria Teresa Babin and Stan Steiner (Alfred A. Knopf, 1974). Excerpted by permission.

Valenzuela, Luisa. "A Story About Greenery" from *Strange Things Happen Here,* trans. Helen Lane. © Luisa Valenzuela. All rights reserved.

Walker, Margaret. "Harriet Tubman" from *October Journey.* Originally published in *Phylon, A Journal of Race and Culture* (Atlanta, 1944). Reprinted by permission of Broadside Press.

Wang, An. *Lessons.* Copyright © 1986 by Wang Institute of Graduate Studies. Excerpted by permission of Addison-Wesley Publishing Company.

White, E. B. Essay in *The New Yorker* July 3, 1944. Reprinted in *The Wild Flag* (Houghton Mifflin). Copyright © 1943, 1971 E. B. White. Reprinted by permission of *The New Yorker.*

Wilbur-Cruce, Eva Antonia. *A Beautiful, Cruel Country.* Copyright © 1987. Excerpted by permission of the University of Arizona Press.

Wright, Orville. *The Papers of Wilbur and Orville Wright, 1899–1905,* ed. Marvin W. McFarland. Excerpted by permission of Ayer Company Publishers, Inc., Salem, New Hampshire.

ABOUT THE AUTHORS

NEIL GRILL is Professor of English at Bronx Community College (City University of New York), where he has taught since 1965. He received his Ph.D. in English from New York University in 1970. He has received an NEH (National Endowment for the Humanities) summer seminar fellowship (1978) and a CUNY-Mellon fellowship (literature, criticism, teaching) for community college teachers (1980). His poetry has appeared in more than twenty periodicals in the U.S. and Canada, and he has published articles on Dickens and Keats. He and Bernard Witlieb are coauthors of *Getting Ready for CUNY-WAT* (1991).

BERNARD WITLIEB is Professor of English at Bronx Community College (City University of New York), where he has taught since 1969. He received his Ph.D. in English from New York University in 1969. He has received two NEH summer seminar fellowships (1984, 1988), an NEH postdoctoral fellowship (1972), a CUNY-Mellon fellowship (literature, criticism, teaching) for community college teachers (1980), and a CUNY research award (1973). He is the author of numerous articles on Chaucer, Richard III, and teaching methods. He has also been an editor of *The New York Times Book of the Environment, 1965–1975;* Cuyás *Spanish-English Dictionary;* and the *World Book Encyclopedia Dictionary*. He is coauthor of a forthcoming book on achievements of U.S. women.

TO THE MEMORIES OF

Belle and Leon Grill
and
Samuel Witlieb and Rhoda Albin

CONTENTS

READING UNITS

LETTER TO STUDENTS

Dear Students,

Welcome to *Americas: A Multicultural Reader for Developmental Writers.*

Throughout the world and especially in the Americas, we seek open societies in which people can think, speak, and write as freely as possible. If information is to be properly understood, students must first filter it through their own experience and express it in their own words. We hope that *Americas* relates to the world you are living in and your vision of the future.

Your experience and knowledge are necessary and valued resources in using this book.

This hemisphere's cultural heritage has been enriched and fed by all those who have settled and lived here.

What and where are the Americas?

The Americas is the large area of the world that covers North, Central, and South America. Although many people think of the United States as America (as in "America the Beautiful"), the Americas has a broader meaning and scope.

The area includes Canada, Mexico, and the United States in North America; such nations as Costa Rica, Guatemala, and Honduras in Central America; islands in the Caribbean, such as Puerto Rico and Antigua; and Brazil, Chile, Peru, Venezuela, and other countries in South America. The Americas has many great cities, mountains, rivers, and beautiful and fertile lands. Its greatest resource, however, is its millions of people with diverse cultures, races, and histories.

What do we mean by culture?

You have heard the word *culture* used in biology. But the word also means the whole makeup of a given people or group. Culture may include history, traditions, customs, myths, language, architecture, and religious and ethical beliefs. It may also include art, music, education, food, clothing, and work. Culture affects our feelings about marriage and family life, attitudes toward birth and death, and ideas about war and peace.

What do we mean by multicultural?

The term *multicultural* refers to the diversity of many cultures—how they blend with one another and how they preserve a separate identity. Multicultural suggests a society that respects and cherishes the gifts and efforts of the full variety of its citizens, and offers all groups the opportunity to contribute to and enrich the entire society.

What will you learn from *Americas?*

Americas will introduce you to many people, documents, events, and ideas in the cultures of the region. Your reading will consist of short selections, the best and most original material we could find, chronologically arranged in thematic units from the moment five centuries ago that Columbus met the original settlers.

At the same time, you will have an opportunity to discuss and write about these selections and the ideas in them with clarity and precision.

How will you use *Americas?*

If you turn to the Contents and then skim the book, you will get an idea of what *Americas* contains.

First, you will find an introductory chapter on reading and writing processes. The connection between reading and writing skills will be explained and demonstrated. A sample reading with filled-in responses provides you with a practical guide to using these processes.

Next, you will find nearly fifty readings in nine units arranged by themes. Each unit begins with an introduction and a list of questions *Before You Read* to help you become familiar with the readings and the important people, events, and ideas in the section.

You will read such documents as the Mayflower Compact and the Declaration of Independence, and speeches by Abraham Lincoln, Martin Luther King, Jr., and Oscar Arias. You will find autobiographical selections by Jackie Robinson, Lee Iacocca, and Eleanor Roosevelt. You will witness events at a slave market in seventeenth-century Barbados, the hardships of a pioneer woman on the Plains, and the arrival in Canada of young Frenchwomen seeking husbands. You will get a glimpse into journals kept by Columbus, Meriwether Lewis, and Orville Wright. You will follow Harriet Tubman's escape to freedom and the Kiowa tribe's search for the home of the sun. You will be present at the explosion of the first atomic bomb and the first landing on the moon.

A Quotation Bank follows the nine reading units. You may wish to use these quotations as inspirations for journals, extemporaneous freewriting, letters or dialogues with historical figures, or springboards to essay writing by using them as thesis statements, topic sentences, supporting evidence, or summary sentences.

The Grammar Handbook in the second part of the book offers detailed chapters on sentence structure, verb forms, punctuation, and parts of speech. Each chapter contains explanations of grammar points using clear examples, followed by a variety of exercises. A unique feature of the handbook is that all the examples and exercises are based on the content of the readings.

The last chapter, "Structure: Paragraph and Essay," uses sentences and paragraphs from the readings to illustrate organization and transition patterns.

In this book, grammar is only one part of writing. It is equally important for you to experience writing as a series of steps or processes that can help you express yourself on subjects that invite your interest.

ACKNOWLEDGMENTS

First, we thank Betty Whitford for bringing our idea to the attention of C. Steven Pensinger, who would become our editor at McGraw-Hill.

Next, our gratitude goes to Steve Pensinger himself for his support of *Americas* from its beginning through all the intermediary stages until its publication. His faith in us was matched by intelligence, sensitivity, and kindness. Authors could have no better editor.

Much appreciated assistance came from our production editor Tom Holton, photo editor Anne Manning, copy editor Laura Daly, and the designers of Caliber Design Planning, Inc.

We especially wish to thank Marlene Griffith of Laney College, California, who reviewed the book at a very early point and gave us invaluable suggestions and encouragement. We also thank those who reviewed drafts of the book, providing us with many suggestions and asking many questions that we ourselves would not have thought of. The completed book owes much to the perceptive readings and comments of Evelyn Ashton-Jones, University of Idaho; Jacqueline Costello, St. John's University (New York); Kathy Fitzgerald, University of Utah; Joseph Harris, University of Pittsburgh; Kate Kiefer, Colorado State University; and Daniel Zimmerman, Middlesex County College of New Jersey.

We also would like to express gratitude to several colleagues at Bronx Community College for their ideas and support, including Professors Ulla Dydo who class tested *Americas,* Mal Nickerson who gave us valuable suggestions throughout, Joe Todaro and Geraldine Diallo who contributed to our awareness of multiculturalism, and Daniel Lowenthal and Phyllis Read. We are grateful to Dean Carl Polowczyk who very early on supported our idea of a multicultural project for developmental students. Our appreciation goes also to secretaries Evelyn Schweidel and Carol Zavin for their kind and able assistance.

For their expert and informed advice on matters north and south, we thank Jeffrey Hoffeld, Jerry Kramer, Carole Lapidus, and Karsten Struhl.

Warm appreciation is extended to Malcolm I. Lewin for his legal advice.

Thanks to Diana Hadgis and Paula Schwartz of the library department at Bronx Community College as well as the staffs of: the University of Toronto, the University of Washington, Tulane University, Queens College, Lehman College, the Centro de Estudios Puertorriqueños at Hunter College, CUNY Graduate School, and the New York Public Library. We are grateful to the National Archives in Washington, D.C., and the Museum of Modern Art as well.

We would like to thank our students at Bronx Community College who over the past twenty-five years have taught us much about living and learning together in a multicultural world.

To our children, Simone and Genese, and Andy and Rachel, for their spirited advice and enthusiastic responses.

And love and respect to Sadie Witlieb.

Finally, we have been incredibly blessed with the encouragement, support, humor, and warmth of our wives, Sima Gerber and Ellen Witlieb.

Neil Grill
Bernard Witlieb

AMERICAS

A Multicultural Reader
for Developmental Writers

READING AND WRITING PROCESSES IN *AMERICAS*

Do you enjoy reading? Do you have different attitudes toward reading for school assignments and reading for pleasure? What do you like to read? Do you have any reading habits or patterns?

How do you become familiar with a reading assignment or a new book or article?

Which of the following do you find most helpful in getting into a reading assignment?

a. introduction and preparation by the instructor

b. class or small group discussion

c. recent books, movies, television shows, and articles on the subject you will read about

d. discussion with family, friends, and fellow workers

e. background or introductory material presented in the textbook

All the readings in *Americas* begin with information to introduce you to the persons, events, and ideas to be found in them. Before you begin to read the sample selection that follows, notice the **title** and **author**: "The First Americans" by George deLucenay Leon. Does the title make you curious?

Next, read the **headnote,** which gives background information about the selection. Have you learned anything new about early voyages and explorers?

Now look at **Words to Notice.** This list defines words or expressions that may be unfamiliar to you. Refer to this list as you read.

The last section before the selection is **Read On.** The activities given here ask you to do specific tasks so that you become involved with what you read. For example, jotting down **margin notes** means writing in the margins short comments, questions, reactions, and so on.

When you have finished these activities, you are ready to tackle the reading selection for the first time.

Now read "The First Americans" at your own pace.

THE FIRST AMERICANS

By George deLucenay Leon

"In the beginning" and "Once upon a time" are phrases that quicken our imaginations.

Columbus's 1492 voyage has become part of what "everyone knows." But obviously, people and civilizations of the Americas were there long before Columbus made his "discovery."

There are legends about other voyagers to the Americas: Saint Brendan of Ireland in the sixth century and Madoc of Wales in the twelfth century, for example. The Norse explorer Leif Ericsson also may have sailed to the northern regions of this hemisphere around the year 1000.

One theory holds that at least 50,000 years ago people living in North America traveled to other continents. After many generations, their descendants returned to North America. But the most widely held belief is that brave venturers had reached the Americas by a different route—more than 10,000 years before Columbus.

Who were these people? Where did they come from? How did they get here? This selection from *Explorers of the Americas Before Columbus* gives some answers to these questions.

WORDS TO NOTICE

eventually: after some time

precipitation: snow, hail, rain, and so on

characterized by: described as

extensive: large, widespread

Siberia: the Soviet Union's northernmost region, extending eastward to the
   Bering Sea and the Pacific Ocean

New England: six northeastern states in the United States

Rockies and Cascades: two mountain ranges in the western and northwestern
   part of the United States

massive: large and solid

interglacial: the time between periods of increased glacier formation

bison: buffalo

predators: anyone or anything that seeks to kill or destroy

Bering Strait: narrow waterway between Alaska and Siberia

glaciation: formation of glaciers

game: animals hunted for food

habitation: place or area to live in

Mayans, Aztecs, and Incas: American Indian tribes of Central America, Mexico, and South America

READ ON

1. What do you think of when you read the **title?**

2. While reading this selection for the first time, jot down **margin notes** on
   facts and ideas that interest you.

About 3.5 to 4 million years ago, the climate on earth started to change slowly. 1
The winters gradually grew longer and colder. More snow fell. The snow on
the ground took longer to melt in spring and summer.

   Eventually, snow began to stay on the ground all year round in many 2
places. Over the years it began piling up. The snow was so packed that it
became ice. Year-round snowfields and ice masses increased in size. In places
the ice formed glaciers—huge sheets as much as 2 miles (3 km) thick and
thousands of miles long and wide.

   Eventually, the snowfall began to decrease, and the process reversed. 3
The temperature of the earth warmed up a little. Less precipitation fell, and
the glaciers began to melt and decrease in size.

Then the earth cooled again, causing the glaciers to grow once more. At **4** least three such warming periods—and at least four glacial periods—occurred during the past million years.

The period characterized by extensive movement of ice sheets is called **5** the Pleistocene Epoch, or Ice Age. During the glacial periods, ice covered Siberia, northern Europe, and parts of North America as far south as the Mississippi Valley. Perhaps a third of the earth was covered with ice. New England was under an ice sheet 1 mile (1.6 km) high. Today, you can see signs of this early glacial activity throughout the upper half of the United States.

Glaciers still exist in North America. There are some big glaciers in Alaska **6** and northern Canada, and smaller ones on mountaintops in the Rockies and Cascades. These glaciers increase and decrease in size depending on the amount of snowfall each year, but they show no signs of turning into the massive glaciers of thousands of years ago.

Some scientists believe that the Ice Age has not ended and that we are **7** now in an interglacial period.

During this period, both human beings and animals began moving east. **8** The larger animals, such as mammoths and bison, were probably searching for new grazing grounds; close on their heels were their predators—cave bears, tigers, and humans.

Tribes from Asia eventually migrated to the Chukchi Peninsula, the point **9** of land in Siberia closest to the North American continent. Probably several times over a period of perhaps as long as thirty thousand years, when travel was easiest, they crossed what is now called the Bering Strait to the North American continent.

The animals also crossed the Strait. Mammoths—huge ancestors of el- **10** ephants—were the favorite target of human hunters. A male mammoth weighed 6 or more tons (5,500 kg) and measured 10 to 14 feet (3 to 4 m) at the shoulder. A single mammoth could provide plenty of meat for many families, as well as ivory for tools and weapons. Humans also wore the hides and fur of other animals, and they turned their ivory and bones into needles, spear-heads, and other tools and weapons.

How did humans and animals cross 125 miles (200 km) of water? Quite **11** simply. At the time of the crossing, a land bridge, now called Beringia, existed across the present Bering Strait. The land bridge between Asia and North America was huge, over 1,200 miles (2,000 km) at its widest point; during periods of glaciation, the ocean level was about 450 feet (140 m) lower than it is today. During warming periods, glacial melting raised the level of the oceans and the present Strait covered the land bridge.

With all the game available, the hunters rarely went hungry. Families grew **12** larger. They spread out, covering more and more territory.

Some of the immigrants settled in what is now called the Yukon Territory **13** (in Canada) and Alaska. Others continued south. As each wave of immigrants arrived, they crowded those who had arrived earlier. Then the first wave would move farther south, or the new wave would keep going past the earlier group.

Eventually some people moved all the way east to the eastern coast of   14
North America, from Newfoundland to Florida. Others continued south until they reached Tierra del Fuego, the southernmost tip of South America. Human bones and other evidence of human habitation have been found in Tierra del Fuego that date to as far back as ten thousand years ago.

Scientists believe that people in early societies moved no farther than   15
they had to. This was usually about 17 miles (27 km) per generation. Traveling the 7,000 miles (11,000 km) from Chukchi to the tip of South America at that rate would have taken about four hundred generations, or over eight thousand years.

What happened to the early Americans? Most scientists believe that the   16
people we call Indians or Native Americans are descended from these ancient Asians. The Mayans, Aztecs, and Incas, as well as their descendants, also share these ancestors.

Now that you have finished this first reading, answer the following questions:

a. Did you like anything in the selection?

b. Did you learn anything new from it?

c. Did anything spark your curiosity or imagination?

d. Did you recall anything you already knew?

e. Did you find anything puzzling or unclear?

f. Did you read carefully or skim? Did you read slowly or quickly?

g. Did you disagree with anything?

h. Did you find something you'd like to discuss further with your class or instructor?

i. As you read, did the title become more understandable?

j. Did you refer to the headnote information?

k. Did you refer to Words to Notice?

l. Did the Read On activities help you?

First readings can give you a lot, and some students read their assignments only once. However, most college students find that they need to read their assignments at least twice. Do you read your work a second time? Why is this a good idea?

Did you reread "The First Americans"? If so, what new information or ideas did you get? What did you notice that you didn't see or realize the first time you read it? Did you identify a main idea, specific examples, a conclusion? Did something that was unclear become understandable to you?

All the reading selections in *Americas* are followed by a series of exercises and activities. Look at the ones prepared for "The First Americans."

IN YOUR OWN VOICE

WHAT DOES IT SAY?

1. How large can glaciers be?

2. How many glacial periods have there been over the past million years?

3. Which animals were most hunted by humans?

4. How did the "first Americans" cross the Bering Strait?

5. Which modern people may be descended from these "first Americans"?

WHAT DOES IT MEAN?

1. Why were climate and weather important factors in the first crossing to the Americas?

2. Why did creatures like the mammoth become extinct?

3. Why could the "first Americans" travel more easily as they moved southward?

4. Why do scientists believe that "people in early societies moved no farther than they had to"?

5. Why might it have taken over eight thousand years for the "first Americans" to travel from the northernmost part of North America to the tip of South America?

STYLE AND SENSE

A **paragraph** is a group of related sentences that state and develop one idea.
   Reread paragraph 6 of "The First Americans" and answer the following questions:

1. Which sentence (called the **topic sentence**) states the general idea of the paragraph?

2. What specific facts do you learn about the topic in another sentence of the paragraph?

3. What additional details do you learn about the topic in yet another sentence of the paragraph?

FROM THE TEXT

The building blocks of sentences are **subjects** and **verbs.** A subject tells *who* or *what* the sentence is about and *does* the action of the sentence. A verb expresses the *action* or *state of being* of the subject.

Read the following sentence:

The animals also crossed the Strait.

a. Who or what is the sentence about? (the subject)

b. What did the subject do? (the verb)

WRITE NOW

Do one of the following activities.

1. **Freewrite** on one of the following Writing Suggestions.

2. Make a list of **journalistic questions** for one of the following Writing Suggestions.

WRITING SUGGESTIONS

1. Imagine that you are an original settler in the Americas. Narrate to your grandchild the story of your journey to this hemisphere.

2. Tell why the original settlers to the Americas made their journey.

3. Describe the feelings of the original settlers as they observed the land, animals, and climate of the Americas.

FURTHER WRITING SUGGESTIONS

4. Although the area of the world known as the Americas was settled at least twelve thousand years ago, tell why many people still say that Columbus "discovered" it.

5. Tell why people would band together to form societies.

The first activity, **In Your Own Voice,** is a space for your immediate impressions of the reading selection. Feel free to use In Your Own Voice in any way you wish. (If you need more room or wish not to write in this book, please use a separate sheet of paper for this exercise.)

After you have completed In Your Own Voice, answer the following questions:

a. Did you have trouble starting to write?

b. How did you begin?

c. Did you surprise yourself?

d. Did you "change gears"?

e. Did you find yourself stopping at certain points?

f. Why did you stop yourself?

g. Did you worry about what you were writing?

h. Did you write about the reading?

i. Did you write about something else?

j. How did it feel to write this way?

Now that you've tried In Your Own Voice, let's look at someone else's response:

IN YOUR OWN VOICE

This is kind of new for me, I feel like I've been thrown in to the middle of the course even tho it's just begun. The reading takes me back millions of yrs — and all I see are sheets of ice, covering everything for thousands of miles. It's *like a movie, shots of a few people and animals looking very small. They're not individual, just groups also I'm confused about whether they came on foot, animals (horses?), or boat — I think by land I also like picturing them heading down all the time until the bottom of South America.*

Following In Your Own Voice are three related exercises that help you to further discover and understand what you have read.

What Does It Say? asks questions that you can answer directly from what you have read.

What Does It Mean? asks questions whose answers are not directly found in the selection. You are asked to consider the meaning and significance of what you have read.

Style and Sense asks you to understand the arrangement, organization, and language of what you have read.

From the Text uses a sentence from the reading selection to review a grammar point.

Your In Your Own Voice responses can stand on their own. They can also be a kind of *prewriting,* that is, writing that contains the seeds for further development.

Write Now is another exercise that uses prewriting activities.

Many instructors and students believe that prewriting activities are the most important ones for beginning college writers. Students at the start of a writing course may say to themselves (and perhaps to the class and teacher), "I have nothing to say or to write about," or "I don't know where to begin," or "My mind's a complete blank."

There are, however, ways in which you can come up with or generate ideas to write about. There are ways for you to put those first words down on paper (or on a word processing screen). In other words, you can express yourself freely in your writing—as you have just done in In Your Own Voice.

In Write Now you begin writing about the topics in **Writing Suggestions** and **Further Writing Suggestions.**

Before you do the Write Now activities, read over the topics on pages 8 and 9.

a. Do any of them interest you?

b. Do you know something about any of them?

c. Which ones don't you like at all?

d. Which one would you like to write about?

Write Now asks you to freewrite or make a list of journalistic questions on the topic you have chosen. You may have heard these terms before and used them as ways of generating ideas or getting something on paper. But if they are new to you, let's introduce them and several other useful prewriting activities.

FREEWRITING AND JOURNALS

These two ways of getting started ask you just to put pen to paper and write whatever comes to mind in whatever way it comes. Just keep writing.

Freewriting is writing without stopping as you freely associate one idea with another, one word or phrase with another. By relaxing and letting go, you can begin writing without the self-criticism and fear of being judged that often stop writers from putting down that first word.

In *Americas,* we want you to freewrite for ten or fifteen minutes. You needn't stick to any topic or stop to make corrections in spelling, grammar, logic, and so on. If you get stuck, you may just write the last word over and over until the next word comes to you.

Journals resemble freewriting but they are often daily records written for yourself alone. Like freewriting, journals are yours to do with as you wish. You may write anything in them, in any way. You should try to write smoothly and naturally, without pausing.

Journals are a good way to communicate with yourself on a regular basis. If written for class, they are a fine way to share your thoughts with others. Again, we suggest that you write for ten or fifteen minutes.

Freewriting and journals may also help you *discover* something that will become part of your composition or essay. However, they need not have any other purpose than helping you dive into the act of writing.

JOURNALISTIC QUESTIONS

Journalistic questions are another way to help you get started writing. Making up your own questions will help you move from reading a selection in *Americas* to writing about it. In freely shaping these questions, you will focus your attention on the key points of what you have read.

Questions often begin with

Who?

What?

Where?

When?

Why?

How?

Starting with these words enables you to jot down quickly in question form the ideas that interested you most, or the ideas that you thought were most significant, or the ideas that puzzled you.

After a few minutes of writing questions, answer them briefly—either in complete sentences or in words and phrases.

When you answer a question clearly, you are well on your way to making what you write understandable to both your readers and yourself. The answers can serve as the springboard to the specific details and examples used in later development.

BRAINSTORM LISTS AND CLUSTER DIAGRAMS

These two ways of getting started ask you to make lists or diagrams to generate ideas for writing. As with freewriting and journalistic questions, these prewriting activities make use of spontaneous thoughts and associations.

Brainstorm lists are a series of words or phrases that freely come to mind as you think about a topic or important idea. You should jot down whatever comes to you even if it seems illogical or unconnected to other words on the list. Just keep writing.

You may find that a word or phrase will set you off on the beginning of a new list on a different aspect of the topic. From the material you have gathered, you may begin to notice some possible sections or divisions for later development.

Let's look at someone else's brainstorm list for Writing Suggestion 1.

decision, good-by, tears, food to take along, icy cold, water/ fog, islands, people suffering, dying, clothes, husband –

wife support, hunt, strange sights, finally a place away from the wind

Cluster diagrams make use of the ability to string together related ideas. Like brainstorming, cluster diagraming (also called mapping) involves freely associated lists of words or phrases. These words are placed in circles or balloons connected to one another by arrows to show the closeness and relatedness of one idea to another.

When you draw a cluster diagram, you write the first word or phrase that comes to you and then circle it. You next draw an arrow and then write and circle the second word that comes to you. You continue this process, being sure to link each circled word or phrase to the one it relates to most closely.

Let's look at someone else's cluster diagram for Writing Suggestion 1.

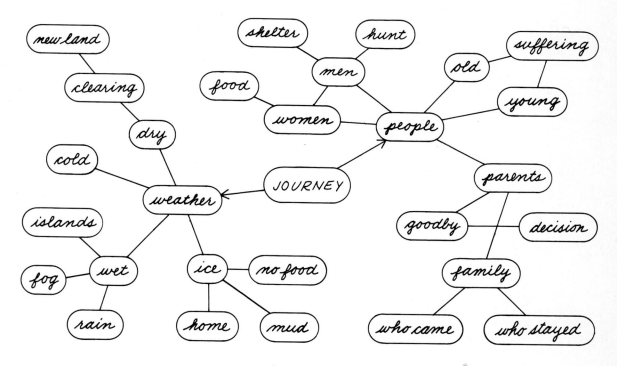

Brainstorm lists and cluster diagrams are prewriting activities used to stimulate your thinking before you write your composition or essay. These activities should take about ten minutes each.

Now you are ready to do some freewriting on the Writing Suggestion topic that you chose earlier. Freewrite now on your own paper.

Then look at someone else's freewriting for Writing Suggestion 1.

I'd tell my grandchild (I'd probably have many) how young I was. My husband + I were married only 6 wks + I was 15! I remember hearing the men up all night + even tho I try to sleep I couldn't. One dawn grandpa came to where I was and said we had to leave that day + head for a new place — he didn't know the name or how long it would take. The place was beyond the ice endless ice. I didn't know what to do, I was frighten to leave my mother and father.

Next, try writing on your own paper some journalistic questions for your topic.

Then look at someone else's journalistic questions for Writing Suggestion 1.

how old was I? why did the men decide to go? when and how did I find out? what were my feelings? which other families were going? how much did anyone know of the new place? how far away was it? where did we rest that first day? what new sights did I see? just how cold did it get? were there strange sea and land animals? did I ever get homesick? Who was born on the way? who died? what did we eat, wear, do to survive?

Prewriting activities should make you feel comfortable and confident about starting quickly. They should help you to come up with a great many useful and interesting ideas to use in shaping your first draft.

FIRST DRAFT

A first draft is an initial try at writing a paragraph or essay. Using your prewriting material as a guide, you create a rough draft to see how it sounds and feels to you.

At this stage, you are not seeking perfection or a finished product. Many students are put off from writing because they believe mistakenly that what they read in books, magazines, and newspapers was written in one smooth and complete effort, rather than in a series of drafts.

Some students write their first draft most easily working from their brainstorm lists, freewriting, and so on. Others plunge into the first draft freshly, without relying directly on their prewriting material. The important thing is to use whatever method is best for you.

You should continue writing without stopping to give much attention to paragraph order, grammar, spelling, or word use. These are matters that involve the revision and editing stages.

In Write Now, first draft activities help you shape opening and development paragraphs.

Let's look at a first draft based on the freewriting sample that you read earlier in this chapter.

I was just 15 and had been married only 6 wks. When the men announced that we were going to travel far. Grandpa said we had to leave and head for a place far from the endless ice. He said he didn't know the name or how far away. Just that I had to go there with my husband. I had not slept one hour I didn't know what to do, I was frighten to leave my mother and father.

We women carried heavy loads. I started to cry because I would never see grandpa again or mother and father. At the edge of the path I kissed mother and father. The long journey was only for the young husbands and wives.

I hated the trip. We walked over ice and frozen ground until finally we saw the frozen waters. My tall husband guided us. He pointed to small, dry hills and flat places like a chain over the icy water. Oh what a terrible wind there was. When we got across I remember I still had to work. Making the fire and cooking the food from our sacks. Each of us women saw to it that the fresh mammoth meat was stripped. Where we arrived their were mountains in the distance. But I remember most of all the ice it did not stop.

Here are some questions about what you have just read.

a. What was carried over from the freewriting?

b. Which new details did you notice?

c. How many paragraphs are there?

d. Which feelings are brought out?

Let's see how a first draft can be revised and edited. Keep what is original and good about the first draft, while reshaping, expanding, changing, and correcting it.

REVISION AND EDITING

Revision teaches you that good writing does not come in one effort. A first step might be to go over your first draft with one of your fellow students. (You may also do this for his or her first draft.) In this peer revision, you both will be putting into practice what you are learning about composing a piece of writing. You may discuss your opening, development paragraphs, details and examples, and closing. You may consider whether paragraphs and sentences belong somewhere else.

This sharing of your work will help you to get a different perspective on your writing. It will also help you to lose your fear of making any changes once you have written something.

Editing or proofreading is reading over your writing to find errors in sentence structure, word use, punctuation, spelling, and so on.

As the writer, you are constantly revising and editing as you go along. Ideas will strike you as you read over a paragraph, or a sentence, or a completed draft. This way of moving back and forth at different stages of your writing is described as *recursive*.

Another way of moving from first to final draft might be to go over the paper with your instructor. He or she will read over the first draft and discuss ways of changing it.

Finally, you should have the last word and decide just what the paper should contain before submitting it.

Let's look at a final draft based on the first draft you read earlier in this chapter.

It was thirty-five years ago, a year before your mother was born, if you can imagine that. I was fifteen and married only six weeks. I hadn't slept all night because the men argued until dawn. They formed a circle and announced that some of us were going to travel far away.

My grandpa Har came over to where I was huddled in a blanket. He said I had to go far from the endless ice. He didn't know this new place's name or how far away it was, but I must go there with my husband. I didn't know what to do, and I was frightened to leave my mother and father.

By noon, we packed all we could. Only then did I cry, knowing I would never see Grandpa again or my mother and father. At the path's edge I kissed my parents for the last time, holding them tight. The long journey was for only the young, childless husbands and wives.

I hated the trip from the beginning. For a few weeks, we walked and walked over ice and frozen ground from dawn to dusk. Each night the women comforted one another. Being the youngest, I got the most attention. I kept wanting to turn back. We went just a few miles a day, and the landscape seemed never to change. We finally saw it—the frozen waters, vast and dangerous.

The next day, my husband, who was the tallest, guided us to the shore. He pointed to small, dry hills and flat places like a chain over the icy water. Oh what a terrible wind there was as we walked to the other side. I'll never forget how it felt on my face. Finally across, we were weary and numb from carrying heavy loads, but still had to build fires. While the men set up shelters, we women stripped and cleaned the fresh mammoth meat we had brought in our sacks.

I had arrived that night at a new place with many mountains in the distance. I was fifteen, but I had grown older in a few weeks. What I remember most, child, about that time was the ice. It did not stop.

Here are some questions about what you have just read.

a. Did you notice any personal details that have been added?

b. Did you notice how the opening paragraph has changed?

c. Did you notice how the number of paragraphs has changed?

d. Did you notice the references to time?

e. Did you notice how the young woman described her feelings in greater detail?

f. Did you notice more attention placed on describing the land?

g. Did you notice how the closing paragraph changed?

h. Did you notice any changes in choice of words?

i. Did you notice how editing led to the correction of major sentence and verb errors?

When you read over the Writing Suggestions and Further Writing Suggestions earlier in this chapter, you saw the kinds of topics found in *Americas*. This final draft is a sample response, just as "The First Americans" is a sample reading.

All of the topics have prompts or directions to help you write. The early ones ask you to describe, narrate, and tell. Later ones ask you to discuss, explain, define, and compare and contrast.

Describe: to create a picture in words.

When you describe something, use details of sight, sound, and smell to make your readers see what you would like them to see. When you describe your reactions to something, make your feelings and ideas clear by using details from your experience.

Narrate: to tell a story.

When you narrate, tell a story or a real experience. Ask yourself, "What happens next?" Use a time sequence from beginning to middle to end (chronological order). Use details to bring the experience to life. Sometimes a story can help support your idea.

Tell: to talk about, to give your opinion about.

When you tell, communicate your experience and ideas in a direct way, as if you were talking to someone.

When you tell what happened or how something happened, give a careful description or narration of facts and events.

When you tell why something happened, give your reasons and views. Use supporting details to back up your opinions.

When you tell whether or not you believe something or agree with something, give your reasons and views. Again, use supporting details to back up your opinions.

Discuss: to talk about something in detail, to give various points of view.

When you discuss an issue, look at several sides and state your own opinion clearly, stressing your main points.

When you discuss what happened or how something happened, give a careful description or narration of facts and events.

When you discuss why something happened, give your reasons and views. Use supporting details to back up your opinions.

When you discuss whether or not you believe something or agree with something, give your reasons and views. Again, use supporting details to back up your opinions.

When you discuss the advantages and disadvantages of something, look at both sides and use examples or other evidence to illustrate each advantage or disadvantage. You may wish to take one side in your conclusion.

Explain: to give reasons for your opinions, actions, or decisions.

When you explain, give reasons based on your own experience or reading why you think or believe something, and take time to expand upon or detail these reasons. Consider whether your explanation will be clear to your readers.

Define: to give the meaning of a word or an idea as clearly as possible.

A definition may be brief, as in a dictionary entry, or extended, as in an essay on "Marriage" or "Senior Citizens." It may be technical and unemotional, as in the meaning of *front-wheel drive,* or full of feeling, as in defining the meaning of *freedom* or *father.*

When you define, generate enough material to give different perspectives on the word or idea, especially if it is an unfamiliar one. Organize this material so that your readers can "get" your meaning. Use details and examples from a variety of sources.

Compare and Contrast: to find similarities and differences between at least two ideas, events, people, or things.

When you compare, find similarities between at least two ideas, events, people, or things.

When you contrast, find differences between at least two ideas, events, people, or things.

When you compare and contrast, organize your material so that ideas, events, people, or things receive balanced attention.

Now that you have been introduced to these sample reading and writing activities, we hope that you find the reading selections and writing assignments in *Americas* challenging and stimulating.

READING
UNITS

Olmec head. Lee Bolton Picture Library.

UNIT 1

Marisol. *Pocohantas.* Photo by Carole and Alex Rosenberg.

BEGINNINGS

The Americas had a rich and complex heritage for thousands of years before Europeans set out for and reached what they called "The New World." Native American tribes like the Iroquois and Pueblos in North America, Aztecs and Mayas in Mexico and Central America, and Incas in South America had evolved both hunting and agriculture-based societies long before the European ships landed at the close of the fifteenth century.

This unit, however, starts with the moment the "old" and "new" worlds meet for the first time: Christopher Columbus's log, or journal, entry for October 12, 1492, a historic date in American and world history.

The section continues with Bartolomé de Las Casas's description of the Spaniards' cruelty to the Indians in Cuba and one Spanish priest's unsuccessful attempt to mediate the conflict.

The chapter continues with the Mayflower Compact (1620), which established the laws of the Pilgrims in their new settlement.

The next selection tells of arranging marriages in seventeenth-century Canada between male Quebec settlers and newly arrived women from the mother country, France.

Then come two views of the West Indian slave trade. The first is a letter from the English company that brought slaves to Jamaica. The second is an eyewitness account of a Barbados slave market written by an English observer.

The unit concludes with the ending of F. Scott Fitzgerald's novel *The Great Gatsby* (1925), which deals with the American dream and looks back to those sailors who came from Europe four or five hundred years ago.

BEFORE YOU READ

What were the Americas like before the arrival of Columbus?

Did Columbus "discover" a "new world"?

Who met the European ships?

Were the inhabitants hospitable to the European explorers?

Which conflicts occurred when different cultures met?

How were or weren't these conflicts resolved?

How did the Europeans control the Americas?

What was the role of European kings and queens in the settlement of the Americas?

Why did men and women leave the lands of their birth to come to the Americas?

What groups of people did not come freely to the Americas?

What do you recall about Columbus, other explorers, the Indians of the Americas, the Pilgrims, the slave trade, and the role and contributions of women?

How do these people and events affect the Americas today?

Would you leave the land of your birth?

Why did you, your family, or your ancestors leave the lands of their birth?

What do you want to learn more about in this unit?

What would you like to study about the Americas on your own? With a group?

Are the Americas a beacon of hope?

THE JOURNAL OF CHRISTOPHER COLUMBUS

"I decided to write down everything that I might do and see and experience on this voyage, from day to day, and very carefully," Christopher Columbus (1451–1506) noted when he began his log, or daily record, on August 3, 1492.

On that day, Columbus (in Spanish, Cristobal Colón) and about ninety crew members set sail from Palos, Spain, on three ships, the *Niña,* the *Pinta,* and the *Santa Maria.*

This log of his first voyage to the Americas seems to be essentially honest. It is therefore invaluable as both a maritime record and a personalized account of Columbus's impressions of the Western Hemisphere and its inhabitants.

The following selection dated October 11-12 records the Europeans' first landing (in the Caribbean) and encounter with the people and culture of the Americas.

WORDS TO NOTICE

unfurled: unrolled, spread

Sovereign: ruler of Spain (*F* for King Ferdinand and *Y* for Queen Isabella)

standard: an official flag

comptroller: controller, person in charge of finances

bore witness: swore

bore: gave birth to (past tense of *to bear*)

marred: disfigured, spoiled

paunch: belly

hank: coiled strands of hair

fluent: smooth, easily flowing

well-dispositioned: mild

dry leaf: tobacco

esteem: respect, admiration

READ ON

1. What do you learn from the title of this selection?

2. What is the first thing you would have done after seeing strange ships approach your island?

Friday, 12 October 1492
(Log entry for 12 October is combined with that of 11 October)

At dawn we saw naked people, and I went ashore in the ship's boat, armed,   1
followed by Martín Alonso Pinzón, captain of the *Pinta*, and his brother,
Vincente Yáñez Pinzón, captain of the *Niña*. I unfurled the royal banner and

the captains brought the flags which displayed a large green cross with the letters *F* and *Y* at the left and right side of the cross. Over each letter was the appropriate crown of that Sovereign. These flags were carried as a standard on all of the ships. After a prayer of thanksgiving I ordered the captains of the *Pinta* and *Niña,* together with Rodrigo de Escobedo (secretary of the fleet), and Rodrigo Sánchez of Segovia (comptroller of the fleet) to bear faith and witness that I was taking possession of this island for the King and Queen. I made all the necessary declarations and had these testimonies carefully written down by the secretary. In addition to those named above, the entire company of the fleet bore witness to this act. To this island I gave the name *San Salvador,* in honor of our Blessed Lord.

No sooner had we concluded the formalities of taking possession of the island than people began to come to the beach, all as naked as their mothers bore them, and the women also, although I did not see more than one very young girl. All those that I saw were young people, none of whom was over 30 years old. They are very well-built people, with handsome bodies and very fine faces, though their appearance is marred somewhat by very broad heads and foreheads, more so than I have ever seen in any other race. Their eyes are large and very pretty, and their skin is the color of Canary Islanders or of sunburned peasants, not at all black, as would be expected because we are on an east-west line with Hierro in the Canaries. These are tall people and their legs, with no exceptions, are quite straight, and none of them has a paunch. They are, in fact, well proportioned. Their hair is not kinky, but straight, and coarse like horsehair. They wear it short over the eyebrows, but they have a long hank in the back that they never cut. Many of the natives paint their faces; others paint their whole bodies; some, only the eyes or nose. Some are painted black, some white, some red; others are of different colors.

The people here called this island *Guanahaní* in their language, and their speech is very fluent, although I do not understand any of it. They are friendly and well-dispositioned people who bear no arms except for small spears, and they have no iron. I showed one my sword, and through ignorance he grabbed it by the blade and cut himself. Their spears are made of wood, to which they attach a fish tooth at one end, or some other sharp thing.

I want the natives to develop a friendly attitude toward us because I know that they are a people who can be made free and converted to our Holy Faith more by love than by force. I therefore gave red caps to some and glass beads to others. They hung the beads around their necks, along with some other things of slight value that I gave them. And they took great pleasure in this and became so friendly that it was a marvel. They traded and gave everything they had with good will, but it seems to me that they have very little and are poor in everything. I warned my men to take nothing from the people without giving something in exchange.

This afternoon the people of San Salvador came swimming to our ships and in boats made from one log. They brought us parrots, balls of cotton

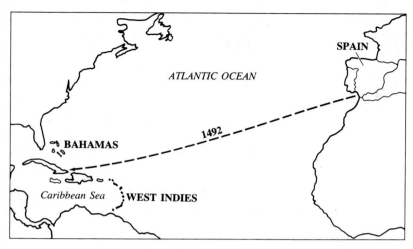

Spain to the Caribbean Sea and the West Indies

thread, spears, and many other things, including a kind of dry leaf that they hold in great esteem. For these items we swapped them little glass beads and hawks' bells.

Many of the men I have seen have scars on their bodies, and when I made signs to them to find out how this happened, they indicated that people from other nearby islands come to San Salvador to capture them; they defend themselves the best they can. I believe that people from the mainland come here to take them as slaves. They ought to make good and skilled servants, for they repeat very quickly whatever we say to them. I think they can easily be made Christians, for they seem to have no religion. If it pleases Our Lord, I will take six of them to Your Highnesses when I depart, in order that they may learn our language.

6

IN YOUR OWN VOICE

WHAT DOES IT SAY?

1. What is displayed on the royal banner?

2. What does Columbus's secretary carefully write down?

3. What favorable first impressions of the inhabitants does Columbus have?

4. How does one inhabitant cut himself?

5. To which religion does Columbus wish to convert the people of the island?

6. Why does Columbus plan to take some of the islanders back to Spain?

WHAT DOES IT MEAN?

1. Why is Columbus armed when he goes ashore?

2. Why is a written document claiming possession of San Salvador of great importance to Columbus and all his crew?

3. How might the inhabitants feel about Columbus's claiming possession of their land?

4. How might the inhabitants feel about Columbus's renaming of their island?

5. Why does Columbus want to convert the natives?

6. What does trading "fairly" mean to Columbus and the crew? To the inhabitants?

7. Why are there no women on the Spanish ships?

STYLE AND SENSE

1. Every kind of writing has a basic organization that begins to form in the opening paragraph. Which words in the first sentence introduce the differences between the Spaniards and the island's inhabitants?

2. Which group is the subject of the rest of the opening paragraph? What evidence supports your answer?

3. How does the opening sentence of the second paragraph remind the reader of the events of the first paragraph?

4. How does the opening sentence of the second paragraph also move toward a description of the second group?

5. How does the closing sentence of the log bring the reader back to the opening sentence?

6. Have you ever kept a diary, journal, or log? What was special about it?

FROM THE TEXT

Subjects and **verbs** together are the building blocks of sentences.

Read the following sentence:

> They hung the beads around their necks, along with some other things of slight value that I gave them.

a. Identify the two verbs (words of action).

b. Identify the two subjects (who or what acts).

c. Do the subjects come before or after their verbs?

See pages 380 and 381 for more on subjects and verbs.

WRITE NOW

Do one of the following activities:

1. Make up a **brainstorm list** of fears and expectations for Writing Suggestion 1 or 2.

2. Write a **journal** on one of the following Writing Suggestions.

WRITING SUGGESTIONS

1. Imagine that you are watching Columbus's ships approach your island. Describe your fears and expectations about the coming events.

2. Imagine that you are a crew member on Columbus's voyage. Describe your fears and expectations about the land you have reached.

3. Describe the scene and narrate the activities when the Europeans and the island's inhabitants meet to trade goods and gifts.

4. Describe Columbus's feelings if he were to arrive in the Americas today.

FURTHER WRITING SUGGESTIONS

5. Tell how your family's traditions and culture contribute to your community.

6. Columbus referred to the Americas as *otro mundo,* "another world." Yet Columbus traditionally is considered the discoverer of the New World. Tell which of these two terms you prefer and why.

THE CONQUEST OF CUBA*

By Bartolomé de Las Casas

Born in Seville, Spain, Bartolomé de Las Casas (1474–1566) became interested in the Americas when he saw Columbus parading through the streets of Seville in 1493 on his return from his first successful voyage. Nearly ten years later, Las Casas sailed to the island of Hispaniola (present-day Dominican Republic and Haiti) in the Caribbean.

Originally a landowner and slaveholder, in 1512 Las Casas became the first priest ordained in the Western Hemisphere. Two years later, he began preaching

*Editors' title

against the Spaniards' cruelty, violence, and greed. Soon he was known as the Protector of the Indians.

This selection comes from his famous *History of the Indies,* begun in 1527 and completed about thirty-five years later. Some modern scholars have disputed the accuracy of Las Casas's account, but pictures and statues in his honor are to be found throughout Latin America today.

Throughout this selection you will notice three dots (...) called ellipsis points. This device tells you that parts of the original have been omitted.

WORDS TO NOTICE

densely: thickly

sagacious: wise

predestined: preplanned, fated

wretched subsistence: few possessions and little food

lodging: housing

prophets: interpreters of God's words

reverence: admiration, adoration, awe

apt: likely

lambs: innocent victims

cleric: priest

commission: reward

wrath: anger

rebukes: criticizes strongly

hindering: blocking, delaying

heap: pile

READ ON

1. What do you learn about the author from the headnote?

2. How is a land conquered and controlled?

The Spaniards entered the province of Camagüey, which is large and densely [1] populated . . . and when they reached the villages, the inhabitants had prepared as well as they could cassava bread from their food; what they called *guaminiquinajes* from their hunting; and also fish, if they had caught any.

Immediately upon arriving at a village, the cleric Casas would have all [2] the little children band together; taking two or three Spaniards to help him, along with some sagacious Indians of this island of Hispaniola, whom he had brought with him, and a certain servant of his, he would baptize the children he found in the village. He did this throughout the island . . . and there were many for whom God provided holy baptism because He had predestined them to glory. God provided it at a fitting time, for none or almost none of those children remained alive after a few months. . . .

When the Spaniards arrived at a village and found the Indians at peace [3] in their houses, they did not fail to injure and scandalize them. Not content with what the Indians freely gave, they took their wretched subsistence from them, and some, going further, chased after their wives and daughters, for this is and always has been the Spaniards' common custom in these Indies. Because of this and at the urging of the said father, Captain Narváez ordered that after the father had separated all the inhabitants of the village in half the houses, leaving the other half empty for the Spaniards' lodging, no one should dare go to the Indians' section. For this purpose, the father would go ahead with three or four men and reach a village early; by the time the Spaniards came, he had already gathered the Indians in one part and cleared the other.

Thus, because the Indians saw that the father did things for them, de- [4] fending and comforting them, and also baptizing their children, in which affairs he seemed to have more command and authority than others, he received much respect and credit throughout the island among the Indians. Further, they honored him as they did their priests, magicians, prophets, or physicians, who were all one and the same.

Because of this . . . it became unnecessary to go ahead of the Spaniards. [5] He had only to send an Indian with an old piece of paper on a stick, informing them through the messenger that those letters said thus and so. That is, that they should all be calm, that no one should absent himself because he would do them no harm, that they should have food prepared for the Christians and their children ready for baptism, or that they should gather in one part of the village, and anything else that it seemed good to counsel them—and that if they did not carry these things out, the father would be angry, which was the greatest threat that could be sent them.

They performed everything with a very good will, to the best of their [6] ability. And great was the reverence and fear which they had for the letters, for they saw that through these what was being done in other, distant regions was known. It seemed more than a miracle to them. . . .

The Spaniards thus passed through certain villages of that province on [7] the road they were taking. And because the folk of the villages . . . were eager to see such a new people and especially to see the three or four mares being taken there, at which the whole land was frightened—news of them flew through the island—many came to look at them in a large town called Caonao, the penultimate syllable long. And the Spaniards, on the morning of the day they arrived at the town, stopped to breakfast in a riverbed that was dry but for a few small pools. This riverbed was full of whetstones, and all longed to sharpen their swords on them [and did]. When they had finished their breakfast, they continued on the road to Caonao.

Along the road for two or three leagues there was an arid plain, where **8** one found oneself thirsty after any work; and there certain Indians from the villages brought them some gourds of water, and some things to eat.

They arrived at the town of Caonao in the evening. Here they found many **9** people, who had prepared a great deal of food consisting of cassava bread and fish, because they had a large river close by and also were near the sea. In a little square were 2,000 Indians, all squatting because they have this custom, all staring, frightened, at the mares. Nearby was a large *bohio,* or large house, in which were more than 500 other Indians, close-packed and fearful, who did not dare come out.

When some of the domestic Indians the Spaniards were taking with them **10** as servants (who were more than 1,000 souls . . .) wished to enter the large house, the Cuban Indians had chickens ready and said to them: "Take these— do not enter here." For they already knew that the Indians who served the Spaniards were not apt to perform any other deeds than those of their masters.

There was a custom among the Spaniards that one person, appointed by **11** the captain, should be in charge of distributing to each Spaniard the food and other things the Indians gave. And while the captain was thus on his mare and the others mounted on theirs, and the father himself was observing how the bread and fish were distributed, a Spaniard, in whom the devil is thought to have clothed himself, suddenly drew his sword. Then the whole hundred drew theirs and began to rip open the bellies, to cut and kill those lambs—men, women, children, and old folk, all of whom were seated, off guard and frightened, watching the mares and the Spaniards. And within two credos, not a man of all of them there remains alive.

The Spaniards enter the large house nearby, for this was happening at **12** its door, and in the same way, with cuts and stabs, begin to kill as many as they found there, so that a stream of blood was running, as if a great number of cows had perished. Some of the Indians who could make haste climbed up the poles and woodwork of the house to the top, and thus escaped.

The cleric had withdrawn shortly before this massacre to where another **13** small square of the town was formed, near where they had lodged him. This was in a large house where all the Spaniards also had to stay, and here about forty of the Indians who had carried the Spaniards' baggage from the provinces farther back were stretched out on the ground, resting. And five Spaniards chanced to be with the cleric. When these heard the blows of the swords and knew that the Spaniards were killing the Indians—without seeing anything, because there were certain houses between—they put hands to their swords and are about to kill the forty Indians . . . to pay them their commission.

The cleric, moved to wrath, opposes and rebukes them harshly to prevent **14** them, and having some respect for him, they stopped what they were going to do, so the forty were left alive. The five go to kill where the others were killing. And as the cleric had been detained in hindering the slaying of the forty carriers, when he went he found a heap of dead, which the Spaniards had made among the Indians, which was certainly a horrible sight.

When Narváez, the captain, saw him he said: "How does Your Honor like **15** what these our Spaniards have done?"

Seeing so many cut to pieces before him, and very upset at such a cruel **16** event, the cleric replied: "That I commend you and them to the devil!"

The heedless Narváez remained, still watching the slaughter as it took **17** place, without speaking, acting, or moving any more than if he had been marble. For if he had wished, being on horseback and with a lance in his hands, he could have prevented the Spaniards from killing even ten persons.

Then the cleric leaves him, and goes elsewhere through some groves **18** seeking Spaniards to stop them from killing. For they were passing through the groves looking for someone to kill, sparing neither boy, child, woman, nor old person. And they did more, in that certain Spaniards went to the road to the river, which was nearby. Then all the Indians who had escaped with wounds, stabs, and cuts—all who could flee to throw themselves into the river to save themselves—met with the Spaniards who finished them.

IN YOUR OWN VOICE

WHAT DOES IT SAY?

1. What does the priest do to the children when the Spaniards first enter a village?

2. What hostile acts do the Spaniards commit against the villagers?

3. What is the purpose of the piece of paper on a stick?

4. How does the massacre begin?

5. What does the priest think of the Spaniards' brutality?

WHAT DOES IT MEAN?

1. Why is the priest eager to baptize the children?

2. Why do the Spaniards injure and take advantage of the villagers?

3. Why do the people respect and fear the priest?

4. Why do the Spaniards draw their swords and continue the slaughter?

5. Why doesn't Captain Narváez stop the killings?

STYLE AND SENSE

1. After the opening two paragraphs, what are the reader's expectations about the relations between the Spaniards and the villagers?

2. In the second paragraph is there any hint that things are not what they seem?

3. How does the first sentence of the third paragraph provide a shocking contrast for the reader?

4. Which words in the first sentences of paragraphs 2, 3, 7, and 8 indicate the order of events in time?

5. How does the description of the priest's actions in paragraphs 11 and 12 return the reader to the ideas of the opening paragraphs?

6. How do the closing two paragraphs serve as a fitting conclusion to the passage?

FROM THE TEXT

Subordinate or dependent clause: a group of related words that contains a subject and verb but that cannot stand alone as a sentence.

Read the following sentences:

When the Spaniards arrived at a village and found the Indians at peace in their houses, they did not fail to injure and scandalize them.

a. List the subjects and verbs.

b. What connection is there between the words *Spaniards* and *they*?

c. Would placing a period after the word *houses* satisfy the reader's curiosity as to what happened?

d. Why does the use of the word *when* in the first part of the sentence require a concluding idea?

e. Why does a writer use (for instance, in a newspaper article) this type of sentence?

See page 383 for more on dependent clauses.

WRITE NOW

Do one of the following activities:

1. Make a list of **journalistic questions** about the events in the reading.

2. Make a **cluster diagram** of acts of either kindness or cruelty.

WRITING SUGGESTIONS

1. Describe your reactions to the massacre.

2. One Spaniard drew his sword, then a hundred, and the massacre began. Narrate a present-day situation in which one act of violence can spark a series of even more violent acts.

3. Describe the scene and people's emotions when the villagers are forced from their homes to make room for the Spaniards (see paragraph 3).

4. Describe the priest's conflicting emotions.

FURTHER WRITING SUGGESTIONS

5. Tell how you would react to a clear and powerful threat to those who depend on you.

6. Tell how community groups can protect the safety and property of their neighborhoods.

THE MAYFLOWER COMPACT

In September 1620 more than a hundred Pilgrims set sail from Plymouth, England, for North America in a small ship called the *Mayflower*. Escaping religious persecution, these men, women, and children hoped to reach Virginia, but storms blew them off course. In December they anchored in Cape Cod Bay in what is now Massachusetts.

On board, forty-one male, adult Pilgrims wrote and signed a document, the Mayflower Compact, in which they pledged themselves to enact "just and equal laws ... for the generall good of the colonie." These principles of government, while limited, were a step toward achieving a representative democracy.

Although half of the Pilgrims died during that first winter, the others chose to remain in the settlement they called Plymouth. After a successful harvest, they celebrated the first Thanksgiving with representatives of a local American Indian tribe, who had helped them survive great hardships.

This reading selection contains spellings that were used in the seventeenth century. For example, *Britaine, doe* (for modern *do*).

WORDS TO NOTICE

compact: agreement

underwritten: signed at the end of the document

subject: person under the rule of a king or queen

dread sovereign: respected or feared ruler

solemnly and mutually: seriously as a group

covenant: swear to an agreement

civil body politic: citizens agreeing to be governed together

ordinance: law or command

meet: ,fitting and proper

submission: agreement to be under the rule of law

reign: period of a ruler's power

Anno Dom(ini): in the year of the Lord (abbreviated A.D.)

READ ON

1. What does the headnote say about the importance of the Mayflower Compact?

2. Why is the pronoun *we* important to the meaning of the Mayflower Compact?

IN the name of God, Amen. We, whose names are underwritten, the loyal subjects of our dread sovereigne Lord, King James, by the grace of God, of Great Britaine, France, and Ireland king, defender of the faith, etc., having undertaken, for the glory of God, and advancement of the Christian faith, and honour of our king and country, a voyage to plant the first colony in the Northerne parts of Virginia, doe, by these presents, solemnly and mutually in the presence of God, and one of another, covenant and combine ourselves together into a civill body politick, for our better ordering and preservation and furtherance of the ends aforesaid; and by virtue hereof to enacte, constitute, and frame such just and equall laws, ordinances, acts, constitutions, and offices, from time to time, as shall be thought most meete and convenient for the generall good of the Colonie unto which we promise all due submission and obedience. In witness whereof we have hereunder subscribed our names at Cap-Codd the 11. of November, in the year of the raigne of our sovereigne lord, King James, of England, France, and Ireland, the eighteenth, and of Scotland the fiftie-fourth. Anno. Dom. 1620.

MR. JOHN CARVER	MR. STEPHEN HOPKINS
MR. WILLIAM BRADFORD	DIGERY PRIEST
MR. EDWARD WINSLOW	THOMAS WILLIAMS
MR. WILLIAM BREWSTER	GILBERT WINSLOW
ISAAC ALLERTON	EDMUND MARGESSON
MILES STANDISH	PETER BROWN
JOHN ALDEN	RICHARD BITTERIDGE
JOHN TURNER	GEORGE SOULE
FRANCIS EATON	EDWARD TILLY
JAMES CHILTON	JOHN TILLY
JOHN CRAXTON	FRANCIS COOK
JOHN BILLINGTON	THOMAS ROGERS
JOSES FLETCHER	THOMAS TINKER
JOHN GOODMAN	JOHN RIDGATE
MR. SAMUEL FULLER	EDWARD FULLER
MR. CHRISTOPHER MARTIN	RICHARD CLARK
MR. WILLIAM MULLINS	RICHARD GARDINER
MR. WILLIAM WHITE	MR. JOHN ALLERTON
MR. RICHARD WARREN	THOMAS ENGLISH
JOHN HOWLAND	EDWARD DOTEN
	EDWARD LIESTER

IN YOUR OWN VOICE

WHAT DOES IT SAY?

1. For which king did the Pilgrims sail?

2. List three reasons why they sailed to North America.

3. Although the first settlement was in Plymouth, Massachusetts, where did the Pilgrims expect to land?

4. Why did the Pilgrims write the Mayflower Compact?

WHAT DOES IT MEAN?

1. What advantages did the Pilgrims gain by agreeing to obey this compact?

2. Why does the compact refer to God and the Christian faith?

3. What does the phrase "just and equall laws" mean to the signers?

4. What is the importance of the signing of one's individual name to a document?

STYLE AND SENSE

1. What is the effect of opening with "In the name of God, Amen" and closing with "Anno. Dom. 1620"?

2. Within the frame of the opening and closing, there are only two sentences. List the subjects and the verbs of both sentences. Note that the same word is used as the subject in both.

3. What makes reading and comprehending the first of the above sentences so difficult?

4. What facts come between the subject and verb in the first of the sentences above?

FROM THE TEXT

Sentence fragment: a portion of a sentence that has been punctuated as if it were a complete sentence.

Read the following:

In the name of God, Amen.

a. List the nouns.

b. Do the nouns perform any action?

c. Do the other words perform any action?

d. Do the words "In the name of God, Amen" form a sentence?

e. When is a sentence fragment an effective means of expression?

See page 401 for more on the sentence fragment.

WRITE NOW

Do one of the following activities:

1. Write a **journal** of your first days after leaving the *Mayflower*.

2. Make a **cluster diagram** of the laws or community responsibilities needed in the new colony.

WRITING SUGGESTIONS

1. Imagine that you are a Pilgrim. Write a letter to your family back home describing your feelings and experiences in the new land.

2. Narrate what happened on the first Thanksgiving.

3. Tell what the new colony's main problem is. Then describe how you would solve this problem.

FURTHER WRITING SUGGESTIONS

4. Narrate a situation in which a person's individual rights may be in conflict with the "general good" of the community.

5. In the Mayflower Compact, forty-one male, adult Pilgrims agree on rules to govern the whole community. Tell:

   a. What might have been the women's reactions to these rules.

   or

   b. Whether the colonists could have survived without the skills and experience of the American Indians.

6. Tell whether governments in the Americas should consider religious values when making laws involving such subjects as divorce, abortion, and prayer in public schools.

FRENCH BRIDES FOR CANADIAN SETTLERS*

By Raymond Douville and Jacques-Donat Casanova

Jacques Cartier led the first French exploration of North America in 1534. Over the next hundred years the French established permanent colonies in Quebec and other parts of Canada.

*Editors' title

In order for these colonies to survive, prosper, and grow, the settlers needed wives. Between 1636 and 1673 about a thousand young Frenchwomen, many of them orphans or widows, agreed to or were encouraged or forced to sail to Canada to fulfill the demand for wives.

Because King Louis XIV endorsed the emigration plan, he was called Father of New France and the women the King's Daughters.

WORDS TO NOTICE

convoys: groups of ships traveling together

frigates: small and fast ships

disembark: go off the ships

rife: widespread

avid: eager

comely: beautiful, attractive

trains: long lines

protégées: women under the king's protection

solemn: serious

chateau: castle or large house

King's Daughters: women from France who agreed to travel to Canada to marry settlers there

accorded: granted, given

discreet: showing good judgment and caution

mutual: shared

notary: public official

betrothed: engaged

consecration: act of making holy or sacred

unduly: overly, excessively

concord: harmony, peace

parties: persons involved

Maine: section of France

spur of the moment: instantly

inevitably: without fail

sheer: absolute, utter

insinuated: hinted with evil intent

pretext: excuse, reason

exceptional: unlike others

inclination: preference, liking

fortitude: courage, strength

READ ON

1. What do the **title** and **headnote** tell about the selection?

2. What roles did women have in colonial Quebec?

From the ports of Dieppe and La Rochelle there sailed each year the convoys 1
of ships which, in Robert de Roquebrune's appropriate words, held the future
of a new nation. When the French frigates were sighted at the approach to
the Gulf the Governor spread throughout the colony news that women were
about to disembark. The priest announced it during the sermon in the Dominican Mass. Seigneurs made it known in the grants of land. Bachelors
flocked to the capital. For a long time a legend was rife which told of avid
colonists, at the sight of a sail, throwing themselves into bark canoes at
breakneck speed, and racing to board the ship in order to seize the healthiest
or the most comely of these girls, according to their several tastes. The perfect
inspiration for a romantic novel, but very far from fact. The trains of immigrants
were put under the authority of a monitress delegated by royal warrant, who
had been ordered to place the King's protégées upon arrival in the care of
the local nuns.

On a day fixed long in advance, a solemn ceremony took place in the 2
great drawing-room of the Governor's chateau, in the presence of the Governor, the Intendant, senior officers and ladies of Society. Madame Bourdon,
who concerned herself particularly in the work of protecting these "King's
Daughters" and other immigrants, was nearly always accorded the honour of
making the official presentations. She knew the name and ancestry of every
girl, which meant that she was able to keep a discreet eye on their activities
from the moment they arrived. She assigned to each immigrant a place to
stay, Quebec, Three Rivers or Montreal.

In the weeks that followed the mutual agreement, the execution and 3
signing of the marriage contract took place at the notary's. It was always a
moving ceremony at which friends and relations gathered. Then, formally
betrothed, the young couple returned to the convent, the almshouse or to the
family which had agreed to house them until the religious consecration of
the marriage. The engaged couple saw each other a little oftener and got to

know each other better. It sometimes happened that one or other of them, occasionally both, regretted their first unduly romantic choice, made in an excess of emotion or nervousness, or for some other reason. Then both would return to the notary where by mutual consent the agreement would be annulled, following a sacred formula: ". . . Whereas there is no longer affection between them and having in mind that this might lead to lack of concord, the parties declare the agreement to be null and void and as if it had never been and without future and that thus the said parties agree to part without further claims on either side." Immediately after an act of this sort had been drawn up to annul a marriage contract between Jean Bellet and Madeleine Beaudouin, the notary Séverin Ameau married the girl himself, and their married life lasted almost half a century. Madeleine Beaudouin had come from Courcival in Maine and had emigrated with her two brothers, Jean and René. The first of these fell victim to the Iroquois and the second became the inseparable companion of the explorer Nicolas Perrot whose sister-in-law he married.

Marie Fayet, who arrived in Quebec in 1661, came of a middle-class family **4** from the parish of Saint-Sauveur in Paris. She agreed to marry the colonist Jean Durand who owned territory in Cap Rouge, a suburb of Quebec. The contract was signed on October 3rd and then revoked on the following January 12th. Marie then agreed to marry Charles Pouliot, but on reflection changed her mind. Again the contract was revoked. She took no definite decision until July 24, 1662, when she married Nicolas Huot, by whom she was to bear eleven children. Her first intended, Jean Durand, not unnaturally of the opinion that Parisian women were very capricious and fickle, preferred to marry a Huron orphan, Catherine Annennontak, who had been brought up by the Ursulines. Another example is that of Anne Guitton whose contract of marriage with Jean Mouflet, otherwise Champagne, was annulled on August 17, 1669, three days after it had been drawn up. Jean Mouflet, on the same day and before the same witnesses François Trotain, Sieur de Saint-Surin, and Jean-Baptiste Gosset, married Anne Dodain before the same notary, Romain Becquet. If we read these stories carefully we learn that between the annulment of the contract with Anne Guitton and the signing of the legal act with Anne Dodain, a religious ceremony had been enacted with the latter. Jean Mouflet and Anne Dodain remained united for the rest of their lives and faced their future in Lachine where they settled down and where later eight children were born to them. During the great massacre in 1689 they were taken prisoner by the Iroquois.

These breakdowns did not often occur, and were invariably settled in a **5** friendly manner. Very few marriages were lightly undertaken on the spur of the moment. The parties preferred to think hard and to ponder on their future. Even in these days it is surprising to read of how successful these unions, upon which depended the future of a whole nation, could prove. Inevitably some dramas arose, often because of the selfishness of narrow-minded people. Sometimes, because of prolonged indecision or sheer bad luck, one of these "King's Daughters" would take a long time to find a spouse. She would then take a job in domestic service until the ideal husband came along. Anne Lejonc, a widow, was engaged to work for Michel Le Neuf for one year. A few months after this agreement, a settler, Jean Desmarais, also widowed, wished to marry her. The wedding was arranged for January 15, 1656. But she was a good housekeeper, and her employer did not want to part with her and so made difficulties. He even insinuated that Desmarais was already married in France. Enquiries showed this to be untrue, but Le Neuf put her clothes and personal belongings under lock and key, forbidding anyone on any pretext whatever to return them to her. This was an exceptional case. More usually the authorities regarded these marriages with favour. Anne Bouyer, born in La Rochelle, was servant to the Governor, Pierre Boucher, when she was wooed by Pierre Pinot, otherwise known as La Perle. The Governor sent for the notary and stood as witness to the couple at a ceremony attended by every prominent person in the neighbourhood.

All these girls had one quality in common—their courage. Constant daily courage. Very few of them failed in the tasks they had to face. And yet it is sometimes tempting to wonder how some of them could have managed to survive the bitter climate and the sort of conditions in which they had to live. A number of them, either by inclination or else because they were less adventurous, preferred to marry settlers from their own provinces, or if possible, from their own villages. But these were a minority. Most of them were more than ready for adventure, and the women helped each other through difficult times. Those who had come from neighbouring regions of France tried to marry settlers living in the same area. The census taken in 1681 makes it plain, for example, that of the fifteen colonists settled in the seigneurie of Lanougère, thirteen married "King's Daughters" who had come from Maine and Poitou. Michel Feulion, who originated from Saint-Pierre-Le-Vieux in Poitou, even married a fellow citizen, Louise Bercier. The two Gautier sisters, Catherine and Anne, married Jean Picart and Pierre Cartier who owned neighbouring farms. Only one of these girls came from Paris. She was Françoise Hobbé, who married the seigneurial notary, Michel Roy. Since she was an educated girl and had been very well brought up, she agreed to become teacher-companion to her friends' children, and she remained to them an unfailing example of intelligence and fortitude.

In this way family life based upon mutual understanding and helpfulness was built up in the new territories. Three immigrants from the recruitment of 1668, Jeanne-Marie Gaultier, Madeleine Philippe and Marguerite Robineau, all went through a form of marriage on the same day, before the same notary, and in the presence of the same witnesses, to Gilles Masson, Pierre Tousignan and Michel Gorron, all colonists. Immediately afterwards they left for the almost virgin seigneurie of Saint-Charles-des-Roches, where their spouses had begun to reclaim small pieces of land. In the early days they had only a temporary hut to shelter them. But children were born, and then after a few years the settlers set out to conquer new territory on the other side of the St. Lawrence river. The young wives bravely followed and took up their pioneering lives once more.

IN YOUR OWN VOICE

WHAT DOES IT SAY?

1. Why are the ships known as "the future of a new nation"?

2. What document had to be signed before a couple married?

3. What work do many women do before they marry?

4. Which quality do these young women share?

5. In what ways are these women adventurous?

6. What two kinds of caring benefit family life?

WHAT DOES IT MEAN?

1. Why are the King's Daughters placed in the care of nuns upon their arrival?

2. Why do many marriages not take place immediately?

3. Why does "every prominent person in the neighbourhood" attend the wedding ceremonies?

4. Why do most of the young women not marry settlers who came originally from their home provinces in France?

5. How does the women's bravery continue throughout the marriage?

6. Why did the King's Daughters decide to leave France?

STYLE AND SENSE

1. What idea is present in the opening and closing sentences of this selection?

2. In paragraph 3, which sentence is supported by the specific example of Jean Bellet and Madeleine Beaudouin?

3. In paragraphs 4, 5, and 6, what specific details or examples support the topic sentence?

4. What words or expressions make the reader care about these young brides?

FROM THE TEXT

Independent clause: a group of related words that contains a subject and a verb and that can stand alone as a sentence.

Read the following sentence:

Most of them were more than ready for adventure, and the women helped each other through difficult times.

a. Identify the two independent clauses.

b. List the subjects and verbs.

c. What is the connection between the words *most of them* and *women*?

d. What word is the connecting link between the two clauses?

e. What punctuation is used at the end of the first independent clause?

f. How does this sentence summarize the main ideas of the selection?

See page 382 for more on the independent clause.

WRITE NOW

Do one of the following activities:

1. Write a **journal** that refers to the women's thoughts and conversations aboard ship.

2. Make a **brainstorm** list of the difficulties or hardships facing the women in colonial Canada.

WRITING SUGGESTIONS

1. Imagine you are a woman coming to a new land for the specific purpose of getting married. Answer one of the following:

    a. Describe the hopes and fears you have about your future life.

or

    b. Describe the reasons you have for leaving home.

2. Tell whether arranged marriages are more likely to be successful than freely entered upon marriages.

3. Write a letter to your family back home, narrating your experiences from the moment you set foot in a new place.

FURTHER WRITING SUGGESTIONS

4. Narrate a situation in which the helpfulness of your neighbors enabled you to overcome the difficulties of being in a new area.

5. Describe the qualities your ideal marriage partner should have.

6. Describe how a woman might feel and act facing the challenges of a new life in the Americas.

SLAVE TRADE IN THE WEST INDIES*

The two connected readings that follow provide insights into European attitudes toward slaves and describe the actual proceedings of a slave market.

The first, a letter written in 1683 from the English-owned Royal African Company, shows the economic basis of the Jamaican-based slave trade.

The second is a selection from Richard Ligon's *True and Exact History of the Island of Barbados,* which describes the young Englishman's experiences in 1647. Ligon gives a stark eyewitness account of the buying and selling of slaves at auction.

Settled by the British in the late 1620s, Barbados played a major role in the commercial trade and slave traffic between Africa and the Western Hemisphere. The island was the first of the English settlements to receive slaves transported by European countries, especially England, Holland, and Portugal. Once in Barbados, the slaves were put up for sale as soon as possible.

WORDS TO NOTICE

(*Royal African Company letter*)

Royal African Company: founded in 1672, this company received a grant from the king of England for an unrestricted monopoly of the West Indian slave trade until 1688

pounds: British units of money

convened: brought before, summoned

l: abbreviation for *pound* (from the Latin *libra*)

interlopers: unauthorized traders

procure: obtain, get

*Editors' title

taxed: blamed, called to account

stipulated: agreed upon (by contract)

dispersed: distributed

monopolists: those with an exclusive license (to traffic in slaves)

chargeable: expensive to maintain, burdensome

impracticable: impractical, bad business

(A True and Exact History of the Island of Barbados)

infirmity: weakness, defect

pound sterling: British unit of money made of silver

desire: ask or request of

bravest: most splendid looking

better: person of greater ability, superior

precedence: priority, privilege

acknowledge: believe in the existence of

thence: that place

chast: chaste, pure, virtuous

breeches: trousers

wanton: immoral, leering

READ ON

1. What do the **title** and **headnote** tell you about the introduction of slavery to the Americas?

2. Which business and monetary terms are found in **Words to Notice**?

Royal African Company letter

October 23, 1683

Reasons advanced by the Royal African Company why the law of Jamaica fixing the price of negroes at eighteen pounds a head should not be continued.

When the Royal Company was convened before the King in November 1680, it agreed to supply three thousand negroes annually at 18 *l.* a head. The Jamaicans turned this into a law, which remains suspended during the King's pleasure. We, the Company, now begged to be released from that agreement, because the terms which were then advantageous are now the reverse. The number of interlopers increases; negroes cost a third to a half more than they did, and are difficult to procure. There is also a loss on the exchange from Jamaica. If it be objected that times may improve, we answer that in that case we shall be ready to lower our rates. We are taxed with having failed to supply the stipulated number. We have made provisions in ships and goods for the full quantity, but many ships have been unable to procure negroes, and after lying many months have left with but half their load of negroes, though with cargo all dispersed. Also, we have often lost a half to a third of the negroes shipped. Even if we had procured all the negroes we wanted, many commanders positively refuse to go to Jamaica in consequence of the laws. As to the objection that if our price were not limited, we might, being monopolists, make it ruinous, we answer that we enjoy far fewer advantages than any other joint stock company. Negroes are not only very chargeable and perishable, but it is impracticable to keep any quantity unsold for many days; we must part with them for what we can get.

From A *True and Exact History of the* Island *of* Barbados by Richard Ligon

When they are brought to us, the Planters buy them out of the Ship, where they find them stark naked, and therefore cannot be deceived in any outward infirmity. They choose them as they do Horses in a Market; the strongest, youthfullest, and most beautiful, yield the greatest prices. Thirty pound sterling is a price for the best man Negroe; and twenty five, twenty six, or twenty seven pound for a Woman; the Children are at easier rates. And we buy them so, as the sexes may be equall; for, if they have more Men than Women, the men who are unmarried will come to their Masters, and complain, that they cannot live without Wives, and desire him, they may have Wives. And he tells them, that the next ship that comes, he will buy them Wives, which satisfies them for the present; and so they expect the good time: which the Master performing with them, the bravest fellow is to choose first, and so in order, as they are in place; and every one of them knows his better, and gives him the precedence, as Cows do one another, in passing through a narrow gate; for, the most of them are as near beasts as may be, setting their souls aside. Religion they know none; yet most of them acknowledge a God, as appears by their motions and gestures: For, if one of them do another wrong, and he cannot revenge himself, he looks up to Heaven for vengeance, and holds up both his hands, as if the power must come from thence, that must do him right. Chast they are as any people under the Sun; for, when the men and women are together naked, they never cast their eyes towards the parts that ought to be covered; and those amongst us, that have Breeches and Petticoats, I never saw so much as a kiss, or embrace, or a wanton glance with their eyes between them.

IN YOUR OWN VOICE

WHAT DOES IT SAY?

1. How many slaves does the Royal African Company promise to supply per year? At what price?

2. How many slaves die on the ships?

3. Which slaves at the auction bring the highest prices?

4. Why do the masters buy an equal number of men and women?

5. Which slave has the first choice of a wife?

6. How do the slaves "acknowledge a God"?

7. Despite their nakedness, what proves that the slaves are modest?

WHAT DOES IT MEAN?

1. Why does the Royal African Company want to change the terms of the agreement?

2. What does "Negroes are not only very chargeable and perishable" suggest about the traders' attitudes toward the slaves?

3. Why do the planters buy the slaves "out of the ship"?

4. Why are the slaves compared to horses and cows?

5. Why do the planters pay less for children?

6. Why are the slaves thought to have no religion?

7. Why is the slaves' modesty praised?

STYLE AND SENSE

These questions are concerned with only the second of the reading selections, Ligon's description of a slave auction.

1. Which details in the opening sentence present a sharp picture of the auction and the participants?

2. Which details after the opening sentence are presented in series of three items?

3. What advantages are there in using series or lists to develop an idea or topic?

FROM THE TEXT

Run-on: two sentences, or two independent clauses, punctuated and written as one sentence. One way to prevent a run-on is to insert a semicolon between the two independent clauses.

Read the following sentence:

> They choose them as they do Horses in a Market; the strongest, youthfullest, and most beautiful, yield the greatest prices.

a. Identify the first independent clause.

b. Identify the second independent clause.

c. Which punctuation separates the two parts of the sentence?

d. What kind of clause is "as they do Horses in a Market"? Why?

See page 389 for more on the run-on sentence.

WRITE NOW

Do one of the following activities:

1. Write at least five **journalistic questions** about the slave trade.

2. **Freewrite** on one of the following Writing Suggestions.

WRITING SUGGESTIONS

1. Imagine that you are transported by a time machine. You are a spectator at a slave market. Describe the scene, the people, and your reactions.

2. Describe the survival skills that slaves possessed or had to develop.

3. Describe the effects that slavery might have on (a) the individual, (b) the family, and (c) the male-female relationship.

FURTHER WRITING SUGGESTIONS

4. Tell which opinions must be held by the buyers before they purchase other human beings.

5. Narrate a situation in which you or someone you know felt powerless against established authority.

6. Slavery has existed under all forms of government. Tell why.

THE GREAT GATSBY

By F. Scott Fitzgerald

This selection is the conclusion of F. Scott Fitzgerald's novel *The Great Gatsby,* published in 1925. It examines the American Dream 430 years after Columbus's arrival. The passage also looks back on the vanished "green" continent that the early European explorers saw stretching before them.

A young midwesterner, Nick Carraway, tells the story of Jay Gatsby, who owns a mansion on Long Island Sound and entertains hundreds of guests at lavish parties there. Gatsby's wealth comes from mysterious (probably illegal) sources.

Gatsby's love affair with a socially prominent married woman, Daisy Buchanan, leads to his covering up of her guilt in a hit-and-run accident. Later, the husband of the woman killed in the accident fatally shoots Gatsby.

Nick's description of the now dark and abandoned mansion casts a shadow on realizing the American Dream in the modern world. But the belief in human possibilities glimpsed in the distant American past still carries men and women forward.

WORDS TO NOTICE

incessant: unstopping, constant

material: real, actual, solid

incoherent: filled with mismatched styles

raspingly: with a harsh sound

inessential: insignificant, meaningless

pandered: slyly hinted

transitory: lasting for a short time

compelled: forced

aesthetic contemplation: thoughts of beauty

commensurate: equal to, measuring up to

brooding: worriedly thinking

obscurity: dimness, gloom

orgiastic: wildly exciting

recedes: goes backwards, retreats

eluded: evaded, escaped

borne: carried (past participle of *to bear*)

READ ON

1. Which of the **Words to Notice** deal with loss of power or direction?

2. What do you know about life in the Jazz Age or the Roaring Twenties?

Gatsby's house was still empty when I left—the grass on his lawn had grown 1
as long as mine. One of the taxi drivers in the village never took a fare past
the entrance gate without stopping for a minute and pointing inside; perhaps
it was he who drove Daisy and Gatsby over to East Egg the night of the
accident, and perhaps he had made a story about it all his own. I didn't want
to hear it and I avoided him when I got off the train.

I spent my Saturday nights in New York, because those gleaming, dazzling 2
parties of his were with me so vividly that I could still hear the music and
the laughter, faint and incessant, from his garden, and the cars going up and
down his drive. One night I did hear a material car there, and saw its lights
stop at his front steps. But I didn't investigate. Probably it was some final
guest who had been away at the ends of the earth and didn't know that the
party was over.

On the last night, with my trunk packed and my car sold to the grocer, 3
I went over and looked at that huge incoherent failure of a house once more.
On the white steps an obscene word, scrawled by some boy with a piece of
brick, stood out clearly in the moonlight, and I erased it, drawing my shoe
raspingly along the stone. Then I wandered down to the beach and sprawled
out on the sand.

Most of the big shore places were closed now and there were hardly any 4
lights except the shadowy, moving glow of a ferryboat across the Sound. And
as the moon rose higher the inessential houses began to melt away until
gradually I became aware of the old island here that flowered once for Dutch
sailors' eyes—a fresh, green breast of the new world. Its vanished trees, the
trees that had made way for Gatsby's house, had once pandered in whispers

to the last and greatest of all human dreams; for a transitory enchanted moment man must have held his breath in the presence of this continent, compelled into an aesthetic contemplation he neither understood nor desired, face to face for the last time in history with something commensurate to his capacity for wonder.

And as I sat there brooding on the old, unknown world, I thought of Gatsby's wonder when he first picked out the green light at the end of Daisy's dock. He had come a long way to this blue lawn, and his dream must have seemed so close that he could hardly fail to grasp it. He did not know that it was already behind him, somewhere back in that vast obscurity beyond the city, where the dark fields of the republic rolled on under the night. **5**

Gatsby believed in the green light, the orgiastic future that year by year recedes before us. It eluded us then, but that's no matter—to-morrow we will run faster, stretch out our arms farther. . . . And one fine morning— **6**

So we beat on, boats against the current, borne back ceaselessly into the past. **7**

IN YOUR OWN VOICE

WHAT DOES IT SAY?

1. What does Nick remember of Gatsby's parties?

2. What does Nick erase from the white steps?

3. Where do the lights on the water come from?

4. What first impression does the new land make on the Dutch sailors?

5. Why couldn't Gatsby grasp his dream?

WHAT DOES IT MEAN?

1. Why does the taxi driver always stop at the entrance gate to Gatsby's property?

2. Which of Nick's actions suggest that he wants to forget his close connection to Gatsby?

3. Why does Nick refer to the island that the Dutch sailors saw as the "new world"?

4. Why doesn't the "enchanted moment" last?

5. What does the last sentence mean?

STYLE AND SENSE

This selection contains contrasts of past and future, dark and light, and emptiness and fullness of life.

1. What do the opening and closing sentences have in common?

2. List at least three words or images indicating darkness; do the same for light.

3. List at least three words or images indicating the emptiness of life; do the same for the fullness of life.

4. Which feelings of the Dutch sailors are similar to Columbus's impressions upon arrival in the Americas?

FROM THE TEXT

> **Compound sentence:** a sentence that contains at least two independent clauses joined by a coordinating conjunction such as *and, but, for, nor, or, so, yet.*

Read the following sentence:

> Most of the big shore places were closed now and there were hardly any lights except the shadowy, moving glow of a ferryboat across the Sound.

a. What are the complete subjects and verbs of the two independent clauses?

b. Which coordinating conjunction joins the two independent clauses?

c. What is the meaning of this coordinating conjunction?

d. Why don't the words beginning with *except* form an independent clause?

See page 386 for more on the compound sentence.

WRITE NOW

1. Freewrite on the American Dream.

2. Make a **cluster diagram** of "natural" or "artificial" environments.

WRITING SUGGESTIONS

1. Tell why you agree or disagree with the statement that the dream of the United States of America still lives for most people.

2. Narrate a situation in which you moved toward a goal because of the strong effect of a past experience.

3. Describe your feelings after achieving a long-hoped-for success. Tell if you had to change your values along the way.

FURTHER WRITING SUGGESTIONS

4. Columbus and the Dutch sailors stood in wonder before the lands they came to. Describe your feelings about the world you live in today, or the world of this passage from *The Great Gatsby*.

5. Narrate a situation in which you overcame personal failure, loss, or disappointment. Tell what you gained from this experience.

6. Trees were destroyed to make way for Gatsby's mansion. Tell how you would balance concern for present comfort with concern for the environment in future generations.

UNIT 2

John Lewis Krimmel. *Fourth of July at Center Square, 1819.* The Historical Society of Pennsylvania.

INDEPENDENCE

The struggle for freedom is part of the history of the Americas. The first selection of this unit, representing the first of these independence movements, is the United States Declaration of Independence (1776). It is followed by a description of a constitutional parade in Philadelphia in 1788. Accompanying this reading is the Bill of Rights, the first ten amendments to the U.S. Constitution.

Also included is Frederick Douglass's July 4, 1852, speech on what that famous holiday means to the American slave. His thoughts reflect the difference between the ideal of freedom and the reality of slavery.

The chapter continues with two Latin American selections: the first is Simón Bolívar's 1814 address to an assembly in Caracas, Venezuela, on his role in helping to free his people from Spanish domination and his position in the new government. The second is a dialogue of ideas from Luis Llorens Torres's early twentieth-century play *El Grito de Lares (The Cry of Lares),* which is about the Puerto Rican uprising against Spain in 1868.

Next is an open letter written in 1907 by Abigail Scott Duniway urging the men of Oregon to approve women's right to vote.

The "I Have a Dream" speech (1963) of Martin Luther King, Jr., concludes this unit on freedom—its promise, its responsibility, its price.

BEFORE YOU READ

What does the word *independence* mean to you? To a nation? To a people?

What is the first modern democracy?

Why did the independence movements in the Americas grow?

What is the Bill of Rights?

Why are constitutions needed?

Why does the reality often conflict with the ideal?

Which qualities must leaders possess?

What is the role of the people in free societies?

How can a defeat be a unifying symbol for a people?

What are civil rights?

Is racial equality possible? Is it easy to achieve?

Do you take your freedoms for granted?

Have you ever lived in a country where your freedoms were denied?

Have you ever read the Declaration of Independence? The Bill of Rights?

What are amendments?

Why was the amendment granting women in the United States the right to vote not approved until this century?

How did the public generally react to suffragettes?

What barriers to freedom in the Americas have existed in the past? What barriers to freedom exist today?

Should there be any limits to freedom?

THE DECLARATION OF INDEPENDENCE

By Thomas Jefferson

July 4, 1776, stands as one of the most important dates in world history. On this day representatives of the thirteen colonies that belonged to England approved the Declaration of Independence. This document, primarily written by Thomas

Jefferson (1743–July 4, 1826), broadcast to the world the intention of the colonies to break away from the rule of King George III.

With the words "All men are created equal," this historic document announces for the first time in modern history a representative democracy. The democratic ideal asserts that the power to govern resides in the will of the people rather than in the age-old Divine Right of Kings.

The Declaration of Independence is also a political document justifying the colonies' revolt, both to American colonists and to governments and peoples of other nations. However, it was not until the conclusion of the Revolutionary War in 1783 that independence was achieved.

WORDS TO NOTICE

impel: force

endowed: blessed, enriched

unalienable: incapable of being taken away

deriving: obtaining, getting

abolish: do away with completely

prudence: caution, discretion

transient: temporary, brief

train: series

usurpations: illegal seizures

invariably: unchangingly

evinces: shows

absolute despotism: complete tyranny

constrains: forces

assent: agreement

relinquish: give up, surrender

inestimable: invaluable

formidable: of great concern

dissolutions: disbandings

annihilation: complete destruction

hither: here

appropriations: takeovers

render: make, cause

quartering: providing housing

abdicated: abandoned

mercenaries: hired soldiers

insurrections: revolts, uprisings

redress: relief, fairness

unwarrantable: unjustifiable

magnanimity: generosity

conjured them: asked them to recall

consanguinity: family ties

acquiesce: give in to

rectitude: rightness

solemnly: seriously

absolved: declared free, acquitted

levy: wage, carry out

READ ON

1. Which of the **Words to Notice** show the hostile feelings between the colonists and England?

2. What does it mean to declare your independence? For an individual? For a nation?

When in the course of human events, it becomes necessary for one people   1
to dissolve the political bands which have connected them with another, and
to assume among the Powers of the earth, the separate and equal station to
which the Laws of Nature and of Nature's God entitle them, a decent respect
to the opinions of mankind requires that they should declare the causes which
impel them to the separation.

        We hold these truths to be self-evident, that all men are created equal,   2
that they are endowed by their Creator with certain unalienable Rights, that
among these are Life, Liberty and the pursuit of Happiness. That to secure
these rights, Governments are instituted among Men deriving their just powers

from the consent of the governed. That whenever any Form of Government becomes destructive of these ends, it is the Right of the People to alter or to abolish it, and to institute new Government, laying its foundation on such principles and organizing its powers in such form, as to them shall seem most likely to effect their Safety and Happiness. Prudence, indeed, will dictate that Governments long established should not be changed for light and transient causes; and accordingly all experience hath shown, that mankind are more disposed to suffer, while evils are sufferable, than to right themselves by abolishing the forms to which they are accustomed. But when a long train of abuses and usurpations pursuing invariably the same Object evinces a design to reduce them under absolute Despotism, it is their right, it is their duty, to throw off such government, and to provide new Guards for their future security. Such has been the patient sufferance of these Colonies; and such is now the necessity which constrains them to alter their former Systems of Government. The history of the present King of Great Britain is a history of repeated injuries and usurpations, all having in direct object the establishment of an absolute Tyranny over these States. To prove this, let Facts be submitted to a candid world.

He has refused his Assent to laws, the most wholesome and necessary 3 for the public good.

He has forbidden his Governors to pass Laws of immediate and pressing 4 importance, unless suspended in their operation till his Assent should be obtained; and when so suspended, he has utterly neglected to attend to them.

He has refused to pass other Laws for the accommodation of large districts 5 of people, unless those people would relinquish the right of Representation in the Legislature, a right inestimable to them and formidable to tyrants only.

He has called together legislative bodies at places unusual, uncomfort- 6 able, and distant from the depository of their Public Records, for the sole purpose of fatiguing them into compliance with his measures.

He has dissolved Representative Houses repeatedly, for opposing with 7 manly firmness his invasions on the rights of the people.

He has refused for a long time, after such dissolutions, to cause others 8 to be elected; whereby the Legislative Powers, incapable of Annihilation, have returned to the People at large for their exercise; the State remaining in the mean time exposed to all the dangers of invasion from without, and convulsions within.

He has endeavoured to prevent the population of these States; for that 9 purpose obstructing the Laws of Naturalization of Foreigners; refusing to pass others to encourage their migration hither, and raising the conditions of new Appropriations of Lands.

He has obstructed the Administration of Justice, by refusing his Assent 10 to Laws for establishing Judiciary Powers.

He has made Judges dependent on his Will alone, for the tenure of their 11 offices, and the amount and payment of their salaries.

He has erected a multitude of New Offices, and sent hither swarms of 12 Officers to harass our People, and eat out their substance.

He has kept among us, in time of peace, Standing Armies without the   **13**
Consent of our Legislature.

He has affected to render the Military independent of and superior to the   **14**
Civil Power.

He has combined with others to subject us to jurisdictions foreign to our   **15**
constitution, and unacknowledged by our laws; giving his Assent to their acts
of pretended Legislation:

For quartering large bodies of armed troops among us: **16**

For protecting them, by a mock Trial, from Punishment for any Murders   **17**
which they should commit on the Inhabitants of these States:

For cutting off our Trade with all parts of the world: **18**

For imposing Taxes on us without our Consent: **19**

For depriving us in many cases, of the benefits of Trial by Jury: **20**

For transporting us beyond Seas to be tried for pretended offenses: **21**

For abolishing the free System of English Laws in a Neighbouring Prov-   **22**
ince, establishing therein an Arbitrary government, and enlarging its boundaries so as to render it at once an example and fit instrument for introducing
the same absolute rule into these Colonies:

For taking away our Charters, abolishing our most valuable Laws, and   **23**
altering fundamentally the Forms of our Governments:

For suspending our own Legislatures, and declaring themselves invested   **24**
with Power to legislate for us in all cases whatsoever.

He has abdicated Government here, by declaring us out of his Protection   **25**
and waging War against us.

He has plundered our seas, ravaged our Coasts, burnt our towns and   **26**
destroyed the Lives of our people.

He is at this time transporting large Armies of foreign Mercenaries to   **27**
compleat works of death, desolation and tyranny, already begun with circumstances of Cruelty & perfidy scarcely paralleled in the most barbarous ages,
and totally unworthy the Head of a civilized nation.

He has constrained our fellow Citizens taken Captive on the high Seas   **28**
to bear Arms against their Country, to become the executioners of their friends
and Brethren, or to fall themselves by their Hands.

He has excited domestic insurrections amongst us, and has endeavoured   **29**
to bring on the inhabitants of our frontiers, the merciless Indian Savages,
whose known rule of warfare, is an undistinguished destruction of all ages,
sexes and conditions.

In every stage of these Oppressions We Have Petitioned for Redress in   **30**
the most humble terms: Our repeated petitions have been answered only by
repeated injury. A Prince, whose character is thus marked by every act which
may define a Tyrant, is unfit to be the ruler of a free People.

Nor have We been wanting in attention to our British brethren. We have   **31**
warned them from time to time of attempts by their legislature to extend an
unwarrantable jurisdiction over us. We have reminded them of the circumstances of our emigration and settlement here. We have appealed to their

native justice and magnanimity and we have conjured them by the ties of our common kindred to disavow these usurpations, which would inevitably interrupt our connections and correspondence. They too have been deaf to the voice of justice and of consanguinity. We must, therefore, acquiesce in the necessity, which denounces our Separation, and hold them, as we hold the rest of mankind, Enemies in War, in Peace Friends.

We, therefore, the Representatives of the United States of America, in **32** General Congress, Assembled, appealing to the Supreme Judge of the world for the rectitude of our intentions, do, in the Name, and by Authority of the good People of these Colonies, solemnly publish and declare, That these United Colonies are, and of Right ought to be Free and Independent States; that they are Absolved from all Allegiance to the British Crown, and that all political connection between them and the State of Great Britain, is and ought to be totally dissolved; and that as Free and Independent States, they have full power to levy War, conclude Peace, contract Alliances, establish Commerce, and to do all other Acts and Things which Independent States may of right do. And for the support of this Declaration, with a firm reliance on the protection of Divine Providence, we mutually pledge to each other our lives, our Fortunes and our sacred Honor.

IN YOUR OWN VOICE

WHAT DOES IT SAY?

1. Why is this document called the Declaration of Independence?

2. Which three rights do all people share?

3. From whom do governments get their power?

4. When can people change their government?

5. What must the people do after abolishing an unjust government?

6. Identify three causes that "impel" the colonies to break away from England.

7. What rights does the newly formed nation declare for itself?

WHAT DOES IT MEAN?

1. What did the words "All men are created equal" mean to the signers of the Declaration of Independence?

2. What is the meaning of "life, liberty and the pursuit of happiness"?

3. How can people exercise and protect their rights in a democracy?

4. Why did it take a long time before the colonists acted to revolt against England?

5. What is unique about the Declaration of Independence in its description of the people's relationship to their government?

STYLE AND SENSE

1. Independence is the main idea of the opening sentence. How is this idea restated in the closing paragraph?

2. What repeated word in paragraph 2 introduces each of the self-evident truths?

3. How does the word *but* in paragraph 2 change the direction and meaning of that paragraph?

4. What repeated word in the closing paragraph introduces the world to the rights of a new nation?

5. Which words and expressions in the document might convince a colonist to fight for freedom and independence and not to remain loyal to the king of England?

FROM THE TEXT

Past participle: the form of a verb that regularly ends in *-ed* and that follows a helping verb, such as *have, be, get,* and *seem.*

Read the following sentence:

We hold these truths to be self-evident, that all men are created equal, that they are endowed by their Creator with certain unalienable Rights, that among these are Life, Liberty and the pursuit of Happiness.

a. Find the two verb forms that end in *-ed.*

b. What is the helping verb that appears before each?

c. Locate at least five more examples in the Declaration of Independence of a helping verb followed by a past participle ending in *-ed.*

See page 429 for more on the past participle.

WRITE NOW

Do one of the following activities:

1. Make a **brainstorm** list of the rights that you consider most important.

2. **Freewrite** on one of the following Writing Suggestions.

WRITING SUGGESTIONS

1. From your experience, tell whether people in this society are created or treated equally.

2. Imagine that you are writing your own declaration of independence. Tell which rights you would guarantee most for yourself and others.

3. Narrate an experience in which you as an individual came into conflict with, disagreed with, or opposed an authority.

FURTHER WRITING SUGGESTIONS

4. Tell how "a decent respect to the opinions of mankind" guides the actions of people and nations.

5. Democracy depends upon "the consent of the governed." Tell why voting is essential to the idea of democracy.

CONSTITUTIONAL MIRACLE*

By Catherine Drinker Bowen

Eleven years after the Declaration of Independence and four years after the treaty ending the Revolutionary War, state delegates met in Philadelphia in May 1787 to prepare a constitution to govern the new nation.

The U.S. Constitution established a federal system of government in which the national government shared power with the governments of the individual states. Not every state would approve or ratify the Constitution until a Bill of Rights was added to protect citizens' individual liberties, such as freedom of speech and press. (The Bill of Rights appears on pages 76–77.)

Catherine Drinker Bowen (1897–1973) was best known as the author of biographies of historical figures, including *Yankee from Olympus,* the life of Justice Oliver Wendell Holmes, Jr., and *John Adams and the American Revolution.*

This selection from *Miracle in Philadelphia* describes a parade in celebration of the ratification of the Constitution.

WORDS TO NOTICE

ratified: approved of

animosity: strong dislike

*Editors' title

endemic: unique, special to

Antifederalists: people opposed to the federal system of government, in which there is one centralized authority

contemporary: one who lives at the same time

circumvented: evaded, sidestepped

wharves: piers, landing places for ships

pennants: banners, flags, standards

dragoons: soldiers

resplendent: decked out, shining

steed: horse

herald: messenger

car: wheeled vehicle

emblazoned: brightly displayed

edifice: building

frieze: decorated horizontal strip

cornucopia: horn of plenty

edifying: uplifting

denomination: religious group

benevolence: goodwill

aurora borealis: northern lights

awed: astonished

conveyed: carried

READ ON

1. What does the **headnote** tell you about the Constitution?

2. Imagine the sights and sounds of a parade in 1788.

By August, 1788, eleven states had ratified: Delaware, Pennsylvania, New   1
Jersey, Georgia, Connecticut, Massachusetts, Maryland, South Carolina, New
Hampshire, Virginia, New York. Rhode Island and North Carolina would come

along in their time. As soon as a majority of nine was assured, state by state held joyful celebration, animosity for the moment forgotten. Perhaps this is endemic to America; once the vote is counted, everybody wants to be in the parade. There was rioting in Albany by Antifederalists, a public burning of the Constitution. Yet in New York City, ten horses had pulled the ship *Hamilton* through the streets—a frigate of thirty-two guns, full-rigged and manned with thirty seamen, "every thing complete and in proportion," a contemporary wrote. Providence, Rhode Island, attempted a Federalist demonstration; it was circumvented when Antifeds, greatly in the majority, advanced upon the scene, forcibly converted the preparations into a July Fourth celebration and helped the Federalists to consume their roasted ox.

The Federal processions were wonderfully ingenious. The ship *Federal Constitution,* the ship *Union,* mounted on wagons, were drawn by horses which bore on their foreheads the names of ratifying states. Philadelphia chose July Fourth for her celebration, and it outdid all the rest. At sunrise a full peal of bells rang out from Christ Church steeple; the ship *Rising Sun,* anchored off Market Street, discharged her cannon in salute to the day. At the wharves all vessels were decorated, and along the harbor from South Street to the Northern Liberties ten ships were ranged, each bearing at its masthead a broad white flag inscribed with the name of a state in gold: *New Hampshire . . . Massachusetts . . . Pennsylvania . . .* A brisk south wind, coming up with the dawn, fluttered the pennants all day.

By eight in the morning the procession was assembling; at nine-thirty it began to move. The First City Troop of Light Dragoons led off, resplendent in their blue coats faced with red, their white saddleclothes edged in blue. After them rode a horseman carrying a flag to symbolize Independence. Next came Thomas Fitzsimons—a member of the Federal Convention—riding Count Rochambeau's steed and bearing a standard with the date of the French Alliance: *Sixth of February, 1778.* Then a horseman carrying a staff twined with olive and laurel, to celebrate the Peace Treaty of 1783; after him a herald with a trumpet, proclaiming a New Era. Next came the Convention of the States, personified by Peter Muhlenberg on horseback; behind him a band of music, playing for dear life a grand march composed for the occasion by Alexander Reinagle.

On they marched, the horses stepping high through streets swept clean for the occasion, under trees neatly trimmed. One rider carried a banner inscribed *Washington, the Friend of his Country.* A big car rumbled by in the shape of an eagle, painted bright blue. On the eagle's breast thirteen stars were emblazoned above thirteen red and white stripes. Six horses drew the vehicle, on which a staff was fixed, holding the Constitution, framed, and crowned with the cap of liberty. Seated within the car, glorious in their robes of office, were Chief Justice McKean and the justices Atlee and Rush.

All along Third Street, up Callowhill to Fourth and west on Market Street went the Grand Procession, a mile and a half of it. Spectators crowded the footways, stood at open windows and on the roofs of the houses, gazing

down at the tramping bright lines of marchers. The consuls and representatives of foreign states passed "in an ornamental car drawn by four horses."
Barbé-Marbois was among them. . . . A citizen and an Indian chief sat side
by side in their carriage, "smoking the Calumet of Peace together—the Sach-
em's head adorned with scarlet and white plumes, ten strings of wampum
round his neck."

But the crowning glory was the Grand Foederal Edifice, set on a carriage   6
drawn by ten white horses. Thirteen Corinthian columns, ten of them complete, three left unfinished, supported the dome. The frieze showed thirteen
stars, and surmounting the dome the figure of *Plenty* bore a cornucopia. *In
Union the Fabric stands firm,* said a device around the pedestal. Ten gentlemen
sat within the Edifice; they represented the citizens at large, to whom the
Constitution had been committed for ratification.

Architects and house carpenters followed on foot, to the number of four   7
hundred and fifty; behind them, sawmakers and filecutters with their flag—
a gold saw on a pink shield. The Agricultural Society was led by "Samuel
Powell, Eq." After him, farmers drove four-ox plows, and a sower spread his
seed. . . . The Manufacturing Society, its insignia a beehive, with bees issuing
in the rays of a rising sun. The Society's horse-drawn platform was thirty feet
long and carried spindles and a carding machine, with women workers drawing cotton, "suitable for blue jeans or federal rib." The float, the whirring
machines were viewed "with astonishment and delight." Citizens could soon
be clothed in cotton, a new fabric, proper for both winter and summer, and
not attractive to moths.

On they came: brickmakers and clockmakers, fringe and ribbon weavers;   8
saddlers and cordwainers; boat builders, sailmakers, ship joiners, ropemak-
ers, carvers, gilders, coopers; blacksmiths and coachmakers, skinners and
glovers; goldsmiths and gunsmiths, the brewers and bakers dressed in spot-
less white; tailors, perukemakers, barber-surgeons and staymakers. "Mr. Francis Serre, with his first journeyman, carried an elegant pair of lady's stays."
Watchmen marched, calling the hour: *"Ten* o'clock, and a glorious star-light
morning." (This, said the *Pennsylvania Gazette,* meant the ten states that had
ratified.)

It was wonderful and heartwarming and edifying, including the ranks of   9
marching clergy, "of almost every denomination, united in charity and broth-
erly love. A circumstance," added the *Gazette,* "which probably never occurred in such extent." The Federal ship *Union,* on its carriage, mounted
twenty guns, "an elegant piece of workmanship," carved and painted, manned
by a crew of twenty-five. Boys trimmed sail as the ship moved along; the pilot
was received on board, and as the procession approached Union Green—
named for the occasion—a sailor threw the leadline and cast anchor.

Union Green lay at the foot of Bush Hill, Mr. William Hamilton's estate.   10
Here, under awnings, tables had been set out, with a "plentiful cold collation."
James Wilson made a speech, after which ten toasts were drunk, in American
porter, beer and cider, each toast being announced by a trumpet and answered

by a discharge of artillery from the ship *Rising Sun* in the harbor. The crowd drank to "The people of the United States." They toasted "Honor and Immortality to the Members of the late Convention." Lastly, with a large benevolence, they drank to "The Whole Family of Mankind."

By six o'clock it was over. "Seventeen thousand" celebrants "*soberly* **11** retired to their respective homes," said the official account, written by Francis Hopkinson, chairman of the committee of arrangement. Hopkinson had labored mightily, including the composition of an *Ode* in four verses, distributed to the crowd as the procession moved along:

> Hail to this festival!—all hail the day!
> Columbia's standard on her roof display!
> And let the people's motto ever be,
> "United thus, and thus united, free!"

The weather had been cloudy, but toward late afternoon the sun came **12** out, and in the evening, "the sky was illuminated by a beautiful aurora borealis." Afterward, people remarked upon the spectators' silence while the procession passed. Benjamin Rush the Philadelphia physician, signer of the Declaration of Independence, called it a "solemn silence," as though citizens were awed, moved by a joy intense and profound. No victory during the late war, Rush said, had brought such deep-seated happiness to every countenance. The sight of the Federal ship *Union*, "complete in all its parts and moving upon dry land conveyed emotions . . . that cannot be described . . . The union of twelve states in the *form*, and of ten states in the *adoption*, of the Constitution in less than ten months, under the influence of local prejudices, opposite interests, popular arts, and even the threats of bold and desperate men, is a solitary event in the history of mankind.

"'Tis done," Rush wrote. "We have become a nation." **13**

THE BILL OF RIGHTS

AMENDMENTS TO THE CONSTITUTION

(The first ten Amendments, usually called the Bill of Rights, went into effect December 15, 1791.)

AMENDMENT I

Congress shall make no law respecting an establishment of religion, or prohibiting the free exercise thereof; or abridging the freedom of speech or of the press; or the right of the people peaceably to assemble, and to petition the government for a redress of grievances.

AMENDMENT II

A well-regulated militia being necessary to the security of a free state, the right of the people to keep and bear arms shall not be infringed.

AMENDMENT III

No soldier shall, in time of peace, be quartered in any house without the consent of the owner, nor in time of war but in a manner to be prescribed by law.

AMENDMENT IV

The right of the people to be secure in their persons, houses, papers, and effects, against unreasonable searches and seizures, shall not be violated, and no warrants shall issue but upon probable cause, supported by oath or affirmation, and particularly describing the place to be searched, and the persons or things to be seized.

AMENDMENT V

No person shall be held to answer for a capital or other infamous crime unless on a presentment or indictment of a grand jury, except in cases arising in the land or naval forces, or in the militia, when in actual service, in time of war or public danger; nor shall any person be subject for the same offence to be twice put in jeopardy of life or limb; nor shall be compelled in any criminal case to be a witness against himself, nor be deprived of life, liberty, or property, without due process of law; nor shall private property be taken for public use without just compensation.

AMENDMENT VI

In all criminal prosecutions, the accused shall enjoy the right to a speedy and public trial, by an impartial jury of the state and district wherein the crime shall have been committed, which district shall have been previously ascertained by law, and to be informed of the nature and cause of the accusation; to be confronted with the witnesses against him; to have compulsory process for obtaining witnesses in his favor, and to have the assistance of counsel for his defence.

AMENDMENT VII

In suits at common law, where the value in controversy shall exceed twenty dollars, the right of trial by jury shall be preserved, and no fact tried by a jury shall be otherwise re-examined in any court of the United States than according to the rules of the common law.

AMENDMENT VIII

Excessive bail shall not be required, nor excessive fines imposed, nor cruel and unusual punishments inflicted.

AMENDMENT IX

The enumeration in the Constitution of certain rights shall not be construed to deny or disparage others retained by the people.

AMENDMENT X

The powers not delegated to the United States by the Constitution, nor prohibited by it to the states, are reserved to the states respectively, or to the people.

IN YOUR OWN VOICE

WHAT DOES IT SAY?

1. How many states were needed to ratify the Constitution?

2. What ships are borne through the streets in the parades celebrating the Constitution?

3. Which city holds the most splendid procession?

4. How does the celebration highlight the number 13?

5. How do ordinary citizens in the parade show their support for the Constitution?

WHAT DOES IT MEAN?

1. How does the ratification vote reveal the democratic process?

2. Why is the Constitution burned in Albany?

3. What is new about the banner proclaiming "Washington, the Friend of his Country"?

4. What does the list of marchers (paragraph 8) tell about the new nation's economic opportunities?

5. How do the floats show the various strengths of the new nation?

6. How does the change in the weather mirror the rising fortunes of the new nation?

STYLE AND SENSE

The description of the Constitution parade in Philadelphia is clear and vivid because of specific details of **time** and **space. Transitional** words and phrases unify and organize the events of this one day.

1. Which words and phrases, often at the openings of paragraphs, show the orderly passage of time during the Philadelphia parade?

2. Which words and phrases show the line of march through the city streets?

3. Which transitional words and phrases in paragraph 3 indicate the order of marchers?

4. How does the use of color give meaning and add vividness to the description of the parade?

5. Why is closing with Rush's quotation effective?

FROM THE TEXT

Subject-verb agreement of indefinite pronouns: words like *everyone, somebody, anyone, anything,* and *nobody* are considered to be third person singular.

Read the following sentence:

Perhaps this is endemic to America; once the vote is counted, everybody wants to be in the parade.

   a. What is the indefinite pronoun?

   b. What is the verb that agrees with it?

   c. Why does the verb end in *-s*?

   See page 412 for more on subject-verb agreement of indefinite pronouns.

WRITE NOW

Do one of the following activities:

1. Make a list of **journalistic questions** about the events in the reading.

2. Make a **cluster diagram** of people's rights or responsibilities in a democracy.

WRITING SUGGESTIONS

1. Imagine that you are a worker mentioned in paragraph 8. Describe the float that your occupational skills would help you to build.

2. In 1788 those who watched the parade were united by patriotism. Describe the feelings and symbols that unite Americans today, two hundred years later.

3. General George Washington rejected an offer to become king of the new nation. Tell how you would have responded to this offer.

FURTHER WRITING SUGGESTIONS

4. An openly racist or anti-American group is scheduled to hold a meeting on your campus. Tell whether its right to hold such a meeting is justified and protected by the First Amendment to the Constitution.

5. The Preamble (Introduction) to the Constitution begins, "We, the People." Narrate a personal experience that involved your constitutional rights.

6. Tell how one amendment in the Bill of Rights is especially important to you as a private citizen.

WHAT, TO THE AMERICAN SLAVE, IS YOUR FOURTH OF JULY?*

By Frederick Douglass

Frederick Douglass (1817?–1895) was born into slavery in Maryland, escaped to New York in 1838, and became a noted antislavery speaker and writer. His best-known work is *Narrative of the Life of Frederick Douglass, An American Slave,* published in 1845. In the decade before the Civil War, he published the antislavery weekly *North Star.*

After the Civil War, Douglass served as a U.S. marshal. In 1889 he became consul general to Haiti, a post he resigned two years later in a dispute over U.S. government policies.

This reading is taken from the July 4, 1852, address delivered by Douglass in Rochester, New York. The subject of this speech is the differences between the ideals of the Declaration of Independence and the realities of slavery. Douglass reminds his listeners that, in part, the Declaration was written by men who were slave owners.

The three periods (...) following the second paragraph let you know that this selection does not contain a portion (four paragraphs) of the original speech.

WORDS TO NOTICE

embodied in: identified with

devout: wholehearted

obdurate: stubborn

stolid: unfeeling

jubilee: special anniversary

servitude: slavery

*Editors' title

hart: male deer

affirm: state as a fact

cyphering: ciphering, doing arithmetic

orators: public speakers

republicans: supporters of the form of representative government found in the United States

beset with: burdened by

discourse: speech

canopy: covering

flay: strip off

sunder: separate

blasphemy: contempt for religion

reproach: disapproval, rebuke

propriety: moral attitude

gross: monstrous

vanity: pride

denunciations: condemnations

brass fronted impudence: total lack of shame

bombast: empty words

impiety: lack of religious values

despotisms: tyrannies, undemocratic governments

revolting barbarity: savage cruelty

READ ON

1. What response do you have to the **title** question?

2. The U.S. Civil War began in 1861. What is important about the time and place of the speech?

Fellow-citizens, pardon me, allow me to ask, why am I called upon to speak   1
here to-day? What have I, or those I represent, to do with your national
independence? Are the great principles of political freedom and of natural

justice, embodied in that Declaration of Independence, extended to us? and am I, therefore, called upon to bring our humble offering to the national altar, and to confess the benefits and express devout gratitude for the blessings resulting from your independence to us?

Would to God, both for your sakes and ours, that an affirmative answer *2* could be truthfully returned to these questions! Then would my task be light, and my burden easy and delightful. For *who* is there so cold, that a nation's sympathy could not warm him? Who so obdurate and dead to the claims of gratitude, that would not thankfully acknowledge such priceless benefits? Who so stolid and selfish, that would not give his voice to swell the hallelujahs of a nation's jubilee, when the chains of servitude had been torn from his limbs? I am not that man. In a case like that, the dumb might eloquently speak, and the "lame man leap as an hart." . . .

For the present, it is enough to affirm the equal manhood of the negro *3* race. Is it not astonishing that, while we are ploughing, planting and reaping, using all kinds of mechanical tools, erecting houses, constructing bridges, building ships, working in metals of brass, iron, copper, silver and gold; that, while we are reading, writing and cyphering, acting as clerks, merchants and secretaries, having among us lawyers, doctors, ministers, poets, authors, editors, orators and teachers; that, while we are engaged in all manner of enterprises common to other men, digging gold in California, capturing the whale in the Pacific, feeding sheep and cattle on the hill-side, living, moving, acting, thinking, planning, living in families as husbands, wives and children, and, above all, confessing and worshipping the Christian's God, and looking hopefully for life and immortality beyond the grave, we are called upon to prove that we are men!

Would you have me argue that man is entitled to liberty? that he is the *4* rightful owner of his own body? You have already declared it. Must I argue the wrongfulness of slavery? Is that a question for Republicans? Is it to be settled by the rules of logic and argumentation, as a matter beset with great difficulty, involving a doubtful application of the principle of justice, hard to be understood? How should I look to-day, in the presence of Americans, dividing, and subdividing a discourse, to show that men have a natural right to freedom? speaking of it relatively, and positively, negatively, and affirmatively. To do so, would be to make myself ridiculous, and to offer an insult to your understanding. There is not a man beneath the canopy of heaven, that does not know that slavery is wrong *for him.*

What, am I to argue that it is wrong to make men brutes, to rob them of *5* their liberty, to work them without wages, to keep them ignorant of their relations to their fellow men, to beat them with sticks, to flay their flesh with the lash, to load their limbs with irons, to hunt them with dogs, to sell them at auction, to sunder their families, to knock out their teeth, to burn their flesh, to starve them into obedience and submission to their masters? Must I argue that a system thus marked with blood, and stained with pollution, is *wrong*? No! I will not. I have better employments for my time and strength, than such arguments would imply.

What, then, remains to be argued? Is it that slavery is not divine; that God **6** did not establish it; that our doctors of divinity are mistaken? There is blasphemy in the thought. That which is inhuman, cannot be divine! *Who* can reason on such a proposition? They that can, may; I cannot. The time for such argument is past.

At a time like this, scorching irony, not convincing argument, is needed. **7** O! had I the ability, and could I reach the nation's ear, I would, to-day, pour out a fiery stream of biting ridicule, blasting reproach, withering sarcasm, and stern rebuke. For it is not light that is needed, but fire; it is not the gentle shower, but thunder. We need the storm, the whirlwind, and the earthquake. The feeling of the nation must be quickened; the conscience of the nation must be roused; the propriety of the nation must be startled; the hypocrisy of the nation must be exposed; and its crimes against God and man must be proclaimed and denounced.

What, to the American slave, is your 4th of July? I answer: a day that **8** reveals to him, more than all other days in the year, the gross injustice and cruelty to which he is the constant victim. To him, your celebration is a sham; your boasted liberty, an unholy license; your national greatness, swelling vanity; your sounds of rejoicing are empty and heartless; your denunciations of tyrants, brass fronted impudence; your shouts of liberty and equality, hollow mockery; your prayers and hymns, your sermons and thanksgivings, with all your religious parade, and solemnity, are, to him, mere bombast, fraud, deception, impiety, and hypocrisy—a thin veil to cover up crimes which would disgrace a nation of savages. There is not a nation on the earth guilty of practices, more shocking and bloody, than are the people of these United States, at this very hour.

Go where you may, search where you will, roam through all the mon- **9** archies and despotisms of the old world, travel through South America, search out every abuse, and when you have found the last, lay your facts by the side of the everyday practices of this nation, and you will say with me, that, for revolting barbarity and shameless hypocrisy, America reigns without a rival.

IN YOUR OWN VOICE

WHAT DOES IT SAY?

1. In which document are the "great principles" of freedom and justice found?

2. What fact does Douglass wish to affirm?

3. What abuses are the slaves victims of?

4. What does the Fourth of July reveal to the American slave?

5. What cover-up are the people of the United States accused of?

6. How do the cruelties of Europe and South America compare with those of the United States?

WHAT DOES IT MEAN?

1. Why does Douglass open the speech with the words "Fellow-citizens, pardon me . . ."?

2. Why is Douglass unable to give voice to a speech celebrating the Fourth of July?

3. Why is it unnecessary to speak against slavery?

4. Why does he consider slavery a crime against God?

5. Why is slavery worse than any other form of tyranny?

STYLE AND SENSE

1. What is the effect of opening the speech with a series of questions?

2. In which other paragraphs do series of questions appear?

3. In which paragraphs are series or lists used in support of Douglass's ideas?

4. The opening paragraph praises independence. Which contrasts to independence are found in the closing paragraph?

5. Why is it an effective closing when Douglass commands the audience to "Go where you may, search where you will, . . ."?

FROM THE TEXT

Subject-verb agreement: the relationship between a subject and a verb in which a singular subject requires a singular verb, a plural subject requires a plural verb.

Read the following sentence:

There is not a nation on the earth guilty of practices, more shocking and bloody, than are the people of these United States at this very hour.

a. Identify the two clauses.

b. Find the first noun in each of these clauses.

c. Which is singular and which is plural?

d. Are these nouns the subjects of their clauses?

e. Which verb goes with which noun?

f. Does the verb usually come before the subject of a sentence?

See page 408 for more on subject-verb agreement.

WRITE NOW

Do one of the following activities.

1. Write a **journal** of a slave's daily activities.

2. Make a **brainstorm** list of your memories of racial or cultural divisions or conflicts.

WRITING SUGGESTIONS

1. This speech by Frederick Douglass cries out against conditions in the United States in 1852. Tell whether or not the ideas of the speech have significance for the present or future of any country in the Americas.

2. Using specific details such as brief lists and series of examples, describe the benefits that independence brings to an individual.

3. In paragraph 3, Douglass mentions the contributions that black workers made to society. Tell how members of minority groups have contributed and continue to contribute to society.

FURTHER WRITING SUGGESTIONS

4. Political candidates make promises. Describe the differences between the promise and the reality in one of the following: housing, employment, education, health care.

5. Tell whether you agree or disagree with the opinion that individuals are responsible for their own fates. Give personal examples or opinions to support your ideas.

6. In paragraphs 4 and 5, Douglass says that slavery is wrong and his audience knows it. Tell why little or no action to eliminate slavery was taken by most of the people in the free states at that time (1852).

INDEPENDENCE OR CONTROL?*

By Simón Bolívar

Known as The Liberator, Simón Bolívar (1783–1830) was the leading soldier and statesman in the Latin American independence movement. He led several campaigns against Spain, which had dominated South America for more than three hundred years.

In the words of the Puerto Rican poet Luis Llorens Torres, Bolívar was "politician, soldier, hero, orator, and poet. Great in everything."

After Venezuela declared its independence in 1811, Bolívar headed a revolutionary army. He proclaimed himself dictator of western Venezuela in 1813, but he was driven out of power the following year.

Over the next decade, Bolívar continued to battle Spain until he achieved decisive victories, liberating Colombia (1819), Venezuela (1821), Ecuador (1822), and Peru (1824). In 1825 the state of Upper Peru was renamed Bolivia in his honor.

This 1814 speech to an informal parliament in Caracas, Venezuela, shows Bolívar's conflicting desires: independence for the Spanish-speaking countries of South America and his personal, absolute control over these new nations.

There is dispute as to whether the speech truly reflects a democratic process or whether Bolívar is manipulating his audience. One fact is clear: the assembly at the end of the meeting granted Bolívar dictatorial powers.

WORDS TO NOTICE

banished: exiled, forcibly removed

redeem: save, deliver

Magdalena: northern coastal area of Colombia

shackle: restrain, hold back

oppressors: cruel, unjust leaders

ignominy: great shame, disgrace

languishing: weakening and suffering

compelled: forced, driven

valorous: brave

just Providence: fair God

*Editors' title

accorded: granted, brought

anarchy: lawless society

sustain: support, supply

sovereign: supreme, kingly; king, ruler

render: present for approval or consideration

stewardship: management, direction

augmenting: increasing

exempt: free; not require to hold

aspire: have ambition for

sheathe: put into the sword's protective cover

succumbing: yielding, surrendering

yoke: control, restraining power

deemed: thought, judged

husband: manage wisely

edifice: foundation of constitutional government; structure

READ ON

1. Which of the **Words to Notice** deal with independence and barriers to independence?

2. Why did Simón Bolívar, unlike George Washington, accept dictatorial powers?

Caracas, January 2, 1814.

Fellow-Citizens: 1

Hatred of tyranny banished me from Venezuela when I saw my country en-chained for the second time; but love of liberty overcame every obstacle in the path which I took to redeem my country from the cruelties and tortures of the Spaniard and brought me back from the distant banks of the Magdalena. My armies, repeatedly triumphant, have everywhere taken possession and have destroyed the powerful foe. Your chains now shackle your oppressors. The Spanish blood that tinges the battlefield has avenged your slain coun-trymen.

I have not given you freedom; for this you are indebted to my fellow-   **2**
soldiers. Behold their noble wounds, which still bleed; recall to mind those
who have perished in battle. My glory has been in the leading of these brave
soldiers. Neither vanity nor lust for power inspired me in this enterprise. The
flame of freedom lighted this sacred fire within me, and the sight of my fellow-
citizens suffering the ignominy of death on the scaffold, or languishing in
chains, compelled me to take up the sword against the enemy. The justice
of our cause united the most valorous soldiers under my banners, and a just
Providence accorded us victory.

My desire to save you from anarchy and to destroy the enemies who were   **3**
endeavoring to sustain the oppressors forced me to accept and retain the
sovereign power. I have given you laws; I have organized for you an administration of justice and finance; in short, I have given you a government.

Citizens, I am not your sovereign. Your representatives must make your   **4**
laws; the national treasury is not the property of him who governs you. Every
administrator of your interests must render you an account of his stewardship.
Judge impartially for yourselves whether I have used the elements of power
for my own advancement, or whether I have devoted my life, my thoughts,
my every moment to make of you a nation by augmenting your resources or,
rather, by creating them.

I yearn for the moment when I can transfer this power to the represen-   **5**
tatives which you will choose. I sincerely trust, Gentlemen, that you will
exempt me from an office which not a few of you could hold with distinction.
Grant me the one honor to which I aspire—that of continuing to fight your
enemies; for I shall never sheathe my sword so long as my country's freedom
is not absolutely assured.

The glory you acquired by expelling your oppressors has been beclouded;   **6**
your honor has been compromised, for you have lost it in succumbing to the
tyrant's yoke. You were the victims of a cruel vengeance. The interests of the
country were in the hands of bandits. Judge, therefore, whether your honor
has been restored; whether your chains have been struck off; whether I have
rid you of your enemies; whether I have given you justice; and whether I have
organized the national treasury.

I submit to you three certified reports by those who have been my deputies   **7**
in exercising the supreme power. The three secretaries of state shall report
whether or not you have taken your place upon the world stage, whether all
the nations that deemed your cause lost once again gaze upon you to admire
the efforts which you are making to insure your existence; whether these
same nations can refuse to respect and recognize your national flag; whether
your enemies have been destroyed as often as they have faced the armies of
the Republic; whether I, at their head, have defended your sacred rights;
whether I have employed your treasury in your defense; whether I have taken
measures to husband and increase it; and whether, on the very field of battle
and in the heat of combat, I have thought of you and of laying the cornerstone

Venezuela

of that edifice which will make of you a free, prosperous, and honored nation. It will then be yours to declare whether or not the plans which have been adopted can carry the Republic to glory and happiness.

IN YOUR OWN VOICE

WHAT DOES IT SAY?

1. Which European nation's troops do Bolívar's armies defeat?

2. What causes Bolívar to fight against the enemy?

3. What does Bolívar claim to give to the Venezuelan people?

4. Which public office does Bolívar not wish to hold?

5. Whose "supreme power" do the three deputies serve?

WHAT DOES IT MEAN?

1. Why does Bolívar praise his soldiers more than himself?

2. Why does Bolívar yearn to transfer "sovereign power" to the future elected representatives?

3. Why have the Venezuelan people lost some glory and honor during the years of Spanish rule?

4. Why does Bolívar not completely trust the Venezuelan people to govern themselves?

5. Why does Bolívar ask the assembly to judge the three "certified reports"?

STYLE AND SENSE

1. Why do paragraphs 1 and 2 highlight past events in the war for Venezuelan independence?

2. Why do paragraphs 3 through 6 focus on current (1814) questions about the formation of an independent government?

3. What future event is emphasized in the speech's closing sentence (see paragraph 7)?

4. How do the other sentences in paragraph 7 restate the main themes of the speech?

5. Why does Bolívar, like Frederick Douglass (see page 81), begin his address with "Fellow-Citizens"?

FROM THE TEXT

Infinitive: the verbal form after the introductory word *to* or after such helping verbs as *will, can,* and *must.* Infinitives do not add *-ed, -s,* or any other ending. Infinitives are not considered to be the verbs of sentences.

Read the following sentence:

My desire to save you from anarchy and to destroy the enemies who were endeavoring to sustain the oppressors forced me to accept and retain the sovereign power.

a. Identify the five infinitives.

b. Which word is understood before the last infinitive?

c. What is the subject of the sentence?

d. What verb does this subject take?

See pages 422 and 436 for more on the infinitive.

WRITE NOW

Do one of the following activities.

1. Make a **brainstorm** list on leadership qualities.

2. **Freewrite** on one of the following Writing Suggestions.

WRITING SUGGESTIONS

1. Describe how a great leader can bring about major changes in national or world events.

2. Describe the steps a country can or must go through so that its honor may be restored after being under the control of another nation.

3. Describe the problems that may result after a nation gains its independence.

FURTHER WRITING SUGGESTIONS

4. Tell whether the same qualities needed to lead a nation in wartime are necessarily as effective in peacetime.

5. Describe a situation in which average persons or public opinion led a nation's leaders to make changes in governmental rules or policies.

6. Describe why freely elected democracies in the Americas have not always survived.

THE CRY OF LARES

By Luis Llorens Torres

On his second voyage to the Americas, Columbus reached Puerto Rico in 1493. The explorer Juan Ponce de León conquered the island soon afterwards, and it remained under Spanish rule until it was ceded to the United States at the end of the Spanish-American War in 1898.

Although much of South America liberated itself from Spain during the nineteenth century, the Spanish government maintained a firm grip on Puerto Rico, supporting the plantation system and not abolishing slavery until 1873. Throughout this period there were numerous revolts against Spanish rule. The most famous began in the town of Lares in 1868. The rebellion was soon defeated, but Lares became for the Puerto Rican people a symbol of the struggle for liberty. As Maria Teresa Babin, the translator of this reading, noted, "In political defeat, Lares lives forever as literature."

This selection from the 1914 play *El Grito de Lares* (The Cry of Lares) by the Puerto Rican essayist and poet Luis Llorens Torres (1878–1944) presents a dialogue between two patriots who debate whether the rebellion at Lares had any value despite its tragic and unsuccessful outcome.

WORDS TO NOTICE

skirmish: minor fight

confirmed: gave proof of

hence: therefore

minimizing: making little of

martyrs: those who die on behalf of a cause

tranquility: peace, serenity

epochs: ages, periods

illustrious: famous

clamorers: loud shouters

feign: pretend

redemption: salvation

rhymester: minor poet

forge: build, create

impotence: lack of power

grimaces: facial expressions of disgust or disapproval

accord: agreement

confederation: united group

READ ON

1. What does the **headnote** say about the importance of Lares?

2. Why can a failed revolt become an inspiration?

DON AURELIO: The rest you already know as well as I. The rebellion failed   1
   after the Pepino skirmish.

DON CHEO: It failed for lack of organization.   2

DON AURELIO: More than that, the failure was due to the lack of response   3
from the rest of the towns. . . . There's no doubt there were people with
push at the head of that rebellion.

DON CHEO: The examples seen later confirmed it. They all behaved like brave   4
patriots. The directors from the capital were the ones who gave no
signs of life anywhere.

DON AURELIO: Hence their insistence on minimizing the importance of and   5
even on ridiculing the patriotism of those men. "It was ridiculous,"
they declare. And they broadcast it so much that I fear those poor
martyrs, the first and perhaps the last of our country, are going to pass
into history as a bunch of fools. They, who gave all, the tranquility of
their homes, the worldly wealth they possessed, and even their lives
for the freedom of this land. They failed? What does failure matter?

DON CHEO: You speak like a patriot. The fact itself of having taken up arms   6
to free the country, exposing themselves to what they did, shows that
they loved this land above all else. And perhaps, as you think, the
future will not do them justice. Always, in all epochs, there will be men
incapable of doing what they did.

DON AURELIO: And to justify themselves they will say that they were lunatics.   7
Heaven knows what will be said of them! There are martyrs who are
martyrs even after death!

DON CHEO: All that means that we have no fatherland. The island, small; the   8
peasant, ignorant. Patriot, but ignorant. Even more, innocent. And the
men from above, the illustrious, the directors will always be what they
are today: a group of shouters, clamorers, but not patriots. They'll grab
hold of anything, this or that reform, any second-class ideal, to feign
that they're doing something. But the essential, fundamental thing,
trying to make a fatherland, like those from Lares tried to do, that . . .
they'll never do. It's sad and discouraging; but it's the truth. There is
no redemption! There will never be!

DON AURELIO: There's no redemption. That is the sentence. Look here now,   9
Manolo el Leñero, that boy who waved a flag for the first time in our
land and with his bloody arm continued waving it and crying "Long
live liberty," who remembers that hero now? Perhaps some town
rhymester. And isn't it sad that a man gives everything to his people,
and that his people aren't even aware, because there are no patriots
to erect his statue, nor historians to reveal his feat, nor poets to sing
of his heroism? Where is this so-called Puerto Rican patriotism? for I
do not find it.

DON CHEO: And the sad fact is, Don Aurelio, that so much misfortune does   10
not depend nor will ever depend on us Puerto Ricans. If it were in our
hands, don't you think there would be thousands of Puerto Ricans
ready to forge the fatherland? Believe it. The same as you and I, Puerto
Ricans think and feel; but neither we, nor anyone, do anything, nor will

anything ever be done. Because we are convinced that it is all impossible. What a tragedy! To be strong and generous and brave, like the Cubans, Dominicans and Venezuelans; love our fatherland, as they love theirs; desire like them to have a homeland to defend and make it great ... and being unable! Not being able! We have, like all men of the earth, a brain to think and a heart to love. But the rest of the men of the earth have a homeland; we Puerto Ricans do not have one, we'll never have one.... Don't you think this cruel impotence? ... Don Aurelio, let's speak no more, for it's the only thing that moves me in life. Life! A clown, yes, but a clown who at times has grimaces and somersaults of tragedy.

DON AURELIO: And are you not consoled in thinking that the leaders of that   11
movement were not only Puerto Ricans? A Venezuelan, a Yankee, and
a Dominican died there, too.

DON CHEO: That may mean, perhaps, a lot more in the future.   12

DON AURELIO: It may symbolize, in the future, the union of America for the   13
freedom of America.

DON CHEO: Such a symbol may console us. Because Puerto Rico is small;   14
but ... America is big.

DON AURELIO: And apart from that idea, the plan of the Puerto Rican rebels,   15
Puerto Ricans, in accord with the Cubans and Dominicans, was the
confederation of the three Antilles.

DON CHEO: Which would be one of the first-rate republics of America.   16

IN YOUR OWN VOICE

WHAT DOES IT SAY?

1. Why does the rebellion fail?

2. Who may "pass into history as a bunch of fools"?

3. What does the rebels' love of country cost them?

4. What do the rebels resent about the Spanish directors?

5. Who is Manolo el Leñero?

6. What political union might have existed if the rebellion had been successful?

WHAT DOES IT MEAN?

1. Why do the Spanish directors pay little attention to the rebellion?

2. Why does the rebels' failure not matter to a patriot like Don Aurelio?

3. How does the failure to honor Manolo el Leñero affect Puerto Rican independence?

4. What is the meaning of "the union of America for the freedom of America"?

STYLE AND SENSE

Patriotism is the central theme of this selection. This main idea is supported by specific examples.

1. How do Don Cheo's words (see paragraph 6) provide vivid examples of patriotism in action?

2. Where else in this selection can the reader find a specific and emotionally powerful example of a patriot?

3. Provide an example in the modern world of a hero, a martyr, and a patriot.

4. How does the naming of a specific example clarify and bring to life a general idea?

5. How do the closing speeches return the reader to the central theme of the opening?

FROM THE TEXT

Subject-verb agreement: often the subject and verb are separated by a phrase. In such cases, the verb must still agree with its subject.

Read the following sentence:

> The directors from the capital were the ones who gave no signs of life anywhere.

a. What is the first verb in the sentence?

b. Is it singular or plural?

c. Which noun is its plural subject?

d. Does the phrase "from the capital" answer the question who or what, as all subjects do?

See page 409 for more on subject-verb agreement with intervening words.

WRITE NOW

Do one of the following activities.

1. **Freewrite** on patriotism.

2. Make a list of **journalistic questions** about the Lares revolt.

WRITING SUGGESTIONS

1. Manolo el Leñero died fighting for a cause that he believed in. Tell whether young people often are more willing to lay down their lives for an ideal than older people.

2. Describe the feelings after defeat and discouragement. Tell what steps can be taken to recover from such a setback.

3. Narrate a situation in which you defended or chose not to defend your patriotic feelings.

FURTHER WRITING SUGGESTIONS

4. Tell how the sparks of rebellion can be set off by **one** of the following: poverty, lack of political power, love of country.

5. Often we hear that experience is the best teacher. Narrate a situation in which a group that you are or were a member of failed to achieve its goals. Tell what the experience taught you.

6. Many times in life we come into conflict with people in authority. The disputes might deal with family, job, or personal rights. Write a short dialogue in which you present both sides of the issue under discussion.

PATH BREAKING: WOMEN AND THE VOTE*

By Abigail Scott Duniway

Abigail Scott Duniway (1834–1915) was a leading feminist and fighter for voting rights for women in the United States. Her independence and determination to achieve women's suffrage (right to vote) stemmed largely from her frontier and pioneer background in her beloved Pacific Northwest.

*Editors' title

Born in a log cabin in Illinois, she and her family made the difficult journey to Oregon. She married at an early age and was the mother of six children. Self-educated, Duniway became a novelist and short story writer before founding in 1871 a newspaper in Portland, the *New Northwest.* Over its brief sixteen-year history the paper gave voice to women's economic and political issues.

The fate of women's suffrage depended, finally, on men: in state legislatures and in the voting booths. This selection, from Duniway's 1914 autobiography *Path Breaking,* is an open letter that she wrote in 1907 to the men of Oregon who would vote on the issue.

In 1912 Oregon voters approved women's right to vote. The Woman Suffrage Proclamation signed by the governor of Oregon was written by Abigail Scott Duniway. Five years after her death, the Nineteenth Amendment to the Constitution made women's suffrage the law of the land.

WORDS TO NOTICE

accorded: granted, given

initiative petitions: signed documents calling for a new law or amendment

elective franchise: freedom to vote

bestowed: gave

solicitation: being asked to (by suffragettes)

sole: alone, by herself

full-fledged: of full status or rank

profoundly: deeply

agitation: stirring up of the public

compel: force

enfranchisement: the voting empowerment of women

encroach: intrude

forsake: give up, abandon

of his own accord: without being told

his delusion is chronic: his long-held false belief

non-partisan, non-sectarian: without regard to political parties or religious affiliation

inalienable: incapable of being taken away

READ ON

1. Why has women's right to vote met with resistance in many countries?

2. Which details in the headnote describe Duniway's strength and determination?

To Every Liberty-Loving Voter of Oregon: 1

The undersigned, representing, as we believe, the large majority of the women of Oregon, are happy to embrace this opportunity, accorded to us through your initiative petitions, to lay before you a few of our many reasons for believing you will be as proud to extend to us, at the coming June election, your courteous invitation to join you in full and free possession of the elective franchise, as were the gallant men of Wyoming, Colorado, Idaho and Utah, who bestowed full rights of citizenship, almost without solicitation, upon every law-abiding woman within her borders.

This movement, which began in Oregon in 1871, grew so rapidly, under   2
the guidance of pioneer men and women and public-spirited law-makers, that the Legislative Assembly enacted, in autumn of 1872, a married woman's sole trader bill, enabling a wife to hold her own earnings, if necessary, as her own property, by registering her intention with the county court. Stimulated by this small beginning, the growth of public sentiment in favor of equal property rights for women has placed Oregon women far in advance, as self-earning propertyholders, of women of any other State in the Union, except the four States wherein they already vote.

But, although we are taxpayers, we are not yet full-fledged voters. This   3
handicap brings the wage earnings of women into ruinous competition with wage-earning voters, and is a disability from which we believe you will be glad to relieve us by your votes next June, in the interest of both halves of the people.

This movement grew from the small official beginning in 1872, above   4
noted, until the year 1884, when your representatives submitted for us, by legislative enactment, a constitutional amendment at the State election of that year, which brought us 11,223 votes. Our proposed amendment was again submitted to a vote of one-half of the people in the year 1900, and the "yes" vote had by that time grown to 26,265. The amendment was again submitted (always by men) in 1906, and the "yes" vote rose to 36,902.

For causes that are wholly eliminated from the present campaign (and   5
we hope from all future State campaigns for equal rights, and, therefore, need not be explained in this letter) the "no" vote of 1906 was for the first time proportionately increased; but the readiness with which men have responded with their signatures to the large initiative petitions, through which you have

reopened our case, is an assurance to us of your success in our behalf at the June election of 1908, for which we are patriotically expectant and profoundly grateful in advance.

If any of you say you are weary of this agitation, we answer in all seriousness, so are we. So weary are we that we believe you will, in mercy, not compel us to repeat this struggle in the year 1910, as we surely must if you fail us this time.   6

If there shall yet remain a few women who should attempt to repeat their former protest against this appeal for equal rights for other women, of which they are unable or unwilling, from their viewpoint, to see the need, we trust your practical good sense will prove to them, through your affirmative votes in our behalf, that our enfranchisement, while enlarging *our* opportunities, will in no way encroach upon their rights or liberties.   7

If any man objects to extending to his wife and mother the power of the ballot from the fear that if they become his equals, they will neglect or forsake the home, we shall depend upon you to divert his mind from such a fallacy, by recalling the fact that the home instinct is inherent in woman, and cannot be created or destroyed by laws of men's or women's making. If he does not know, of his own accord, that there are many hundreds of men and women in Oregon, who could not have the semblance of a home to keep, under present industrial conditions, if women did not go outside to earn or help to earn the means to rent or support a home in ruinous competition with balloted men, just let him alone; his delusion is chronic, and he is past recovery.   8

This movement for the enfranchisement of your closest friends, the mother-half of the people of Oregon, is wholly non-partisan, non-sectarian and non-political. We are not seeking to make laws to govern men. We believe as implicitly in men's fundamental right to self-government as in our own, and we are awaiting your invitation, through the ballot box, to the possession of our inalienable right to equality with you before the law, which we prize for the same reasons that you prize it, and we believe it will be a pleasure to you to bestow it upon us exactly as it would be our pleasure to extend it to you under reversed conditions.   9

ABIGAIL SCOTT DUNIWAY,
PRESIDENT OREGON STATE EQUAL SUFFRAGE ASSOCIATION.

MRS. HENRY WALDO COE, HONORARY PRESIDENT.
MRS. ELIZABETH LORD, VICE-PRESIDENT.
MRS. C. M. CARTWRIGHT, SECOND VICE-PRESIDENT.
SARAH A. EVANS, MEMBER OF NATIONAL EXEC. COM.
MISS ELMA BUCKMAN, RECORDING SECRETARY.

MRS. W. E. POTTER, TREASURER.
MRS. A. BONHAM, FINANCIAL SECRETARY.
MYRTLE E. PEASE, CORRESPONDING SECRETARY.
MRS. ELIZABETH EGGERT, FIRST AUDITOR.
MARTHA DALTON, SECOND AUDITOR.
MRS. IMOGENE BATH, THIRD AUDITOR.

LIST OF VICE-PRESIDENTS BY COUNTIES:

Baker, Mrs. Harvey K. Brown; Benton, Prof. Helen Crawford; Clackamas, Mrs. Eva Emery Dye; Clatsop, Mrs. J. H. Trullinger; Columbia, Mrs. E. H. Flagg; Coos, Mrs. Henry Sengstaken; Crook, Mrs. Ada Millican; Curry, Mrs. H. A. Stewart; Douglas, Mrs. Ida Marsters; Gilliam, Mrs. Clay Clark; Grant, Mrs. Ida Niven; Harney, Mrs. Frank Davey; Jackson, Mrs. Hattie S. Day; Josephine, Mrs. L. L. Mangum; Klamath, Mrs. O. C. Applegate; Lake, Mrs. C. U. Snider; Lane, Mrs. Minnie Washburne; Lincoln, Mrs. R. A. Bensell; Linn, Dr. Anna B. Reed; Malheur, Mrs. Tina Chambers; Marion, Mrs. Clara H. Waldo; Morrow, Mrs. Florence Whitehead; Multnomah, Mrs. C. M. Cartwright; Polk, Mrs. Walter L. Tooze; Sherman, Mrs. Ella Slayback; Tillamook, Mrs. Emma Morrison; Umatilla, Mrs. S. A. Lowell; Union, Mrs. Minerva B. Eaton; Wallowa, Mrs. Elizabeth Oakes; Wasco, Mrs. Elizabeth Lord; Washington, Mrs. Imogene Bath; Yamhill, Mrs. Emma Galloway; Wheeler, Mrs. J. S. Stewart.

IN YOUR OWN VOICE

WHAT DOES IT SAY?

1. As of 1907, in which states could women vote?

2. What does the sole trader bill enable married women to do?

3. When was a constitutional amendment on suffrage first presented to the Oregon voters?

4. What do men fear if women become their equals?

5. What is women's "inalienable right"?

WHAT DOES IT MEAN?

1. Why is the open letter addressed to "Every Liberty-Loving Voter of Oregon"?

2. Why did women first gain the right to vote in four new western states?

3. Why is the sole trader bill essential for wives?

4. Why do women's contributions at home, on the farm, and in the workplace earn them the right to vote?

5. Why does Duniway use the phrase "inalienable right"?

STYLE AND SENSE

An open letter is usually printed in a newspaper and comments on a current issue.

1. In paragraph 1, why does Duniway write that she represents "the large majority of the women of Oregon"?

2. In paragraph 1, why is the word "reasons" mentioned?

3. Why do paragraphs 2 through 5 summarize the reasons?

4. Why does Duniway use the word *if* repeatedly in paragraphs 6 through 8?

5. Why does Duniway use the word *we* repeatedly in the closing paragraph?

FROM THE TEXT

Present participle: the form of a verb ending in *-ing* that follows the helping verb *to be* in any of its forms: *am, are, is, was, were, been.*

Read the following sentence:

We are not seeking to make laws to govern men.

a. What form of *to be* is used?

b. Is it singular or plural? Why?

c. What present participle completes the meaning of the verb?

d. Why is *not* not a verb?

e. Identify two infinitives in the sentence.

WRITE NOW

Do one of the following activities.

1. Make a **brainstorm** list for the expression "path breaking."

2. Make a **cluster diagram** of the full rights of citizenship.

WRITING SUGGESTIONS

1. Imagine you are a suffragette striving for women's right to vote. Answer **one** of the following:

    a. Describe the personal qualities that you need to pursue your goals in a society hostile to the justice of your cause.

or

    b. Describe how and why you would continue fighting for your goals over many years despite constant defeat, ridicule, and even arrest and imprisonment.

2. Once the Fifteenth Amendment to the Constitution was approved in 1870, all citizens of any state in the United States had the legal right to vote—all citizens, that is, except women. Answer **one** of the following:

a. Tell why women were the last to gain the vote.

or

b. Describe how a woman would have felt knowing she was the last to gain the vote.

FURTHER WRITING SUGGESTIONS

3. Many people today continue to work for the passage of the Equal Rights Amendment. Tell why equal rights remains an issue seventy years after the ratification of the Nineteenth Amendment guaranteeing women's suffrage.

4. Duniway wrote in one of her novels: "When woman's true history shall have been written, her part in the upbuilding of this nation will astound the world." Tell how one woman or a group of women contributes or has contributed to the building up of your community, nation, or homeland.

5. Duniway stressed women's economic independence and security. Tell whether this issue is of similar importance today.

I HAVE A DREAM

By Martin Luther King, Jr.

On August 28, 1963, the leader of America's civil rights movement, Dr. Martin Luther King, Jr. (1929–1968), delivered a speech in Washington, D.C., before a quarter of a million people who had assembled that day to dramatize the need for prompt civil rights action and legislation. In his address, he stressed the importance of achieving the goals of racial equality and social justice through nonviolent actions and protest.

In 1964 Dr. King was awarded the Nobel Peace Prize for his efforts. He was assassinated in 1968 after leading a rally in support of striking sanitation workers in Memphis, Tennessee.

This final reading of Unit 2 looks at the evolving American dream 187 years after the Declaration of Independence stated that "all men are created equal," an ideal that Dr. King held dear.

WORDS TO NOTICE

five score: 100

Emancipation Proclamation: document issued by President Abraham Lincoln on January 1, 1863, during the Civil War freeing slaves in the Confederacy

momentous: of great importance

beacon light: guiding signal

seared: scorched, burned

withering: severely destructive

manacles: handcuffs, shackles

languishing: wasting away

exile: outsider, alien

promissory note: signed promise to pay an amount of money

fall heir: inherit

unalienable: incapable of being taken away

hallowed: holy, sacred

desolate: dismal, empty

sweltering: uncomfortably hot

invigorating: giving strength and courage

plane: level surface

militancy: active participation

engulfed: surrounded, swamped

inextricably: forever entwined

devotees: supporters

trials and tribulations: sufferings, ordeals

redemptive: worthwhile

creed: belief, principle

interposition and nullification: actions taken by states in opposition to the law of the land

exalted: elevated

jangling discords: noisy disagreements

prodigious: vast, of great size

curvaceous: shapely, attractively rounded

hamlet: little town

spiritual: religious folksong of black Americans

READ ON

1. Which of the **Words to Notice** deal with the oppressive and unjust effects of racial inequality?

2. What do you know about Martin Luther King, Jr.?

I am happy to join with you today in what will go down in history as the greatest demonstration for freedom in the history of our nation. 1

Five score years ago, a great American, in whose symbolic shadow we stand, signed the Emancipation Proclamation. This momentous decree came as a great beacon light of hope to millions of Negro slaves who had been seared in the flames of withering injustice. It came as a joyous daybreak to end the long night of captivity. 2

But one hundred years later, we must face the tragic fact that the Negro is still not free. One hundred years later, the life of the Negro is still sadly crippled by the manacles of segregation and the chains of discrimination. One hundred years later, the Negro lives on a lonely island of poverty in the midst of a vast ocean of material prosperity. One hundred years later the Negro is still languishing in the corners of American society and finds himself an exile in his own land. So we have come here today to dramatize an appalling condition. 3

In a sense we have come to our nation's Capital to cash a check. When the architects of our republic wrote the magnificent words of the Constitution and the Declaration of Independence, they were signing a promissory note to which every American was to fall heir. This note was a promise that all men would be guaranteed the unalienable rights of life, liberty, and the pursuit of happiness. 4

It is obvious today that America has defaulted on this promissory note insofar as her citizens of color are concerned. Instead of honoring this sacred obligation, America has given the Negro people a bad check; a check which has come back marked "insufficient funds." But we refuse to believe that the bank of justice is bankrupt. We refuse to believe that there are insufficient funds in the great vaults of opportunity of this nation. So we have come to cash this check—a check that will give us upon demand the riches of freedom and the security of justice. We have also come to this hallowed spot to remind America of the fierce urgency of *now*. This is no time to engage in the luxury of cooling off or to take the tranquilizing drug of gradualism. *Now* is the time 5 to make real the promises of Democracy. *Now* is the time to rise from the dark and desolate valley of segregation to the sunlit path of racial justice. *Now* is the time to open the doors of opportunity to all of God's children. *Now* is the time to lift our nation from the quicksands of racial injustice to the solid rock of brotherhood.

It would be fatal for the nation to overlook the urgency of the moment **6** and to underestimate the determination of the Negro. This sweltering summer of the Negro's legitimate discontent will not pass until there is an invigorating autumn of freedom and equality. 1963 is not an end, but a beginning. Those who hope that the Negro needed to blow off steam and will now be content will have a rude awakening if the Nation returns to business as usual. There will be neither rest nor tranquility in America until the Negro is granted his citizenship rights. The whirlwinds of revolt will continue to shake the foundations of our Nation until the bright day of justice emerges.

But there is something that I must say to my people who stand on the **7** warm threshold which leads into the palace of justice. In the process of gaining our rightful place we must not be guilty of wrongful deeds. Let us not seek to satisfy our thirst for freedom by drinking from the cup of bitterness and hatred. We must forever conduct our struggle on the high plane of dignity and discipline. We must not allow our creative protest to degenerate into physical violence. Again and again we must rise to the majestic heights of meeting physical force with soul force. The marvelous new militancy which has engulfed the Negro community must not lead us to a distrust of all white people, for many of our white brothers, as evidenced by their presence here today, have come to realize that their destiny is tied up with our destiny and their freedom is inextricably bound to our freedom. We cannot walk alone.

And as we walk, we must make the pledge that we shall march ahead. **8** We cannot turn back. There are those who are asking the devotees of civil rights, "When will you be satisfied?" We can never be satisfied as long as the Negro is the victim of the unspeakable horrors of police brutality. We can never be satisfied as long as our bodies, heavy with the fatigue of travel, cannot gain lodging in the motels of the highways and the hotels of the cities. We cannot be satisfied as long as the Negro's basic mobility is from a smaller ghetto to a larger one. We can never be satisfied as long as a Negro in Mississippi cannot vote and a Negro in New York believes he has nothing for which to vote. No, no, we are not satisfied, and we will not be satisfied until justice rolls down like waters and righteousness like a mighty stream.

I am not unmindful that some of you have come here out of great trials **9** and tribulations. Some of you have come fresh from narrow jail cells. Some of you have come from areas where your quest for freedom left you battered by the storms of persecution and staggered by the winds of police brutality. You have been the veterans of creative suffering. Continue to work with the faith that unearned suffering is redemptive.

Go back to Mississippi, go back to Alabama, go back to South Carolina, **10** go back to Georgia, go back to Louisiana, go back to the slums and ghettos of our modern cities, knowing that somehow this situation can and will be changed. Let us not wallow in the valley of despair.

I say to you today, my friends, that in spite of the difficulties and frustra- **11** tions of the moment I still have a dream. It is a dream deeply rooted in the American dream.

I have a dream that one day this nation will rise up and live out the true **12** meaning of its creed: "We hold these truths to be self-evident; that all men are created equal."

I have a dream that one day on the red hills of Georgia the sons of former **13** slaves and the sons of former slaveowners will be able to sit down together at the table of brotherhood.

I have a dream that one day even the state of Mississippi, a desert state **14** sweltering with the heat of injustice and oppression, will be transformed into an oasis of freedom and justice.

I have a dream that my four little children will one day live in a nation **15** where they will not be judged by the color of their skin but by the content of their character.

I have a dream today. **16**

I have a dream that one day the state of Alabama, whose governor's lips **17** are presently dripping with the words of interposition and nullification, will be transformed into a situation where little black boys and black girls will be able to join hand with little white boys and white girls and walk together as sisters and brothers.

I have a dream today. **18**

I have a dream that one day every valley shall be exalted, every hill and **19** mountain shall be made low, the rough places will be made plains, and the crooked places will be made straight, and the glory of the Lord shall be revealed, and all flesh shall see it together.

This is our hope. This is the faith with which I return to the South. With **20** this faith we will be able to hew out of the mountain of despair a stone of hope. With this faith we will be able to transform the jangling discords of our nation into a beautiful symphony of brotherhood. With this faith we will be able to work together, to pray together, to struggle together, to go to jail together, to stand up for freedom together, knowing that we will be free one day.

This will be the day when all of God's children will be able to sing with **21** new meaning "My country 'tis of thee, sweet land of liberty, of thee I sing. Land where my fathers died, land of the pilgrim's pride, from every mountainside, let freedom ring."

And if America is to be a great nation this must become true. So let **22** freedom ring from the prodigious hilltops of New Hampshire. Let freedom ring from the mighty mountains of New York. Let freedom ring from the heightening Alleghenies of Pennsylvania!

Let freedom ring from the snowcapped Rockies of Colorado! **23**

Let freedom ring from the curvaceous peaks of California! **24**

But not only that; let freedom ring from Stone Mountain of Georgia!   **25**
Let freedom ring from Lookout Mountain of Tennessee!   **26**
Let freedom ring from every hill and mole hill of Mississippi. From every   **27**
mountainside, let freedom ring.

When we let freedom ring, when we let it ring from every village and   **28**
every hamlet, from every state and every city, we will be able to speed up
that day when all of God's children, black men and white men, Jews and
Gentiles, Protestants and Catholics, will be able to join hands and sing in the
words of the old Negro spiritual, "Free at last! free at last! thank God almighty,
we are free at last!"

IN YOUR OWN VOICE

WHAT DOES IT SAY?

1. Why were the listeners assembled in Washington?

2. What would be fatal for the nation to overlook?

3. How should Dr. King's listeners respond to the use of physical force against them?

4. Which specific acts of segregation are mentioned?

5. What is the creed of the United States?

6. From which regions will freedom ring?

7. Who will join hands when his dream is fulfilled?

WHAT DOES IT MEAN?

1. Why is it time to "cash a check"?

2. Why does Dr. King insist on nonviolence?

3. Why is the dream for all Americans?

4. Why does Dr. King include "to go to jail together" in a list of worthwhile group actions?

5. Why has reaching Dr. King's goals been delayed?

STYLE AND SENSE

1. The speech is organized around the repetition of several vivid expressions. Identify at least three of these. Why are they used in the speech?

2. Dr. King uses many contrasts and opposites. Identify at least three of these. Why are they important to the meaning of the speech?

3. Dr. King was a minister. Which parts of the speech sound like passages from the Bible? Why?

4. How do the words "Let freedom ring" serve as a fitting close to the repeated phrase "I have a dream"?

FROM THE TEXT

Subject-verb agreement of relative pronouns: *who, which, that,* or other relative pronoun may be singular or plural, depending upon the **antecedent**

(the noun or word group to which the pronoun refers). The verb will be singular or plural accordingly.

Read the following sentence:

But there is something that I must say to my people who stand on the warm threshold which leads into the palace of justice.

a. Identify the antecedent of the relative pronoun *who*.

b. Is it singular or plural?

c. Which verb agrees with *who*? Is it singular or plural?

d. Identify the antecedent of the relative pronoun *which*.

e. Is it singular or plural?

f. Which verb agrees with *which*? Is it singular or plural?

See page 410 for more on subject-verb agreement of relative pronouns.

WRITE NOW

Do one of the following activities.

1. Freewrite your reactions to the speech.

2. Make a **brainstorm** list on the idea of equality.

WRITING SUGGESTIONS

1. Tell how far the people of the United States have come in achieving Dr. King's dream.

2. Dr. King had a dream for his own children. Describe your dream for your children's future and what they will have to do to fulfill these expectations.

3. Narrate a situation in which a nonviolent response can bring about a positive social change.

FURTHER WRITING SUGGESTIONS

4. The famous American folksinger Woody Guthrie composed "This Land Is Your Land." Tell whether you believe the title of this song applies or does not apply to you and your loved ones.

5. Listen to a recording of the "I Have a Dream" speech. Describe your reaction to Dr. King's words and voice. Tell if hearing the speech produces a different effect from just reading it.

6. Both the Declaration of Independence and Dr. King's address speak of the rights of the people under God. Tell in what ways religious faith does or does not support and reinforce the freedoms of a democratic society.

UNIT 3

Joseph Becker. *Snow Sheds on the Central Pacific Railroad in the Sierra Nevada Mountains, May 18, 1869.* The Thomas Gilcrease Institute of American History and Art, Tulsa, Oklahoma.

ACROSS A
CONTINENT

North, Central, and South America lie between the Atlantic and Pacific oceans. This unit deals with the contributions, sacrifices, and losses of individuals and groups in the movement to build and settle the American hemisphere from coast to coast.

The first selection is from Meriwether Lewis's journal (1805). Lewis and his co-leader, William Clark, were sent to explore the western regions by President Thomas Jefferson following the Louisiana Purchase, which extended the U.S. boundaries from the Mississippi to the Rocky Mountains.

This expansion in territory was matched by an expansion in language as words were added or their meanings changed to fit new circumstances. The second reading is from the preface to Noah Webster's *American Dictionary of the English Language* (1828).

Next is William Least Heat Moon's modern reflection on the youthful Pony Express riders.

The price of expansion across a huge continent is vividly expressed in Chief Ten Bears' "I Don't Want to Settle There" (1867), a speech in which "progress" or "manifest destiny" is seen from the perspective of the Native Americans forced to give up traditional lands and ways of life.

The section continues with an account of the Chinese-American contribution to the building of the transcontinental railroad (1869), and the lack of due recognition for this achievement. You will also find the November and December 1891 diary entries of a pioneer woman who accompanies her husband on a wagon trip across the Kansas prairies.

The last piece from David McCullough's *Path Between the Seas* (1977) describes the achievement of the building of the Panama Canal, with a mostly West Indian labor force, at the start of this century.

BEFORE YOU READ

Why was westward expansion the policy of the U.S. government?

What happened to the peoples of the western U.S. territories during the expansion period?

How should a country treat its natural resources, abundance, beauty, and so on?

Do you know of some generally unrecognized achievements of groups in the building of their country?

Have you spoken to your grandparents or other older relatives about their youthful experiences?

Have you thought of traveling to distant parts of your country?

Have you ever read any of the journals kept by women pioneers?

Should a country have one official, standard language?

Is a country weakened by cultural diversity?

Why were the horse and railway important in the growth of the United States?

Why were the ship, canoe, and rifle also important in the Western Hemisphere's history?

Do the Indians of the Americas have claims on the lands from which they were removed?

How are business and commerce factors in the growth of a country?

Have television, movies, and books given fair and accurate accounts of all groups affected by westward expansion?

Does the movement across a continent enhance the opportunities for a multicultural society?

THE JOURNAL OF LEWIS AND CLARK

By Meriwether Lewis

In 1804 President Thomas Jefferson asked his private secretary, Meriwether Lewis (1774–1809), and William Clark (1770–1838) to explore the western territories acquired by the Louisiana Purchase and to find a land route to the Pacific Ocean.

Leaving St. Louis, Missouri, in May, the two army officers and the forty-two soldiers and civilians who accompanied them endured many hardships. Aided by Sacajawea, a Shoshone (American Indian) woman who served as their interpreter, they traveled to North Dakota, Montana, and Idaho, where they crossed the Rocky Mountains before reaching the Columbia River headwaters at the Pacific Ocean a year and a half later.

On their return in 1806, Lewis and Clark carried maps, reports on the American Indians, descriptions of the land, and specimens of plant and animal life. This selection from Lewis's journals gives a firsthand account of what is needed to survive the dangers of the Montana wilderness.

This selection contains spellings that were acceptable in the early nineteenth century.

WORDS TO NOTICE

reconnoiters: surveys, scouts

intervening: lying between

decended: descended, went down

semblance: appearance

recolected: recollected, remembered, recalled

pitched: attacked forcibly

espontoon: spearlike weapon

accordingly: for that reason

precipitation: haste, speed

novil: novel, strange, new

indeavoured: endeavored, tried

tallons: talons, claws

burrow: hole in the ground

couched: bent ready to attack

league: alliance

disposed: ready

prudent: wisely cautious

READ ON

1. What information does the **headnote** contain about the places that Lewis and Clark explored?

2. After reading Lewis's journal for the first time, ask yourself how you would respond to a sudden threat to your life.

Friday June 14th 1805.

1   [On this day Lewis reconnoiters the remaining four falls and the intervening rapids which compose the Great Falls, going as far as Sun River, which during the winter they had named Medicine River. He is on the way to the latter as the entry continues.] I decended the hill and directed my course to the bend of the Missouri near which there was a herd of at least a thousand buffaloe; here I thought it would be well to kill a buffaloe and leave him untill my return from the river and if I then found that I had not time to get back to camp this evening to remain all night here there being a few sticks of drift wood lying along shore which would answer for my fire, and a few s[c]attering cottonwood trees a few hundred yards below which would afford me at least the semblance of a shelter. under this impression I scelected a fat buffaloe and shot him very well, through the lungs; while I was gazeing attentively on the poor anamal discharging blood in streams from his mouth and nostrils, expecting him to fall every instant, and having entirely forgotten to reload my rifle, a large white, or reather brown bear, had perceived and crept on me within 20 steps before I discovered him; in the first moment I drew up my gun to shoot, but at the same instant recolected that she was not loaded and that he was too near for me to hope to perform this opperation before he reached me, as he was then briskly advancing on me; it was an open level plain, not a bush within miles nor a tree within less than three hundred yards of me; the river bank was sloping and not more than three feet above the level of the water; in short there was no place by means of which I could conceal myself from this monster untill I could charge my rifle; in this situation I thought of retreating in a brisk walk as fast as he was advancing untill I could reach a tree about 300 yards below me, but I had no sooner terned

myself about but he pitched at me, open mouthed and full speed, I ran about 80 yards and found he gained on me fast, I then run into the water the idea struk me to get into the water to such debth that I could stand and he would be obliged to swim, and that I could in that situation defend myself with my espontoon; accordingly I ran haistily into the water about waist deep, and faced about and presented the point of my espontoon, at this instant he arrived at the edge of the water within about 20 feet of me; the moment I put myself in this attitude of defence he sudonly wheeled about as if frightened, declined to combat on such unequal grounds, and retreated with quite as great precipitation as he had just before pursued me.

As soon as I saw him run in that manner I returned to the shore and **2** charged my gun, which I had still retained in my hand throughout this curious adventure. I saw him run through the level open plain about three miles, till he disappeared in the woods on medecine river; during the whole of this distance he ran at full speed, sometimes appearing to look behind him as if he expected pursuit. I now began to reflect on this novil occurence and indeavoured to account for this sudden retreat of the bear. I at first thought that perhaps he had not smelt me bofore he arrived at the waters edge so near me, but I then reflected that he had pursued me for about 80 or 90 yards before I took the water and on examination saw the grownd toarn with his tallons immediately on the imp[r]ession of my steps; and the cause of his allarm still remains with me misterious and unaccountable, so it was and I felt myself not a little gratifyed that he had declined the combat. my gun reloaded I felt confidence once more in my strength.

in returning through the level bottom of Medecine river and about 200 **3** yards distant from the Missouri, my direction led me directly to an anamal that I at first supposed was a wolf; but on nearer approach or about sixty paces distant I discovered that it was not, it's colour was a brownish yellow; it was standing near it's burrow, and when I approached it thus nearly, it couched itself down like a cat looking immediately at me as if it designed to spring on me. I took aim at it and fired, it instantly disappeared in it's burrow; I loaded my gun and ex[a]mined the place which was dusty and saw the track from which I am still further convinced that it was of the tiger kind. whether I struck it or not I could not determine, but I am almost confident that I did; my gun is true and I had a steady rest by means of my espontoon, which I have found very serviceable to me in this way in the open plains. It now seemed to me that all the beasts of the neighbourhood had made a league to distroy me, or that some fortune was disposed to amuse herself at my expence, for I had not proceded more than three hundred yards from the burrow of this tyger cat, before three bull buffaloe, which wer feeding with a large herd about half a mile from me on my left, seperated from the herd and ran full speed towards me, I thought at least to give them some amusement and altered my direction to meet them; when they arrived within a hundred yards they mad[e] a halt, took a good view of me and retreated with precipitation. I then continued my rout homewards passed the buffaloe which I had killed, but did not think it prudent to remain all night at this place which really from the succession of curious adventures wore the impression on my mind of inchantment; at sometimes for a moment I thought it might be a dream, but the prickley pears which pierced my feet very severely once in a while, particularly after it grew dark, convinced me that I was really awake, and that it was necessary to make the best of my way to camp.

IN YOUR OWN VOICE

WHAT DOES IT SAY?

1. Which animal does Lewis kill?

2. What will Lewis rely on to survive in the woods overnight?

3. Why is Lewis unable to kill the bear?

4. Where does the "tyger cat" escape to?

5. Why does Lewis decide to leave the wilderness area?

6. What convinces Lewis that this adventure was not a dream?

WHAT DOES IT MEAN?

1. What reasons might Lewis have had for shooting the buffalo?

2. What do Lewis's actions in the bear chase reveal about his character?

3. Do Lewis's weapons put him on equal terms with the animals in the wilderness? Explain.

4. Why does Lewis find some of his adventures risky and others amusing?

5. Why does Lewis think these incidents could have been a dream?

6. What do Lewis's actions suggest about his attitude toward or feelings about nature?

STYLE AND SENSE

A **narrative** is a story that tells of events as they happen, happened, or will happen.

1. Which tense did Lewis use in narrating his adventures?

2. From the reading list five words or expressions referring to time that direct the reader from the first event to the last.

3. How does the use of chronological order in this selection create interest and allow the narrative to unfold?

4. How does Lewis tell the reader that he is moving from one place to another during the day?

5. What place does Lewis mention in the opening and closing of the narrative?

FROM THE TEXT

Past tense: the verb form that indicates that the action, or state of being, started and ended at an earlier time.

Read the following sentence:

I loaded my gun and examined the place which was dusty and saw the track.

a. Identify the four verbs in this sentence.

b. What does an *-ed* ending indicate about the time (tense) of two of these verbs?

c. What is the present tense form of the other two verbs?

d. Because the vowel sound has changed from present to past tense of these two verbs, is an *-ed* ending necessary in the past tense?

e. List five verbs in paragraph 1 that use an *-ed* ending to indicate the past tense.

f. List five verbs in paragraphs 2 and 3 that form the past tense without the *-ed* ending.

See page 420 for more on the past tense.

WRITE NOW

Do one of the following activities.

1. Make a **brainstorm** list of skills you need in new circumstances.

2. Write a **topic sentence** for any of the following Writing Suggestions.

WRITING SUGGESTIONS

1. Tell how your experiences and observations on a trip to a place that you had never been before brought about changes in your perceptions of the world.

2. Describe how you would react if you were alone and faced with a sudden, life-threatening situation.

3. Describe the risks and rewards of a life choice that will lead you on a path that no one else in your family has taken.

FURTHER WRITING SUGGESTIONS

4. Narrate in the past tense a significant moment or occasion in your life. Provide details that help the reader follow the events from beginning to end. You may wish to use words referring to time.

5. To reach the Pacific Ocean, Lewis and Clark crossed thousands of miles of land inhabited by Native Americans. Discuss why the government considered these lands the property of the United States.

LANGUAGE AND COUNTRY*

By Noah Webster

Noah Webster (1758–1843) was a teacher and lawyer who believed that an independent United States needed "to have a system of [its] own, in language as well as government." His *American Speller* (1783) was the first schoolbook published in the United States, selling more than 75 million copies in over a century of use. Published at the end of the Revolutionary War, the book simplified spellings (for example, *color* for *colour*) and accepted American usage as standard and proper.

It was not until 1828 that Webster's monumental *An American Dictionary of the English Language* was published. This selection from the preface to the dictionary expresses Webster's desire for a uniquely American English.

Over the past 175 years, however, Webster's goal of a standard, uniform language, which may be thought of as monocultural, has sometimes been viewed as a societal barrier by cultural or ethnic groups and by non-English-speaking Americans.

WORDS TO NOTICE

perpetuate: continue

retain: keep

conversant: familiar with

*Editors' title

heraldry: symbols by which noble families were recognized

feudal system: economic and social system of the Middle Ages

obsolete: out of date

civil institutions: public customs

phraseology: the way something is worded

unexampled: without a previous model

orthography: correct spelling

palpable: obvious

anomalies: irregularities

vernacular tongue: everyday language of a country

bequeath: hand down

jurisdiction: power or extent (of the dictionary)

READ ON

1. Why is Webster's dictionary a political statement?

2. While reading Webster's preface for the first time, make margin notes on what you consider to be important.

It is not only important, but, in a degree necessary, that the people of this country, should have an *American Dictionary* of the English Language; for, although the body of the language is the same as in England, and it is desirable to perpetuate that sameness, yet some differences must exist. Language is the expression of ideas; and if the people of one country cannot preserve an identity of ideas, they cannot retain an identity of language. Now an identity of ideas depends materially upon a sameness of things or objects with which the people of the two countries are conversant. But in no two portions of the earth, remote from each other, can such identity be found. Even physical objects must be different. But the principal differences between the people of this country and of all others, arise from different forms of government, different laws, institutions and customs. Thus the practice of hawking and hunting, the institution of heraldry, and the feudal system of England origi-nated terms which formed, and some of which now form, a necessary part of the language of that country; but, in the United States, many of these terms are no part of our present language,—and they cannot be, for the things which they express do not exist in this country. They can be known to us only as obsolete or as foreign words. On the other hand, the institutions in this country which are new and peculiar, give rise to new terms or to new applications of old terms, unknown to the people of England; which cannot be explained by them and which will not be inserted in their dictionaries, unless copied from ours. Thus the terms, *land-office; land-warrant; location of land; consociation* of churches; *regent* of a university; *intendant* of a city; *plantation, selectmen, senate, congress, court, assembly, escheat,* &c. are either words not belonging to the language of England, or they are applied to things in this country which do not exist in that. No person in this country will be satisfied with the English definitions of the words *congress, senate* and *assembly, court,,* &c. for although these are words used in England, yet they are applied in this country to express ideas which they do not express in that country. With our present constitutions of government, *escheat* can never have its feudal sense in the United States.

But this is not all. In many cases, the nature of our governments, and of our civil institutions, requires an appropriate language in the definition of words, even when the words express the same thing, as in England. Thus the English Dictionaries inform us that a *Justice* is one deputed by the *King* to do right by way of judgment—he is a *Lord* by his office—Justices of the peace are appointed by the *King's commission*—language which is inaccurate in respect to this officer in the United States. So *constitutionally* is defined by Todd or Chalmers, *legally,* but in this country the distinction between *constitution* and *law* requires a different definition. In the United States, a *plantation* is a very different thing from what it is in England. The word *marshal,* in this country, has one important application unknown in England or in Europe. 2

A great number of words in our language require to be defined in a phraseology accommodated to the condition and institutions of the people in these states, and the people of England must look to an American Dictionary for a correct understanding of such terms. 3

The necessity therefore of a Dictionary suited to the people of the United States is obvious; and I should suppose that this fact being admitted, there could be no difference of opinion as to the *time,* when such a work ought to be substituted for English Dictionaries. 4

There are many other considerations of a public nature, which serve to justify this attempt to furnish an American Work which shall be a guide to the youth of the United States. Most of these are too obvious to require illustration. 5

One consideration however which is dictated by my own feelings, but which I trust will meet with approbation in correspondent feelings in my fellow citizens, ought not to be passed in silence. It is this. "The chief glory of a nation," says Dr. Johnson, "arises from its authors." With this opinion deeply impressed on my mind, I have the same ambition which actuated that great man when he expressed a wish to give celebrity to Bacon, to Hooker, to Milton and to Boyle. 6

I do not indeed expect to add celebrity to the names of *Franklin, Washington, Adams, Jay, Madison, Marshall, Ramsay, Dwight, Smith, Trumbull, Hamilton, Belknap, Ames, Mason, Kent, Hare, Silliman, Cleaveland, Walsh, Irving,* and many other Americans distinguished by their writings or by their science; but it is with pride and satisfaction, that I can place them, as authorities, on the same page with those of *Boyle, Hooker, Milton, Dryden, Addison, Ray, Milner, Cowper, Davy, Thomson* and *Jameson.*   **7**

A life devoted to reading and to an investigation of the origin and principles of our vernacular language, and especially a particular examination of the best English writers, with a view to a comparison of their style and phraseology, with those of the best American writers, and with our colloquial usage, enables me to affirm with confidence, that the genuine English idiom is as well preserved by the unmixed English of this country, as it is by the best *English* writers. Examples to prove this fact will be found in the Introduction to this work. It is true, that many of our writers have neglected to cultivate taste, and the embellishments of style; but even these have written the language in its genuine *idiom*. In this respect, Franklin and Washington, whose language is their hereditary mother tongue, unsophisticated by modern grammar, present as pure models of genuine English, as Addison or Swift. But I may go farther, and affirm, with truth, that our country has produced some of the best models of composition. The style of President Smith; of the authors of the Federalist; of Mr. Ames; of Dr. Mason; of Mr. Harper; of Chancellor Kent; [the prose] of Mr. Barlow; of the legal decisions of the Supreme Court of the United States; of the reports of legal decisions in some of the particular states; and many other writings; in purity, in elegance and in technical precision, is equaled only by that of the best British authors, and surpassed by that of no English compositions of a similar kind.   **8**

The United States commenced their existence under circumstances wholly novel and unexampled in the history of nations. They commenced with civilization, with learning, with science, with constitutions of free government, and with that best gift of God to man, the christian religion. Their population is now equal to that of England; in arts and sciences, our citizens are very little behind the most enlightened people on earth; in some respects, they have no superiors; and our language, within two centuries, will be spoken by more people in this country, than any other language on earth, except the Chinese, in Asia, and even that may not be an exception.   **9**

It has been my aim in this work, now offered to my fellow citizens, to ascertain the true principles of the language, in its orthography and structure; to purify it from some palpable errors, and reduce the number of its anomalies, thus giving it more regularity and consistency in its forms, both of words and sentences; and in this manner, to furnish a standard of our vernacular tongue, which we shall not be ashamed to bequeath to *three hundred millions of people,* who are destined to occupy, and I hope, to adorn the vast territory within our jurisdiction.   **10**

IN YOUR OWN VOICE

WHAT DOES IT SAY?

1. What does the dictionary seek to preserve?

2. Why is the language of Americans different from that of other English-speaking people?

3. Why are some British words "obsolete" in the United States?

4. Give examples from the reading selection of words that changed their meanings after crossing from England to the United States.

5. Why would English people need to use this American dictionary?

6. With what advantages did the United States begin?

7. Which language will be used by the most people two centuries after the dictionary's publication?

8. What are Webster's expressed aims in compiling this dictionary?

WHAT DOES IT MEAN?

1. Why is language as the expression of ideas important for the development of a nation's identity?

2. How do changes in government and society affect language?

3. What does the existence of an American dictionary say to the English people or other foreigners about the prospects of the young nation?

4. What does the existence of an American dictionary say to non-English-speaking Americans?

5. Why has Webster's prediction (see paragraph 9) about the growth of English in the United States become true?

STYLE AND SENSE

1. Dictionaries are used for many purposes. Name three ways in which dictionaries can help improve your writing.

2. A prefix is a syllable placed at the beginning of a word or root to change the meaning of the original. Find the meanings of the prefixes *un-* in *unknown* (paragraph 1), *in-* in *inaccurate* (paragraph 2), and *con-* in *constitutions* (paragraph 9).

3. A suffix is a syllable placed at the end of a word or root to change the meaning of the original. Find the meanings of the suffixes *-ness* in *sameness* (paragraph 1), *-tion* in *definition* (paragraph 2), and *-fy* in *purify* (paragraph 3).

4. What are the differences between a dictionary and a thesaurus?

5. If dictionaries did not exist, how could people reach agreement on word or language usage?

FROM THE TEXT

Helping or auxiliary verbs: such words as *can, could, may, might, shall, should, will, would, must,* and *ought* used in combination with completer verbs to express time relationships, possibility, obligation, necessity, or permission.

Read the following sentence:

> Language is the expression of ideas; and if the people of one country cannot preserve an identity of ideas, they cannot retain an identity of language.

a. Identify the two helping verbs and their completers.

b. What purpose is expressed by the helping verbs?

c. Do the completer verbs have endings?

See page 437 for more on helping verbs.

WRITE NOW

Do one of the following activities.

1. In small groups, discuss the differences between spoken and written language.

2. Choose the Writing Suggestion that interests you most. Explain why.

WRITING SUGGESTIONS

1. Narrate a situation in which you were not satisfied with the way that you used language. Describe your feelings.

2. Discuss the impact of establishing language standards.

3. California has passed a law making English the official state language. Tell whether such a law is needed for your country, state, or province.

FURTHER WRITING SUGGESTIONS

4. Webster says that a single shared language provides a foundation for bringing together the people of a nation. Discuss factors besides language that give people a sense of common identity. You may wish to consider traditions, history, patriotism, economics, religion, or social values. Be sure to include specific evidence to support your ideas.

5. Even the most common words may not have exactly the same meaning to two different people. Define one emotion, such as *love, anger, jealousy,* or *fear,* or one abstract noun, such as *freedom, democracy, friendship, loyalty, sympathy,* or *loneliness.* Use examples, personal experiences, and other supporting details to extend and clarify your definition.

6. Webster wrote a dictionary of the American language of his time. Compile your own "dictionary" of five words or expressions that you cannot find in your own dictionary. Define each term and provide a sentence, situation, or brief dialogue that shows how the term is used.

THE PONY EXPRESS*

By William Least Heat Moon

In his book *Blue Highways* (1982), William Least Heat Moon (b. 1939) records in his journal what he sees and experiences on a cross-country automobile trip.

During his western travels, the American Indian author comes upon a deserted stagecoach stop in Nevada. After describing what he sees, he writes about the Pony Express, a relay mail service that operated between Missouri and California from April 3, 1860, to October 24, 1861. In addition, the Pony Express helped to maintain the antislavery North's link to California during the Civil War.

The service was discontinued after the completion of the first transcontinental telegraph line. Despite its brief existence, the Pony Express has remained a vivid part of U.S. history.

WORDS TO NOTICE

willow-thatch: covered with leaves of the willow tree

compost: decayed substances

Overland: stagecoach company

*Editors' title

transcontinental: extending across the continent

Forty-niners: prospectors in the 1849 California gold rush

archaeological: ancient, historical

utter: complete

wiry: skinny but strong

mochila: saddle covering

Inaugural Address: President's first speech

comprised: made up

contraptions: devices

touchstones: standards

READ ON

1. What does the **headnote** say about the Pony Express?

2. While reading William Least Heat Moon's description for the first time, underline the most interesting sections.

New Pass Station, under cliffs of the Desatoya Mountains and half an hour **1**
west of Austin, used to be a stagecoach stop. The cold morning I pulled in
to make breakfast, it was a tumble of stone walls and the willow-thatch roof
had long since gone to compost. These stations were crude shelters even
when the Overland ran the route; a traveler in 1861 described Cold Spring,
the next stop west, as a "wretched place, half-built and wholly unroofed." He
spent the night in a haystack. What I took for a ruin was, perhaps, a reconstruction.

I found my cooler empty except for some sardines and the can of chopped **2**
liver, so I went on along the stage road, also once the Pony Express trail and
the route of the first transcontinental telegraph. Add to those the journeys of
Indians and Forty-niners, and highway 50 is one archaeological layer of communication upon another.

Regardless of the utter fierceness of desert winters and summers, the **3**
Pony Express riders, they say, always rode in shirt-sleeves; considering the
real hazards of the job, that may be true. The Central Overland California and
Pike's Peak Express (the actual name of the Pony Express) used to run notices
that are models for truth in advertising. An 1860 San Francisco newspaper
printed this one:

WANTED
Young, skinny, wiry fellows not
over eighteen. Must be expert
riders willing to risk death
daily. Orphans preferred.

Despite or because of such ads, never was there a shortage of riders.

The only baggage the boys carried—in addition to the mail mochila— **4**
was a kit of flour, cornmeal, and bacon, and a medical pack of turpentine,
borax, and cream of tartar. Not much in either one to keep a rider alive. A
letter cost $2.50 an ounce, and, if the weather and horses held out and the
Indians held off, it might go the two thousand miles from Missouri to California
in ten days, as did Lincoln's Inaugural Address. But the primary purpose of
the service was neither the speedy delivery of news or correspondence; rather,
the Express comprised part of the Northern defense strategy during the Civil
War by providing a fast, central link with California that Southern raiders
couldn't cut. For the seventeen months the Pony Express existed, it helped
to hold California in the Union; what's more, this last of the old-world means
of communication before mechanical contraptions took over left a deep mark
on the American imagination. The riders, going far on little, became touchstones of courage and strength.

IN YOUR OWN VOICE

WHAT DOES IT SAY?

1. What remains of the original stagecoach stop?

2. For which two purposes is the stage road later used?

3. What kind of person does the Pony Express advertise for?

4. How long might it take a letter to reach California from Missouri?

5. What important role did the Pony Express play in the Civil War?

WHAT DOES IT MEAN?

1. How does the stage road become an "archaeological layer of communication"?

2. Why does the advertisement say "Orphans preferred"?

3. Why has the Pony Express, which lasted only seventeen months, "left a deep mark on the American imagination"?

STYLE AND SENSE

1. Closing sentences often open up to the reader why the topic of the essay is important. How does the final sentence declare the author's main intention?

2. In the middle of the essay, there is a brief advertisement. How does the wording of the advertisement capture the harsh and dangerous reality of the Old West?

3. The opening paragraph describes the end of a way of life. By beginning this way, how is the road paved for the heroic closing sentence?

FROM THE TEXT

Sentence fragment: a portion of a sentence that has been punctuated as if it were a complete sentence.

Read the following advertisement:

WANTED
Young, skinny, wiry fellows not
over eighteen. Must be expert
riders willing to risk death
daily. Orphans preferred.

a. Are any of these three statements complete sentences?

b. Add a subject to make the second statement complete.

c. Add a helping verb to make the third statement complete.

d. Using the first two statements, write a complete sentence. You may wish to add words or change the forms of words in the advertisement.

e. Advertisements like this one use sentence fragments. Why are sentence fragments sometimes effective?

f. Why are such sentence fragments inappropriate for essays?

See page 401 for more on the sentence fragment.

WRITE NOW

Do both of the following activities.

1. Make a **brainstorm** list of heroic persons or heroic qualities.

2. Organize this list into logically related groups.

WRITING SUGGESTIONS

1. The Pony Express riders are thought of as heroes. However, their individual names are mostly lost to history. Tell why a heroic individual or group outside your family who is unknown or unsung deserves to be famous.

2. The Pony Express stop described in this reading selection is now an abandoned ruin. Describe your feelings about a place, a job, or an object that has lost its former importance or fame.

3. William Least Heat Moon refers to modern methods of communication as "mechanical contraptions." Discuss how these new devices have changed people's relationships for better or worse.

FURTHER WRITING SUGGESTIONS

4. History seems to be filled with the stories of famous men. Women's contributions, however, have not been fully recognized. Discuss what changes in traditional attitudes toward women are needed to provide a fairer historical balance.

5. No one could accuse the Pony Express of not obeying truth in advertising laws. Choose a television commercial or magazine advertisement. Explain whether it meets your standards for truth and fairness.

6. The advertisement seeks "fellows not over eighteen . . . willing to risk death daily." In the United States, eighteen-year-olds must register for the military draft. Discuss why age eighteen is considered so important in defining adulthood.

I DON'T WANT TO SETTLE THERE*

By Chief Ten Bears

In October 1867, Chief Ten Bears (1792?–1873), the principal leader of the Yamparika tribe of the Comanche nation, came to Medicine Lodge Creek, Kansas, with more than 4,000 Kiowa Apaches, Kiowas, Cheyennes, Arapahoes, and other Comanches to meet with a U.S. government peace commission, dominated by military personnel.

The commission did not budge from its demands: the tribes were to keep the peace, and they would be given lands away from pioneer settlements and

*Editors' title

travel routes. In return, the federal government would supply food and seeds, offer farming and carpentry instruction, build schools, furnish doctors, and provide $25,000 annually for clothing and other needs. At the end of the council, ten chiefs signed the peace treaty.

As a result, the tribes could no longer freely hunt the Central Plains. Dissatisfied, Ten Bears and other chiefs later went to Washington, D.C., in a futile attempt to have the treaty changed. He died soon after, on the reservation at Fort Sill (Oklahoma), Indian Territory.

No stranger to treaty negotiations and broken promises, Chief Ten Bears, who had met with President Abraham Lincoln in the White House in 1863, was the major advocate for the assembled tribes in Kansas. This selection is his speech to Nathaniel G. Taylor, the commissioner of Indian Affairs.

Although American Indians have a great oral tradition, this speech, like many others, was written down by a white listener on the scene.

WORDS TO NOTICE

lodges: Indian dwellings

gourds: hard-rinded inedible fruits

reservation: land area for Indian tribes

prairie: large, flat grassland

Great Father: American Indian term for the President of the United States

hinder: prevent

grievances: complaints

disposed to: in favor of

papooses: young American Indian children

hearken: listen

lance: spear

READ ON

1. What does the **title** suggest about Ten Bears' attitude and situation?

2. After reading Ten Bears' speech for the first time, tell what the main idea of the reading is.

My heart is filled with joy when I see you here, as the brooks fill with water   1
when the snow melts in the spring; and I feel glad as the ponies do when
the fresh grass starts in the beginning of the year. I heard of your coming

when I was many sleeps away, and I made but few camps when I met you. I know that you had come to do good to me and to my people. I looked for benefits which would last forever, and so my face shines with joy as I look upon you.

My people have never first drawn a bow or fired a gun against the whites.   2
There has been trouble on the line between us, and my young men have danced the war-dance. But it was not begun by us. It was you who sent the first soldier and we who sent out the second. Two years ago I came upon this road, following the buffalo, that my wives and children might have their cheeks plump and their bodies warm. But the soldiers fired on us, and since that time there has been a noise like that of a thunderstorm, and we have not known which way to go. So it was upon the Canadian.

Nor have we been made to cry once alone. The blue dressed soldiers   3
and the Utes came from out of the night when it was dark and still, and for campfires they lit our lodges. Instead of hunting game they killed my braves, and the warriors of the tribe cut short their hair for the dead. So it was in Texas. They made sorrow come into our camps, and we went out like the buffalo bulls when the cows are attacked. When we found them, we killed them, and their scalps hang in our lodges.

The Comanches are not weak and blind, like the pups of the dog when   4
seven sleeps old. They are strong and farsighted, like grown horses. We took their road and we went on it. The white women cried and our women laughed.

But there are things which you have said to me which I do not like. They   5
were not sweet like sugar, but bitter like gourds. You said that you wanted to put us upon a reservation, to build our houses and make us medicine lodges. I do not want them. I was born upon the prairie where the wind blew free and there was nothing to break the light of the sun.

I was born where there were no inclosures and where everything drew a   6
free breath. I want to die there and not within walls. I know every stream and every wood between the Rio Grande and the Arkansas, I have hunted and lived over that country. I lived like my fathers before me, and, like them, I lived happily.

When I was at Washington the Great Father told me that all the Coman-   7
ches' land was ours and that no one should hinder us in living upon it. So why do you ask us to leave the rivers and the sun and the wind and live in houses? Do not ask us to give up the buffalo for the sheep. The young men have heard talk of this, and it has made them sad and angry. Do not speak of it more. I love to carry out the talk I get from the Great Father. When I get goods and presents I and my people feel glad, since it shows that he holds us in the eye.

If Texans had kept out of my country there might have been peace. But   8
that which you now say we must live on is too small. The Texans have taken away the places where the grass grew the thickest and the timber the best. Had we kept that, we might have done the things you ask. But it is too late. The white man has the country which we loved, and we only wish to wander on the prairies until we die. Any good thing you say to me shall not be

forgotten. I shall carry it as near to my heart as my children, and it shall be as often on my tongue as the name of the Great Father. I want no blood upon my land to stain the grass. I want it all clear and pure, and I wish it so that all who go through among my people may find peace when they come in and leave it when they go out.

The commissioners have come afar to listen to our grievances. My heart **9** is glad, and I shall hide nothing from you. I understood that you were coming down here to see us. I moved away from those disposed to war, and I also came from afar to see you. The Kiowas and Comanches have not been fighting. We were away down south when we heard that you were coming to see us.

The Cheyennes are those that have been fighting you. They did it in broad **10** daylight, so that all could see them. If I had been fighting I would have done so also. Two years ago I made peace with General Harney, Sanborn, and Colonel Leavenworth at the mouth of the Little Arkansas. That peace I have never broken. When the grass was growing this spring a large body of soldiers came along on the Santa Fe road. I had not done anything and therefore was not afraid.

All the chiefs of the Kiowas, Comanches, and Arapahoes are here today. **11** They have come to listen to the good word. We have been waiting here a long time to see you, and we are getting tired. All the land south of the Arkansas belongs to the Kiowas and Comanches, and I don't want to give away any of it. I love the land and the buffalo, and will not part with any. I want you to understand also that the Kiowas do not want to fight and have not been fighting since we made the treaty. I hear a good deal of fine talk from these gentlemen, but they never do what they say. I don't want any of these medicine homes built in the country; I want the papooses brought up just exactly like I am. When I make peace, it is a long and lasting one; there is no end to it. We thank you for your presents.

All these chiefs and headmen feel happy. They will do what you want. **12** They know that you are doing the best you can. I and they will do so also. There is one big chief lately died—Jim Pockmark, of the Caddoes—he was a great peacemaker, and we are sorry he is dead.

When I look upon you I know you are all big chiefs. While you are in **13** the country we go to sleep happy and are not afraid. I have heard that you intend to settle us on a reservation near the mountains. I don't want to settle there. I love to roam over the wide prairie, and when I do it I feel free and happy, but when we settle down we grow pale and die.

Hearken well to what I say. I have laid aside my lance, my bow, and my **14** shield, and yet I feel safe in your presence. I have told you the truth. I have no little lies hid about me, but I don't know how it is with the commissioners; are they as clear as I am? A long time ago this land belonged to my fathers, but when I go up to the river I see a camp of soldiers, and they are cutting my wood down or killing my buffalo. I don't like that, and when I see it my heart feels like bursting with sorrow. I have spoken.

IN YOUR OWN VOICE

WHAT DOES IT SAY?

1. Who first used weapons?

2. Which tribe helped to burn the Comanche lodges?

3. Where are the Comanches told to live?

4. Where does Chief Ten Bears want to die?

5. Why are the young American Indians sad and angry?

6. What does Chief Ten Bears want for the tribes' children?

7. What does the chief see the U.S. soldiers doing?

WHAT DOES IT MEAN?

1. Why does Chief Ten Bears begin his speech by praising the U.S. commissioners?

2. Although they have been defeated, why does the chief say that the Comanches are strong?

3. Why do the Comanches want to remain "where the wind blew free"?

4. Why do the U.S. commissioners want to place the American Indian tribes on reservations?

5. What does Chief Ten Bears hope to gain by his willingness to remain at peace?

STYLE AND SENSE

1. Chief Ten Bears speaks on behalf of several tribes. Yet the opening and closing paragraphs repeat a word that makes his message personal. Identify the word and tell why it is effective.

2. Often a speech points out differences between opposing viewpoints. Find three places in the speech where differences are clearly presented.

3. Which words or expressions give a sympathetic picture of the American Indian way of life?

FROM THE TEXT

Word endings: Final *-s* or *-es* is added to the basic word to show

1. a change from singular to plural, as in *girl/girls, box/boxes.*

2. the present tense verb agrees with its third person subject, as in *he says, she goes, it works.*

Read the following sentence:

My heart is filled with joy when I see you here, as the brooks fill with water when the snow melts in the spring; and I feel glad as the ponies do when the grass starts in the beginning of the year.

a. What are the verbs that agree with these subjects: *heart, snow, grass?*

b. Are these subjects and verbs singular or plural?

c. What ending do all of these present tense verbs have?

d. What are the two plural nouns in this sentence?

e. What endings do these nouns have?

f. Do the verbs that agree with these nouns end in *-s* or *-es*?

See pages 408 and 420 for more on word endings.

WRITE NOW

Do both of the following activities.

1. Make a **cluster diagram** on one of the following Writing Suggestions.

2. Using your cluster diagram, write a **topic sentence.**

WRITING SUGGESTIONS

1. Every group seeks to keep alive important cultural customs and traditions. Describe how these customs are handed down to the younger generation.

2. Discuss the effects of westward expansion on the Native American peoples who already inhabited the land.

3. Chief Ten Bears stated: "When I make peace, it is a long and lasting one." Tell if there are times when the price of peace is too great.

FURTHER WRITING SUGGESTIONS

4. Chief Ten Bears stated: "I want the papooses brought up just exactly like I am." Explain why the younger generation may not agree with this hope.

5. Imagine that you are the commissioner for Indian Affairs representing the U.S. government. Explain why it is necessary for the American Indians to agree to the treaty's terms.

6. People are often forced to resettle or move to unfamiliar areas because of government policy. Discuss the reasons why a person or a family adapts or does not adapt to such an experience. You may wish to use examples from history or current events.

THE GREAT RAILWAY COMPETITION
By Jack Chen

After California became a state in 1850, it became clear that a transcontinental railroad was needed to profitably carry agricultural products eastward and consumer goods westward, especially since the railroad would hasten the populating of the West.

In 1862 the federal government agreed to subsidize the construction of the railroad. The Central Pacific, working eastward from California, and the Union Pacific, working westward from Nebraska, began the task of laying track. Competition between the Chinese workers of the Central Pacific and the "Irish terriers" of the Union Pacific spurred on the construction of the line.

On May 10, 1869, the two groups met at Promontory, Utah.

Born in Port-of-Spain, Trinidad, in 1908, Jack Chen worked as a journalist and cartoonist in China, the Soviet Union, and England from 1927 to 1972. Since then he has spent much of his time in the United States writing and preparing historical and cultural projects.

Chen was the senior researcher and coordinator of the Chinese of America Exhibition, 1785–1980. Among his numerous books are *The Chinese Theatre* (1948), *Inside the Cultural Revolution* (1975), and *The Chinese of America: From the Beginnings to the Present* (1981), from which this selection is taken.

WORDS TO NOTICE

in tandem: together

Crocker: Charles Crocker, construction boss of the Central Pacific Railway Company

entice: persuade, lure

exploits: great achievements

taunted: provoked and teased

surpassed: bettered

advent: coming

keen: intense, sharp

careered: moved forward quickly

amicable: friendly, peaceful

tie: crossbeam supporting the rails

laurel: evergreen shrub

consternation: anxiety, dismay

Stanford: Leland Stanford, president of the Central Pacific

fidelity and industry: loyalty and hard work

Judah: Theodore Judah, engineer who envisioned a transcontinental railroad, but who could not gain investor support for his idea

formidable: impressive, hard to beat

complemented: worked together as a unit

feat: noteworthy achievement

agitators: troublemakers

straw bosses: assistant foremen

pidgin English: simplified form of English used between people speaking different languages

regaled: entertained

diaspora: movement to scattered places

tycoons: very wealthy business leaders

coffers: money boxes, treasuries

to boot: in addition

glut: oversupply

scapegoats: persons unjustifiably blamed

READ ON

1. While reading this selection for the first time, jot down margin notes about what you consider to be most important.

2. Whom did you expect to be in the snapshot commemorating the completion of the railway?

On the plains, the Chinese worked in tandem with all the Indians Crocker   **1**
could entice to work on the iron rails. They began to hear of the exploits of
the Union Pacific's "Irish terriers" building from the east. One day, the Irish
laid six miles of track, they were told. The Chinese of the Central Pacific
topped this with seven. "No Chinaman is going to beat us," growled the Irish,
and the next day, they laid seven and a half miles of track. They swore that
they would outperform the competition no matter what it did.

Crocker taunted the Union Pacific that his men could lay ten miles of   **2**
track a day. Durant, president of the rival line, laid a $10,000 wager that it
could not be done. Crocker took no chances. He waited until the day before
the last sixteen miles of track had to be laid and brought up all needed
supplies for instant use. Then he unleashed his crews. On April 28, 1869,
while Union Pacific checkers and newspaper reporters looked on, a combined
gang of Chinese and eight picked Irish rail handlers laid ten miles and 1,800
feet more of track in twelve hours. This record was never surpassed until the
advent of mechanized track laying. Each Irishman that day walked a total
distance of ten miles, and their combined muscle handled sixty tons of rail.

So keen was the competition that when the two lines approached each   **3**
other, instead of changing direction to link up, their builders careered on and
on for 100 miles, building lines that would never meet. Finally, the government
prescribed that the linkage point should be Promontory, Utah.

Competition was keen, but there seems to be no truth in the story that   **4**
the Chinese and Irish in this phase of work were trying to blow each other
up with explosives. It is a fact, however, that when the two lines were very
near each other, the Union Pacific blasters did not give the Central Pacific
men timely warning when setting off a charge, and several Chinese were hurt.
Then a Central Pacific charge went off unannounced and several Irishmen
found themselves buried in dirt. This forced the foremen to take up the matter
and an amicable settlement was arranged. There was no further trouble.

On May 10, 1869, the two lines were officially joined at Promontory, north   **5**
of Ogden in Utah. A great crowd gathered. A band played. An Irish crew and
a Chinese crew were chosen to lay the last two rails side by side. The last
tie was made of polished California laurel with a silver plate in its center
proclaiming it "The last tie laid on the completion of the Pacific Railroad,
May 10, 1869." But when the time came it was nowhere to be found. As
consternation mounted, four Chinese approached with it on their shoulders
and they laid it beneath the rails. A photographer stepped up and someone
shouted to him "Shoot!" The Chinese only knew one meaning for that word.
They fled. But order was restored and the famous ceremony began; Stanford
drove a golden spike into the last tie with a silver hammer. The news flashed
by telegraph to a waiting nation. But no Chinese appears in that famous
picture of the toast celebrating the joining of the rails.

Crocker was one of the few who paid tribute to the Chinese that day: "I   **6**
wish to call to your minds that the early completion of this railroad we have
built has been in large measure due to that poor, despised class of laborers

called the Chinese, to the fidelity and industry they have shown." No one even mentioned the name of Judah.

The building of the first transcontinental railway stands as a monument **7** to the union of Yankee and Chinese-Irish drive and know-how. This was a formidable combination. They all complemented each other. Together they did in seven years what was expected to take at least fourteen.

In his book on the building of the railway, John Galloway, the noted **8** transportation engineer, described this as "without doubt the greatest engineering feat of the nineteenth century," and that has never been disputed. David D. Colton, then vice-president of the Southern Pacific, was similarly generous in his praise of the Chinese contribution. He was asked, while giving evidence before the 1876 congressional committee, "Could you have constructed that road without Chinese labor?" He replied, "I do not think it could have been constructed so quickly, and with anything like the same amount of certainty as to what we were going to accomplish in the same length of time."

And, in answer to the question, "Do you think the Chinese have been a **9** benefit to the State?" West Evans, a railway contractor, testified, "I do not see how we could do the work we have done, here, without them; at least I have done work that would not have been done if it had not been for the Chinamen, work that could not have been done without them."

It was heroic work. The Central Pacific crews had carried their railway **10** 1,800 miles through the Sierra and Rocky mountains, over sagebrush desert and plain. The Union Pacific built only 689 miles, over much easier terrain. It had 500 miles in which to carry its part of the line to a height of 5,000 feet,

San Francisco to Promontory, Utah

with another fifty more miles in which to reach the high passes of the Black Hills. With newly recruited crews, the Central Pacific had to gain an altitude of 7,000 feet from the plain in just over 100 miles and make a climb of 2,000 feet in just 20 miles.

All this monumental work was done before the age of mechanization. It was pick and shovel, hammer and crowbar work, with baskets for earth carried slung from shoulder poles and put on one-horse carts. **11**

For their heroic work, the Chinese workmen began with a wage of $26 a month, providing their own food and shelter. This was gradually raised to $30 to $35 a month. Caucasians were paid the same amount of money, but their food and shelter were provided. Because it cost $0.75 to $1.00 a day to feed a white unskilled worker, each Chinese saved the Central Pacific, at a minimum, two-thirds the price of a white laborer (1865 rates). Chinese worked as masons, dynamiters, and blacksmiths and at other skilled jobs that paid white workers from $3 to $5 a day. So, at a minimum, the company saved about $5 million by hiring Chinese workers. **12**

Did this really "deprive white workers of jobs" as anti-Chinese agitators claimed. Certainly not. In the first place, experience had proved that white workers simply did not want the jobs the Chinese took on the railroad. In fact, the Chinese created jobs for white workers as straw bosses, foremen, railhandlers, teamsters, and supervisors. **13**

The wages paid to the Chinese were, in fact, comparable to those paid unskilled or semiskilled labor in the East (where labor was relatively plentiful), and the Chinese were at first satisfied. Charles Nordhoff estimated that the frugal Chinese could save about $13 a month out of those wages. The *Alta California* estimated their savings at $20 a month and later, perhaps, as wages increased, they could lay aside even more. With a bit of luck, a year and a half to two years of work would enable them to return to China with $400 to buy a bit of land and be well-to-do farmers. **14**

But the Chinese began to learn the American way of life. On one occasion in June 1867, 2,000 tunnelers went on strike, asking for $40 a month, an eight-hour day in the tunnels, and an end to beating by foremen. "Eight hours a day good for white man, all same good for Chinese," said their spokesman in the pidgin English common in the construction camps. But solidarity with the other workers was lacking, and after a week the strike was called off when the Chinese heard that Crocker was recruiting strikebreakers from the eastern states. **15**

When the task was done, most of the Chinese railwaymen were paid off. Some returned to China with their hard-earned savings, and the epic story of building the Iron Horse's pathway across the continent must have regaled many a family gathering there. Some returned with souvenirs of the great work, chips of one of the last ties, which had been dug up and split up among them. Some settled in the little towns that had grown up along the line of the railway. Others took the railway to seek adventure further east and south. Most made their way back to California and took what jobs they could find in that state's growing industries, trades, and other occupations. Many used **16** their traditional and newly acquired skills on the other transcontinental lines and railways that were being swiftly built in the West and Midwest. This was the start of the diaspora of the Chinese immigrants in America.

The Union and Central Pacific tycoons had done well out of the building **17** of the line. Congressional investigation committees later calculated that, of $73 million poured into the Union Pacific coffers, no more than $50 million could be justified as true costs. The Big Four and their associates in the Central Pacific had done even better. They had made at least $63 million and owned most of the CP stock worth around $100 million and 9 million acres of land grants to boot.

Ironically, the great railway soon had disastrous results for the Chinese **18** themselves. It now cost only $40 for an immigrant to cross the continent by rail and a flood of immigrants took advantage of the ease and cheapness of travel on the line the Chinese had helped to build. The labor shortage (and resulting high wages) in California turned into a glut. When the tangled affairs of the Northern Pacific line led to the stock market crash of Black Friday, September 19, 1873, and to financial panic, California experienced its first real economic depression. There was devastating unemployment, and the Chinese were made the scapegoats.

IN YOUR OWN VOICE

WHAT DOES IT SAY?

1. Which two companies are building the transcontinental railroad?

2. Where and when do the two railroad lines meet?

3. What makes the Chinese accomplishment "heroic work"?

4. Which tools and equipment do the workers use in building the railroad?

5. Why do the Chinese workers strike in June 1867?

WHAT DOES IT MEAN?

1. Why do the Irish workers say, "No Chinaman is going to beat us"?

2. Why must the government force the two railroad lines to link up with one another?

3. Why do no Chinese appear in the famous photograph celebrating the joining of the rails?

4. Why are the Chinese willing to take jobs that white workers refuse?

5. Why is the transcontinental railroad essential to the growth of the United States?

STYLE AND SENSE

A **paragraph** is a group of related sentences about one major point. Read paragraph 5 of this selection.

1. What is the function of the first four sentences?

2. Why are these sentences of varying lengths?

3. Which details indicate the historic value of this occasion?

4. What is surprising about the closing sentence?

5. How is the paragraph's arrangement similar to that of a snapshot?

FROM THE TEXT

Subject-verb agreement: The verb must agree with its subject in number and not with a prepositional phrase or with any other intervening words that modify the subject.

Read the following:

But solidarity with the other workers was lacking

a. What is the subject?

b. Is the subject singular or plural?

c. What is the complete verb that agrees with the subject?

d. Is the verb singular or plural?

e. Identify the prepositional phrase.

See page 409 for more on subject-verb agreement with an intervening prepositional phrase.

WRITE NOW

Do both of the following activities.

1. Freewrite on one of the following Writing Suggestions.

2. From your freewriting, take one main idea and write a **topic sentence**.

WRITING SUGGESTIONS

1. The Chinese rail workers made an immediate and visible contribution to their new nation. Describe the values that enabled them to succeed despite prejudice, hardship, and unfamiliarity with the English language.

2. Some of the Chinese workers returned to China after the completion of the railroad project; most, however, stayed in the United States. Discuss the conflict within individuals in deciding whether to leave a place or remain.

3. Discuss the advantages and disadvantages of competition between two persons or groups.

FURTHER WRITING SUGGESTIONS

4. The Chinese workers received little recognition for their hard work and bravery. Tell whether individuals or groups need society's praise and support to attain long-term goals.

5. Just thirteen years after the completion of the transcontinental railroad, the U.S. Congress passed the Chinese Exclusion Act in 1882 barring any future immigration from China.

   a. Tell how you would feel about this act if you were a Chinese-American living in the United States at that time.

   or

   b. Tell whether a nation has the right to decide who can and cannot be permitted to live within its borders.

6. Explain if you would take a job, knowing that others were earning more for the same work although you had equal qualifications and experience.

A PIONEER WOMAN'S DIARY: KANSAS TO COLORADO*

By Martha Shaw

"These stories are the record of the woman side of pioneer life. They picture the deprivations, the cruel hardships, the sacrifices, the dangers as no other

*Editors' title

history ever has done or could do," said Lilla Day Monroe of her collection of Kansas women's diaries.

The diaries of one pioneer woman, Martha Shaw (1867–1924), total more than 4,000 pages covering a forty-year period. They describe her life as a teenager at home, her years living on her own, her bitterly unhappy first marriage and covered-wagon journey to the Colorado frontier, her widowhood, and her successful second marriage.

In these diaries, which she kept secret, Shaw does not flinch from telling the harsh realities of pioneer life for a woman. Her story of a covered-wagon journey from Kansas to Colorado in 1891 is no exception.

Shaw underlined many words in her diary. In this book, italics represent the underlinings.

WORDS TO NOTICE

thro': through

ought: anything

surly: rude, unfriendly

compel: force

Topeka: capital of Kansas

utter: complete

thrifty: successful, prosperous

gale: strong wind

lest: in order that (an event) not happen

enquire: inquire, ask

imminent: about to happen

Team: horses harnessed together

"Claim Shanty": miners' cabin

profane: obscene

vileness: disgusting character

unendurable: impossible to live with

READ ON

1. What would you include in your own diary?

2. When you read this diary for the first time, underline words that tell what Martha feels about Johnny.

November

Sun. 1

Been *so sick* today. I am getting so poor some are afraid, my little one will not live to come to me, but what can one do.

Sat. 7

Sewing at Mrs. Baker's again today. *Everyone thinks* it *is dreadful* that Johnny *intends to make me drive thro' to Colo.* with him *in a big wagon and especially this late* in *the Fall. I have asked him* to *let me go on the Train,* if *I must go at this time,* but *he won't even let me do that. I never quarrel* with him and he *never sees ought but a smiling face, however much my heart may ache,* but *this heartless treatment is beginning to make me lose my love for him.*

Wed. 11

Our last night in this house, and God only knows what is before me, but I shall *trust* Him to take care of me and my unborn Babe.

Thurs. 12

We ate dinner with the Bakers today, finished packing and loading our wagon this afternoon, and bid all our neighbors goodbye this evening; even the surly Geo. Weymouth, came over and shook hands with me and had kissed me goodbye, before I knew his intentions, but not a word passed between us. We drove down to brother Jim Shaw's to stay all night and we told them of our expected little one and Oh! their surprise; and so at last, it is good-bye to home and friends, and away to the West, for a *new* home and *new* friends, in a *new* country, almost a Desert. But I am *willing* to make the sacrifice, if it will but restore my husband's health. Our friends think him very selfish to *compel* me to take such a trip in my condition especially, when I could as well go on the train. This late in the Fall will even be harmful to him and I will suffer greatly. Woman will sacrifice everything for the man she loves, why will *he* not do *half* as much for her.

Fri. 13

Well at last, our journey has commenced and tonight after only a few miles of travel, I am *very* tired and the jolting of the wagon, caused me to *suffer much.* We were late in getting away from Topeka, leaving about 3 o'clock; the weather fine and a lovely evening. From our camp tonight at Mulhollen Hill, or a little West, we can see the lights of my beloved Topeka, and it makes my heart ache; when shall I see them again, if ever: my husband in poor health and at the end of a *long hard* journey, my little one to be born, without the help of Doctor or Nurse. But *for an ever present* God, I would be in *utter despair.*

Sat. 14

A cold, chilly drive. Rained all day and the roads terribly, hilly—we got *"stuck"* on one hill. With our heavily loaded wagon, we only reached Dover, 20 miles from Topeka, at dark this evening, and I am so weary and heart sick.

Mon. 16

Passed thro' *Harveyville* at noon. Bought some good, *Home-made bread,* at a little house in the Village. Very cold today and snowed some, but we keep warm as we have a stove in the wagon; how *hard* this *shaking,* as we drive along over *rough, frozen roads* and never a word of sympathy. Johnny gets so cross, if he *even* thinks I feel badly; well, I thank God, for giving me a heart, that can keep its sorrow to itself.

Sat. 21

We passed thro' *Marian,* a nice, thrifty looking, little town, late this afternoon and are in camp, three miles West tonight. Turned *very cold* and *wind blows a gale* and only that we are in a *hollow* I believe it would blow our wagon over, heavy as it is. We see some fine country and some especially pretty place, but the trip *is so hard,* I can't enjoy *anything.* I am not so sick any more, but I *suffer dreadfully,* from the *jolting* of the wagon, so I get out and walk as much as I can, but I am getting so heavy and it is *so hard* for me to climb in and out of our high wagon over the side-boards. It is cruel of Johnny to make me *suffer such torture* by this trip.

Sun. 22

Passed thro' *Hillsboro* and *Lehigh* today and tonight are stopping over night with a young couple by the name of Drew, three miles East of Canton. They are strangers, but insisted on our coming in and sleeping in a bed and I am so *grateful.*

Mon. 23

Drove thro' the "outskirts" of Canton, McPherson Co., this morning and 7 miles beyond to the Ritz farm by noon, and are "laying over" here, to rest and visit and "re-adjust" our load, which has become badly shaken apart. Mrs. Ritz is a cousin of Mother Shaw's. So tonight again, I will get to straighten by tired body in a bed, with room to turn over, and I am *so* tired and worn I could cry, if I could only get away by myself. Mrs. Ritz had such a *splendid* supper and I ate heartily without getting sick.

December

Wed. 2

Passed thro' *Dodge City,* this morning and tonight are camped 20 miles West at *Cimarron. Cold* and the *wind blows a gale.* We *drove in beside a large empty store building* and are *pretty well protected.* The roads are *something terrible* and *sometimes* it is *wholly unsafe* for me to be in the wagon. The journey is *so hard,* that *many times,* I *lie on the mattress* behind Johnny and *cry my heart out* and *he* thinks *I'm sleeping.* How *blind most* men *are* and *how utterly indifferent, to what women suffer. Some times, after a hard days journey,* I can feel no life and my *heart* is *agonized, lest my little one be dead.*

Sat. 5

Passed thro' Deerfield and Lakin today: *Six degrees below zero last night* and we had no shelter whatever, but was no wind. About 4 o'clock, we came to a Ranch house and stopped to enquire the *better* road, as *two roads forked here.* It was *commencing to snow* and the people *advised us to stay* with them *over night,* as a *Blizzard* was *imminent,* but Johnny *would not listen* to them. Oh! *I would give the World to have stayed.* They said *but one* house in 18 miles and that an *empty one* and Johnny understood them to say, *but one empty house* in 18 miles. Well, we drove on and the *storm grew worse,* and *soon* was *dark* and the *little travelled* road, began to *fill,* and my *heart beat anxiously; finally* when we could *no longer follow* the *dim trail,* to *either go ahead or turn back,* and the *wind, snow* and *ice* was suffocating us and we *could hardly force our Team against it,* we *made out* a *dim black shadow,* near the road, which *proved,* an *empty* and *locked "Claim Shanty,"* so we drove up beside it and are camped, with *no other protection* and *completely lost and only those who have been lost in a Blizzard know the agony.*

Sun. 6

The wind was *blowing so hard* this morning, that I *feared* to look out of our *closed wagon,* lest the storm *still be raging,* but when I *found heart* to do so, the sun was shining and a dim depression, showed we were near the road, but Oh! the *terrible anxiety* of the past night. Lost in a *terrible storm,* that might last, on *these barren Plains, for days* and our poor horses, tho blanketed, had to *stand out in it all, as also our faithful Watch dog,* Joe, a fine New-foundland, whom we *might* have *kept* in wagon, with us only for Johnny's *impatience*: and we might all have been comfortably housed, had Johnny but listened to the *kindly* Ranch people. I am *sure* I did not sleep a moment all night: our horses and dog suffered *dreadfully,* and Johnny *froze* his hands a little "unhitching". And we had very little fuel too: Oh! it was a night of *torture,* but God *graciously* spared us, and my unborn Babe, that I *so feared* would come to me last night God has been *merciful* and I *cannot thank* Him *enough.* We drove to *Kendall* for dinner and six miles only farther West, to camp tonight—deep snow—hard traveling.

Mon. 7

We reached Syracuse, our last City in Ks. nearly noon, and found my father there, with Team, to meet us and take part of our load. And he took a *mighty big load,* off my heart, for there will be no more anxiety, about roads. After dividing our load with Pa and eating our dinner and getting some supplies, we started out on the last hundred miles of our journey. Crossing the Arkansas River and driving 8 miles S.W. we are *cozily* camped among some low, sand Hills, and I can sleep happily because Pa is here and I feel safer. He protested about starting out with us after dinner as we could reach no house, to make our camp tonight, but we told him we were used to it. He was *shocked* to think we had not camped each night in a town, where I could have had some comfort, and care if needed.

Tues. 8

Have driven *all* day, today, without a *sight* of a *living* thing; *not a bird,* bush or tree; the Plain as level as a floor, with only Buffalo grass growing; not the *slightest hollow* or *raise* of ground—just a *monotony* of *"distance"*. We camped tonight at Pettit's Ranch and my father insisted on my going in to visit Mrs. Pettit who *seldom* sees a woman in her Ranch life. I was very sick all day.

Thurs. 10

Commenced our journey this morning before Sunrise and reached Pa's Ranch, Belle View, at 11:10 A.M. and I *could have cried with joy,* that my *long hard journey was ended, only I was too tired and sick.* My sister and family (May and Lyman, and little James and Zaidee) were all at Pa's to meet us. Little Zaidee is five years old today. We were *four long weeks* on the journey, who would not rejoice at the end of it.

Fri. 11

Enjoying *blessed rest* at Pa's today; I *wonder* if it *won't seem like this* in Heaven, when our Earthly journey is ended. Not a very pleasant day, almost a storm. Oh! it's been so hard, and I am sure my unborn little one, became tired to, because some nights, after a *hard* day, there would be no pulse of life and I would fear lest my little one would *never* come to me.

Sat. 19

At Pa's, just *resting, resting resting.*

Sat. 26

We went over to Mr. James Wilson's this afternoon, to complete arrangements for the renting of his farm as doctor told Johnny to go on a farm, so to be out in open air much as possible.

Thurs. 31

Pa, Ma, Vella, Johnny and I, all went to sisters today to help celebrate, her *6th Wedding Anniversary.* Lyman is so good to her and their two little ones. And so ends another year of my life: I *think* the *most unhappy, I have ever known.* Johnny is so *unkind* to me, but *more* through his *selfish, indifferent, nature,* than that he *willfully means* to be unkind; but *it is not possible* to live *happily* with him and *were it not* for God's *mercy, I could pray to die.* My *greatest joy* is my *expected Motherhood* and one would *think, this coming joy,* would make him kinder, but it *does not. He does not spare me in the least:* there *is not a profane, low, vulgar, filthy name he has not called me. His vileness is almost unendurable.*

IN YOUR OWN VOICE

WHAT DOES IT SAY?

1. Why does Martha want to go to Colorado by train, and not by wagon?

2. Why is Martha willing "to make the sacrifice" of going on the trip?

3. Why does Martha worry about giving birth in the new place?

4. Where do the Shaws spend the night during the blizzard?

5. Whom does Martha meet in Syracuse, Kansas?

6. Why is 1891 the *"most unhappy"* year of Martha's life?

WHAT DOES IT MEAN?

1. Why does Martha always show *"a smiling face"* to Johnny?

2. Why does Martha look back at Topeka?

3. Why do strangers offer help to the Shaws?

4. Why is Martha comforted by her father's expression of concern?

5. Why does Martha use the diary to express her true feelings about Johnny?

STYLE AND SENSE

1. How does keeping a diary help you understand yourself?

2. Why is a diary usually kept secret?

3. How can a diary be a companion?

4. Why are the feelings and events described in a diary assumed to be true?

5. How does keeping a diary affirm your own voice and identity?

FROM THE TEXT

Read the following sentence:

> We see some fine country and some especially pretty place, but the trip is *so hard*, I can't enjoy *anything*.

a. Why is there no -s ending on the verb *see*?

b. Which verb agrees with the subject *trip*?

c. Why is there no -s ending on *enjoy*?

d. What is the tense of these verbs?

See page 408 for more on subject-verb agreement.

WRITE NOW

Do both of the following activities.

1. Write a **journal** on one of the following Writing Suggestions.

2. Write a **topic sentence** based on a main idea found in your journal.

WRITING SUGGESTIONS

1. Keep a dated diary for one week. Try to express your feelings about events and people mentioned in it.

2. On the journey, Martha visits Mrs. Pettit, "who *seldom* sees a woman in her Ranch life." Tell why both Martha and Mrs. Pettit welcome the opportunity to share experiences and feelings.

3. Lilla Day Monroe, who collected Kansas pioneer women's diaries, wrote of these women: "Their troubles were so close at hand, their sacrifices cut to the quick, their surroundings were so drab and disheartening that it always brought a lump to one's throat to think of the old days. But the women were so brave." Describe the ways in which women were brave and made significant contributions to pioneer life.

FURTHER WRITING SUGGESTIONS

4. The word *hospitality* is related to *host* and *guest.* Answer one of the following:

    a. Tell whether you would have opened your home to strangers passing through on their way west.

    or

    b. Tell how you would have acted while under the roof of your hosts.

5. Martha describes Johnny as cruel and vile, yet she feels some loyalty to him as her husband and the father of her unborn child. Tell what you would do about such a situation if you were Martha.

THE CULEBRA CUT*

By David McCullough

Imagine two vast oceans separated by an immense land mass. There had to be a way for ships to cross it without having to sail around it for months on end.

For centuries explorers, merchants, and nations sought a "path between the seas," a route across Central America connecting the Atlantic and Pacific oceans. In the late-nineteenth century, France tried unsuccessfully to build a canal.

From 1821 to 1903 Panama was part of Colombia. In 1903 Colombia refused to sign a treaty allowing the United States to build a canal through the area. With the political and military support of the United States, Panama successfully gained its independence. The new nation then leased an area called the Canal Zone to the United States, which completed the Panama Canal after a monumental effort of more than ten years.

The canal work force was composed of about 30,000 black men and women from the Caribbean and 6,000 workers from the United States. They faced deadly diseases, such as malaria and yellow fever, and sudden death by dynamite explosion.

This selection is from David McCullough's *Path Between the Seas,* which won the 1978 National Book Award.

WORDS TO NOTICE

Culebra Cut: the major excavation or dig near the village of Culebra

locks: canal sections with gates to adjust water levels enabling ships to pass through

colossal: huge, gigantic

vantage points: places providing good views

panoramic: wide-angle

vibrant: lively, vivid

veritable Pittsburgh: truly resembling Pittsburgh, a city known for its steel industry

crevice: opening, split

reverberating: echoing loudly

tend: look after

*Editors' title

spurs: mountain ridges

eerily: mysteriously

I.C.C.: Interoceanic Canal Commission, established to evaluate construction plans

Goethals: George Washington Goethals, chief engineer of the Panama Canal

nimbly: quickly and athletically

Bishop: Joseph Bucklin Bishop, journalist, Panama Canal administrator

magazines: storage houses for powder and other explosives

congested: overly crowded

aggregate: total, combined

tamping: packing tightly

premature: earlier than expected

READ ON

1. What does the **headnote** say about the difficulty in building a canal to link the Atlantic and Pacific?

2. While reading about the Culebra Cut for the first time, what did you discover about the building of the canal?

The "special wonder of the canal" was Culebra Cut. It was the great focus of attention, regardless of whatever else was happening at Panama. The building of Gatun Dam or the construction of the locks, projects of colossal scale and expense, were always of secondary interest so long as the battle raged in that nine-mile stretch between Bas Obispo and Pedro Miguel. The struggle lasted seven years, from 1907 through 1913, when the rest of the world was still at peace, and in the dry seasons, the tourists came by the hundreds, by the thousands as time went on, to stand and watch from grassy vantage points hundreds of feet above it all. Special trains had to be arranged to bring them out from Colón and Panama City, tour guides provided, and they looked no different from the Sunday crowds on the Boardwalk at Atlantic City. Gentlemen wore white shoes and pale straw hats; ladies stepped along over the grass in ankle-length skirts and carried small, white umbrellas as protection from the sun. . . .

Panoramic photographs made at the height of the work gave an idea of how tremendous that canyon had become. But the actual spectacle, of course, was in vibrant color. The columns of coal smoke that towered above the shovels and locomotives—"a veritable Pittsburgh of smoke"—were blue-black turning to warm gray; exposed clays were pale ocher, yellow, bright orange, slate blue, or a crimson like that of the soil of Virginia; and the vibrant green of the near hills was broken by cloud shadow into great patchworks of sea blue and lavender.

The noise level was beyond belief. On a typical day there would be more **3** than three hundred rock drills in use and their racket alone—apart from the steam shovels, the trains, the blasting—could be heard for miles. In the crevice between Gold Hill and Contractors Hill, where the walls were chiefly rock, the uproar, reverberating from wall to wall, was horrible, head-splitting.

For seven years Culebra Cut was never silent, not even for an hour. Labor **4** trains carrying some six thousand men began rolling in shortly after dawn every morning except Sunday. Then promptly at seven the regular work resumed until five. But it was during the midday break and again after five o'clock that the dynamite crews took over and began blasting. At night came the repair crews, men by the hundreds, to tend the shovels, which were now being worked to the limit and taking a heavy beating. Night track crews set off surface charges of dynamite to make way for new spurs for the shovels, while coal trains servicing the shovels rumbled in, their headlights playing steadily and eerily up and down the Cut until dawn. And though it was official I.C.C. policy that the Sabbath be observed as a day of rest, there was always some vital piece of business in the Cut that could not wait until Monday.

Among the most fascinating of the surviving records of the work is a **5** series of Army Signal Corps films made down in the Cut. Watching these rare old motion pictures (now in a collection at the National Archives), seeing the trains cut back and forth across the screen, seeing the dynamite go off and tiny human figures rush about through clouds of dust and smoke, one senses too how extremely dangerous it all was. At one point, when a shovel suddenly swings, Goethals can be seen to jump nimbly out of the way.

Bishop and those others who described the spectacle from the cliffs above **6** had very little to say about such hazards. But year after year hundreds of men were being killed or hideously injured. They were caught beneath the wheels of trains or struck by flying rock, crushed to death, blown to bits by dynamite. "Man die, get blow up, get kill or get drown," recalled one black worker; "during the time someone asked where is Brown? He died last night and bury. Where is Jerry? He dead a little before dinner and buried. So on and so on all the time."

Construction of the canal would consume more than 61,000,000 pounds **7** of dynamite, a greater amount of explosive energy than had been expended in all the nation's wars until that time. A single dynamite ship arriving at Colón carried as much as 1,000,000 pounds—20,000 fifty-pound boxes of dynamite in one shipload—all of which had to be unloaded by hand, put aboard special trains, and moved to large concrete magazines built at various points back from the congested areas.

At least half the labor force was employed in some phase of dynamite **8** work. Those relatively few visitors permitted to walk about down in the Cut saw long lines of black men march by with boxes of dynamite on their heads, gangs of men on the rock drills, more men doing nothing but loading sticks of dynamite into the holes that had been drilled. The aggregate depth of the dynamite holes drilled in an average month in Culebra Cut (another of those statistics that defy the imagination) was 345,223 feet, or more than sixty-five miles. In the same average month more than 400,000 pounds of dynamite were exploded, which meant that all together more than 800,000 dynamite sticks with their brown paper wrappings, each eight inches long and weighing half a pound, had been placed in those sixty-five miles of drill holes, and again all by hand.

Difficulty was had at first in determining how much dynamite to use in **9** a single shot, depending on the depth of the holes, the spacing of the holes, and the character of the rock, which could be anything from basalt to the softest shale. The foremen responsible for the loading and tamping learned by trial and error. Different grades of powder were tried, different kinds of fuses and methods of firing.

Premature explosions occurred all too often as the pace of work in- **10** creased. "We are having too many accidents with blasts," Goethals noted in June 1907. "One killed 9 men on Thursday at Pedro Miguel. The foreman blown all to pieces." Several fatal accidents were caused when shovels struck the cap of an unexploded charge. Another time a twelve-ton charge went off prematurely when hit by a bolt of lightning, killing seven men. Looking back years later, one West Indian remembered, "The flesh of men flew in the air like birds many days."

The worst single disaster occurred on December 12, 1908, at Bas Obispo. **11** More than fifty holes had been drilled in the solid rock on the west bank of the Cut and these had been loaded with some twenty-two tons of dynamite. The charges had been tamped, the fuses set, but none of the holes had been wired since the blast was not scheduled until the end of the day. As the foreman and one helper were tamping the final charge, the whole blast went off, by what cause no one was ever able to determine. Twenty-three men were killed, forty injured.

As time went on the men became extremely proficient and accidents **12** became comparatively rare considering the volume of explosives being used and the numbers of laborers involved. Still, more men would be killed, and very often, as at Bas Obispo, there would be too little left of them to determine who they were.

IN YOUR OWN VOICE

WHAT DOES IT SAY?

1. How many years does it take to complete work on the Culebra Cut?

2. From which vantage points do the tourists watch?

3. When do the dynamite crews begin blasting each day?

4. How many pounds of dynamite are used in the construction of the canal?

5. Why is the policy of not working on the Sabbath disregarded?

6. Why can't those who die in the explosions be identified?

WHAT DOES IT MEAN?

1. Why is the Culebra Cut called the special wonder of the canal?

2. What event in 1914 ended the peaceful period from 1907 to 1913?

3. What seems strange about the tourists' clothing?

4. Why do writers and observers like Bishop "have very little to say about such hazards" as dynamite explosions?

5. Why must the foremen use the risky method of trial and error in handling dynamite?

STYLE AND SENSE

A **topic sentence** contains the main idea of a paragraph and is often the first sentence. The rest of the paragraph contains specific details to support the topic sentence.

1. Identify the topic sentence of paragraph 4.

2. Which specific supporting details does the next sentence provide?

3. How does the naming of the crews support the topic sentence?

4. How do the references to time support the topic sentence?

5. Which repeated word in the second and next-to-last sentences shows the never-ending cycle of work?

6. How does the last sentence serve as a summary and a comment on the topic sentence?

FROM THE TEXT

Subject-verb agreement with collective nouns: as a subject, the collective noun is considered to be third person singular. The verb, therefore, is also third person singular.

Read the following sentence:

Among the most fascinating of the surviving records of the work is a series of Army Signal Corps films made down in the Cut.

a. What is the verb?

b. What is the subject?

c. Is it singular or plural?

d. Does the prepositional phrase "of Army Signal Corps films" affect the choice of verb?

e. Rewrite the sentence so that the subject is near the beginning.

See page 411 for more on subject-verb agreement with collective nouns.

WRITE NOW

Do both of the following activities.

1. Make a list of **journalistic questions** about the building of the Panama Canal.

2. Write the **first draft** of a paragraph that answers one of the journalistic questions.

WRITING SUGGESTIONS

1. Discuss why individuals or nations pursue great dreams and ambitions despite disappointment, failure, and tragedy.

2. Imagine that you are one of the workers in the Culebra Cut being observed by tourists protected from the sun. Describe your feelings about yourself and the tourists.

3. McCullough states that the building of the Panama Canal was "the adventure of a lifetime." Tell what would be the adventure of a lifetime for you. Explain why.

FURTHER WRITING SUGGESTIONS

4. Discuss whether you would prefer a job situation in which several workers plan and carry out a task by themselves, or one in which the workers are under the direction of a supervisor or an executive.

5. Building the canal was in many ways a battle between human beings and the natural world. Explain why and how people challenge the environment and the forces of nature.

6. The West Indians building the canal were paid at a much lower rate than the other laborers. Discuss the advantages and disadvantages of "cheap labor" in the world today.

UNIT 4

THE UNITED STATES CIVIL WAR

The Civil War in the United States occurred between 1861 and 1865. The opposing forces were the North (Union), comprising the free states, and the South (Confederacy), comprising the states where slavery was legal. Another issue was the continuing conflict about the limit of the power of the federal government and the limit of the power of the states.

This section begins with a poem by Margaret Walker depicting Harriet Tubman's escape to freedom and her forays back to the South to free other slaves.

Next is an eyewitness account by Emma Holmes of Charleston, South Carolina of the attack on Fort Sumter, the start of the Civil War.

The unit ends with Abraham Lincoln's famous Gettysburg Address, a tribute to those who fought and died in the battle of Gettysburg, Pennsylvania (July 1863).

The Union victory was shadowed by Lincoln's assassination in April 1865. The U.S. Civil War took the lives of more Americans than any other war in U.S. history.

BEFORE YOU READ

What does the word *civil* mean?

Why are civil wars fought?

What do you know about the Civil War in the United States? What were its causes?

What was the role of Abraham Lincoln in the Civil War?

How can the healing process of a divided nation begin?

Should the living praise those who die in war?

Is combat for men only?

What is women's role in wartime?

Why should the President of the United States speak to the public?

Would you endanger your own life to rescue slaves?

Did people avoid compromise on national issues?

What was the Underground Railroad?

Is war too glorified?

Is a civil war worse than any other?

Was the Civil War worth fighting?

HARRIET TUBMAN

By Margaret Walker

Born into slavery in Maryland about 1820, Harriet Tubman escaped in 1849. She became one of the most successful "conductors" on the Underground Railroad, a system for helping runaway slaves escape to the North and Canada. Among the slaves she was known as Moses, and her successes led the abolitionist John Brown to call her General Tubman.

In the Civil War she was a scout and spy for the Union Army. Her story was recorded by her friend Sarah Bradford in *Scenes from the Life of Harriet Tubman* (1869). In later years, Tubman helped found the National Association of Colored Women. She died in 1913.

Margaret Walker was born in Birmingham, Alabama, in 1915. After being educated in the South, she received a Ph.D. from the University of Iowa and worked as a college English professor, newspaper reporter, and social worker.

She received the Yale Younger Poets Award for *For My People* (1942). Her novel *Jubilee* (1966) deals with the decade of the Civil War. Her most recent books are a biography of the author Richard Wright and a collection of essays.

WORDS TO NOTICE

slavers: slave owners

bleak: grim, cheerless

bonded: enslaved

lash: whip

grubber: digger

marster: master

sullen: resentful

yonder: over there

ransom: reward, price

stills: equipment for distilling homemade whiskey

Uncle Sam: the United States

Harpers Ferry: site in West Virginia of famous raid by the antislavery leader **John Brown** (1800–1859)

Fred Douglass: Frederick Douglass (1817–1895), former slave who became a leading abolitionist and editor of the *North Star*

Abolitionists: antislavery supporters

READ ON

1. What does the **headnote** say about Harriet Tubman?

2. While reading the poem, **star** the words that evoke an emotional response in you.

Dark is the face of Harriet,
Darker still her fate
Deep in the dark of Southern wilds
Deep in the slavers' hate.

Fiery the eye of Harriet,   5
Fiery, dark, and wild;
Bitter, bleak, and hopeless
Is the bonded child.

Stand in the fields, Harriet,
Stand alone and still   10
Stand before the overseer
Mad enough to kill.

This is slavery, Harriet,
Bend beneath the lash;
This is Maryland, Harriet,   15
Bow to poor white trash.

You're field hand, Harriet,
Working in the corn;
You're a grubber with the hoe
And a slave child born.   20

You're just sixteen, Harriet,
And never had a beau;
Your mother's dead long time ago,
Your daddy you don't know.

This piece of iron's not hard enough   25
To kill you with a blow,
This piece of iron can't hurt you,
Just let you slaves all know.

I'm still the overseer,
Old marster'll believe my tale;   30
I know that he will keep me
From going to the jail.

Get up, bleeding Harriet,
I didn't hit you hard;
Get up, bleeding Harriet,   35
And grease your head with lard.

Get up, sullen Harriet,
Get up and bind your head.
Remember this is Maryland
And I can beat you dead.   40

The Underground Railroad—Maryland to Canada

How far is the road to Canada?
How far do I have to go?
How far is the road from Maryland
And the hatred that I know?

I stabbed that overseer;   45
I took his rusty knife;
I killed that overseer;
I took his lowdown life.

For three long years I waited,
Three years I kept my hate,   50
Three years before I killed him,
Three years I had to wait.

Done shook the dust of Maryland
Clean off my weary feet;
I'm on my way to Canada   55
And Freedom's golden street.

I'm bound to git to Canada
Before another week;
I come through swamps and mountains,
I waded many a creek.   60

Now tell my brothers yonder
That Harriet is free;

Yes, tell my brothers yonder
No more auction block for me.

Come down from the mountain, Harriet,   65
Come down to the valley at night,
Come down to your weeping people
And be their guiding light.

Sing Deep Dark River of Jordan,
Don't you want to cross over today?   70
Sing Deep Wide River of Jordan,
Don't you want to walk Freedom's way?

I stole down in the night time,
I come back in the day,
I stole back to my Maryland   75
To guide the slaves away.

I met old marster yonder
A-coming down the road,
And right past me in Maryland
My old marster strode.   80

I passed beside my marster
And covered up my head;
My marster didn't know me
I guess he heard I'm dead.

I wonder if he thought about   85
That overseer's dead;
I wondered if he figured out
He ought to know this head?

You'd better run, brave Harriet,
There's ransom on your head;   90
You better run, Miss Harriet,
They want you live or dead.

Been down in valleys yonder
And searching round the stills,
They got the posse after you,   95
A-riding through the hills.

They got the blood hounds smelling,
They got their guns cocked too;
You better run, bold Harriet,
The white man's after you.   100

They got ten thousand dollars
Put on your coal-black head;
They'll give ten thousand dollars;
They're mad because you fled.

I wager they'll be riding   105
A long, long time for you.
Yes, Lord, they'll look a long time
Til Judgment Day is due.

I'm Harriet Tubman, people,
I'm Harriet the slave,   110
I'm Harriet, free woman,
And I'm free within my grave.

    Come along, children, with Harriet
    Come along, children, come along
    Uncle Sam is rich enough   115
    To give you all a farm.

I killed the overseer.
I fooled old marster's eyes,
I found my way to Canada
With hundreds more besides.   120

    Come along to Harpers Ferry
    Come along to brave John Brown
    Come along with Harriet, children,
    Come along ten million strong.

I met the mighty John Brown,   125
I know Fred Douglass too
Enlisted Abolitionists
Beneath the Union Blue.

I heard the mighty trumpet
That sent the land to war;   130
I mourned for Mister Lincoln
And saw his funeral car.

    Come along with Harriet, children,
    Come along to Canada.
    Come down to the river, children,   135
    And follow the northern star.

I'm Harriet Tubman, people,
I'm Harriet, the slave,
I'm Harriet, free woman,
And I'm free beyond my grave.   140

    Come along to freedom, children,
    Come along ten million strong;
    Come along with Harriet, children,
    Come along ten million strong.

IN YOUR OWN VOICE

WHAT DOES IT SAY?

1. Why must the young Harriet Tubman "bend beneath the lash"?

2. What happens to the overseer?

3. Where does Harriet Tubman seek freedom?

4. Why does she return to Maryland?

5. How much is the reward for her capture?

6. List the famous people mentioned in this poem.

WHAT DOES IT MEAN?

1. Why does the future seem "bitter, bleak, and hopeless" to Harriet Tubman?

2. Why does she think of going to Canada?

3. Why is the River Jordan associated with freedom?

4. Why does Tubman risk her life to free hundreds of slaves?

5. Why does Tubman state, "I'm free beyond my grave"?

STYLE AND SENSE

1. The poem repeats such words as *dark, deep, fiery,* and *come.* Discuss whether this repetition adds to or takes away from the emotional power of the piece.

2. Discuss whether Harriet Tubman's spoken language (for example, lines 41 through 64) adds to or takes away from the emotional power of the poem.

3. This poem begins with one young woman and ends with "ten million strong." Which of Tubman's words show identification with all the slaves?

FROM THE TEXT

Apostrophe: a punctuation mark used (1) to show possession and (2) to indicate a letter or letters missing when a contraction is formed.

Read the following line:

Don't you want to walk Freedom's way?

a. Why is there an apostrophe in *don't?*

b. In the following examples, use apostrophes to form contractions:

   1. they are

   2. he will

   3. it has been raining

   4. a person might have

c. Why is there an apostrophe in *Freedom's way?*

d. Why is the apostrophe after the *m* and not after the *s?*

See page 460 for more on the apostrophe.

WRITE NOW

Do both of the following activities.

1. **Freewrite** on the poem's theme, events, or the emotions aroused in you.

2. Write the **first draft** of a paragraph on one of the ideas from your freewriting.

WRITING SUGGESTIONS

1. "Harriet Tubman" is a poem that tells a story. Narrate the story of Harriet Tubman and the Underground Railroad. Add enough details so that the reader has a more complete picture of several events of the poem. Do not quote lines from the poem.

2. Tubman frees herself but returns to free others. Tell whether or not you would do the same.

3. Discuss how the lessons learned from the freedom struggles of the past affect either people or nations today.

FURTHER WRITING SUGGESTIONS

4. Tubman is proud to have met such famous people as John Brown, Frederick Douglass, and Abraham Lincoln. Explain why you would like to meet and talk to a specific famous person of the past or present.

5. The escaping slaves followed the North Star to freedom. A famous folksong, "Follow the Drinking Gourd," brings this historical event to life. Discuss how a song of today deals with an important contemporary event or concern.

6. Tubman killed the overseer. Discuss whether violence is ever necessary to bring about changes in society.

THE CIVIL WAR BEGINS*

By Emma Holmes

Emma Edwards Holmes (1838–1910) was a member of one of the leading families of South Carolina, the first state to secede, or withdraw, from the Union.

*Editors' title

Her *Diary* (1861–1866) covers Civil War events that she witnessed or read about in Charleston newspapers or letters from friends and relatives in the Confederate Army. It includes descriptions of Southern women's contributions to the war effort and accounts of their social life. She also provides a slave owner's perspective on the changing relationship between whites and blacks during the Civil War.

These diary selections from April 11 to 13, 1861, vividly describe the first battle between the North and South.

WORDS TO NOTICE

annals: year-by-year history

despatch: dispatch, military report

Jeff Davis: Jefferson Davis, president of the Confederacy

aid-de-camps: aides-de-camp, junior officers

Anderson: Major Robert Anderson, commander of the Union forces at Fort Sumter in Charleston

battery: area of town where artillery guns are mounted

thronged: crowded

bar: sandbar at the mouth of a harbor

Beauregard: Pierre G. T. Beauregard, Confederate general

grave: serious

"Palmetto boys": soldiers from South Carolina, whose nickname is the Palmetto State

cove: small bay

breaches: openings, gaps

husbanding: saving up

magazines: ammunition storage areas

spire: pointed structure on a house or tower

promenade: seaside public walking area

opera glasses: small binoculars

report: loud noise from gunfire

"magic seven": the seven Confederate states

riddled: damaged by many bullet holes

1. Which of the **Words to Notice** deal with the battle and the onlookers?

2. What feelings would you have about the outbreak of war?

April 11, Thursday

[This] is a day never to be forgotten in the annals of Charleston. A   **1**
despatch was received from Jeff Davis with orders to demand the surrender
of the Fort immediately at 2 P.M. Two aid-de-camps went to Anderson with
the summons, giving him until six to decide. The whole afternoon & night
the Battery was thronged with spectators of every age and sex, anxiously
watching and awaiting with the momentary expectation of hearing the war of
cannon opening on the fort or on the fleet which was reported off the bar.
Every body was restless and all who could go were out. . . .

April 12, Friday

. . . The first time Anderson said, if the fort was not battered, he would   **2**
have to surrender in three days for want of food. Beauregard went the second
time last night at ten to urge the surrender, but Anderson refused. All last
night the troops were under arms, and, at half past four this morning, the
heavy booming of cannons woke the city from its slumbers. The battery was
soon thronged with anxious hearts, and all day long they have continued, a
dense quiet orderly mass, but not a sign of fear or anguish is seen. Every
body seems relieved that what has been so long dreaded has come at last
and so confident of victory that they seem not to think of the danger of their
friends. Every body seems calm & grave. I am writing about half past four in
the afternoon, just about twelve hours since the first shot was fired. And,
during the whole time, shot & shell have been steadily pouring into Ft. Sumter
from Fort Stevens where our "Palmetto boys" have won the highest praise
from Beauregard, from Ft. Moultrie, & [from] the floating battery placed at
the cove. These are the principal batteries & just before dinner we received
despatches saying *no one* has been hurt on either Morris or Sullivan's Islands,
and, though the floating battery & Fort Stevens have both been hit several
times, *no damage* has been done, while two or three breaches have been
made in Ft. Sumter. For more than two hours our batteries opened on Anderson before he returned a single shot, as if husbanding his resources. At
times his firing has been very rapid, then slow & irregular and at times
altogether upon Ft. Moultrie. Though every shot is distinctly heard & shakes
our house, I feel calm and composed. This morning I was so very restless
because I was not able to go out, though the Dr. let me go down stairs, that
I felt almost sick, but some one came constantly to tell us the news, & we
were comforted by hearing "all well" at Fort Stevens. . . . At one time it was
reported between twenty & thirty regulars had been killed at Fort Moultrie by

the bursting of one of their own shells, but a subsequent despatch showed it to be false.

There are some few ladies who have been made perfectly miserable and nearly frantic by their fears of the safety of their loved ones, but the great body of citizens [seems] to be so impressed with the justice of our cause that they place entire confidence in the God of Battles. Every day brings hundreds of men from up country, & the city is besides filled with their anxious wives and sisters and mothers, who have followed them.

April 13, Saturday

All yesterday evening and during the night our batteries continued to fire 4 at regular intervals. About six in the afternoon the rain commenced and poured for some hours. The wind rose & it became quite stormy. But this morning rose clear & brilliantly beautiful. Yesterday was so misty it was difficult to see what was going on at the forts. The wind was from the west today, which prevented us from hearing any firing, and we were becoming anxious to know the meaning of the stillness when Uncle James sent to tell us Fort Sumter was on fire. I could not wait for the Dr.'s permission but drove hurriedly to cousin Sallie's [DeSaussure] where I had a splendid view of the harbor with the naked eye. We could distinctly see the flames amidst the smoke. All the barracks were on fire. Beyond lay the fleet of four or five vessels off the bar, their masts easily counted. They did not make the slightest effort to go to Anderson's relief. We could only tell when a gun was fired by the smoke or a white cloud as "big as a man's hand" floating for a few moments along the blue sky marked where a shell had burst. Occasionally when the fire reached the temporary magazines, or a shell struck them, an explosion followed which was felt in the city. The scene at Fort Sumter must have been awful beyond description. . . . Both on Friday and Saturday Anderson put his flag at half mast as a signal of distress, the barracks being on fire three times on Friday. "His friends" took no notice of it & [the distress signal] was not understood by our men though all sympathized deeply with him and shouted applause every time he fired.

In the meantime the scene to the spectators in the city was intensely 5 exciting. The Battery and every house, housetop and spire, was crowded. On White Point Garden were encamped about fifty cadets, having in charge, five, six and twelve pounders placed on the extreme of the eastern promenade. It was thought the vessels might attempt to come in and bombard the city, and workmen were busy all day in mounting four twenty-fours directly in front of cousin T[a]'s [DeSaussure]. With the telescope I saw the shots as they struck the fort and [saw] the masonry crumbling. . . . We [also] saw the men moving about on the sand hills [on Morris Island]. All [there] were anxious to see, and most had opera glasses which they coolly used till they heard a report from Sumter when they dodged behind the sand hills. On Friday, when a shot struck the iron-battery, battering in one of the trapdoors, [Capt. George] Cuthbert walked coolly amidst the thickest of the fire on the outside, to examine it, and, during the whole battle, the Palmetto Guard, 135 strong, behaved with the greatest coolness, skill and gallantry. They had in charge Steven's Battery (Cuthbert), a mortar battery (Rutledge), and Point Battery (T. S. Brownfield commanding), where were two 42's & the rifled cannon just sent on by Charles K. Prioleau from England a most destructive weapon, whose every shot told with dreadful effect. During the morning a demand for cartridge bags for the Dahlgreen guns was made. The elder ladies cut and about twenty girls immediately went to work, all seated on the floor, while we set one to watch and report. Soon the welcome cry was heard, "the flag is down.". . .

What a change was wrought in a few moments in the appearance of the   **6**
harbor. Steamers with fire engines were immediately despatched to the fort. The garrison gathered on the wharf to breathe the fresh air, & numbers of little sailing boats were seen to dart like sea-gulls in every direction conveying gentlemen to the islands to see their friends.

During the afternoon a small boat came with a white flag from the fleet   **7**
bearing an officer who wished to make arrangements with Anderson about his removal.

As soon as the surrender was announced, the bells commenced to ring   **8**
and in the afternoon salutes of the "magic seven" were fired from the *Cutter Lady Davis School* ship and "Cadet's Battery" in honor of the one of the most brilliant & bloodless victories in the records of the world. After thirty three hours consecutive cannonading, not one man hurt on either side, no damage of any consequence done to any of our fortifications, though the officers' quarters at Fort Moultrie & many of the houses on Sullivan's [Island] were riddled & though the outer walls of Fort Sumter were much battered & many of the guns disabled besides the quarters burnt, still as a military post it is uninjured.

I have tried to give an outline of this ever memorable day but find it   **9**
difficult to do justice to the subject and to the gallant men who achieved the independence of our beloved State. Another difficulty is, among the thousand different rumors each day circulated, always to find out which is the true tale even about things occurring before our own eyes.

IN YOUR OWN VOICE

WHAT DOES IT SAY?

1. Which weapon is used by the Confederate forces in the attack on Fort Sumter?

2. Why is everyone in Charleston relieved that war has begun?

3. How can the spectators tell when a gun is fired?

4. What job is performed by the women in the city to assist the military?

5. How many men on both sides are killed or wounded?

WHAT DOES IT MEAN?

1. Why is April 11, 1861, "a day never to be forgotten in the annals of Charleston"?

2. Why are the citizens "so confident of victory"?

3. Why are Holmes and other civilians generally unafraid to be close to the battle?

4. Why do the Confederate forces have great sympathy for Major Anderson's distress?

5. Why does Holmes find it difficult to believe the truth about things she sees?

STYLE AND SENSE

Paragraph 1 of the April 13, 1861, entry of Emma Holmes's diary describes her feelings and observations about the attack on Fort Sumter, the first battle of the Civil War.

1. Why do the opening sentences of paragraph 1 refer to time?

2. Why are the weather conditions described in detail?

3. What can Holmes see "with the naked eye"?

4. What value is an ordinary person's diary of a historical event?

FROM THE TEXT

Subject-verb agreement: the verb agrees with its subject even when the subject follows the verb.

Read the following:

On White Point Garden were encamped about fifty cadets

a. What is the complete verb?

b. Is the verb singular or plural?

c. What is the subject?

d. Is the subject singular or plural?

e. Rewrite the From the Text statement so that the subject precedes the verb.

See page 415 for more on subject-verb agreement and inverted word order.

WRITE NOW

Do both of the following activities.

1. Make a list of **journalistic questions** about the events in the diary.

2. Write a **first draft** of a paragraph based on one of the journalistic questions.

WRITING SUGGESTIONS

1. A civil war is fought by people of the same nation, on their very own soil. Discuss the impact of a civil war on the people and the nation.

2. The sight and sound of war brought crowds of enthusiastic spectators to the Charleston waterfront. Tell whether or not you would be one of these spectators.

3. Describe the emotions that are aroused when "our boys" go off to war.

FURTHER WRITING SUGGESTIONS

4. Television brings images of war into millions of homes. Discuss how seeing "things occurring before our own eyes" may or may not change our attitude toward war.

5. Some countries forbid women from participating in combat. Explain why you agree or disagree with this policy.

6. Describe the steps that opposing groups in a nation or community can take to reach a harmonious or peaceful compromise.

THE GETTYSBURG ADDRESS

By Abraham Lincoln

At Gettysburg, Pennsylvania, in early July 1863, the Union Army defeated the Confederate forces in a crucial battle in which losses on both sides totaled nearly 50,000.

Abraham Lincoln (1809–1865), the sixteenth president of the United States, spoke at the dedication of the national cemetery in Gettysburg on November 19, 1863. Lincoln's speech, one of the most famous in history, honors the dead for their heroism and sacrifice, and seeks to heal the wounds of a divided nation.

WORDS TO NOTICE

address: speech

fourscore: eighty (four times twenty)

proposition: principle, idea

altogether: entirely, completely

consecrate: make sacred or holy

hallow: make holy

detract: take away from

note: notice, pay attention to

resolve: state firmly

perish: die, disappear

READ ON

1. What do you know about Abraham Lincoln and the Gettysburg Address?

2. Read the speech aloud. **Underline** key words and phrases.

Fourscore and seven years ago our fathers brought forth on this continent, a   **1**
new nation, conceived in Liberty, and dedicated to the proposition that all
men are created equal.

Now we are engaged in a great civil war, testing whether that nation or   **2**
any nation so conceived and so dedicated, can long endure. We are met on
a great battle-field of that war. We have come to dedicate a portion of that
field, as a final resting place for those who here gave their lives that that
nation might live. It is altogether fitting and proper that we should do this.

But, in a larger sense, we can not dedicate—we can not consecrate—   **3**
we can not hallow—this ground. The brave men, living and dead, who struggled here, have consecrated it, far above our poor power to add or detract.
The world will little note, nor long remember, what we say here, but it can
never forget what they did here. It is for us the living, rather, to be dedicated
here to the unfinished work which they who fought here have thus far so
nobly advanced. It is rather for us to be here dedicated to the great task
remaining before us—that from these honored dead we take increased devotion to that cause for which they gave the last full measure of devotion—
that we here highly resolve that these dead shall not have died in vain—that
this nation, under God, shall have a new birth of freedom—and that government of the people, by the people, for the people, shall not perish from the
earth.

IN YOUR OWN VOICE

WHAT DOES IT SAY?

1. What event occurred "fourscore and seven years ago"?

2. Who are buried at Gettysburg?

3. What must the living do in order to honor the dead?

4. What "shall not perish from the earth"?

WHAT DOES IT MEAN?

1. Why does Lincoln emphasize nationhood at a Civil War memorial?

2. Why does Lincoln believe that the living cannot dedicate the burial ground?

3. How is "a new birth of freedom" possible?

4. Why does a speech delivered by a President have special impact?

STYLE AND SENSE

A **transition** is a bridge created by repeating words and phrases, using synonyms and pronouns, and placing key informational words between sentences and paragraphs. A transition produces clear, coherent writing.

1. Which three key words in the second sentence also appear in the first sentence?

2. Which pronoun is repeated in the second paragraph? Where else does it appear?

3. Which words in the first sentence contrast with the first word *now* in the second sentence?

4. What is the function of the word *but* at the start of the third paragraph?

5. Which words in the opening and closing sentences of the speech suggest a contrast to death?

FROM THE TEXT

Relative pronouns: *who, whom, whose, which,* and *that* are pronouns that refer to their preceding nouns or pronouns (**antecedents**).

Read the following sentence:

It is for us, the living, rather, to be dedicated here to the unfinished work which they who fought here have thus far so nobly advanced.

a. Identify the two relative pronouns.

b. Identify the noun and pronoun antecedents.

c. Identify the relative pronoun that refers to people.

d. Identify the relative pronoun that refers to a thing.

e. Can the word *that* be substituted for both relative pronouns?

See page 453 for more on relative pronouns.

WRITE NOW

1. In small groups, talk about the meaning of these words: "All men are created equal."

2. Write a **topic sentence** based on your discussion.

WRITING SUGGESTIONS

1. In the eighteenth century, the Declaration of Independence declared that "all men are created equal." In the nineteenth century, Abraham Lincoln used these exact words in the Gettysburg Address. In the twentieth century, Martin Luther King, Jr., also quoted these words. Discuss one of the following:

   a. The reasons why these words have remained the cornerstone of American democracy.

   b. How the meaning of these words has changed over the course of time.

   c. How these words speak to the hopes and yearnings of people in many countries of the world today.

FURTHER WRITING SUGGESTIONS

2. Discuss how a President of the United States can influence public opinion.

3. Discuss whether honoring those who died in war makes the idea of war more acceptable.

UNIT 5

Artist unknown. Navajo blanket. 1880–90. Natural History Museum of Los Angeles County.

BORDERS:
REAL AND
IMAGINED

Does the word *borders* suggest a crossing over to a new land, or a protective boundary against the unknown? Or something else?

Borders—geographical, emotional, generational—are the theme of this unit.

The section opens with "Fauna of the United States," a fanciful, yet mysterious tall tale about "creatures" in the Minnesota and Wisconsin woods by the Argentinean writer Jorge Luis Borges. This is followed by a folktale by the Native American writer N. Scott Momaday about the Kiowas' search for the home of summer.

The southwestern United States at the turn of this century is the locale for the next piece, a woman's memory of her grandparents' house.

The unit then moves to the Midwest for a train ride across the Mississippi, marking a transition from adolescence to adulthood for Ernest Hemingway's fictional character Nick Adams.

A different kind of border is crossed in Jackie Robinson's autobiographical account of his signing of a contract with the Brooklyn Dodgers organization in 1945, the first step to breaking the color barrier in major league baseball.

Finally, the Canadian sense of place, identity, and boundary is explored in Margaret Atwood's "True North."

BEFORE YOU READ

Why are geographical borders important?

What do borders represent?

What kinds of borders do folktales, tall tales, and myths cross?

What are some important borders in the life cycle?

What problems exist in crossing from adolescence to adulthood?

What borders do you want to cross?

What borders do you fear to cross?

Are they the same?

How can you reach across borders?

What is gained or lost by crossing a border?

How does breaking new ground in one field or profession carry over into society as a whole?

Would you like to live on or near a border? Which one?

Which personal borders are important to you?

Which borders will be crossed in the twenty-first century?

Do "good fences make good neighbors," as the poet Robert Frost wrote?

Are borders needed between the nations of the Americas? Why or why not?

FAUNA OF THE UNITED STATES

By Jorge Luis Borges

Blending fantasy and reality, mixing essay and narrative, the stories of the Argentinean writer Jorge Luis Borges (1899–1986) create their own imaginative world. The events in his stories do not often occur in the same order that they would in real life, if they could happen at all.

Borges's two most famous collections of short narratives, *Labyrinths* and *Ficciones,* have had a significant influence on fiction writing throughout the world. His award-winning poetry and essays also established him as a major literary figure.

This selection from *The Book of Imaginary Beings,* a wide-ranging collection of animal tales, fables, folklore, and oddities, shows Borges's appreciation of the tall tales of the north-central United States.

WORDS TO NOTICE

fauna: the animals of a region

yarns: exaggerated or invented tales

singular: one-of-a-kind

beak: bill

snare: trap, capture

fleetest: fastest

vaporous: steamlike

dachshund: short-legged, long-bodied dog

incline: slope

coveted: strongly desired

pinnacle: peak, highest point

plumage: feathers

READ ON

1. Make up and then name one imaginary creature.

2. While rereading this selection, **find** details that are more realistic than fantastic.

The yarns and tall tales of the lumber camps of Wisconsin and Minnesota include some singular creatures, in which, surely, no one ever believed. **1**

There is the *Hidebehind,* which is always hiding behind something. No matter how many times or whichever way a man turns, it is always behind him, and that's why nobody has been able to describe it, even though it is credited with having killed and devoured many a lumberjack. **2**

Then there is the *Roperite.* This animal is about the size of a pony. It has a ropelike beak which it uses to snare even the fleetest of rabbits. **3**

The *Teakettler* owes its name to the noises it makes, much like those of **4**

a boiling teakettle. Vaporous clouds fume from its mouth and it walks backward. It has been seen very few times.

The *Axehandle Hound* has a hatchet-shaped head, a handle-shaped body,   5
and stumpy legs. This North Woods dachshund eats only the handles of axes.

Among the fish of this region we find the *Upland Trout.* They nest in trees   6
and are good fliers but are scared of water.

There's another fish, the *Goofang,* that swims backward to keep the water   7
out of its eyes. It's described as "about the size of a sunfish, only much
bigger."

We shouldn't forget the *Goofus Bird* that builds its nest upside down and   8
flies backward, not caring where it's going, only where it's been.

The *Gillygaloo* nested on the slopes of Paul Bunyan's famed Pyramid   9
Forty, laying square eggs to keep them from rolling down the steep incline
and breaking. These eggs were coveted by lumberjacks, who hard-boiled them
and used them as dice.

And finally there's the *Pinnacle Grouse,* which had a single wing. This   10
enabled it to fly in one direction only, circling the top of a conical hill. The
color of its plumage varied according to the season and according to the
condition of the observer.

IN YOUR OWN VOICE

WHAT DOES IT SAY?

1. Where do the tall tales originate?

2. How are rabbits caught?

3. What is strange about the *Upland Trout*?

4. What do the lumberjacks use as dice?

5. On which two factors does the plumage of the *Pinnacle Grouse* depend?

WHAT DOES IT MEAN?

1. Why do the lumberjacks invent imaginary creatures?

2. How does the *Hidebehind* reveal the dangers in the lumberjacks' own minds?

3. How is the *Teakettler* similar to the *Hidebehind*?

4. Why does the *Goofus Bird* build its nest upside down?

5. Which human traits do some of the imaginary creatures embody?

STYLE AND SENSE

1. In the opening paragraph, how does the phrase "singular creatures" suggest the topic of every paragraph that follows?

2. Why are no specific names for creatures given in the opening paragraph?

3. What do the first sentences of paragraphs 2 through 10 have in common?

4. How do the other sentences in each of these paragraphs make the creature's name appropriate?

5. The words *then* (paragraph 3), *another* (paragraph 7), *finally* (paragraph 10) have a special purpose. What is it?

FROM THE TEXT

Pronoun: a word that takes the place of a noun. A singular pronoun replaces a singular noun. A plural pronoun replaces a plural noun.

Read the following sentence:

The *Teakettler* owes its name to the noises it makes, much like those of a boiling teakettle.

a. To which noun do both *its* and *it* refer?

b. Is this noun singular or plural?

c. Which pronoun replaces *the noises*?

d. Is this pronoun singular or plural?

e. List five pronouns besides *its* that do not need an apostrophe before the final -*s*.

See page 198 for more on pronouns.

WRITE NOW

Do both of the following activities.

1. Write a **topic sentence** for one of the Writing Suggestions below.

2. Make a list of examples to support the topic sentence.

WRITING SUGGESTIONS

1. Each of us was given a name at birth. Tell whether that name suits you or your personality and whether you have ever wanted to change it. You may wish to consider its sound and length, its family history, its origin, or any other factor influencing your attitude.

2. This selection contains imaginary creatures used to explain real events and feelings. Explain why a child similarly may select a particular object, toy, doll, or stuffed animal to act out or "work through" real questions or fears.

3. Paul Bunyan was a legendary, giant lumberjack who performed superhuman deeds. For example, with his pick he was said to have carved out the Grand Canyon. Narrate a tall tale in which you account for the creation of one of these: a river, a mountain, a star, a flower.

FURTHER WRITING SUGGESTIONS

4. Narrate a story about the imaginary creature you made up in Read On, or one of those in the reading.

5. Tell how you would explain to a child the difference between fantasy and reality.

6. Discuss the importance of an individual's imagination in a technological world.

KIOWA SUMMER: THE SETTING OUT

By N. Scott Momaday

N. Scott Momaday (born 1934) is a Kiowa Indian whose book *House Made of Dawn* received the Pulitzer Prize in 1968. One year later, he wrote *The Way to Rainy Mountain,* a work that evokes memories of his own past and the culture and way of life of his tribal ancestors.

This selection from *The Way to Rainy Mountain* retells a traditional Kiowa folktale. The story relates a journey or quest to discover the home of summer. To reach it, the Kiowas follow the sun.

Momaday writes elsewhere in the book, "My grandmother had a reverence for the sun, a holy regard that now is all but gone out of mankind."

WORDS TO NOTICE

Kiowas: an American Indian tribe of the southwestern United States

thicket: dense growth of trees and shrubs

limb: branch

darted: moved rapidly

breaking camp: preparing to leave a campsite

READ ON

1. What different meanings can the word *setting* have in the title?

2. When you **reread** this selection, what new details or ideas did you discover?

You know, the Kiowas are a summer people. Once upon a time a group of young men sat down in a circle and spoke of mighty things. This is what they said: "When the fall of the year comes around, where does the summer go? Where does it live?" They decided to follow the sun southward to its home, and so they set out on horseback. They rode for days and weeks and months, farther to the south than any Kiowa had ever gone before, and they saw many strange and wonderful things. At last they came to the place where they saw the strangest thing of all. Night was coming on, and they were very tired of riding; they made camp in a great thicket. All but one of them went right to sleep. He was a good hunter, and he could see well in the moonlight. He caught sight of something: men were all about in the trees, moving silently from limb to limb. They darted across the face of the full moon, *and he saw that they were small and had tails!* He could not believe his eyes, but the next morning he told the others of what he had seen. They only laughed at him and told him not to eat such a large supper again. But later, as they were breaking camp, a certain feeling came over them all at once: they felt that they were being watched. And when they looked up, the small men with tails began to race about in the limbs overhead. That is when the Kiowas turned around and came away; they had had quite enough of that place. They had found the sun's home after all, they reasoned, and they were hungry for the good buffalo meat of their homeland.

IN YOUR OWN VOICE

WHAT DOES IT SAY?

1. Which questions do the young Kiowas want answered?

2. How many Kiowas stay awake during the night?

3. What is strange about the men in the trees?

4. What do all the Kiowas see in the morning that makes them return home?

WHAT DOES IT MEAN?

1. Why do the Kiowas follow the sun southward?

2. Why do they make camp in a thicket?

3. Why do the others change their minds about what the waking man told them?

4. Why do the Kiowas say they have reached the sun's home?

5. What kinds of borders do the Kiowas come upon?

STYLE AND SENSE

Folktales are short fictional narratives that are often passed down from one generation to another, either orally or in written form. A folktale may contain imaginary animals and people, supernatural happenings, and sudden changes of shape and identity.

1. Which words and expressions show the passage of time until the Kiowas make camp for the night?

2. Which words and expressions build suspense until the reader learns what the hunter sees that night?

3. Why does the scene change to daylight before the Kiowas break camp?

4. How does the last sentence answer the Kiowas' questions?

5. The English language uses words of light and dark, day and night to reveal the extent of knowledge. For example, *shed light on, be in the dark about.* List at least three other words or expressions that use images of light and dark.

FROM THE TEXT

Run-on sentence: sentence error resulting from the inclusion of two or more independent clauses in one sentence without the correct connecting word or punctuation.

Comma splice: a type of sentence error resulting from the use of a comma by itself without a connecting word between two independent clauses.

Read the following sentence:

Night was coming on, and they were very tired of riding; they made camp in a great thicket.

a. Identify the three independent clauses.

b. Identify the subject and verb of each clause.

c. To prevent a comma splice, what is used between the first two independent clause?

d. To prevent a run-on sentence, what is used between the second and third independent clauses?

See page 389 for more on the run-on sentence and comma splice.

WRITE NOW

Do both of the following activities.

1. **Freewrite** on one of the following Writing Suggestions.

2. Write a **thesis statement** on one idea from your freewriting.

WRITING SUGGESTIONS

1. Each individual has a cultural heritage. Narrate one family story that has been passed down to you by your parents or grandparents. Explain how this story connects your family to its cultural traditions.

2. When faced with something different, unusual, or unknown, people may hide from, run from, ridicule, confront, or accept it. Discuss your own experience or observation of others in such circumstances and explain why people might react so differently.

3. The young Kiowas, without the advice or supervision of their elders, set out and return on their own. Discuss whether teenagers and young adults should make important life decisions independently.

FURTHER WRITING SUGGESTIONS

4. Narrate a folktale that tells about the search for the home of either fall, winter, or spring. Describe the season's home.

5. The Kiowas set out to find summer's home. In the closing sentence, they

head for home. Explain what the word *home* or *homeland* means to a person or a people.

6. Most of the Kiowas did not believe the hunter's story until with their own eyes they saw the small men with tails. Discuss the saying "Seeing is believing." You may wish to use examples or experiences to develop your ideas.

MY GRANDPARENTS' HOUSE*

By Eva Antonia Wilbur-Cruce

In this selection from *A Beautiful, Cruel Country,* Eva Antonia Wilbur-Cruce recalls scenes from her early childhood. Growing up at the turn of the century, the young ranch girl observes warmly her grandparents' home, traditions, and faith, their three strengths against the hardships of life in the rugged, lonely borderlands between Sonora in northern Mexico and Arizona, still a territory of the United States but soon to become a state.

WORDS TO NOTICE

oregano: herb used to season foods

pelts: animal skins

rheumatic: arthritic, stiff

panacea: cure-all

amber: yellowish-brown

ingestive: taken in by mouth

liniment: liquid rubbed into the body as a pain reliever

jojoba: small shrub bearing seeds used to make an oil

eaves: overhanging edges of a roof

poultices: soft heated packs applied to heal inflammation

bunk house: dwelling for hired or ranch hands

ramada: arbor, tree-lined area

olla: large, open-mouthed pot for storing water

doggerel: bad verse

*Editors' title

enlighten: give knowledge to

indulgences: (in Roman Catholicism) pardons of punishment that is due for
sins

contrition: repentance

READ ON

1. While you read this selection for the first time, **star** or **underline** words that
help to describe the personalities of both grandparents.

2. What interests you most about each grandparent?

My grandparents' house was across the creek, just a stone's throw from ours. 1
Their house consisted of three large rooms, the kitchen, the *sala* (living room),
and my grandparents' bedroom.

The kitchen had a dirt floor, a wood stove, and a large window which 2
was loaded with geraniums and cans that held mint, oregano, and winter
onions. A long table sat in the middle of the room with wooden boxes pushed
under it to be pulled out and used as seats.

The floor of the *sala* was carpeted with goat pelts and held a couch which 3
made up into a bed for Rita and Che who used the *sala* as a bedroom at
night.

The main feature of my grandparents' bedroom was the many prints of 4
santos that covered all the walls. Sometimes a *santero*, a peddler of religious
articles, would come by the ranch, and my Grandmother Vilducea would
always buy the image of some saint from him that she did not yet have in
her sacred collection. Room on the wall would somehow be made for it,
usually by crowding the other images.

Under the window on the south side of their house was my grandmother's 5
jardín de savila. The *savila* (aloe) was the favorite healing herb. My grandmother called it the *protectora*. The furniture one had in the house was much
less important to us in those days than the medicinal herbs that one grew in
one's garden and the knowledge to use these effectively, for there were no
doctors within a reasonable distance.

And so my grandmother took great care of her garden of medicinal herbs 6
and plants. The leaves of the *savila* were cut, peeled, and applied to cuts,
burns, or painful rheumatic joints. Then there was the true panacea of the
Vilducea family garden—garlic. Garlic was used for everything. We chopped
clubs of garlic into tiny little pieces and drank them down with a glass of
warm water, both to thin the blood and to enrich the blood. We used it as a
disinfectant for insect bites and stings. My mother used it often for scorpion
stings. Grandfather chopped whole heads of garlic and put them in a jar of
pure alcohol. He placed the jar in the sun until it took on an amber color.

The Arizona-Mexico border

Then he divided the contents between two jars. One he used as an ingestive for internal troubles; the other as a liniment for massaging his joints and muscles. Grandfather never complained of muscular pains.

I can still remember my grandfather hurriedly cutting small branches or   **7** twigs from the *romero* (rosemary) plants, crushing them and dropping them into boiling water. He would cook them and let them simmer for awhile. Then he would seat whoever was having an asthmatic attack at the table and put a towel over his head until my grandmother could bring the steaming dish of romero tea and place it under the patient's nose so that he could breathe and inhale the steam. As the patient laboriously inhaled and exhaled, Grandfather and Grandmother would pound his back. I can still hear my grandfather saying to her, "Rhythm, Margarita, rhythm. Rhythm is important." I liked hearing the rhythmic, clapping sound of their hands as they moved them back and forth over the back of the asthmatic, who was gasping for breath. Then there would be the joyful announcement: "He is breathing! He is over the attack!" Grandmother would run and kneel before the picture of the Holy Trinity and thank the Lord for helping them to help the patient.

Grandmother's garden also boasted a big jojoba. Jojobas didn't usually   **8** grow at this altitude, so Grandmother took special care of hers, which was under the eaves on the north side of the house. It spent the winter under a tent of old burlap sacks and old quilts, but during the summer rains, it was always luscious and beautiful. We used the jojoba nuts to make poultices, and many times my mother would also use them to make "coffee." She didn't like the brew they made, but she would make it in desperation, when real coffee was not available.

My uncles had made a large bunk house that faced the kitchen of my   **9** grandparents' house, and they built their ramada so that it joined my grandparents' ramada. This made what we called a *ramadon*, a very spacious ramada with entrances at both ends, north and south. Here, my grandmother had more savila plants in cans hanging from the beams. These particular savila plants were supposed to keep the evil spirits away, and they may have done that, but they also kept the insects away from the other plants growing in the ramadon. From the beams on the north side of the ramadon hung a *filtro*, a specially made clay vessel, through which the water seeped and fell, one drop at a time, into an olla in which my grandmother had dropped a cupful of diced savila as a purifier. This was the drinking water for the day.

On the right-hand side of his own door to the ramadon, Grandfather had **10** nailed a large cardboard on which he had copied some doggerel he had once seen on the main door of the great hacienda of Señor Calderon, in Mexico. Grandfather called it a *poesía*, and when some friend tried to enlighten him, he would become angry and say that it *was* a poesía, so great that one could gain 200 indulgences by reciting it—and that was something no poet would sneer at. So when he returned from a hard day's work in his truck garden, he would stand, wiping the sweat off his face, and read aloud these words written before him on his door:

> ¿Quién llena esta casa de luz? Jesús.
> ¿Quién la llena de alegría? María.
> ¿Quién la abraza en la fe? José.
> Luengo bien claro se ve
> Que siempre habra contrición,
> Tieniendo en el corazón,
> A Jesús, María, y José.

> (Who fills this house with light? Jesus.
> Who fills it with happiness? Mary.
> Who embraces it in faith? Joseph.
> Then we clearly see that there will always be
>   contrition,
> Having Jesus, Mary, and Joseph in our hearts.)

IN YOUR OWN VOICE

WHAT DOES IT SAY?

1. Which three rooms make up the house?

2. What is the main feature of the grandparents' bedroom?

3. What does Grandmother grow in her garden?

4. Why does Grandmother kneel before the picture of the Holy Trinity?

5. What purpose do the *savila* (aloe) plants hanging in cans serve?

6. What does Grandfather recite after a hard day's work?

WHAT DOES IT MEAN?

1. What does the description of the kitchen imply about the way that the grandparents live?

2. What connection is there between the images of the *santos* (saints) and the grandmother's *jardín de savila* (aloe garden)?

3. How is this connection continued in the treatment of the asthmatic?

4. How are the family's workaday and spiritual lives brought together by the poem?

5. How are the family's workaday and spiritual lives brought together by descriptions of the interior and exterior of the grandparents' house?

STYLE AND SENSE

1. What is the general topic of the opening paragraph?

2. How do the next three paragraphs specifically develop this general topic?

3. Which words introduce the change of scene in paragraph 5?

4. In which paragraphs does the scene change from outdoors to indoors?

5. How does the closing paragraph return the reader to the general topic of the opening paragraph?

6. How does the vocabulary in the sentence preceding the poem reflect the simplicity of the family's life and house?

FROM THE TEXT

Past participle after the verb *to be*: the past participle, with or without the -*ed* or -*d* ending, completes the meaning of verbs of being, such as *be, get, feel,* and *become.*

Read the following sentence:

> The leaves of the *savila* were cut, peeled, and applied to cuts, burns, or painful rheumatic joints.

a. Identify the form of *be* in the sentence.

b. Which past participles complete the meaning of the helping verb?

c. Why are the endings not the same for all of the past participles?

d. Is the word *cuts* a verb? Why?

See page 429 for more on the past participle after *to be.*

WRITE NOW

Do both of the following activities.

1. Write the **first draft** of an opening paragraph for one of the following Writing Suggestions.

2. List several examples that can develop the ideas found in your first draft.

WRITING SUGGESTIONS

1. Describe a house, apartment, or other dwelling that you have lived in. Use details in such a way that your positive, negative, or mixed feelings toward the place become clear.

2. Discuss how spiritual beliefs affect and influence your daily life. Identify these beliefs and provide specific examples.

3. Wilbur-Cruce's narrative recreates a warm memory. Narrate the story of a moment in your past that remains vivid to you. Explain why this moment is still significant.

FURTHER WRITING SUGGESTIONS

4. After a hard day's work, the author's grandfather always recited poetry. Describe how a work of literature or a movie can be a release from pressure or an emotional outlet.

5. In this selection, disease and physical pain are treated with homemade remedies not prescribed by a physician. Discuss present-day attitudes to doctors, hospitals, and medications.

6. Discuss how living on or near the border between two countries can affect a family or individuals in the family.

CROSSING THE MISSISSIPPI

By Ernest Hemingway

Ernest Hemingway (1899–1961) is one of the twentieth century's most famous authors. In World War I (1917), Hemingway volunteered for service with an ambulance unit in France. Later he was seriously wounded during combat duty with an Italian infantry battalion.

His wartime experiences were the basis for his 1929 masterpiece *A Farewell to Arms*. *The Sun Also Rises* (1926) expressed the sense of loss and absence of faith for Hemingway's postwar generation. His short stories and novels were most notable for their direct, simple vocabulary and realistic dialogue.

Hemingway's life and writings later centered on his experiences during the Spanish Civil War (1936–1939) and on his celebrated hunting expeditions in Africa.

Cuba was the setting for his finest later novel, *The Old Man and the Sea* (1952). Hemingway received the Pulitzer Prize for this novel in 1953 and was awarded the Nobel Prize in literature one year later.

This fictional selection is narrated by Nick Adams, a young man whose experiences in the Midwest and elsewhere mirror those of Hemingway's youth and early adulthood.

WORDS TO NOTICE

siding: railroad track to the side of the main track

lurched: moved unsteadily to one side

reins: guiding straps

trajectory: curved path through space

exulting: rejoicing

commenced: started

dope: (*slang*) information

butcher: (*slang*) vendor on a train

sea-legs: balanced (as if walking on the rolling deck of a ship)

bluffs: cliffs

bayou: marshy creek or inlet

desolate: uninhabited and lonely

abutments: solid supports of a bridge

jutted: extended out

READ ON

1. When you read this story for the first time, **underline** words or expressions dealing with movement or lack of movement.

2. As part of your rereading, find the sentence containing the story's main idea.

The Kansas City train stopped at a siding just east of the Mississippi River   **1**
and Nick looked out at the road that was half a foot deep with dust. There
was nothing in sight but the road and a few dust-grayed trees. A wagon lurched
along through the ruts, the driver slouching with the jolts of his spring seat
and letting the reins hang slack on the horses' backs.

Nick looked at the wagon and wondered where it was going, whether the   **2**
driver lived near the Mississippi and whether he ever went fishing. The wagon
lurched out of sight up the road and Nick thought of the World Series game
going on in New York. He thought of Happy Felsch's home run in the first
game he had watched at the White Sox Park, Slim Solee swinging far forward,
his knee nearly touching the ground and the white dot of the ball on its far
trajectory toward the green fence at center field, Felsch, his head down, tear-
ing for the stuffed white square at first base and then the exulting roar from
the spectators as the ball landed in a knot of scrambling fans in the open
bleachers.

As the train started and the dusty trees and brown road commenced to   **3**
move past, the magazine vendor came swaying down the aisle.

"Got any dope on the Series?" Nick asked him.   **4**

"White Sox won the final game," the news butcher answered, making his   **5**
way down the aisle of the chair car with the sea-legs roll of a sailor. His
answer gave Nick a comfortable glow. The White Sox had licked them. It was
a fine feeling. Nick opened his *Saturday Evening Post* and commenced reading, occasionally looking out of the window to watch for any glimpse of the
Mississippi. Crossing the Mississippi would be a big event he thought, and
he wanted to enjoy every minute of it.

The scenery seemed to flow past in a stream of road, telegraph poles,   **6**
occasional houses and flat brown fields. Nick had expected bluffs for the
Mississippi shore but finally, after an endless seeming bayou had poured past
the window, he could see out of the window the engine of the train curving
out onto a long bridge above a broad, muddy brown stretch of water. Desolate
hills were on the far side that Nick could now see and on the near side a flat
mud bank. The river seemed to move solidly downstream, not to flow but to
move like a solid, shifting lake, swirling a little where the abutments of the
bridge jutted out. Mark Twain, Huck Finn, Tom Sawyer, and LaSalle crowded
each other in Nick's mind as he looked up the flat, brown plain of slow-
moving water. Anyhow I've seen the Mississippi, he thought happily to himself.

IN YOUR OWN VOICE

WHAT DOES IT SAY?

1. In which direction is Nick heading?

2. Whom does Nick see from the train window?

3. What exciting event does Nick ask the magazine vendor about?

4. What surprises Nick about the scenery as the train approaches the Mississippi?

5. What surprises Nick about the movement of the river?

6. Whom does Nick think of when he glimpses the Mississippi for the first time?

WHAT DOES IT MEAN?

1. Why does the narrative begin "just east of the Mississippi River"?

2. Why is the word *dust* repeated in the first description?

3. Why is the memory of the long home run important to Nick?

4. Why is he happy that the Chicago White Sox won the World Series?

5. Why is crossing the Mississippi "a big event" in Nick's life?

6. How does the real Mississippi compare to Nick's dream of it?

STYLE AND SENSE

1. How does Nick change as the train crosses the Mississippi from east to west?

2. How does nature change as the train crosses the Mississippi from east to west?

3. What similarity is there between the path of the home run and the route of the train?

4. How is Nick's journey from east to west reminiscent of events in U.S. history?

5. Mark Twain and Robert LaSalle were an author and an explorer, respectively; Twain wrote extensively about the Mississippi, and La Salle sailed down the Mississippi to the sea. Huckleberry Finn and Tom Sawyer were fictional characters created by Twain. Why do these names cross Nick's mind?

FROM THE TEXT

Past perfect tense: a tense using the helping verb *had* and the past participle to express action completed in the past *before* another past action occurred.

Read the following two sentences:

His answer gave Nick a comfortable glow. The White Sox had licked them.

a. Are both the ballgame and the news vendor's answer past events?

b. Which of the two actions occurred first?

c. Which tense is used to indicate the earlier action?

d. Why is *had* used instead of *have* or *has*?

See page 431 for more on the past perfect tense.

WRITE NOW

Do both of the following activities.

1. Make a **brainstorm** list based on one word or idea in the following Writing Suggestions.

2. Write the **first draft** of a paragraph based on one word from the list.

WRITING SUGGESTIONS

1. People must make choices at all stages of life. Discuss the reasons for a significant decision that you have made, and describe the expected and unexpected results of that decision.

2. The narrative ends, "Anyhow I've seen the Mississippi, he thought happily to himself." Each reader may judge whether Nick is truly happy at this moment. Discuss how even an unsuccessful or disappointing outcome can be a hard-earned, but worthwhile learning experience.

3. News of the Chicago White Sox winning the World Series "gave Nick a comfortable glow." Explain why people's moods are often closely intertwined with the success or lack of success of a favorite team, show business personality, political party or figure, and so on.

FURTHER WRITING SUGGESTIONS

4. The college years are often a time of transition. Describe how the college experience has changed your personality, your perception of the outside world, or your interaction with others.

5. People often have mixed feelings when they are on their own for the first time. Describe the border between childhood and adulthood.

6. Dreams, new experiences, and ambitions are not limited to young people Nick's age. Discuss the dreams, hopes, and ambitions that senior citizens have.

I NEVER HAD IT MADE

By Jackie Robinson

> In 1947 Jackie Robinson (1919–1972) became the first black baseball player to break the color barrier in the major leagues.
>
> Two years earlier, Robinson had joined the Kansas City Monarchs in the segregated Negro league. Unknown to Robinson, Branch Rickey, the president of the Brooklyn Dodgers, had been conducting a secret search throughout the Americas for a player of color with the potential to play in the major leagues.
>
> This selection from Robinson's autobiography *I Never Had It Made* recounts the historic interview between Robinson and Rickey. Two months later, on October 23, 1945, Robinson signed a contract to play for the Montreal Royals, the farm team of the Brooklyn Dodgers. He went on to lead the Dodgers to six World Series appearances and was the first black ballplayer to be voted into the National Baseball Hall of Fame.

WORDS TO NOTICE

classic: of recognizable high quality

red tape: official delay in procedures

speculating: guessing

Clyde Sukeforth: Brooklyn Dodger scout

churning: tossing violently

incredulous: unbelieving

abruptly: suddenly, without warning

insinuation: insulting suggestion

exhaustive: complete, thorough

agitator: one who stirs up

on face value: as genuine

transfixed: frozen, motionless

beanballs: pitches deliberately thrown at a batter's head

infuriate: anger, enrage

steadfastly: firmly

guardedly: cautiously

READ ON

1. While reading this selection for the first time, make **margin notes** about Robinson's different reactions to Rickey's words.

2. While rereading, **summarize** the shifts in Robinson's reactions.

Branch Rickey was an impressive-looking man. He had a classic face, an air   1
of command, a deep, booming voice, and a way of cutting through red tape
and getting down to basics. He shook my hand vigorously and, after a brief
conversation, sprang the first question.

"You got a girl?" he demanded.   2

It was a hell of a question. I had two reactions: why should he be con-   3
cerned about my relationship with a girl; and, second, while I thought, hoped,
and prayed I had a girl, the way things had been going, I was afraid she might
have begun to consider me a hopeless case. I explained this to Mr. Rickey
and Clyde.

Mr. Rickey wanted to know all about Rachel. I told him of our hopes and   4
plans.

"You know, you *have* a girl," he said heartily. "When we get through   5
today you may want to call her up because there are times when a man needs
a woman by his side."

My heart began racing a little faster again as I sat there speculating. First   6
he asked me if I really understood why he had sent for me. I told him what
Clyde Sukeforth had told me.

"That's what he was supposed to tell you," Mr. Rickey said. "The truth   7
is you are not a candidate for the Brooklyn Brown Dodgers. I've sent for you
because I'm interested in you as a candidate for the Brooklyn National League
Club. I think you can play in the major leagues. How do you feel about it?"

My reactions seemed like some kind of weird mixture churning in a   8
blender. I was thrilled, scared, and excited. I was incredulous. Most of all, I
was speechless.

"You think you can play for Montreal?" he demanded.   9

I got my tongue back. "Yes," I answered.   10

Montreal was the Brooklyn Dodgers' top farm club. The players who went   11
there and made it had an excellent chance at the big time.

I was busy reorganizing my thoughts while Mr. Rickey and Clyde Sukeforth   12
discussed me briefly, almost as if I weren't there. Mr. Rickey was questioning
Clyde. Could I make the grade?

Abruptly, Mr. Rickey swung his swivel chair in my direction. He was a   13
man who conducted himself with great drama. He pointed a finger at me.

"I know you're a good ballplayer," he barked. "What I don't know is   14
whether you have the guts."

I knew it was all too good to be true. Here was a guy questioning my   15
courage. That virtually amounted to him asking me if I was a coward. Mr.
Rickey or no Mr. Rickey, that was an insinuation hard to take. I felt the heat
coming up into my cheeks.

Before I could react to what he had said, he leaned forward in his chair   16
and explained.

I wasn't just another athlete being hired by a ball club. We were playing   17
for big stakes. This was the reason Branch Rickey's search had been so
exhaustive. The search had spanned the globe and narrowed down to a few
candidates, then finally to me. When it looked as though I might be the
number-one choice, the investigation of my life, my habits, my reputation,
and my character had become an intensified study.

"I've investigated you thoroughly, Robinson," Mr. Rickey said.   18

One of the results of this thorough screening was reports from California   19
athletic circles that I had been a "racial agitator" at UCLA. Mr. Rickey had
not accepted these criticisms on face value. He had demanded and received
more information and came to the conclusion that, if I had been white, people
would have said, "Here's a guy who's a contender, a competitor."

After that he had some grim words of warning. "We can't fight our way   20
through this, Robinson. We've got no army. There's virtually nobody on our
side. No owners, no umpires, very few newspapermen. And I'm afraid that
many fans will be hostile. We'll be in a tough position. We can win only if
we can convince the world that I'm doing this because you're a great ballplayer
and a fine gentleman."

He had me transfixed as he spoke. I could feel his sincerity, and I began   21
to get a sense of how much this major step meant to him. Because of his
nature and his passion for justice, he had to do what he was doing. He
continued. The rumbling voice, the theatrical gestures, were gone. He was
speaking from a deep, quiet strength.

"So there's more than just playing," he said. "I wish it meant only hits,   22
runs, and errors—only the things they put in the box score. Because you
know—yes, you would know, Robinson, that a baseball box score is a democratic thing. It doesn't tell how big you are, what church you attend, what
color you are, or how your father voted in the last election. It just tells what
kind of baseball player you were on that particular day."

I interrupted. "But it's the box score that really counts—that and that   **23**
alone, isn't it?"

"It's all that *ought* to count," he replied. "But it isn't. Maybe one of these   **24**
days it *will* be all that counts. That is one of the reasons I've got you here,
Robinson. If you're a good enough man, we can make this a start in the right
direction. But let me tell you, it's going to take an awful lot of courage."

He was back to the crossroads question that made me start to get angry   **25**
minutes earlier. He asked it slowly and with great care.

"Have you got the guts to play the game no matter what happens?"   **26**

"I think I can play the game, Mr. Rickey," I said.   **27**

The next few minutes were tough. Branch Rickey had to make absolutely   **28**
sure that I knew what I would face. Beanballs would be thrown at me. I would
be called the kind of names which would hurt and infuriate any man. I would
be physically attacked. Could I take all of this and control my temper, remain
steadfastly loyal to our ultimate aim?

He knew I would have terrible problems and wanted me to know the   **29**
extent of them before I agreed to the plan. I was twenty-six years old, and all
my life back to the age of eight when a little neighbor girl called me a nigger—
I had believed in payback, retaliation. The most luxurious possession, the
richest treasure anybody has, is his personal dignity. I looked at Mr. Rickey
guardedly, and in that second I was looking at him not as a partner in a great
experiment, but as the enemy—a white man. I had a question and it was the
age-old one about whether or not you sell your birthright.

"Mr. Rickey," I asked, "are you looking for a Negro who is afraid to fight   **30**
back?"

I never will forget the way he exploded.   **31**

"Robinson," he said, "I'm looking for a ballplayer with guts enough not   **32**
to fight back."

IN YOUR OWN VOICE

WHAT DOES IT SAY?

1. Why does Rickey send for Robinson?

2. Why is Montreal a good place for Robinson to begin?

3. Which doubt of Rickey's upsets Robinson greatly?

4. What doesn't Rickey accept "on face value"?

5. What is democratic about a baseball box score?

6. What must Robinson have "guts enough" not to do?

WHAT DOES IT MEAN?

1. Why is Rickey's first question, "You got a girl?"

2. Why is Robinson surprised and speechless at Rickey's proposal?

3. Why must Robinson be both "a great ballplayer and a fine gentleman"?

4. Why does Robinson accept the challenge?

5. What does Rickey hope to accomplish by hiring Robinson? Was Rickey's hope realized?

STYLE AND SENSE

This selection presents not only the conversation or dialogue between the participants of the interview, but also a description of their personalities and emotions.

1. How does the description of Rickey in the opening paragraph prepare the reader for the way he conducts the interview?

2. Which verbs show Rickey's intense nature and command of the interview?

3. How does the description of Robinson in paragraph 3 prepare the reader for the way he responds to the interview questions?

4. Which later paragraphs contain similar descriptions of Robinson as he undergoes Rickey's questioning? What portrait of Robinson emerges?

5. How does the dialogue in paragraphs 30 and 32 show that the men are evenly matched?

FROM THE TEXT

Complex sentence: A sentence containing an independent clause and at least one dependent clause.

Read the following sentence:

If you're a good enough man, we can make this a start in the right direction.

a. Identify the dependent clause.

b. Which word makes the clause dependent?

c. Which punctuation mark follows the dependent clause?

d. If the clauses are reversed, is there still a complex sentence?

e. Is the sentence written with a comma if the clauses are reversed?

f. Find at least two more complex sentences in this selection.

Note: A **sentence fragment** results if a dependent clause stands alone and is punctuated as a complete sentence.
See page 401 for more on the sentence fragment.

WRITE NOW

Do both of the following activities.

1. **Freewrite** on one of the following Writing Suggestions.

2. Write the **first draft** of a paragraph based on a main idea from your free-writing.

WRITING SUGGESTIONS

1. Jackie Robinson entered major league baseball more than forty years ago. Discuss whether or not his career and those of other great minority athletes have had an impact on racial and social progress in the United States.

2. Until his interview with Rickey, Robinson had responded to racist acts and remarks by "payback, retaliation." Rickey demands that Robinson control his temper "no matter what happens." Answer one of the following:

   a. Explain which course of action more effectively deals with prejudice.

   or

   b. Discuss whether or not Rickey has the right to make such a demand of Robinson.

3. Describe the border that Robinson and Rickey crossed. Discuss whether such a border is ever erased or is ever the same again.

FURTHER WRITING SUGGESTIONS

4. Rickey believes that even a strong man "needs a woman by his side." Compare and contrast the perceptions of women's roles in 1945 with those of today.

5. Robinson writes, "The most luxurious possession, the richest treasure anybody has, is his personal dignity." Explain why this statement is especially

true for an individual in conflict with his peers, family, employers, or government agencies.

6. Before Robinson was hired, Rickey had him thoroughly investigated. Discuss whether government or private employers have the right to conduct such investigations of prospective employees.

TRUE NORTH

By Margaret Atwood

Margaret Atwood (born 1939) is one of Canada's most acclaimed literary figures. She is the recipient of numerous awards for her novels, poetry, short stories, and essays.

In her writings, she explores the tensions and contrasts between human feelings and achievements and nature. Both have their rewards and risks. Her novels, including *The Edible Woman* (1969), *Bodily Harm* (1982), and *The Cat's Eye* (1989), deal with female-male relationships, alienation, and other stresses in modern life.

In this selection from a 1987 essay, which appeared in a magazine issue devoted entirely to Canada and its people, Atwood seeks the roots of her Canadian heritage and traces the geographical and emotional boundaries of a place she calls True North.

WORDS TO NOTICE

relative: thought of in relation to something else

latitude: distance from the equator

Mercator projection: type of map with latitude and longitude at right angles to each other

nape: back part

retrospect: examination of the past

Shield granite: hard, gray stone found in a vast Canadian plateau

wigwam: hut of the Indian tribes of the Great Lakes region

coniferous: bearing cones

deciduous: shedding leaves yearly

scraggier: barer, less filled in

Dionne Quints: the first quintuplets to live beyond infancy were born in Ontario May 28, 1934

silhouettes: dark outlines against a light background

prams: baby carriages

flourishing: going strong, continuing to prosper

pike: a large freshwater fish

personified: embodied, symbolized

unprecedented: never before taken

precarious: risky, uncertain

sledges: heavy sleds

aqueducts: artificial water channels, usually above ground

blitzed shambles: totally destroyed area

scrim: thin curtain

catch phrase: slogan, popular saying

READ ON

1. While reading this essay for the first time, jot down **margin notes** about what or where True North is.

2. While rereading, what facts about Canada do you discover?

Where is the north, exactly? It's not only a place but a direction, and as such 1 its location is relative: to the Mexicans, the United States is the north, to Americans Toronto is, even though it's on roughly the same latitude as Boston.

Wherever it is for us, there's a lot of it. You stand in Windsor and imagine 2 a line going north, all the way to the pole. The same line going south would end up in South America. That's the sort of map we grew up with, at the front of the classroom in Mercator projection, which made it look even bigger than it was, all that pink stretching on forever, with a few cities sprinkled along the bottom edge. It's not only geographical space, it's space related to body image. When we face south, as we often do, our conscious mind may be directed down there, towards crowds, bright lights, some Hollywood version of fame and fortune, but the north is at the back of our minds, always. There's something, not someone, looking over our shoulders, there's a chill at the nape of the neck.

The north focuses our anxieties. Turning to face north, face the north, **3**
we enter our own unconscious. Always, in retrospect, the journey north has
the quality of dream.

Where does the north begin? **4**

Every province, every city, has its own road north. From Toronto you go **5**
up the 400. Where you cross the border, from here to there, is a matter of
opinion. Is it the Severn River, where the Shield granite appears suddenly out
of the earth? Is it the sign announcing that you're halfway between the equator
and the North Pole? Is it the first gift shop shaped like a wigwam, the first
town—there are several—that proclaims itself The Gateway to the North?

As we proceed, the farms become fewer, rockier, more desperate-looking, **6**
the trees change their ratios, coniferous moving in on deciduous. More lakes
appear, their shorelines scraggier. Our eyes narrow and we look at the clouds:
the weather is important again.

One of us used to spend summers in a cottage in Muskoka, before the **7**
road went in, when you took the train, when there were big cruise ships there,
and matronly motor launches, and tea dances at the hotels, and men in white
flannels on the lawns, which there may still be. This was not just a cottage
but a Muskoka cottage, with boathouse and maid's quarters. Rich people
went north in the summers then, away from cities and crowds; that was before
the cure for polio, which has made a difference. In this sort of north, they
tried to duplicate the south, or perhaps some dream of country life in England.
In the living room there were armchairs, glass-fronted bookcases, family
photos in silver frames, stuffed birds under glass bells. The north, as I said,
is relative.

For me, the north used to be completely in force by the Trout Creek **8**
planing mill. Those stacks of fresh-cut lumber were the true gateway to the
north, and north of that was North Bay, which used to be, to be blunt, a bit
of an armpit. It was beef-sandwich-on-white-bread-with-gravy-and-canned-peas
country. But no more. North Bay now has shopping malls, and baskets of
flowers hanging from lampposts above paving-stone sidewalks, downtown.
It has a Granite Club. It has the new, swish, carpeted buildings of Laurentian
University. It has gourmet restaurants. And in the airport, where southbound
DC-9s dock side by side with northbound Twin Otters, there's a book rack in
the coffee shop that features Graham Greene and Kierkegaard, hardly standard
airport fare.

The south is moving north. **9**

We bypass North Bay, which now has a bypass, creeping southerliness, **10**
and do not go, this time, to the Dionne Quints Museum, where five little
silhouettes in black play forever beside an old log cabin, complete with the
basket where they were packed in cotton wool, the oven where they were
warmed, the five prams, the five Communion dresses.

Beyond North Bay there is a brief flurry of eccentricity—lawns populated **11**
with whole flocks of wooden-goose windmills—and then we go for miles and
miles past nothing but trees, meeting nothing but the occasional truck loaded

with lumber. This area didn't used to be called anything. Now it's the Near North Travel Area. You can see signs telling you that. Near what, we wonder uneasily? We don't want to be near. We want to be far.

At last we see the Ottawa River, which is the border. There's a dam across **12** it, two dams, and an island between them. If there were a customs house it would be here. A sign faces us saying *Bienvenue;* out the back window there's one saying *Welcome.* This was my first lesson in points of view.

And there, across the border in Québec, in Témiscaming, is an image **13** straight from my childhood: a huge mountain made of sawdust. I always wanted to slide down this sawdust mountain until I finally did, and discovered it was not like sand, dry and slippery, but damp and sticky and hard to get out of your clothes. This was my first lesson in the nature of illusion.

Continue past the sawdust mountain, past the baseball diamond, up the **14** hill, and you're in the centre of town, which is remarkable for at least three things: a blocks-long public rock garden, still flourishing after more than forty-five years; a pair of statues, one a fountain, that look as if they've come straight from Europe, which I think they did; and the excellent, amazingly low-priced hamburgers you can get at the Boulevard Restaurant, where the décor, featuring last year's cardboard Santa Claus and a stuffed twenty-three-pound pike, is decidedly northern. Ask the owner about the pike and he'll tell you about one twice as big, forty-five pounds in fact, that a fellow showed him strapped to the tailgate of his van, and that long, too.

You can have this conversation in either French or English: Témiscaming **15** is a border town and a northern one, and the distinctions made here are as likely to be north-south as French-English. Up in these parts you'll hear as much grumbling, or more, about Québec City as you will about Ottawa, which is, after all, closer. Spit in the river and it gets to Ottawa, eh?

For the north, Témiscaming is old, settled, tidy, even a little prosperous- **16** looking. But it's had its crises. Témiscaming is the resource economy personified. Not long ago it was a company town, and when the company shut down the mill, which would have shut down the town too, the workers took the unprecedented step of trying to buy it. With some help they succeeded, and the result was Tembec, still going strong. But Témiscaming is still a one-industry town, like many northern towns, and its existence is thus precarious.

Not so long ago, logging was a different sort of business. The men went **17** into the woods in winter, across the ice, using horse-drawn sledges, and set up camp. (You still come across these logging camps now and then in your travels through the lakes, abandoned, already looking as ancient as Roman aqueducts; more ancient, since there's been no upkeep.) They'd cut selectively, tree by tree, using axes and saws and the skills that were necessary to avoid being squashed or hacked. They'd skid the trees to the ice; in the spring, after the ice went out, there would be a run down the nearest fast river to the nearest sawmill.

Now it's done with bulldozers and trucks, and the result is too often a **18** blitzed shambles; cut everything, leave a wreck of dead and, incidentally, easily flammable branches behind. Time is money. Don't touch the shoreline though, we need that for tourists. In some places, the forest is merely a scrim along the water. In behind it's been hollowed out.

Those who look on the positive side say it's good for the blueberries.   **19**

Sometimes we went the other way, across to Sudbury, the trees getting   **20**
smaller and smaller and finally disappearing as you approached. Sudbury was another magic place of my childhood. It was like interplanetary travel, which we liked to imagine, which was still just imagination in those days. With its heaps of slag and its barren shoulders of stone, it looked like the moon. Back then, we tell the children, before there were washer-dryers and you used something called a wringer washer and hung the sheets out on something called a clothesline, when there weren't even coloured sheets but all sheets were white, when Rinso white and its happy little washday song were an item, and Whiter than White was a catch phrase and female status really did have something to do with your laundry, Sudbury was a housewife's nightmare. We knew people there; the windowsills in their houses were always grey.

Now the trees are beginning to come back because they built higher   **21**
smokestacks. But where is all that stuff going now?

IN YOUR OWN VOICE

WHAT DOES IT SAY?

1. Where does the imaginary line going north through Windsor reach? Going south?

2. Who went north to the summer cottages in Muskoka?

3. Which words on signs near the Ottawa River indicate that Canada has two official languages?

4. What is the major industry of Témiscaming?

5. To what is the barren, stony land near Sudbury compared?

WHAT DOES IT MEAN?

1. Why is the north "at the back of our minds, always"?

2. Why do summer vacationers to the north furnish their cottages in an English style?

3. Why are the stacks of lumber called the true gateway to the north?

4. What lesson about illusion is learned by sliding down the sawdust mountain?

5. Why is the future precarious for Témiscaming and other northern logging towns?

6. Why is Sudbury "a housewife's nightmare"?

STYLE AND SENSE

1. Why is it effective to start paragraph 1 with a question followed immediately by an answer?

2. How would a reader be affected if the writer did not answer the question immediately?

3. Which words in paragraph 6 contrast the landscapes on the journey north?

4. Which paragraphs contrast past and present Canadian life?

5. Which place names and spellings suggest the many cultures of Canada?

6. How do all these contrasts combine to produce a portrait of True North?

FROM THE TEXT

Compound verb: two or more verbs joined by *and* or *or* having the same subject. Each verb must agree with the subject.

Read the following sentence:

You stand in Windsor and imagine a line going north, all the way to the pole.

a. What is the subject?

b. What is the compound verb?

c. Why is there no need to write the subject twice?

d. Why is there no *-s* ending on these present tense verbs?

See page 416 for more on the compound verb.

WRITE NOW

Do both of the following activities.

1. Make a **cluster diagram** of the word *border*.

2. Write the **first draft** of a paragraph based on the part of the cluster that interests you most.

WRITING SUGGESTIONS

1. Define and describe one of the following: True North, True East, True South, or True West. You may wish to include landscape, people, customs, occupations, and so on.

2. Margaret Atwood retains many childhood memories of northern Canada.

Describe how your memories of a particular time and place influence you today and may continue to do so in the future.

3. A border is an imaginary line or boundary dividing countries, states, provinces, and so on. Discuss why countries and peoples sometimes go to war because of a border dispute or crossing.

FURTHER WRITING SUGGESTIONS

4. Explain how an area or country's weather and climate can affect the behavior and attitude of an individual, group, or community.

5. Atwood observes two customs house signs, one saying *Bienvenue* and the other saying *Welcome*. Discuss the advantages and disadvantages of living in a multicultural society.

6. Not only countries but people have borders. Discuss the borders that may separate people or that may not be crossed by other people.

UNIT 6

Ben Shahn. *For Full Employment after the War Register to Vote.* 1944. Offset lithograph, printed in color, 30 × 39⅞". Collection, The Museum of Modern Art, New York. Gift of the CIO Political Action Committee.

for full employment after the war
REGISTER·VOTE
CIO POLITICAL ACTION COMMITTEE

BUSINESS AND WORK

Rapid industrial growth, increasing urbanization, and advances in manufacturing and technology marked the business climate of the post–Civil War United States. This, in turn, led to the rise of entrepreneurs and the formation of labor unions to secure workers' rights.

Walt Whitman's "I Hear America Singing" (1855) opens this section. The poem, though pre–Civil War, is an anthem celebrating American artisans and workers of all ages, both men and women.

This is followed by the concluding pages of Horatio Alger's 1868 novel *Fame and Fortune.* The book tells of how its hero's diligence and honesty enabled him to rise from an impoverished boyhood on the streets to success and wealth in the business world.

Sixty years later, with the United States in its greatest economic crisis, the Great Depression, Will Rogers proposes "A Cure for the Depression" (1931) involving the basic faith and potential of the American worker.

Next comes Ruth Wolf's account of her jobs during World War II. Like other Rosie the Riveters, she worked in factories and met up with unfairness and harassment.

Lee Iacocca, in the early 1980s, writes of the "equality of sacrifice" between management and labor he witnessed as head of the ailing Chrysler Corporation.

The section on business and work ends with an excerpt from An Wang's autobiography telling how he began and developed Wang Laboratories in 1951.

BEFORE YOU READ

Why is work important to the individual? To society?

What kind of work have you done?

What kind will you do after graduation?

What kinds of work did your parents do? Your grandparents?

Can people find joy in working?

Should government be involved in business? In which ways and to what extent?

Does everyone have an equal opportunity for economic success?

How can a person's cultural heritage be both an asset and a liability in starting a business?

What qualities should a good worker possess?

Are these qualities the same ones needed in management?

How do the skills needed for employment today differ from those of a century ago?

What do you know about the Great Depression?

Did the Depression affect anyone in your family?

What is more important: formal education or job experience?

What is management's responsibility to workers? Workers to management?

Who's to blame for economic troubles?

What do you see as your economic future?

I HEAR AMERICA SINGING

By Walt Whitman

Walt Whitman (1819–1892) is the poet of America and democracy. His major poetic work, *Leaves of Grass,* first published in 1855, was revised and enlarged over the next thirty years. His poetic voice is revolutionary: in an unrhymed, personal style, it celebrates the self, equality, the universe, and the optimism of the expanding nation.

Whitman served as a nurse in the U.S. Civil War, writing prose and poetry that depicted war in realistic terms. The assassinated president Abraham Lincoln is honored in the poem "When Lilacs Last in the Dooryard Bloom'd" (1865).

The original version of "I Hear America Singing" was first published in the 1860 edition of *Leaves of Grass*.

WORDS TO NOTICE

varied: different, many

carols: joyful songs

blithe: happy, carefree

mason: one who builds with stone

ploughboy: young farmer

party: group

robust: strong, vigorous

READ ON

1. What does the poem's **title** mean?

2. While reading the poem for the first time, **underline** who the singers are.

I hear America singing, the varied carols I hear,
Those of mechanics, each one singing his as it should
   be blithe and strong,
The carpenter singing his as he measures his plank or
   beam,
The mason singing his as he makes ready for work, or
   leaves off work,
The boatman singing what belongs to him in his boat,
   the deckhand singing on the steamboat deck,
The shoemaker singing as he sits on his bench, the
   hatter singing as he stands,
The wood-cutter's song, the ploughboy's on his way in
   the morning, or at noon intermission or at sundown,
The delicious singing of the mother, or of the young
   wife at work, or of the girl sewing or washing,

Each singing what belongs to him or her and to
    none else,
The day what belongs to the day—at night the
    party of young fellows, robust, friendly,
Singing with open mouths their strong melodious
    songs.

IN YOUR OWN VOICE

WHAT DOES IT SAY?

1. Who are the singers?

2. Who sings from morning until night?

3. Who sing at night?

4. Which qualities do the songs share?

WHAT DOES IT MEAN?

1. Why is America singing carols?

2. Why are materials such as wood and stone mentioned in the poem?

3. Why does each song belong to its singer?

4. Why are all the day songs sung by people who work with their hands?

5. Why are "strong melodious" night songs mentioned?

STYLE AND SENSE

---

1. In what way are the opening and closing lines similar?

2. In what identical way is each individual introduced?

3. In what way do the poem's words express a democratic spirit?

4. What do songs and poems have in common?

FROM THE TEXT

Read the following:

> The shoemaker singing as he sits on his bench

a. Do these words form a complete sentence?

b. Create complete sentences by

    1. Inserting a helping verb before *singing*.

    2. Changing *singing* to a present tense verb.

    3. Adding an independent clause before *the shoemaker*.

See page 401 for more on the sentence fragment.

WRITE NOW

Do both of the following activities.

1. Write a **journal** of your working day.

2. **Organize** your journal material into categories for development in one of the following Writing Suggestions.

WRITING SUGGESTIONS

1. Describe how working with one's hands may be a joyful experience.

2. Discuss how the words and music of a song or other musical piece reflect contemporary attitudes toward work.

3. Narrate an experience in the workplace that developed a spirit of harmony and cooperation.

FURTHER WRITING SUGGESTIONS

4. Explain how the contribution and accomplishment of an individual worker benefit the entire society.

5. Whitman's poem is optimistic. Answer one of the following:

   a. Discuss the outlook for the peoples of the Americas in the twenty-first century.

   or

   b. Describe typical nineteenth-century working conditions for those who earned their living at home or in the factory.

FAME AND FORTUNE

By Horatio Alger

Fame and Fortune, published in 1868, is one of the more than 100 popular novels Horatio Alger (1832–1899) wrote about what "energy, ambition, and an honest purpose may achieve" even for poor young men and boys.

The modern reader may well wonder at Alger's limited and restricted vision of who can achieve success: women and minority groups do not figure prominently in his novels. It is a reflection on nineteenth-century attitudes that Alger's novels were, nevertheless, immensely popular.

This selection concludes *Fame and Fortune,* a story of how Richard Hunter, a poor, studious, and hard-working boy, became successful after rescuing the drowning son of his future employer, Mr. Rockwell. This rags-to-riches theme continues when Richard, in his turn, extends a helping hand to Micky Maguire, a recently released young pickpocket.

WORDS TO NOTICE

expiration: end, conclusion

commence: begin

plying the trade of: working as

boot-black: person who shines shoes for a living

fidelity: loyalty, faithfulness

confederate: partner in crime

Island: site of reformatory (Blackwell's Island in New York City)

consequentially: seriously

upstart: snob

ejaculated: exclaimed, said suddenly

prowess: skill

incontinently: recklessly

incredulity: disbelief

wayward: straying from virtue

vagabond: wandering vagrant

chequered: checkered, inconsistent, up-and-down

vista: prospect, future

unbounded: unlimited

wavered: changed, shifted

trials and privations: troubles and deprivations

READ ON

1. While reading this story for the first time, **star** all the words dealing with money and a business career.

2. While rereading, **find** the places in the story where the opinions of the author Horatio Alger are stated directly.

. . . When Micky had gone out, Mr. Rockwell said, "Well, Richard, I have lost my book-keeper."   **1**

"Yes, sir," said Dick.   **2**

"And I can't say I am sorry. I will do Mr. Gilbert the justice to say that he understood his business; but he was personally disagreeable, and I never liked him. Now I suppose I must look out for a successor."   **3**

"Yes, sir, I suppose so."   **4**

"I know a very competent book-keeper, who is intending to go into business for himself at the expiration of six months. Until that time I can secure his services. Now, I have a plan in view which I think you will approve. You shall at once commence the study of book-keeping in a commercial school in the evening, and during the day I will direct Mr. Haley to employ you as his assistant. I think in that way you will be able to succeed him at the end of his term."   **5**

Dick was completely taken by surprise. The thought that he, so recently plying the trade of a boot-black in the public streets, could rise in six months to the responsible post of a book-keeper in a large wholesale house, seemed almost incredible.   **6**

"I should like nothing better," he said, his eyes sparkling with delight, "if you really think I could discharge the duties satisfactorily."   **7**

"I think you could. I believe you have the ability, and of your fidelity I feel assured."   **8**

"Thank you, sir; you are very kind to me," said Dick, gratefully.   **9**

"I have reason to be," said Mr. Rockwell, taking his hand. "Under God it is to your courage that I owe the life of my dear boy. I shall never forget it. One thing more. I intend Michael to undertake most of your present duties, such as going to the post-office, etc. Do you think he will answer?"   **10**

"I think so," said Dick. "He has been a rough customer, but then he has **11** never had a chance. I believe in giving everybody a chance."

"So do I," said Mr. Rockwell. "Michael shall have his chance. Let us hope **12** he will improve it."

There are many boys, and men too, who, like Micky Maguire, have never **13** had a fair chance in life. Let us remember that, when we judge them, and not be too hasty to condemn. Let us consider also whether it is not in our power to give some one the chance that may redeem him.

That afternoon Micky Maguire was provided with a new suit of clothes, **14** of which he felt very proud. The next morning, on his way to the post-office, he fell in with his old confederate, Limpy Jim, who regarded him with a glance of the most bewildering surprise.

"It aint you, Micky,—is it?" he asked, cautiously, surveying his old com- **15** rade's neat appearance. "When did you come back from the Island?"

"Shut up about the Island, Jim," said Micky. "Do I look as if I had been **16** there?"

"You look nobby," said Jim. "Where's your brush?" **17**

"I've give up the blackin' business," said Mickey. **18**

"You have? What are you going to do? Sell papers?" **19**

"No," said Micky, consequentially. "I'm in business on Pearl Street." **20**

"Why," said Limpy Jim, surprised, "that's where that upstart Ragged Dick **21** works."

"He aint an upstart, an' he aint ragged," said Micky. "He's a friend of **22** mine, an' if you insult him, I'll lam' ye."

"O my eyes!" ejaculated Jim, opening the organs of vision to a very wide **23** extent; "that's the biggest joke I ever heerd of."

"You'll hear of a bigger one pretty quick," said Micky, rolling up his **24** sleeves, and squaring off scientifically.

Limpy Jim, who had a respect for Micky's prowess, incontinently fled, **25** surveying Micky from a safe distance, with a look in which surprise seemed to mingle with incredulity.

It may seem strange, but, from that time forth, Dick had no firmer friend **26** than Micky Maguire, who, I am glad to say, though occasionally wayward, improved vastly, and became a useful employé of the establishment which he had entered. Of course both in ability and education, though in the last he gained considerably, he was quite inferior to Dick; but he was advanced as he grew older to the position of porter, where his strength stood him in good stead. His pay increased also, and through Dick's influence he was saved from vicious habits, and converted from a vagabond to a useful member of society.

And now, almost with regret, I find myself closing up the record of Dick's **27** chequered career. The past with its trials is over; the future expands before him, a bright vista of merited success. But it remains for me to justify the title of my story, and show how Dick acquired "Fame and Fortune." I can only hint briefly at the steps that led to them.

In six months, at the age of seventeen, Dick succeeded to Mr. Gilbert's **28** place with a salary, to commence with, of one thousand dollars. To this an annual increase was made, making his income at twenty-one, fourteen hundred dollars. Just about that time he had an opportunity to sell his up-town lots, to a gentleman who had taken a great fancy to them, for five times the amount he paid, or five thousand dollars. His savings from his salary amounted to about two thousand dollars more.

Meanwhile Mr. Rockwell's partner, Mr. Cooper, from ill health felt obliged **29** to withdraw from business, and Richard, to his unbounded astonishment and gratification, was admitted to the post of junior partner, embarking the capital he had already accumulated, and receiving a corresponding share of the profits. These were so large that Richard was able to increase his interest yearly by investing his additional savings, and three years later he felt justified in offering his hand to Ida Greyson, whose partiality to Dick had never wavered. He was no longer Ragged Dick now, but Mr. Richard Hunter, junior partner in the large firm of Rockwell & Hunter. Mr. Greyson felt that even in a worldly way Dick was a good match for his daughter; but he knew and valued still more his good heart and conscientious fidelity to duty, and excellent principles, and cheerfully gave his consent. Last week I read Dick's marriage in the papers, and rejoiced in his new hopes of happiness.

So Dick has achieved FAME and FORTUNE,—the fame of an honorable and **30** enterprising man of business, and a fortune which promises to be very large. But I am glad to say that Dick has not been spoiled by prosperity. He never forgets his humble beginnings, and tries to show his sense of God's goodness by extending a helping hand to the poor and needy boys, whose trials and privations he understands well from his own past experience.

IN YOUR OWN VOICE

WHAT DOES IT SAY?

1. What is Mr. Rockwell's plan for Richard?

2. Who will take over Richard's duties?

3. Which event leads to Richard's becoming a junior partner?

4. How does Richard remember his "humble beginnings"?

WHAT DOES IT MEAN?

1. Why is a business career suitable for Richard?

2. Why does Richard say, "I believe in giving everybody a chance"?

3. Why is Limpy Jim upset at seeing Micky in a new suit?

4. Why are Richard's financial affairs given in such detail (see paragraph 28)?

5. Why does the story have a happy ending?

STYLE AND SENSE

Time is always present in a story **(narrative)**. When readers ask themselves, "What happens next?" or "What happened earlier?" they are responding to the order of the story's events.

1. Identify those paragraphs that open with words referring to time.

2. Locate at least six more references to time.

3. How do these references to time show what is involved in Richard's path to success?

FROM THE TEXT

Modifier: word or group of words describing some other word or words in the sentence.

Read the following sentence:

"You'll hear of a bigger one pretty quick," said Micky, rolling up his sleeves, and squaring off scientifically".

a. Which word is modified by "rolling up his sleeves" and "and squaring off scientifically"?

b. Why can't a period be placed between *Micky* and *rolling*?

c. Create a complete sentence after *Micky* by adding whatever words are necessary before *rolling*.

d. Create a complete sentence after *Micky* by changing *rolling* to the past tense.

Note: Words ending in *-ing* often are modifiers. Known as **present participles,** these words cannot be punctuated as if they were a complete sentence. A **sentence fragment** will result, such as *Micky rolling up his sleeves, and squaring off scientifically.*
See page 404 for more on the present participle.

WRITE NOW

Do both of the following activities.

1. Write the **thesis statement** of the opening paragraph of an essay based on one of the following Writing Suggestions.

2. **Outline** the rest of the essay, showing your development of the main ideas.

WRITING SUGGESTIONS

1. Richard Hunter's story suggests that the doorway to success is open to all Americans, regardless of their backgrounds. Do you agree or disagree? Explain your answer.

2. The orphaned Richard Hunter earned his living as a boot-black in the city streets. He is then offered the chance to work in an office and "commence commercial school in the evening." Answer one of the following:

    a. Discuss whether colleges should give credit to students for work or life experience.

or

    b. Discuss whether formal education is more valuable than work or life experience for career success.

3. Describe the role that businesses play or should play in the educating and training of their employees.

FURTHER WRITING SUGGESTIONS

4. Donald Trump and Lee Iacocca are among the most admired people in the United States today. Are successful business leaders good role models? Explain your answer.

5. Mr. Rockwell takes the responsibility for the welfare of Richard and Micky. Discuss whether government or private agencies should aid today's underprivileged youngsters.

6. The successful Richard Hunter "never forgets his humble beginnings." Describe the ways those who have achieved financial success can contribute to the well-being of their original communities.

A CURE FOR THE DEPRESSION*

By Will Rogers

Will Rogers (1879–1935) was a noted humorist, actor, and writer. Born in Oologah, Indian Territory (now Oklahoma), he began his career with a rope-twirling act performed in Wild West shows and vaudeville.

On stage he commented with humor and gentle satire on the events, politics, and personalities of the day. From 1923 on he wrote weekly articles in the *New York Times* and other newspapers.

This selection, taken from Rogers's October 25, 1931, radio broadcast, con-

---

*Editor's title

siders ways to overcome the harmful effects of the Great Depression on the average person. The Depression was a time of dramatic economic crisis marked by breadlines, high unemployment, lost production, and personal and corporate bankruptcy.

This broadcast transcription omits some apostrophes (*cant*) and uses spellings (*hasent, dident*) to suggest the spoken language.

WORDS TO NOTICE

two-bit: twenty-five cent; cheap, ordinary

rompers: child's one-piece garment

calloused: hardened

Mr. Mellon: Andrew Mellon, U.S. secretary of the treasury (1921–1931)

League of Nations: international organization formed after World War I to promote cooperation and peace

silver question: economic dispute concerning the United States' guarantees of its currency by silver, instead of gold

Prohibition: period (1920–1933) when alcoholic beverages could not be legally manufactured and sold in the United States

potter's fields: burial grounds for those without money, friends, or family

"cockeyed": foolish, contradictory

capitalized: provided with wealth or property as investments

drunk: (*slang*) spending spree

arrogant: proud and superior

liberal: generous, giving freely

"hooey": nonsense

READ ON

1. While reading this broadcast transcription for the first time, **underline** the causes of the Great Depression.

2. While rereading, **summarize** the main idea of the broadcast.

October 25, 1931 [radio broadcast]

We used to be told that depression was just a state of mind but starvation **1** has changed that impression. Depression is a state of health. It's moved from the mind to the stomach. And it aint really depression either: it's just a return to normalcy. We are just getting back to earth. We are back to two-bit meals and cotton underwear and off $1.50 steaks and silk under rompers. The trouble is America is just muscle bound from holding a steering wheel. The only place we are calloused from work is the bottom of our driving toe.

This country has just got one problem: it's not the balancing of Mr. **2** Mellon's budget (that's his problem); it's not the League of Nations; it's not the silver question; not a one of those problems mean a thing in the world to us *as long as we have seven million of our own out of work.* Our only problem is to arrange the affairs of this prosperous country (yes, prosperous right now) so that a man that wants to work can get work and give him a more equal division of the wealth the country produces.

Now if our big men in the next year cant fix that, well they just aint big **3** men, that's all.

What does prohibition amount to if your neighbor's children are not **4** eating? It's food, not drink is our problem now. We were so afraid the poor people might drink, now we fixed it so they cant eat.

We got more wheat, more corn, more food, more cotton, more money **5** in the banks, more everything in the world than any nation that ever lived ever had, yet we are starving to death.

We are the first nation in the history of the world to go to the poor house **6** in an automobile.

Our potter's fields are surrounded by granaries full of grain. Now if there **7** ain't something "cockeyed" in an arrangement like that, then this microphone in front of me is a mousetrap.

Now a miracle can't happen and all these people get a job over night. **8** It's going to take time. So they must be fed and cared for perhaps all winter.

Every one of us that have anything got it by the aid of these very people. **9** There is not an unemployed man in the country that hasent contributed to the wealth of every millionaire in America.

The working classes dident bring this one. It was the big boys that thought **10** the financial drunk was going to last forever and over bought, over merged and over capitalized.

Now the people are not asking for money. They are asking for a job. But **11** there is no job, towns and cities cant say they havent got the money. For the same amount of money is in the country as when these folks had their share. Somebody's got it.

Last winter we dident realize the need. But this winter we got no excuse. **12** Its been shown to us all summer.

Now dont wait for the government to feed these people. I have seen lots **13** of audiences and heard lots of appeals, but I have yet to see one where the people knew the need, and the cause was there, that they dident come through. Even Europe who hates us and thinks we are arrogant, bad-mannered and everything else, will tell you that we are liberal.

    Dog-gone it, our folks are liberal. I don't know anything about America's being "fundamentally sound" and all that after-dinner "hooey," but I do know that America is "fundamentally generous."   **14**

IN YOUR OWN VOICE

WHAT DOES IT SAY?

1. What has changed the Depression from "just a state of mind"?

2. What is the country's only problem?

3. Even in the Great Depression, what assets and resources does the United States still possess?

4. What are the people asking for?

5. Which quality makes America "fundamentally sound"?

WHAT DOES IT MEAN?

1. Why does Rogers consider the Depression as a return to a normal way of life?

2. Why is providing jobs the cure for the Depression?

3. How have the unemployed contributed to the wealth of "every millionaire in America"?

4. Why should the people not wait for the government to feed them?

5. Why does Rogers praise America for being liberal?

STYLE AND SENSE

1. What is the effect on the radio audience of Rogers's use of *we, us, our*?

2. Which words identify those who are different from Rogers and his audience?

3. Which contrasts reveal the gap between the haves and the have-nots?

4. Why does Rogers often use informal language like "well they just ain't big men, that's all"? List other examples of this type of language.

FROM THE TEXT

Subject-verb agreement: In the present tense, the verb that agrees with the third person singular subject usually has an *-s* or *-es* ending.

Read the following sentence:

> Even Europe who hates us and thinks we are arrogant, bad-mannered and everything else, will tell you that we are liberal.

a. What is the subject?

b. Is it singular or plural?

c. Which relative pronoun refers to the subject?

d. Is it singular or plural?

e. Which verbs does the relative pronoun take?

f. Are they singular or plural?

See page 408 for more on subject-verb agreement.

WRITE NOW

Do both of the following activities.

1. Write a **first draft** of a paragraph based on one of the following Writing Suggestions.

2. **Revise** the paragraph—alone or with another student.

WRITING SUGGESTIONS

1. Rogers places great reliance on the average person's willingness to help himself or herself when he writes, "Now dont wait for the government to feed these people." Explain whether in any or all countries in the Americas today, such confidence in individual effort is preferable to government assistance.

2. During the Depression radio comedy shows helped people to laugh at their troubles. Discuss how today's television comedies reflect society's values and concerns.

3. Rogers describes the people of the United States as being basically generous, even in the midst of the Depression. Describe how the people of the United States or the people of your homeland act(ed) in the face of an economic, political, or military crisis.

FURTHER WRITING SUGGESTIONS

4. The Great Depression ended fifty years ago. Since then, many people of the United States have achieved economic prosperity. Answer one of the following:

   a. Discuss how and why this prosperity has enabled the United States to help solve many of its social problems.

or

   b. Discuss how and why social problems persist despite these generally prosperous conditions.

5. Describe the effects that a prolonged Depression or period of financial decline may have on a family or a community.

WORKING IN A WARTIME FOUNDRY AND A STEEL MILL*

By Ruth Wolf

World War II (1939–45) saw millions of women move into skilled factory and industrial defense jobs in support of the war effort. Some replaced men who served in the military, and others trained for and became experts in shipbuilding, weapons and aircraft manufacture, and other important industries.

Rosie the Riveter was the name given to these women workers. While they endured harassment in the workplace and earned lower wages than men for performing the same job, many of these women received decent wages for the first time and union support against unfair treatment. Although indispensable to the nation, as soon as the war ended and the men came home, most of these women found themselves no longer needed or wanted on the job.

This selection from *The Life and Times of Rosie the Riveter* is Ruth Wolf's own account of her experiences working at a foundry in Ohio and a steel mill in Pennsylvania during the war.

*Editors' title

WORDS TO NOTICE

sweat shop: workplace characterized by low wages, long hours, and substandard working conditions

affair: *(slang)* thing

milling machine and a lathe: machines for grinding tools and holding them

foundry: factory where metal or glass is melted

quotas: set amounts

apprentice: beginner learning a trade

piecework: work in which a person is paid by the number of items produced

Croatian: a person from Croatia (the second largest of the republics within Yugoslavia)

walkout: sudden walking off the job

thorn in their side: continual source of annoyance

jig: device to hold and guide tools

annealing: heating and cooling process to toughen metal or glass

ware: manufactured goods

READ ON

1. While reading this selection for the first time, **underline** any event or experience that shows workers supporting each other.

2. While rereading, **find** examples of unequal or unfair treatment of the women workers.

Before the war I worked in the pottery trade. East Liverpool, Ohio, is the 1
pottery center of the world. I worked there from the seventh grade. It's a
woman's industry. There were two women to every man. It was a sweat shop
affair and the wages were very low.

Shortly after Pearl Harbor had been bombed, I saw an ad in the daily 2
paper which said, "Anyone interested in doing defense work, call or come
in to the unemployment office." So I went downtown before work one day,
and I signed up. I would work a shift in the pottery shop and then do a session
in the training school. They taught us how to run a milling machine and a
lathe. After about six weeks' time, they sent me and about twenty other women
to report at the Patterson Foundry Company.

I was put on a milling machine, making small pieces for machine guns. **3** It had to be very exact. They told us, "If you don't make these pieces exactly right, it may cost some soldier his life."

Our production quotas were based according to the piece. You had to **4** work exceedingly hard to make the average wage, much less anything over. You were also paid according to the size of the piece, and men always got the bigger pieces which brought more money. One day I turned to this older man, who was working right alongside me. He was very old, and he was handling just the same size pieces I was. I was shocked to find out that he was making much more than I was. Turns out they had kept me on this apprentice wage, even though I'd been there longer than he had. I was spitting mad. Here I was, doing the same work at the same time, and him making more than me!

They had never had women in that foundry before, and both the foremen **5** and the other men there resented us terribly and did all sorts of things against us. We were not allowed to do anything with the machines, only to operate them. If it went bad, we had to call the machinist, who, of course, was a man. And since it was piecework it was very important to get your machine fixed fast. If a man's machine broke down, the machinist would go right away and fix it, but a woman could wait longer than a day.

They timed us so that we could not go to the restroom. At first, we did **6** not even have a restroom—then finally they built one for us. But if the foreman saw you going down those steps more than once or twice in a morning, he'd say, "Why are you leaving that job?"

There was one lady there, Julia, a very big Croatian woman. She worked **7** like a man, and they put her on men's jobs, doing heavy lifting. But they did not pay her as much as they did the men.

One day, she was talking to a union man who was trying to organize the **8** plant. She knew him, and she saw him on this sound truck outside, and so she went over to say hello. The owner of the plant saw her, and they fired her on the spot!

We were all outraged. We said, "No, you will not fire her. She works too **9** hard for you. She is the best worker in the plant. If you fire her, we'll all walk out." And we did! The walkout lasted maybe a day, and then they backed down. But from then on Julia was always a thorn in their side.

I got a taste of that kind of treatment myself, after the union came in. **10** Most of the women there had no experience with unions. But I had been a trustee in the pottery union, so I ended up representing them. That was when the foreman we worked for really started making things rough for me.

I had been working on this milling machine, which I did very well on. **11** But then one morning, he said, "You go work on that big machine." It was a newer electrical milling machine, which made much bigger pieces. I knew it would be hard for me to handle. I had to stand on a box to reach it.

The girl next to me was a friend, and gave me a few instructions about **12** what to do. She pushed the button to show me something, and then suddenly the machine caught the pieces of the jig and broke them. I wasn't about to say that she had done it, because there was a rule in the shop that no one is to operate another person's machine. She would have lost her job.

The foreman was furious with me, though he could not fire me. Instead, he gave me a five-day suspension. But I knew that many men had broken jigs and that they hadn't done anything to them, so I demanded a release from the company. At that time, the government would not allow you to leave a plant, if you were working on war orders, without a special release.   **13**

I had heard that the Crucible Steel mill across the state line, in Midland, Pennsylvania, was thinking of taking women, so I went there once I got my release, and I was in one of the first groups of women they hired. I ran into many of the same things there as in the foundry. Steel, too, had always been a man's industry, and the men were against having us in the plant, even though it was necessary, because so many men were at war. The foreman presented the same problem as the one in the foundry. He couldn't see a woman in there for nothing.   **14**

When I hired in, I told them that I knew how to fire an annealing furnace. My husband had taught me years before. I used to bring him his dinner in the furnace room on the nights when he worked overtime, and sometimes I'd stay and keep him company there while he worked. I was interested in what he did, you know, and so he explained to me how it all worked.   **15**

I surprised them all at the Crucible mill—they never expected to find a woman who knew how to operate the furnace!   **16**

The work I did there was not nearly so hard as in the pottery factory, where you had to lift big loads, and heavy boxes of ware. We used to stand all day long on concrete floors in the pottery factory, which really ruins your feet. In the steel mill, we did not have anything like that. It was easy work, more intelligent work. You weren't just standing up all day and working like a robot.   **17**

IN YOUR OWN VOICE

WHAT DOES IT SAY?

1. Which event causes Wolf and other women to take on defense jobs?

2. How did the foundry foremen and male workers react to the presence of female workers?

3. Why is Julia fired?

4. Why is Wolf suspended?

5. What surprises the steel mill workers about Wolf?

WHAT DOES IT MEAN?

1. Why does the advertisement say "Anyone interested in doing defense work" can apply?

2. Why is Wolf shocked at the salary the older man receives?

3. Why are the men's machines repaired faster than the women's?

4. Why is Julia "fired on the spot" for talking to a union organizer?

5. Why couldn't the steel mill foreman "see a woman in there for nothing"?

STYLE AND SENSE

To answer questions 1 through 3, reread paragraph 7.

1. What does the word *lady* mean? Does it mean the same as *woman*?

2. What does "she worked like a man" mean?

3. What does "men's jobs" mean?

4. In paragraph 12, what does *girl* mean?

5. Wolf mentions *foremen* (paragraph 5) and *union man* (paragraph 8). Are these terms acceptable to you? If not, provide substitute terms.

FROM THE TEXT

Read the following sentence:

It was a sweat shop affair and the wages were very low.

a. Identify the independent clauses.

b. Which conjunction prevents a run-on sentence?

c. Identify the subject and verb of each clause.

d. Which verb is singular? Which is plural?

WRITE NOW

Do both of the following activities.

1. **Freewrite** on one of the following Writing Suggestions.

2. Write a **first draft** of a paragraph based on a main idea from the freewriting.

WRITING SUGGESTIONS

1. In *The Second Stage* (1981), Betty Friedan writes, "The woman will find and use her own strength and style at work, instead of trying so hard to do it man's way." Answer one of the following questions:

    a. Discuss the "strength and style" that women bring into the workplace.

    or

    b. Discuss whether or not women have strengths and styles at work which are different from those of men.

2. When Ruth Wolf became a trustee of the pottery union, she followed in the footsteps of people like Sarah Bagley, who founded the first significant union, the Lowell (Massachusetts) Female Labor Reform Association (1845). Answer one of the following questions:

   a. Discuss the importance of unions to workers.

   or

   b. Discuss why you would or would not join a union today.

3. More and more women are entering the work force, and more and more women hold managerial positions. Describe the changes in society that have occurred and will continue to occur because of this increased presence of women.

FURTHER WRITING SUGGESTIONS

4. Interview a retired worker. You may wish to ask about the working conditions and pay, equal treatment on the job, male and female interaction, job satisfaction and support networking.

5. At present, U.S. women earn about 60 percent of what men earn for doing the same job. Discuss the effects on women and men when equal pay for equal work becomes a reality.

6. Wolf refers to "men's work" and "women's work." Tell whether these terms have meaning today or had meaning in the past.

EQUALITY OF SACRIFICE

By Lee Iacocca

The son of Italian immigrants, Lee Iacocca was born in 1924 in Allentown, Pennsylvania. At the age of twenty-two, Iacocca began working at the Ford Motor Company as a student engineer. He rose to become a major executive at Ford, best known for creating the highly successful Mustang.

In November 1978, Iacocca joined the Chrysler Corporation, which was near bankruptcy. On January 7, 1980, President Jimmy Carter signed the Chrysler Corporation Loan Guarantee Act, a $3.5 billion aid package to help the ailing company survive. Under Iacocca's leadership, Chrysler recovered and repaid the loans well before they were due.

In his autobiography, Iacocca focuses on the "equality of sacrifice" and the cooperative spirit needed to bring about Chrysler's recovery. However, the rescue effort was a painful process that involved the loss of jobs, salary reductions, cutbacks in management, and labor concessions.

WORDS TO NOTICE

equivalent of: synonym for

concessions: rights given up

coalition: a unified group formed out of diverse groups

martyr: one who sacrifices for a cause

go into the pits: get ready for drastic action

pragmatic: practical

austerity: economic belt-tightening

Lynn Townsend: Chrysler Corporation chairman who retired in 1975

unraveled: undone, apart

fat cats: *(slang)* millionaires

saga: long, involved story

accordingly: appropriately

hecklers: loud, abusive persons who interrupt speakers

stock options: opportunities to buy shares in a company

serenely: calmly

grit their teeth: endure trouble

READ ON

1. While reading this essay for the first time, jot down **margin notes** of acts of cooperation and acts of sacrifice.

2. While rereading, ask yourself if "equality" accurately describes the sacrifices that were made.

With the passage of the Loan Guarantee Act, we now had a fighting chance   1
to survive. And I do mean "fighting"!

Our mission was the economic equivalent of war. Although no one was   2
getting killed for Chrysler, the economic survival of hundreds of thousands
of people depended on whether we could arrange the various concessions
that the Loan Guarantee Act required.

I was the general in the war to save Chrysler. But I sure didn't do it alone.   3
What I'm most proud of is the coalition I was able to put together. It shows
what cooperation can do for you in hard times.

I began by reducing my own salary to $1.00 a year. Leadership means   4
setting an example. When you find yourself in a position of leadership, people
follow your every move. I don't mean they invade your privacy, although there's
some of that, too. But when the leader talks, people listen. And when the
leader acts, people watch. So you have to be careful about everything you
say and everything you do.

I didn't take $1.00 a year to be a martyr. I took it because I had to go into   5
the pits. I took it so that when I went to Doug Fraser, the union president, I
could look him in the eye and say: "Here's what I want from you guys as
your share," and he couldn't come back to me and ask: "You SOB, what
sacrifice have *you* made?" That's why I did it, for good, cold, pragmatic
reasons. I wanted our employees and our suppliers to be thinking: "I can
follow a guy who sets that kind of example."

Unfortunately, austerity was a new idea at Chrysler. When I came in, I   6
heard all kinds of horror stories about the extravagance of the previous administration. But I wasn't impressed. After all, I had lived for years with Henry
Ford, who thought he owned the company and who was powerful enough to
act as if he did. Henry spent enough money to make Lynn Townsend look
like a beggar. He made the head of General Motors look like he was on
welfare.

Although my reduced salary didn't mean I had to skip any meals, it still   7
made a big statement in Detroit. It showed that we were all in this together.
It showed that we could survive only if each of us tightened his belt. It was
a dramatic gesture, and word of it got around very quickly.

I learned more about people in three years at Chrysler than in thirty-two   8
years at Ford. I discovered that people accept a lot of pain if everybody's
going through the chute together. If everybody is suffering equally, you can
move a mountain. But the first time you find someone goofing off or not
carrying his share of the load, the whole thing can come unraveled.

I call this equality of sacrifice. When I started to sacrifice, I saw other   9
people do whatever was necessary. And that's how Chrysler pulled through.
It wasn't the loans that saved us, although we needed them badly. It was the
hundreds of millions of dollars that were given up by everybody involved. It
was like a family getting together and saying: "We got a loan from our rich
uncle and now we're going to prove that we can pay him back!"

This was cooperation and democracy at their best. I'm not talking about   10
a Bible lesson here. I'm talking about real life. We went through it. It works.
It's like magic and it awes you.

But our struggle also had its dark side. To cut expenses, we had to fire   11
a lot of people. It's like a war: we won, but my son didn't come back. There
was a lot of agony. People were getting destroyed, taking their kids out of
college, drinking, getting divorced. Overall we preserved the company, but
only at enormous personal expense for a great many human beings.

Our task was made a little easier by the knowledge that much of America   12
was rooting for us. We were no longer seen as the fat cats asking for welfare.
With the congressional hearings behind us, that part of the saga was over.
By now, our advertising campaign was beginning to get results. We were the
underdog engaged in a heroic struggle, and the public responded accordingly.

Many unknown people wrote to us, saying in a hundred different ways   13
that they were with us, that Henry Ford's loss was Chrysler's gain. The little
people said a lot, and they said it well. They understood what we were doing.

Some pretty big people helped us, too. Bob Hope came to see me. He   14
told me that while having a massage he'd seen one of my commercials on
television. Now he wanted to do something for us.

I ran into Bill Cosby at dinner one night in Las Vegas. That same night,   15
he called me in my hotel at 1:00 A.M.

I said, "Hey man, you woke me up."   16

He said: "Hell, we're just getting going. We're up all night. Anyway, I   17
admire what you're doing, and I appreciate how much you're helping the
black people. I'd like to do something for you. I make a lot of money and
other people are starving." He came to Detroit to do a show for our workers—
20,000 of them. Then he got on a plane and left. He never asked for a dime.
He never asked for a car. He just wanted to help us out and show his support.

One night Pearl Bailey came up to me at a diabetes function in downtown   18
Detroit. She said she just had to talk to me. She thanked me for trying to
preserve jobs and for giving people hope. Instead of doing a concert, she
wanted to give a lecture to our workers at the Jefferson Avenue plant.

She made a rousing speech about patriotism and the need to sacrifice.   19
But while she was talking, a couple of hecklers started in: "Easy for you to
say, Pearl, you're rich!"

Before we knew it, we almost had a riot on our hands. I had to jump up   20
and bring the meeting to a close. But it was a great gesture, and I really
appreciated it.

Frank Sinatra wanted to help, too. He said: "Lee, if you're working for a   21
dollar, I will, too." He did some commercials for us, and during the second
year we gave him some stock options. I hope Frank held on to them, because
if he did, he made a bundle.

There were a number of these cases. During that period, I got to see the   22
positive side of human beings. I had never really known how people would
act when the chips were down. I learned that the majority will rally around.

They won't think about greed, even though the media seem to believe that greed is the only motivating force in business. Most people, when called upon, will serve—so long as they're not being singled out to get the short end of the stick.

I also learned that people can act very serenely in a crisis. They accept **23** their fate. They know it's going to be a tough grind, but they grit their teeth and go with it. Watching that happen was the pleasant part—maybe the only pleasant part—of this whole episode.

IN YOUR OWN VOICE

WHAT DOES IT SAY?

---

1. By what gesture does Iacocca show his leadership?

2. Under which circumstances can people "move a mountain"?

3. What is the "dark side" of saving the Chrysler Corporation?

4. What does Bill Cosby do to help?

5. What seems to have been the only pleasant part of the crisis for Iacocca?

WHAT DOES IT MEAN?

1. Why does Iacocca consider himself an army general?

2. Why is Iacocca's dollar-a-year salary significant?

3. Why are the federal loans not enough to save the company?

4. How is Chrysler's position as "underdog" valuable?

5. How does Chrysler's experience disprove the media belief that "greed is the only motivating force in business"?

STYLE AND SENSE

Iacocca writes, "Our mission was the economic equivalent of war." This metaphor comparing an economic battle with a military one is developed throughout the selection.

1. List at least five words or expressions of this kind to dramatize Chrysler's struggle for survival.

2. How does Iacocca's use of the word *I* at the start of nine paragraphs show his intention to lead?

3. How does the title "Equality of Sacrifice" show the relationship of Iacocca and other individuals and groups working toward Chrysler's recovery?

4. What is the effect of the repeated use of the military metaphor?

FROM THE TEXT

Complex sentence: A sentence containing an independent clause and at least one dependent clause.

Read the following:

I took it because I had to go into the pits.

a. Identify the dependent clause.

b. Which word makes this clause dependent?

c. Which punctuation mark follows the dependent clause?

d. If the clauses are reversed, is there still a complex sentence?

e. Is the sentence written with a comma if the clauses are reversed?

f. Find at least two other complex sentences in this selection.

Note: A **sentence fragment** results when a dependent clause stands alone and is punctuated as a complete sentence.

See page 405 for more on the dependent clause sentence fragment.

WRITE NOW

Do both of the following activities.

1. Write a **first draft** of an opening paragraph based on one of the following Writing Suggestions.

2. **Revise** this paragraph—alone or with another student.

WRITING SUGGESTIONS

1. Describe a situation in your life in which teamwork accomplished more than what could have been achieved individually. Describe your feelings throughout.

2. Iacocca uses the word *I* often but states that the whole recovery effort was a triumph of teamwork. Discuss whether the presence of a leader helps or hinders teamwork.

3. Compare and contrast the leadership qualities of a business executive with those of a school official, a politician, a military officer, or any other person in authority.

FURTHER WRITING SUGGESTIONS

4. Explain why you chose or chose not to sacrifice your time, money, and energy when you were asked to do so for the good of your school, community, or place of employment.

5. Famous entertainers helped the Chrysler Corporation. Explain why celebrities make themselves available for charity and benefit performances and other kinds of socially responsible activities.

6. People go into business to make money. Discuss what a business or company owes to the public in return for the opportunity to make a profit.

A CALCULATED RISK*

By An Wang

An Wang was born in 1920 in Shanghai, China. After achieving the highest college entrance examination scores, he graduated from Chiao Tung University in 1940.

In 1945 he entered Harvard University for further engineering training. His interests turned to physics, and he earned his master's and doctoral degrees in less than three years. In 1948 he became research fellow at the Harvard Computation Laboratory, under the leadership of Dr. Howard Aiken. He married Lorraine Chiu in 1949.

Two years later, Wang invested his entire savings of $600 in his first business venture, a one-person electronics company in Boston. Wang Laboratories grew to be one of the world's major computer and information processing firms. In 1986 Dr. Wang and eleven other famed naturalized American citizens in the arts and sciences were awarded the Medal of Liberty. He died in 1990.

This selection from Dr. Wang's autobiography, *Lessons,* starts with his decision to take a risk and start a business.

WORDS TO NOTICE

pros and cons: positive and negative points

sole proprietorship: one owner

incorporation: formation of a corporation

unduly: overly

*Editors' title

accommodate: allow room for

conviction: firm belief

province: area of interest under the control of someone else

academia: college or university environment

arena: area of activity

prestigious: much admired

cosmopolitan: made up of groups from all over the world

insulated: separated and protected

subtle: hard to detect

turmoil: upheaval, agitated state

Confucianism: teachings of the Chinese philosopher Confucius (551–479 B.C.E.)

assimilate: absorb, take in

disciplines: fields of study

hence: therefore

menial: lowly, subservient

prudence: good judgment

READ ON

1. While you read this selection for the first time, **underline** all the decisions Wang made.

2. While rereading, **discover** instances in which Wang's Chinese heritage became a factor in his decisions.

This was a big decision, and I did not make it in a day. But as with most of my major decisions since, I did not spend more than a couple of weeks thinking through the pros and cons, and once I had made the decision, rather than worry about whether it was right or wrong, I devoted all my energy to making that decision work.   1

  I discovered that a form of business called a sole proprietorship made the most sense for what I wanted to accomplish. A sole proprietorship is not actually a form of incorporation. At that time, all I had to do to set up a sole proprietorship was go to City Hall and pay a small registration fee, and give my company a name.   2

  In April 1951, I notified the Computation Laboratory that I would be leaving. My one-year contract with them was due to expire in June 1951, so   3

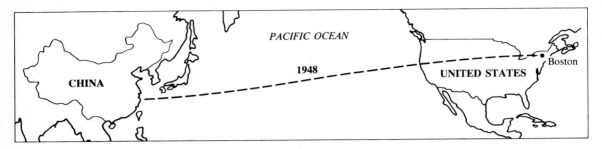

From China across the Pacific to Boston

there was nothing unusual about the timing of my decision. Because of the news that the laboratory would be getting out of computer research, a number of other research fellows were leaving as well, and so Dr. Aiken was not unduly surprised. On June 22, I received the papers which certified that I, Dr. An Wang, would be doing business as Wang Laboratories.

In the years since 1951, I have occasionally been asked why I called the company Wang Laboratories, which some people feel makes the company sound like it is in the pharmaceutical business. I could have called it Digital Electronics or Cyberdyne or some other high-tech name. I used my own name in part because at that point my expectations were that I would *be* the company since it was a sole proprietorship, and perhaps in part out of pride. I wanted the company to reflect my values and my origins—and in truth I could not think of a better name. Working at the Computation Laboratory had given me the idea of calling the company Wang Laboratories; while the two laboratories would be very different in scale, I would be doing work at my laboratory that was similar to the work I had done at the Computation Laboratory. I used the plural, *laboratories,* rather than the singular because I thought the company would expand over the years, and I wanted a name that would accommodate growth. I was indeed very naive: I did not think about marketing studies, the reaction of the investment community, or anything else that goes into naming a company these days.   **4**

I quickly found very inexpensive office space—at about seventy dollars a month—on Columbus Avenue in the South End of Boston, and I was officially in business. My capital was six hundred dollars in savings, and I had no orders, no contracts, and no office furniture.   **5**

My conviction that I was taking a reasonable risk given the potential rewards was not shared by my acquaintances, particularly our Chinese friends. They were sensitive to discrimination against Asians, and they did not think it wise to start a business in an area still perceived to be the province of the establishment. At that time most of the Chinese who had come to the United States for graduate studies chose academia as the arena in which they might prove themselves. To be a full professor at a prestigious university was the summit of success. Lorraine remembers that Professor L. J. Chu, who became a full professor at MIT, was regarded as the most successful member of the Chinese community. Our friends reminded us that the only businesses Chinese-   **6**

Americans seemed to be involved in provided services of one sort or another. I think many of them expected me to fail.

Once I began Wang Laboratories, Chinese friends called regularly to see **7** how I was doing. When it became clear that I was making a go of it, some of those following my progress decided to try the same thing themselves. Two brothers we knew named Li, both professors at MIT, left academia to found a company soon after I founded mine.

I was certainly aware that at that time there was some discrimination **8** against Chinese, but in the cosmopolitan Cambridge community, my wife and I were somewhat insulated from that discrimination. In the nineteenth century, Chinese had been treated quite badly in the United States, even, on occasion, being attacked by lynch mobs. While things were no longer as violent when I arrived, other, more subtle forms of discrimination persisted. I remember on one occasion we answered an advertisement for an apartment, only to be told when we showed up to inspect it that the apartment was not available. I am convinced that the apartment became unavailable when the superintendent saw that we were Chinese. When I encountered this type of discrimination, my response was to take it as an unpleasant fact of life and then, to redouble my efforts to succeed.

Despite the political turmoil of my youth, I have always felt intense pride **9** in the historical depth of Chinese culture. A Chinese can never outgrow his roots. Ancient ideas such as Confucianism are as relevant today as they were twenty-five hundred years ago. There is also a practical genius to Chinese culture that allows it to assimilate new ideas without destroying old ones. As a Chinese, I had also mastered some of the scientific disciplines that have been the special strength of Western societies. In other words, I felt I had succeeded on the West's own terms. Hence I was distressed to see the menial role Americans assigned to Chinese back then, and a small part of the reason I founded Wang Laboratories was to show that Chinese could excel at things other than running laundries and restaurants. Of course, there is no question about that today, but in 1950, things were very different.

However, though the desire to change the image of Chinese in America **10** was a part of my motivation to start my company, it would be a mistake to conclude that I was founding a company to prove anybody wrong; I was founding the company primarily because it seemed like a smart thing to do.

Although I felt my decision was based on prudence, I do not underesti- **11** mate the role of confidence. My confidence had been built by the risks I had taken in my youth, and now it pushed me to act on my judgment. A number of other researchers may have seen the same opportunities that I did but failed to act. It is necessary to gather facts, and to analyze those facts when considering a course of action, but the world is shaped only by actions, and to take action requires confidence.

Today, thirty-five years after I founded the company, I continually hear **12** people question whether Wang Laboratories can survive the competition with mighty IBM. My response is that the odds against Wang Laboratories surviving in 1951, and then growing to the size it has, were a lot worse than the odds of the company's successfully competing against IBM today.

IN YOUR OWN VOICE

WHAT DOES IT SAY?

1. What does Wang do instead of worrying whether his decision to start a business is right or wrong?

2. Why is the company named Wang Laboratories?

3. What is the reaction of most of Wang's Chinese friends to his starting a business?

4. What is Wang's response to acts of discrimination?

5. What must be done when considering a course of action?

WHAT DOES IT MEAN?

1. Why is starting a business "a big decision"?

2. Which values are suggested by the name Wang Laboratories?

3. How does discrimination interfere with Chinese-Americans' starting their own companies?

4. Why is the Chinese cultural tradition important to Wang?

5. Why did Wang feel proud of his success?

STYLE AND SENSE

1. Which is the most important word in the opening paragraph?

2. In paragraphs 2 through 5, what process does Wang describe?

3. In paragraphs 6 through 9, which contrasting attitudes of Chinese-Americans does Wang discuss?

4. How do the closing paragraphs 10 through 12 come back to the main idea of the opening paragraph?

FROM THE TEXT

Gerund: a verbal noun that ends in -*ing* and functions as a subject, or as the object of a verb or a preposition, or in any other way that a noun functions.

Read the following sentence:

Working at the Computation Laboratory had given me the idea of calling the company Wang Laboratories.

a. What is the complete verb of the sentence?

b. What is the complete subject?

c. What is the gerund?

d. What is the other gerund in the sentence?

e. Is this gerund the object of a verb or of a preposition?

See page 380 for more on subjects of sentences.

WRITE NOW

Do both of the following activities.

1. Make a **brainstorm** list of the qualities and characteristics necessary for success in business.

2. Write a **first draft** of a paragraph based on a main idea from the brainstorming.

WRITING SUGGESTIONS

1. Describe the qualities and values that one must have to be a success in business.

2. Decisions are often made after considering the advice of family, friends, and peers. Compare and contrast the advantages and disadvantages of listening to such advice.

3. Wang writes, "To take action requires confidence." Explain how having confidence in yourself can produce both better decision-making and better results.

FURTHER WRITING SUGGESTIONS

4. Explain how being discriminated against may be a motivating force in a person's striving to better himself or herself.

5. As the saying goes, "Build a better mousetrap, and the world will beat a path to your door." Discuss whether the door of opportunity is open to all people in the Americas.

6. Describe the riskiest decision that you will make in the next five years.

7. Wang writes, "A Chinese can never outgrow his roots." Discuss whether this idea is true for you in terms of your own ethnic group or ancestry.

UNIT 7

CITIES AND TOWNS

Just as there are diversity and unity among the peoples of the Americas, so are there diversity and unity in the places where they live. From the mid-nineteenth century to the 1920s, many immigrants, chiefly from Europe, came to the cities of this hemisphere.

Jane Addams's "Hull House" discusses a humanitarian response to the problems inevitably caused by having large numbers of persons from different ethnic groups living next to each other in overcrowded neighborhoods.

The second selection, from Mary Antin's autobiography, tells of the new immigrant's joy in discovering new heroes and values in the adopted country.

This is followed by the former Speaker of the U.S. House of Representatives "Tip" O'Neill's reminiscence of his immigrant ancestors and an illustration of the use of political organization to break through the walls of prejudice.

Next is Margaret Laurence's short story "A Bird in the House," which tells of a father and daughter's relationship in a small Canadian town.

Concluding the unit is Luisa Valenzuela's imaginative short story of the conflicts between city and countryside and between governmental authority and individual freedom.

BEFORE YOU READ

Are you an immigrant to the United States or any other country in the Americas? Are any members of your family immigrants?

What hopes and expectations do new arrivals bring to their adopted country?

How do the immigrants change their new country?

What problems and prejudices do immigrants face?

What do you know about the Statue of Liberty? Ellis Island? The point of entry in San Francisco?

After graduation, where would you like to live—in a city or a small town?

What problems exist in modern cities? In modern small towns?

What is the future for the small town? The large city?

What stereotypes do people have about city life or small town life?

Why is elementary school important to newcomers to the Americas?

What are your memories of elementary school?

What is the importance of national holidays?

How can an immigrant keep the traditions and customs of his or her native land while adapting to the new land?

How does political life in a democracy help newcomers to survive and prosper in a new land?

In what ways do new arrivals help each other?

HULL HOUSE*

By Jane Addams

Jane Addams (1860–1935) was a world-renowned social reformer. In 1889 she and Ellen Gates Starr founded Hull House in Chicago. This neighborhood settlement house with its trained resident workers provided many necessary social, educational, and cultural services.

*Editors' title

Addams wrote *Twenty Years at Hull-House* (1910), an autobiographical narrative. She assumed leadership roles in obtaining the vote for women and in gaining labor and welfare reforms. For her work on behalf of immigrants and the poor and for her efforts in the peace movement, Addams shared the 1931 Nobel Peace Prize.

This selection from an essay in *Philosophy and Social Progress* (1893) describes the site of Hull House and the living and working conditions of its neighboring residents.

WORDS TO NOTICE

ample: large

ornately: elaborately

vicissitudes: changes in fortune

aspect: look, appearance

Bohemian: Czechoslovakian

clannish: keeping to themselves

ward: a political district of a city

aldermen: elected ward representatives

are unchecked: go unwatched

initiative: first step

civic duties: responsibilities as citizens

sweating system: factories or businesses that exploit their workers (long hours, low pay, poor conditions)

unscrupulous: dishonest, immoral

shanty: shack

provisional: temporary

abound: exist in large number

READ ON

1. Jot down **margin notes** on the various groups served by Hull House.

2. While rereading, **summarize** the problems of the community.

Hull House is an ample old residence, well built and somewhat ornately 1 decorated after the manner of its time, 1856. It has been used for many purposes, and although battered by its vicissitudes, is essentially sound and has responded kindly to repairs and careful furnishing. Its wide hall and open fires always insure it a gracious aspect. It once stood in the suburbs, but the city has steadily grown up around it and its site now has corners on three or four more or less distinct foreign colonies. Between Halsted Street and the river live about ten thousand Italians: Neapolitans, Sicilians, and Calabrians, with an occasional Lombard or Venetian. To the south on Twelfth Street are many Germans, and side streets are given over almost entirely to Polish and Russian Jews. Still farther south, these Jewish colonies merge into a huge Bohemian colony, so vast that Chicago ranks as the third Bohemian city in the world. To the northwest are many Canadian-French, clannish in spite of their long residence in America, and to the north are many Irish and first-generation Americans. On the streets directly west and farther north are well-to-do English-speaking families, many of whom own their houses and have lived in the neighborhood for years. I know one man who is still living in his old farm-house. This corner of Polk and Halsted Streets is in the fourteenth precinct of the nineteenth ward. This ward has a population of about fifty thousand, and at the last presidential election registered 7072 voters. It has had no unusual political scandal connected with it, but its aldermen are generally saloon-keepers and its political manipulations are those to be found in the crowded wards where the activities of the petty politician are unchecked.

The policy of the public authorities of never taking an initiative, and always 2 waiting to be urged to do their duty, is fatal in a ward where there is no initiative among the citizens. The idea underlying our self-government breaks down in such a ward. The streets are inexpressibly dirty, the number of schools inadequate, factory legislation unenforced, the street-lighting bad, the paving miserable and altogether lacking in the alleys and smaller streets, and the stables defy all laws of sanitation. Hundreds of houses are unconnected with the street sewer. The older and richer inhabitants seem anxious to move away as rapidly as they can afford it. They make room for newly arrived immigrants who are densely ignorant of civic duties. This substitution of the older inhabitants is accomplished industrially also in the south and east quarters of the ward. The Hebrews and Italians do the finishing for the great clothing-manufacturers formerly done by Americans, Irish, and Germans, who refused to submit to the extremely low prices to which the sweating system has reduced their successors. As the design of the sweating system is the elimination of rent from the manufacture of clothing, the "outside work" is begun after the clothing leaves the cutter. An unscrupulous contractor regards no basement as too dark, no stable loft too foul, no rear shanty too provisional, no tenement room too small for his workroom, as these conditions imply low rental. Hence these shops abound in the worst of the foreign districts, where the sweater easily finds his cheap basement and his home finishers. There is a constant tendency to employ school-children, as much of the home and shop work can easily be done by children.

IN YOUR OWN VOICE

WHAT DOES IT SAY?

1. In the years between 1856 and 1893, when this selection was written, how did the neighborhood surrounding Hull House change?

2. Which groups of people live in the neighborhood of Hull House?

3. Which daily problems face the neighborhood's residents?

4. What kinds of workplaces exist under the "sweating system"?

WHAT DOES IT MEAN?

1. Why is Hull House established in that neighborhood?

2. Why is the neighborhood divided into "more or less distinct foreign colonies"?

3. Why is a lack of initiative by politicians and citizens "fatal in a ward"?

4. Why do the new arrivals accept the harsh working conditions of the "sweating system"?

5. Why are schoolchildren also employed?

STYLE AND SENSE

1. Draw a map of the streets and neighborhood surrounding Hull House. Indicate where Hull House stands and where the various ethnic groups live.

2. Which words in paragraph 1 enable you to locate Hull House and its surroundings?

3. Which words in paragraph 2 enable you to locate the various ethnic groups?

FROM THE TEXT

Read the following sentence:

On the streets directly west and farther north are well-to-do English-speaking families, many of whom own their houses and have lived in the neighborhood for years.

a. What is the subject of the first clause?

b. Which verb agrees with the subject?

c. What is unusual about the placement of the subject?

d. What is the subject of the second clause?

e. Which two verbs (compound verb) agree with the second subject?

f. Is the second clause independent? Why?

WRITE NOW

Do both of the following activities.

1. **Freewrite** on one of the following Writing Suggestions.

2. Write a **thesis statement** for an essay based on a main idea that you discovered during freewriting.

WRITING SUGGESTIONS

1. Discuss whether or not social agencies are effective in combating community and family problems.

2. Social work was pioneered by women and traditionally has been a career field dominated by women. Discuss the advantages and disadvantages of this historical fact.

3. One hundred years ago Hull House was located in a crowded section of Chicago, where "the older and richer inhabitants" moved away, making room for new arrivals. Answer one of the following:

   a. Discuss the positive and negative effects of this type of population shift in cities today.

   or

   b. Discuss why, despite their problems, major cities continue to attract not only immigrants, but also young people, suburbanites, and those from small town and agricultural communities.

FURTHER WRITING SUGGESTIONS

4. Explain how a community or after school center, "Y," or similar neighborhood resource supports the appreciation of and participation in the performing and fine arts, and so on.

5. Compare and contrast the working conditions existing in Chicago's Hull House neighborhood in 1893 with those in a similar urban setting today.

6. Some countries require all young people between the ages of eighteen and twenty-one to devote at least one year to community or public service. Do you agree or disagree with this policy? Explain your answer.

THE PROMISED LAND

By Mary Antin

Mary Antin (1881–1949) was born in the Jewish section of Polotzk, a small town in Russia. Her father emigrated to Boston, Massachusetts, in 1891, but it was not until three years later that the rest of the family was able to join him in the United States.

In 1912 Antin completed *The Promised Land,* an autobiography. The book describes life in czarist Russia as a mix of poverty, mental depression, isolation, and stifled opportunity. On the other hand, the United States is presented as a place where, despite life's hardships, individuals have opportunities for self-fulfillment and personal success.

Beyond this, *The Promised Land* is a powerful statement of the benefits that the United States provides for its immigrants, and of the cultural enrichment that the immigrants bring to the United States.

WORDS TO NOTICE

wrought: shaped, brought about

comrades in adoption: new immigrants

rehearsal: rehearing, repeat

sober: serious

wherewith: with which

hew: cut

songs of David: Book of Psalms

utter reverence: total respect

formerly: before, previously

detained: kept for a short period

Day of Atonement: Yom Kippur, the holiest of the Jewish holidays

mimicry: close imitation

precept: principle

incarnation: bodily form

piety: devotion to religious principles

inimitable: not capable of being imitated

irreproachable: blameless, not capable of being criticized

paradoxical: contradictory

consequence: importance

naturalization: legal process of becoming a citizen

glutton: greedy eater

advent: arrival, coming

common: public park or open area

in very earnest: in great seriousness

READ ON

1. What do the title and **headnote** of Antin's autobiography suggest to you?

2. While rereading this selection, **find** the indications of Antin's joy in her new land.

The public school has done its best for us foreigners, and for the country, 1
when it has made us into good Americans. I am glad it is mine to tell how
the miracle was wrought in one case. You should be glad to hear of it, you
born Americans; for it is the story of the growth of your country; of the flocking
of your brothers and sisters from the far ends of the earth to the flag you love;
of the recruiting of your armies of workers, thinkers, and leaders. And you
will be glad to hear of it, my comrades in adoption; for it is a rehearsal of
your own experience, the thrill and wonder of which your own hearts have
felt.

How long would you say, wise reader, it takes to make an American? By 2
the middle of my second year in school I had reached the sixth grade. When,
after the Christmas holidays, we began to study the life of Washington, running
through a summary of the Revolution, and the early days of the Republic, it
seemed to me that all my reading and study had been idle until then. The

reader, the arithmetic, the song book, that had so fascinated me until now, became suddenly sober exercise books, tools wherewith to hew a way to the source of inspiration. When the teacher read to us out of a big book with many bookmarks in it, I sat rigid with attention in my little chair, my hands tightly clasped on the edge of my desk; and I painfully held my breath, to prevent sighs of disappointment escaping, as I saw the teacher skip the parts between bookmarks. When the class read, and it came my turn, my voice shook and the book trembled in my hands. I could not pronounce the name of George Washington without a pause. Never had I prayed, never had I chanted the songs of David, never had I called upon the Most Holy, in such utter reverence and worship as I repeated the simple sentences of my child's story of the patriot. I gazed with adoration at the portraits of George and Martha Washington, till I could see them with my eyes shut. And whereas formerly my self-consciousness had bordered on conceit, and I thought myself an uncommon person, parading my schoolbooks through the streets, and swelling with pride when a teacher detained me in conversation, now I grew humble all at once, seeing how insignificant I was beside the Great.

As I read about the noble boy who would not tell a lie to save himself **3** from punishment, I was for the first time truly repentant of my sins. Formerly I had fasted and prayed and made sacrifice on the Day of Atonement, but it was more than half play, in mimicry of my elders. I had no real horror of sin, and I knew so many ways of escaping punishment. I am sure my family, my neighbors, my teachers in Polotzk—all my world, in fact—strove together, by example and precept, to teach me goodness. Saintliness had a new in-

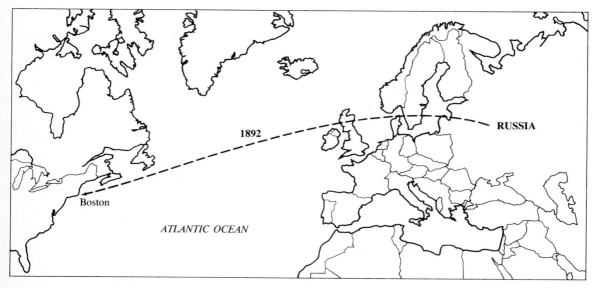

From Russia across the Atlantic to Boston

carnation in about every third person I knew. I did respect the saints, but I could not help seeing that most of them were a little bit stupid, and that mischief was much more fun than piety. Goodness, as I had known it, was respectable, but not necessarily admirable. The people I really admired, like my Uncle Solomon, and Cousin Rachel, were those who preached the least and laughed the most. My sister Frieda was perfectly good, but she did not think the less of me because I played tricks. What I loved in my friends was not inimitable. One could be downright good if one really wanted to. One could be learned if one had books and teachers. One could sing funny songs and tell anecdotes if one travelled about and picked up such things, like one's uncles and cousins. But a human being strictly good, perfectly wise, and unfailingly valiant, all at the same time, I had never heard or dreamed of. This wonderful George Washington was as inimitable as he was irreproachable. Even if I had never, never told a lie, I could not compare myself to George Washington; for I was not brave—I was afraid to go out when snowballs whizzed—and I could never be the First President of the United States.

So I was forced to revise my own estimate of myself. But the twin of my   **4** new-born humility, paradoxical as it may seem, was a sense of dignity I had never known before. For if I found that I was a person of small consequence, I discovered at the same time that I was more nobly related than I had ever supposed. I had relatives and friends who were notable people by the old standards,—I had never been ashamed of my family,—but this George Washington, who died long before I was born, was like a king in greatness, and he and I were Fellow Citizens. There was a great deal about Fellow Citizens in the patriotic literature we read at this time; and I knew from my father how he was a Citizen, through the process of naturalization, and how I also was a citizen, by virtue of my relation to him. Undoubtedly I was a Fellow Citizen, and George Washington was another. It thrilled me to realize what sudden greatness had fallen on me; and at the same time it sobered me, as with a sense of responsibility. I strove to conduct myself as befitted a Fellow Citizen.

Before books came into my life, I was given to stargazing and daydream-   **5** ing. When books were given me, I fell upon them as a glutton pounces on his meat after a period of enforced starvation. I lived with my nose in a book, and took no notice of the alternations of the sun and stars. But now, after the advent of George Washington and the American Revolution, I began to dream again. I strayed on the common after school instead of hurrying home to read. I hung on fence rails, my pet book forgotten under my arm, and gazed off to the yellow-streaked February sunset, and beyond, and beyond. I was no longer the central figure of my dreams; the dry weeds in the lane crackled beneath the tread of Heroes.

What more could America give a child? Ah, much more! As I read how   **6** the patriots planned the Revolution, and the women gave their sons to die in battle, and the heroes led to victory, and the rejoicing people set up the Republic, it dawned on me gradually what was meant by *my country*. The people all desiring noble things, and striving for them together, defying their oppressors, giving their lives for each other—all this it was that made *my country.* It was not a thing that I *understood;* I could not go home and tell Frieda about it, as I told her other things I learned at school. But I knew one could say "my country" and *feel* it, as one felt "God" or "myself." My teacher, my schoolmates, Miss Dillingham, George Washington himself could not mean more than I when they said "my country," after I had once felt it. For the Country was for all the Citizens, and *I was a Citizen.* And when we stood up to sing "America," I shouted the words with all my might. I was in very earnest proclaiming to the world my love for my new-found country.

IN YOUR OWN VOICE

WHAT DOES IT SAY?

1. What is the best thing the public school has done?

2. What effect does the name of George Washington have on Antin?

3. Which of Washington's qualities does Antin most admire?

4. How does her father become a United States citizen?

5. What does Antin think "made *my country*"?

WHAT DOES IT MEAN?

1. Why is becoming an American of great importance to Antin?

2. Why does Antin compare her "utter reverence" for George Washington with her prayers?

3. Why does Antin consider goodness "not necessarily admirable"?

4. How does the term *Fellow Citizen* affect Antin's behavior and thinking?

5. How does the knowledge of American heroes affect Antin?

6. Would all immigrants be as optimistic as Antin? Why?

STYLE AND SENSE

1. What is the main idea of the opening paragraph?

2. What is the purpose of the question at the beginning of paragraph 2?

3. How do paragraphs 2 through 5 develop the main idea?

4. What is the purpose of the question at the beginning of paragraph 6?

5. Which repeated words of the closing paragraph emphasize the main idea?

FROM THE TEXT

Read the following sentence:

My sister Frieda was perfectly good, but she did not think the less of me because I played tricks.

a. Identify the two independent clauses.

b. Which coordinating conjunction introduces the second independent clause?

c. Is there any punctuation mark before the second independent clause? Why?

d. Identify the dependent clause.

e. Which subordinating conjunction introduces the dependent clause?

f. Is there any punctuation before the dependent clause? Why?

See page 465 for more on comma use to separate clauses.

WRITE NOW

Do both of the following activities.

1. Make a **brainstorm** list of the word *citizen*.

2. Use the brainstorm list to write a **topic sentence** of a paragraph for one of the following Writing Suggestions.

WRITING SUGGESTIONS

1. Discuss the courses or subjects you would take to become a better citizen.

2. Explain how a "sense of dignity" develops from a combination of personal qualities and social conditions.

3. This selection is from a chapter entitled "My Country." Discuss why a new land has such a hold on immigrants.

FURTHER WRITING SUGGESTIONS

4. Most countries allow immigrants to become citizens. Explain why immigrants would or would not want to become citizens of the country they are living in.

5. Antin values education greatly. Discuss one of the following:

    a. Whether a public school education prepares students for their future.

or

    b. If a college education can equalize opportunities for success.

6. In *The Promised Land,* Antin praises George Washington. Discuss the barriers faced by a woman seeking election as the leader of her nation today.

7. Discuss whether it is better for an immigrant to settle in a big city or in a small town.

ALL POLITICS IS LOCAL

By Thomas P. O'Neill

Thomas P. ("Tip") O'Neill (born 1912) became the elected Speaker of the United States House of Representatives in 1977, serving for a decade.

Exactly fifty years earlier on a June day in 1927, the fourteen-year-old O'Neill, working as a groundskeeper at Harvard University, observed the graduating class. He vowed, "I would work to make sure my people could go to places like Harvard."

In this selection, the lifelong Democrat recalls his Irish heritage and how his career evolved from the neighborhood political system of his day.

WORDS TO NOTICE

potato famine: agricultural disaster in Ireland in the 1840s that caused nearly a million deaths, leading to increased immigration to the United States

picks: pointed tools for breaking up ground and hard surfaces

kiln: oven for hardening and drying bricks

tram: open car on rails designed for hauling

Brahmins: upper-class society, aristocracy

Yankees: New Englanders, Brahmins

Gaelic: Irish language

Cork: a city in Ireland

redcoats: British soldiers in the American Revolution

skirmishes: minor battles

commemorated: honored, served as a memorial to

menial: insignificant, lowly

literally: actually

bigoted: prejudiced, biased

run on bank: sudden, mass withdrawal of funds by depositors

READ ON

1. While you read this selection for the first time, jot down **margin notes** on words, phrases, or situations involving prejudice.

2. While rereading, what did you **discover** about ways to deal with prejudice?

I knew I was Irish even before I knew I was American. Back in 1845, my grandfather and his two brothers had been brought over from Ireland by the New England Brick Company. I still have a deed for the plot that my grandfather bought in the Cambridge cemetery. The immigrants had seen so much death during the potato famine that the first thing they did when they came to America was to buy a plot to be buried in—just in case.   1

My grandfather settled in North Cambridge and worked in the brickyards, where they made bricks with nothing more than picks, shovels, and wheelbarrows. They would mix the clay, soften it, throw it in the kiln, and then bake the bricks. My father was born in 1874, and as a young man he, too, worked in the brickyards—digging with a pick and an ax and loading the clay on a tram, with a horse to pull it up the slope from the pit.   2

But the Irish didn't want their kids in the clay pits, and by around 1900 these jobs were taken over by the French Canadians. Twenty years later it was the Italians, with each successive generation moving their own kids out and getting them educated as clergymen, lawyers, or doctors. Banking and insurance, however, remained closed to the ethnics. The old aristocracy, the Brahmins of Boston, the Yankees, held those for themselves.   3

There was one section of our neighborhood, around Clay Street and Montgomery, where some of the old-timers still spoke Gaelic. But they never encouraged their kids to speak it, because we in the younger generation were expected to be "real" Americans.   4

Still, at the age of seven I was sent to Gaelic school, which met on Sunday afternoons. We learned a few Gaelic phrases and a couple of songs and step dances, but my Irish education didn't last very long. In 1920 Terrence MacSweeney, the lord mayor of Cork, died of a hunger strike. Our teacher   5 was MacSweeney's sister-in-law, and on the following Sunday she wouldn't allow me back. Because my parents had been born in America, I was considered a "narrowback"—somebody who wasn't really fit for good labor. And narrowbacks were no longer welcome at the MacSweeneys'.

We had a tremendous hatred of the English. In addition to our fierce Irish   6
pride, there was our American heritage as well. Kids in other cities were playing cops and robbers, or cowboys and Indians, but with us it was patriots and redcoats. During the Revolutionary War there had been skirmishes right in our own neighborhood between the British soldiers and the colonials. There was a store on Massachusetts Avenue on the spot where the redcoats had cut through as they rode into Cambridge from Arlington, and every day we passed by the stone markers that commemorated the dead. Bunker Hill, the Old North Church, the U.S.S. *Constitution,* Paul Revere's house, the site of the Boston Tea Party—these were familiar landmarks, and we felt a firsthand connection to the brave men and women who fought the American Revolution. This wasn't just history; it was real life.

One of the favorite topics in our neighborhood was how the Yankees in   7
Boston had burned down the Ursuline Convent over in Charlestown, just a few miles from where we lived. People would talk about that terrible deed, about what the Protestant Yankees had done to those poor Irish Catholic nuns, and they'd stir themselves up into a frenzy.

I heard so much about that incident that one day, when I was in my teens,   8
I decided to look it up in a book. To my shock, the burning of the convent had occurred back in the summer of 1834! But to hear people talk about it, you would have thought it happened the day before yesterday.

But not all of our problems with the English were in the past. There were   9
businesses in Boston that needed employees but put up signs in the windows saying NINA, which, as we all knew, meant No Irish Need Apply. And each year on Easter Sunday, men in our neighborhood would go from door to door, collecting money for the Irish Republican Army. On the front window of almost every house you would see a sticker: "I gave to the Army." In those days, of course, the IRA was a very different organization from what it is today; back then, it simply stood for the united freedom of Ireland.

More than any other group I know of, the Irish in this country have used   10
the ballot box to improve their lives. When I was growing up, one of the real powers in Boston politics was an Irishman named Martin Lomasney, who worked out of the Hendricks Club in the West End. It was said that Martin would meet the new immigrants at the boat and take them straight over to register to vote. Then he'd bring them over to the gas works and get them a job. Finally, he'd take them to the West End and he'd show them where they were going to live until they had earned enough money to find their own place.

The old-timers used to tell stories of how Martin would greet them at the   11
polls on election day. "Here's your ballot," he'd say. "I've already marked it

for you. When you get in there, pick up the ballot they give you and give them back this one." When you came out you'd give Martin the clean ballot, and he'd mark it off and give it to the next guy in line.

In the 1930s, when I first entered politics, all the financial institutions in   **12** the city of Boston were closed to my people. Today, of course, that's only a bad memory. It was the politicians who made the difference, who took their people out of the menial jobs and gave them better opportunities.

I'm proud that I was able to play a role in that process. Although it   **13** happened gradually, there was one occasion when I literally used my political power to force a change in the system. In 1950, when I was Speaker of the Massachusetts Legislature, I had business to attend to one day in the North Avenue Savings Bank in North Cambridge. As I was climbing the stairs, I saw a fellow coming down with tears in his eyes.

"What's the matter?" I asked him.   **14**

"You're Tip O'Neill, aren't you?" he said. "Then you probably know my   **15** father, Billy Askin. We're from Worcester, and he used to be in the State House."

"Sure I know your father," I said. "But what happened to you?"   **16**

"Last week I gave up my job at another bank because this place promised   **17** to make me a vice president. But this morning, when I came in, they found out I was a Catholic and now they won't hire me. So instead of a promotion, I'm out of a job!"

I was furious. I ran up the stairs and into the office of the bank president,   **18** a German fellow named Karstein, whose family had run the local coal-and-oil company back when Cambridge was a Yankee town.

"Mr. Karstein," I said, "my name is Tip O'Neill."   **19**

"Yeah? What do you want?"   **20**

"I'm the Speaker of the Massachusetts legislature and I'm also your local   **21** representative. I grew up around here, and when I went to St. John's Grammar School, every Tuesday we'd put a dime in the bank. Today, all my children have accounts in this bank, and so do most of the people in North Cambridge. Our St. Vincent de Paul fund at the church has thirty-three thousand dollars on deposit here.

"Now I understand that you just refused to hire a man because he's   **22** Catholic. I can't believe it, and I'm going to give you until Monday to change your mind. If my friend doesn't get the job, I'm going to walk the streets from here to Fresh Pond Parkway, and I'm going to tell every person I meet along the way that you're a bigoted son of a bitch who won't hire Catholics. And I can guarantee you'll have the biggest run on your bank that you've ever seen in your life!"

When I returned to the bank a few days later, Billy Askin's son was sitting   **23** in his office as the new vice president. There was also a new teller named O'Connor, and a third Catholic whose name I no longer remember. A lot had changed since that commencement day at Harvard in 1927.

IN YOUR OWN VOICE

WHAT DOES IT SAY?

1. What is the first job in America for O'Neill's grandfather?

2. Who control the banking and insurance industries?

3. Which childhood game do O'Neill and his friends play?

4. What does NINA mean?

5. How does Martin Lomasney ensure that new immigrants will vote the way he wants them to?

6. Why does O'Neill confront the bank president?

WHAT DOES IT MEAN?

1. What does O'Neill mean when he says, "I knew I was Irish even before I knew I was American"?

2. Why does O'Neill say, "We had a tremendous hatred of the English"?

3. Why do people in O'Neill's neighborhood still talk about the burning of the Ursuline Convent?

4. How does the ballot box offer opportunities for advancement for the Irish?

5. What makes a local politician effective?

STYLE AND SENSE

Topic sentence: A sentence expressing the one main idea of a paragraph. The topic sentence announces that what follows will develop this idea in more specific detail.

1. Identify the topic sentence of paragraph 1.

2. How is this topic sentence developed in paragraphs 1, 2, and 3?

3. Identify the topic sentence of paragraph 6.

4. Which details in paragraph 6 develop the topic sentence?

5. Identify the topic sentence in paragraph 10.

6. How is this topic sentence developed in paragraphs 10, 11, and 12?

FROM THE TEXT

Read the following sentence:

The old aristocracy, the Brahmins of Boston, the Yankees, held those for themselves.

a. What is the subject of the verb *held*?

b. Which other nouns identify the subject?

c. Can these nouns be omitted from the sentence without changing its basic meaning?

d. Which marks of punctuation appear between the related nouns?

See page 468 for more on comma use with phrases that come between subject and verb.

WRITE NOW

Do both of the following activities.

1. Make a list of **journalistic questions** about local politics.

2. Use the list of journalistic questions to write the **first draft** of an opening paragraph for one of the following Writing Suggestions.

WRITING SUGGESTIONS

1. O'Neill writes, "I knew I was Irish even before I knew I was American." Identify the group or groups of which you are a member. Discuss the qualities or characteristics that define the group or groups.

2. This selection appears in a chapter entitled "All Politics Is Local." Explain how local politicians can help people in their communities.

3. O'Neill believes that the doors of opportunity in the United States continually open to each successive generation (paragraph 3). Explain how this optimistic view can benefit you as an individual.

FURTHER WRITING SUGGESTIONS

4. Define *prejudice* and explain why it exists.

5. O'Neill mentions Boston landmarks that give him and his friends "a firsthand

connection" to U.S. history. Describe how you felt a link to the past when you visited a landmark or specific place.

6. Discuss the role or importance of ethnic pride in a multicultural society.

A BIRD IN THE HOUSE
By Margaret Laurence

Margaret Laurence (1926–1987), one of Canada's finest writers, was born in the small prairie town of Neepawa, Manitoba. She recreated that town, calling it Manawaka in a series of four novels.

Laurence began writing in childhood. She developed as a novelist during her stay in the countries of Somaliland and Ghana (1949–1957). Africa became the setting of her early books.

This selection is from the title story of *A Bird in the House.* The story recreates the twelve-year-old heroine's changing feelings and family relationships on one Remembrance Day, a Canadian holiday to honor its major contributions to the winning cause in World War I (called the "Great War") at the great cost of 60,000 lives.

As one character says later in this story, "A bird in the house means a death in the house."

WORDS TO NOTICE

resigned: sorrowfully accepting

civic: municipal, city

invariably: unchangingly

chidingly: disapprovingly, scoldingly

lanky: long and thin

Blackfoot or Cree: Canadian Indian

withdrawn: isolated

a patch on: a comparison to

imposters: pretenders to jobs or titles not their own

spindly: tall and extremely thin

caricatures: distortions, exaggerations

the last Post: closing bugle call

gabbling: gabbing, chatting noisily

newel post: post at the bottom of a staircase

talons: claws

etched: marked

Great War: World War I

enormity: overwhelming seriousness

mantelpiece: shelf above a fireplace

sheath: case for a sword

poignant: deeply moving

awe: great fear and respect

simultaneously: at the same time

READ ON

1. While you read this selection for the first time, jot down **margin notes** of all instances of obeying and disobeying orders.

2. While rereading, **find** the words and phrases showing the changing relationship between Vanessa and her father.

The parade would be almost over by now, and I had not gone. My mother   1
had said in a resigned voice, "All right, Vanessa, if that's the way you feel,"
making me suffer twice as many jabs of guilt as I would have done if she had
lost her temper. She and Grandmother MacLeod had gone off, my mother
pulling the low boxsleigh with Roddie all dolled up in his new red snowsuit,
just the sort of little kid anyone would want people to see. I sat on the lowest
branch of the birch tree in our yard, not minding the snowy wind, even
welcoming its punishment. I went over my reasons for not going, trying to
believe they were good and sufficient, but in my heart I felt I was betraying
my father. This was the first time I had stayed away from the Remembrance
Day parade. I wondered if he would notice that I was not there, standing on
the sidewalk at the corner of River and Main while the parade passed, and
then following to the Court House grounds where the service was held.

I could see the whole thing in my mind. It was the same every year. The   2

Manawaka Civic Band always led the way. They had never been able to afford full uniforms, but they had peaked navy-blue caps and sky-blue chest ribbons. They were joined on Remembrance Day by the Salvation Army band, whose uniforms seemed too ordinary for a parade, for they were the same ones the bandsmen wore every Saturday night when they played "Nearer My God to Thee" at the foot of River Street. The two bands never managed to practise quite enough together, so they did not keep in time too well. The Salvation Army band invariably played faster, and afterwards my father would say irritably, "They play those marches just like they do hymns, blast them, as though they wouldn't get to heaven if they didn't hustle up." And my mother, who had great respect for the Salvation Army because of the good work they did, would respond chidingly, "Now, now, Ewen—" I vowed I would never say "Now, now" to my husband or children, not that I ever intended having the latter, for I had been put off by my brother Roderick, who was now two years old with wavy hair, and everyone said what a beautiful child. I was twelve, and no one in their right mind would have said what a beautiful child, for I was big-boned like my Grandfather Connor and had straight lanky black hair like a Blackfoot or Cree.

After the bands would come the veterans. Even thinking of them at this 3 distance, in the white and withdrawn quiet of the birch tree, gave me a sense of painful embarrassment. I might not have minded so much if my father had not been among them. How could he go? How could he not see how they all looked? It must have been a long time since they were soldiers, for they had forgotten how to march in step. They were old—that was the thing. My father was bad enough, being almost forty, but he wasn't a patch on Howard Tully from the drugstore, who was completely grey-haired and also fat, or Stewart MacMurchie, who was bald at the back of his head. They looked to me like imposters, plump or spindly caricatures of past warriors. I almost hated them for walking in that limping column down Main. At the Court House, everyone would sing *Lord God of Hosts, be with us yet, lest we forget, lest we forget.* Will Masterson would pick up his old Army bugle and blow the last Post. Then it would be over and everyone could start gabbling once more and go home.

I jumped down from the birch bough and ran to the house, yelling, making 4 as much noise as I could.

> I'm a poor lonesome cowboy
> An' a long way from home—

I stepped inside the front hall and kicked off my snow boots. I slammed the 5 door behind me, making the dark ruby and emerald glass shake in the small leaded panes. I slid purposely on the hall rug, causing it to bunch and crinkle on the slippery polished oak of the floor. I seized the newel post, round as a head, and spun myself to and fro on the bottom stair.

I ain't got no father
To buy the clothes I wear.
I'm a poor lonesome—

At this moment my shoulders were firmly seized and shaken by a pair of hands, white and delicate and old, but strong as talons.   **6**

"Just what do you think you're doing, young lady?" Grandmother MacLeod   **7**
enquired, in a voice like frost on a windowpane, infinitely cold and clearly etched.

I went limp and in a moment she took her hands away. If you struggled,   **8**
she would always hold on longer.

"Gee, I never knew you were home yet."   **9**

"I would have thought that on a day like this you might have shown a   **10**
little respect and consideration," Grandmother MacLeod said, "even if you couldn't make the effort to get cleaned up enough to go to the parade."

I realised with surprise that she imagined this to be my reason for not   **11**
going. I did not try to correct her impression. My real reason would have been even less acceptable.

"I'm sorry," I said quickly.   **12**

In some families, *please* is described as the magic word. In our house,   **13**
however, it was *sorry.*

"This isn't an easy day for any of us," she said.   **14**

Her younger son, my Uncle Roderick, had been killed in the Great War.   **15**
When my father marched, and when the hymn was sung, and when that unbearably lonely tune was sounded by the one bugle and everyone forced themselves to keep absolutely still, it would be that boy of whom she was thinking. I felt the enormity of my own offence.

"Grandmother—I'm sorry."   **16**

"So you said."   **17**

I could not tell her I had not really said it before at all. I went into the   **18**
den and found my father there. He was sitting in the leather-cushioned arm-chair beside the fireplace. He was not doing anything, just sitting and smoking. I stood beside him, wanting to touch the light-brown hairs on his forearm, but thinking he might laugh at me or pull his arm away if I did.

"I'm sorry," I said, meaning it.   **19**

"What for, honey?"   **20**

"For not going."   **21**

"Oh—that. What was the matter?"   **22**

I did not want him to know, and yet I had to tell him, make him see.   **23**

"They look silly," I blurted. "Marching like that."   **24**

For a minute I thought he was going to be angry. It would have been a   **25**
relief to me if he had been. Instead, he drew his eyes away from mine and fixed them above the mantelpiece where the sword hung, the handsome and evil-looking crescent in its carved bronze sheath that some ancestor had once brought from the Northern Frontier of India.

"Is that the way it looks to you?" he said.   26

I felt in his voice some hurt, something that was my fault. I wanted to   27
make everything all right between us, to convince him that I understood, even
if I did not. I prayed that Grandmother MacLeod would stay put in her room,
and that my mother would take a long time in the kitchen, giving Roddie his
lunch. I wanted my father to myself, so I could prove to him that I cared more
about him than any of the others did. I wanted to speak in some way that
would be more poignant and comprehending than anything of which my
mother could possibly be capable. But I did not know how.

"You were right there when Uncle Roderick got killed, weren't you?" I   28
began uncertainly.

"Yes."   29

"How old was he, Dad?"   30

"Eighteen," my father said.   31

Unexpectedly, that day came into intense being for me. He had had to   32
watch his own brother die, not in the antiseptic calm of some hospital, but
out in the open, the stretches of mud I had seen in his snapshots. He would
not have known what to do. He would just have had to stand there and look
at it, whatever that might mean. I looked at my father with a kind of horrified
awe, and then I began to cry. I had forgotten about impressing him with my
perception. Now I needed him to console me for this unwanted glimpse of
the pain he had once known.

"Hey, cut it out, honey," he said, embarrassed. "It was bad, but it wasn't   33
all as bad as that part. There were a few other things."

"Like what?" I said, not believing him.   34

"Oh—I don't know," he replied evasively. "Most of us were pretty young,   35
you know, I and the boys I joined up with. None of us had ever been away
from Manawaka before. Those of us who came back mostly came back here,
or else went no further away from town than Winnipeg. So when we were
overseas—that was the only time most of us were ever a long way from
home."

"Did you want to be?" I asked, shocked.   36

"Oh well—" my father said uncomfortably. "It was kind of interesting to   37
see a few other places for a change, that's all."

Grandmother MacLeod was standing in the doorway.   38

"Beth's called you twice for lunch, Ewen. Are you deaf, you and Vanessa?"   39

"Sorry," my father and I said simultaneously.   40

Then we went upstairs to wash our hands.   41

IN YOUR OWN VOICE

WHAT DOES IT SAY?

1. Where is Vanessa during the parade?

2. Which two bands played during the parade?

3. Who follow the bands?

4. Why is Remembrance Day painful to Grandmother MacLeod?

5. Where was Vanessa's father when Uncle Roderick was killed?

WHAT DOES IT MEAN?

1. Why doesn't Vanessa go to the parade?

2. Why is Vanessa's baby brother named Roderick?

3. Why do the marching veterans embarrass Vanessa?

4. Why does Vanessa cry after talking to her father?

5. Why do most of the veterans return to the Canadian prairies?

STYLE AND SENSE

1. How do the words "I had not gone" in the opening sentence separate Vanessa from the rest of her family?

2. In paragraphs 2 and 3, how does Vanessa's description of the marchers suggest reasons for her not going?

3. How does the conversation with Grandmother MacLeod help Vanessa to begin to understand what the day means to the family?

4. How do the closing two lines suggest that Vanessa and her father have reached an understanding?

5. How has Vanessa changed from the beginning of the story?

FROM THE TEXT

Sentence structure: a sentence can consist of one independent clause and one or several dependent clauses or phrases that might be needed to add to the information contained in the independent clause.

Read the following sentence:

I sat on the lowest branch of the birch tree in our yard, not minding the snowy wind, even welcoming its punishment.

a. What is the independent clause?

b. What are the subject and verb?

c. Which information is contained in the prepositional phrases "on the lowest branch," "of the birch tree," "in our yard"?

d. What are the two participial phrases?

e. Why are they not independent clauses?

f. Which noun or pronoun do these participial phrases modify?

See page 386 for more on the complex sentence.

WRITE NOW

Do both of the following activities.

1. After doing any prewriting activity on one of the following Writing Suggestions, write a **first draft** of an opening paragraph.

2. **Revise** the paragraph—alone or with the help of another student.

WRITING SUGGESTIONS

1. Describe a time when you realized you had begun to develop a separate personality or point of view from that of older persons in your family.

2. Discuss ways in which parent-child conflicts can be resolved successfully.

3. Discuss what is gained and what is lost when grandparents live in the same household with their children and grandchildren.

FURTHER WRITING SUGGESTIONS

4. Vanessa's father left his small town in the Canadian prairies only when he served as a soldier in World War I. Discuss why people often live out their entire lives in one locale, even when the opportunity to live elsewhere is possible.

5. Discuss whether Remembrance Day and other memorials and honors for a nation's dead help to heal an individual's or a family's or a community's loss.

6. Interview an older person. Describe his or her childhood remembrances of a holiday celebration.

A STORY ABOUT GREENERY

By Luisa Valenzuela

Many of the novels and short stories of Luisa Valenzuela (born 1938) are imaginative fantasies that confront the harsh realities of life in her beloved South America, especially her homeland of Argentina: dictatorship, repression of women, sudden violence, and the unexplained disappearances of people who in some way or another offended government authorities.

She writes about a world in which things are often not what they seem. For example, Valenzuela collected her favorite short stories in a book invitingly called *Open Door*. But she notes in the book's preface that *Open Door* is the name of a lunatic asylum in Argentina.

During Valenzuela's lifetime, Argentina has been the scene of much political turmoil: military takeovers; dictatorships, especially Juan Peron's; and occasionally and most recently, democratic elections.

This story tells of a governmental outlawing of a color. It describes a plant of that color that survives despite the decree, and people's varied responses to the presence of the plant within the walls of their city.

WORDS TO NOTICE

pampas: (in South America) vast grassy plains

subjective: based on personal feelings

objective: not influenced by personal feelings

crevices: narrow cracks in walls

thistle: plant with purple, yellow, or white flowers

thriving: growing well

eradicated: removed, eliminated

decree: governmental order

yank: tug suddenly

prickles: small thorns

self-abnegating: self-denying

engendered: created, given birth to

greenhorn: inexperienced person

proscribed: forbade, banned

evokes: brings to the surface, calls up

hypothetical: supposedly true

chlorophyll: green matter found in plants

sect: religious or political group

emblem: symbol

Scotch separatists: group supporting an independent Scotland

maté: aromatic beverage made from a plant

affinities: similarities, connections

dissident: disagreeing

amnesty: general pardon

revere: worship, adore

READ ON

1. While reading this selection for the first time, **underline** all words and phrases that refer to or suggest color.

2. While rereading, **discover** the changing responses individuals and groups have toward *green*.

Walls have been built to contain the pampas but once upon a time a little seed outdid all those massed tons of cement, even though the verb *to outdo* is highly subjective and permits a vast range of interpretations. The objective fact is this: the walls don't let even a breath of pampas greenery through but they can't keep the wind from stealing in through the crevices. The wind is individualistic and thistle seeds are stubborn, and one finally managed to float windborne through the air and land in the urban zone. Today we can see a thistle thriving in a city that has eradicated green by decree.   1

In the beginning it was easy. People avoided looking down as they turned the corner, but now that the thistle has grown—favored by rains so surprising at this time of year—it's no longer so easy to avoid that sight, especially for those who work in the nearby skyscrapers and can't help but be dazzled as they cast a sidelong glance at its green radiance.   2

The mayor is fit to be tied. He thinks of all the money spent to change the traffic lights so that they turn from red to blue, and now this . . .   3

(Nobody has the courage to yank the thistle out, even with welding glasses on, for fear of being contaminated by the color or attacked by prickles.)   4

A new decree has just appeared in the *Official Journal*, stating that un-   **5**
officially everything is permitted us, provided it doesn't lead to abuses. In this
way they hope that some self-abnegating citizen will rid us of the thistle. This
business about abuses sounds fishy; since it can be interpreted most any
way, it's better to stick to the old procedures until we get clearer instructions.
But most citizens feel liberated, a sensation almost unknown to those under
fifteen.

The state of war began in the sixties, and it was never officially ended   **6**
for the simple reason that it had never been officially declared. It's rumors
that hang heaviest over us—rumors engendered by fear, and phrases that
sometimes begin as an innocent joke then grow until they claim a great many
victims. Perhaps the best example is the color that's now unmentionable: it
all began because someone let it be known that the president didn't like
being thought a gr . . . horn in politics. Then his successor had a daughter
skinny as a rail who didn't look good in gr . . . , so it was declared unfash-
ionable. After a while the wife of a minister was seen with another man in a
park, and immediately parks, squares, and other gr . . . spaces were eliminated
from the federal district. Then the mayor I referred to earlier came along and
proscribed the pampas for reasons that were never explained, and finally the
color of the traffic lights was changed and everything would be right except
for the thistle. It disturbs many people; it evokes memories. There are even
those who allow themselves to become nostalgic about billiard tables or the
hypothetical benefits of chlorophyll. All on account of a prickly, ugly little
thistle, which even so looks radiantly beautiful to many. Moreover, a secret
sect has sprung up with the thistle as its emblem, and its members have
recently been in contact with Scotch separatists—can you imagine? They
began by pursuing noble ends: freedom from discrimination on the basis of
color or religion, and social justice and equality of the sexes. Little by little
they've become fanatics. Now they say that if they win they'll make all citizens
wear green uniforms, and the national beverage will be a soft drink made
from green maté syrup.

The government already feels certain affinities with this dissident group   **7**
and there is talk of an alliance soon. Meanwhile large groups of citizens make
pilgrimages to the sacred thistle and bring it offerings of animal manure
obtained on the black market. They have taken the clever precaution of
covering the thistle with a white cloth so as not to be dazzled by it, and are
organizing processions and singing hymns in the hope of an amnesty that
will allow them to revere the thistle as a great monument to national harmony.

IN YOUR OWN VOICE

WHAT DOES IT SAY?

1. Why did the mayor order the walls to be built?

2. What was the only green thing in the city?

3. Why was the mayor "fit to be tied"?

4. Which rumors led to the banishment of green?

5. What were the original goals of the secret sect?

WHAT DOES IT MEAN?

1. Why was the government afraid of the pampas?

2. Why was the wind described as "individualistic"?

3. Why did the city residents at first accept the decree against green?

4. Why did they later change their minds?

5. Why is it a danger to "make all citizens wear green uniforms"?

STYLE AND SENSE

In the story, the physical characteristics of the city are described directly. The world beyond the city limits is only hinted at.

1. List at least three words that describe the city or parts of it as hard or solid or with sharp corners.

2. Why is the city described this way?

3. List the words that describe nature or natural things.

4. What qualities or characteristics of nature are suggested by these descriptive words?

FROM THE TEXT

Read the following sentence fragment:

All on account of a prickly, ugly thistle, which even so looks radiantly beautiful to many.

a. Why is it a fragment?

b. Adding words, rewrite as a complete sentence.

c. Adding and changing words, rewrite as *two* complete sentences.

See page 401 for more on the sentence fragment.

WRITE NOW

Do both of the following activities.

1. Write a **thesis statement** as part of an opening paragraph for one of the following Writing Suggestions.

2. **Revise** the paragraph—alone or with the help of another student.

WRITING SUGGESTIONS

1. Discuss the importance of greenery in a city.

2. Explain why a governmental policy based on color discrimination does not make sense.

3. Individuals give up total freedom in order to live with their fellow human beings in society. For example, people generally obey traffic signals. Answer one of the following:

   a. Discuss why people obey laws that they believe to be just.

or

   b. Discuss why people obey laws that they believe to be unjust.

FURTHER WRITING SUGGESTIONS

4. In the story, nature is a positive, life-giving force. Describe how one natural phenomenon, like rain, wind, fire, and so on, is both beneficial and harmful.

5. Explain why the banning of a particular movie, record, book, or other creative work often creates increased interest in that work.

6. Valenzuela writes of a city in which the younger residents have never experienced freedom. Describe the kind of society in which young people would feel liberated.

UNIT 8

W. Eugene Smith. *Monsanto Inspector.* 1952. *Life Magazine.* Time Warner Inc.

PROMISE AND PERIL

The twentieth century has seen great scientific discoveries and advances. Yet with each scientific or technological gain, there seemed to come along a threat to human existence.

Three of the selections in this unit are personal accounts of events that changed the way people live and think. Another selection imagines an unnaturally silent and dying world.

The unit begins with the diary entry of Orville Wright on the day he and his brother Wilbur became the first to fly an airplane.

Next is a reporter's description of the first atomic bomb explosion at Los Alamos, New Mexico, in 1945, the beginning of the nuclear age.

This is followed by the first chapter of Rachel Carson's *Silent Spring,* entitled "A Fable for Tomorrow," in which pesticides slowly but surely bring an end to nature's bounty and animal life.

Also included is a vivid description of the tension and excitement on earth and in space the day U.S. astronauts first set foot on the moon.

The unit ends with a survey of the perils to the lives of very young children in the Americas and the promising steps being taken to assure them of full and healthy lives.

BEFORE YOU READ

How has the world changed over the past hundred years?

How will it change in your lifetime?

Should money be spent to solve problems on earth or to explore outer space?

Have you ever flown in a plane? If not, why not?

Have you ever visited the Smithsonian Institution in Washington, D.C.?

What qualities are needed to be a successful inventor?

What do you know about the atomic bomb attacks on Hiroshima and Nagasaki in 1945?

How did these bombings change the world forever?

How did the bombings appear to the Japanese? To the rest of the world?

What do you know about the first person to set foot on the moon?

Should space missions continue in the wake of the *Challenger* tragedy?

Would you volunteer for a trip to outer space?

What threats to the environment exist today?

What should the government do to protect the air we breathe and the water we drink?

What should individuals and private organizations do to preserve the environment?

Will the twenty-first century hold promise or peril for you?

THE WRIGHT BROTHERS AT KITTY HAWK*

By Orville Wright

On December 17, 1903, near Kitty Hawk, North Carolina, Orville (1871–1948) and Wilbur (1867–1912) Wright made the first successful flights in a power-driven airplane with a person aboard.

*Editors' title

Just ten years before, the Wrights had begun to learn about and to design aircraft, using the facilities of their bicycle business in Dayton, Ohio. Writing to his father in 1900, Wilbur stated, "It is my belief that flight is possible and while I am taking up the investigation for pleasure rather than profit, I think there is a slight possibility of achieving fame and fortune from it."

Orville Wright's diary entry dramatically recreates that momentous day in world history.

WORDS TO NOTICE

anemometers: instruments that measure the force of the wind

truck: a wheeled open vehicle that carried the plane

rudder: a vertical piece in the plane's tail used for steering

dart: move suddenly and rapidly

ways: tracks

gust: sudden, forceful wind

sidled: moved sideways

lateral: of or to the side

hummock: small, rounded hill

pitching: tossing in alternate directions

jar: jolt

spars: upright poles

ribs: narrow, curved parts

READ ON

1. While reading this diary entry for the first time, **underline** the words and phrases dealing with obstacles to a successful flight.

2. While rereading, **discover**—alone or with another student—ways in which these obstacles were overcome.

Thursday, December 17, 1903

When we got up a wind of between 20 and 25 miles was blowing from the north. We got the machine out early and put out the signal for the men at the station. Before we were quite ready, John T. Daniels, W. S. Dough,

A. D. Etheridge, W. C. Brinkley of Manteo, and Johnny Moore of Nags Head arrived. After running the engine and propellers a few minutes to get them in working order, I got on the machine at 10:35 for the first trial. The wind, according to our anemometers at this time, was blowing a little over 20 miles (corrected) 27 miles according to the Government anemometer at Kitty Hawk. On slipping the rope the machine started off increasing in speed to probably 7 or 8 miles. The machine lifted from the truck just as it was entering on the fourth rail. Mr. Daniels took a picture just as it left the tracks. I found the control of the front rudder quite difficult on account of its being balanced too near the center and thus had a tendency to turn itself when started so that the rudder was turned too far on one side and then too far on the other. As a result the machine would rise suddenly to about 10 ft. and then as suddenly, on turning the rudder, dart for the ground. A sudden dart when out about 100 feet from the end of the tracks ended the flight. Time about 12 seconds (not known exactly as watch was not promptly stopped). The lever for throwing off the engine was broken, and the skid under the rudder cracked. After repairs, at 20 min. after 11 o'clock Will made the second trial. The course was about like mine, up and down but a little longer over the ground though about the same in time. Dist. not measured but about 175 ft. Wind speed not quite so strong. With the aid of the station men present, we picked the machine up and carried it back to the starting ways. At about 20 minutes till 12 o'clock I made the third trial. When out about the same distance as Will's, I met with a strong gust from the left which raised the left wing and sidled the machine off to the right in a lively manner. I immediately turned the rudder to bring the machine down and then worked the end control. Much to our surprise, on reaching the ground the left wing struck first, showing the lateral control of this machine much more effective than on any of our former ones. At the time of its sidling it had raised to a height of probably 12 to 14 feet. At just 12 o'clock Will started on the fourth and last trip. The machine started off with its ups and downs as it had before, but by the time he had gone over three or four hundred feet he had it under much better control, and was traveling on a fairly even course. It proceeded in this manner till it reached a small hummock out about 800 feet from the starting ways, when it began

Kitty Hawk, North Carolina

its pitching again and suddenly darted into the ground. The front rudder frame was badly broken up, but the main frame suffered none at all. The distance over the ground was 852 feet in 59 seconds. The engine turns was 1071, but this included several seconds while on the starting ways and probably about a half second after landing. The jar of landing had set the watch on machine back so that we have no exact record for the 1071 turns. Will took a picture of my third flight just before the gust struck the machine. The machine left the ways successfully at every trial, and the tail was never caught by the truck as we had feared.

After removing the front rudder, we carried the machine back to camp. **2** We set the machine down a few feet west of the building, and while standing about discussing the last flight, a sudden gust of wind struck the machine and started to turn it over. All rushed to stop it. Will who was near one end ran to the front, but too late to do any good. Mr. Daniels and myself seized spars at the rear, but to no purpose. The machine gradually turned over on us. Mr. Daniels, having had no experience in handling a machine of this kind, hung on to it from the inside, and as a result was knocked down and turned over and over with it as it went. His escape was miraculous, as he was in with the engine and chains. The engine legs were all broken off, the chain guides badly bent, a number of uprights, and nearly all the rear ends of the ribs were broken. One spar only was broken.

After dinner we went to Kitty Hawk to send off telegram to M. W. While **3** there we called on Capt. and Mrs. Hobbs, Dr. Cogswell and the station men.

IN YOUR OWN VOICE

WHAT DOES IT SAY?

1. What is the machine?

2. What is the plane's speed during the first flight?

3. How long does the first flight last?

4. Who pilots the plane during the second flight?

5. How far does the plane go on its longest flight?

6. What altitude does the plane reach?

WHAT DOES IT MEAN?

1. Why are wind conditions important that morning?

2. Why does Mr. Daniels photograph the event?

3. Although the four flights last fewer than two minutes, why do the brothers need ninety minutes to complete them?

4. What is remarkable about the statement "we picked the machine up and carried it back to the starting ways"?

STYLE AND SENSE

Diary: a written, personal daily record of thoughts and events. The word *diary* is derived from the Latin word meaning "day"; similarly, the word *journal* is derived from the French word meaning "day."

1. Why is the opening sentence a good way to begin a diary?

2. How does the mention of the exact takeoff time of each flight contribute to the narrative's effectiveness?

3. Why are all four flights described in one long paragraph?

4. Why does Wright start a second paragraph? A third paragraph?

5. Why does Wright alternate the pronouns *we* and *I*?

FROM THE TEXT

Sentence fragment: a portion of a sentence that has been punctuated as if it were a complete sentence. A complete sentence requires subject, verb, and independent clause.

Read the following:

Dist. not measured but about 175 ft. Wind speed not quite so strong.

a. Which requirement for a complete sentence is absent in both fragments?

b. Correct each fragment by adding the missing requirement.

c. Why were two additions needed in the first fragment?

d. Why is a fragment more acceptable in a diary than in an essay or other more formal writing?

See page 401 for more on the sentence fragment.

WRITE NOW

Do both of the following activities.

1. Make a list of **journalistic questions** about the events of December 17, 1903.

2. Use the list of journalistic questions to write a **first draft** of an opening paragraph for one of the following Writing Suggestions.

WRITING SUGGESTIONS

1. Describe your thoughts and experiences on the day of your first airplane flight. You may wish to include details of the airport and plane and preparations for the flight.

2. The airplane is the fastest way to travel, yet many people prefer to go long distances by car, bus, train, or ship. Compare and contrast the advantages and disadvantages of two of these means of transportation.

3. Imagine you are Orville Wright. Write a diary entry for either the day before this first flight or the day after.

FURTHER WRITING SUGGESTIONS

4. Like other important inventions, the airplane has changed the ways people and nations around the world live, act, and think. Answer one of the following:

   a. Discuss how the military use of the airplane has affected and continues to affect life on this planet.

   or

   b. Discuss how the airplane has affected and continues to affect business and commerce, personal travel, or international relations.

5. Discuss how a specific invention has changed people's lives.

6. Each person is born with a unique gift or talent. Explain what your gift is and tell how you may develop it in the future for pleasure or profit.

DAWN OVER ZERO: THE STORY OF THE ATOMIC BOMB

By William L. Laurence

On July 16, 1945, during World War II, in a remote area of New Mexico, a group of scientists and members of the military waited at dawn for the first testing of the atomic bomb.

The *New York Times* correspondent William L. Laurence was an observer that morning. His description captures the awesome reality and power of the explosion. Surprisingly, the immense destructive force of the bomb is not high-lighted or emphasized in the account of that July day.

Less than one month later, President Harry Truman ordered the atomic bombing of Japan. On August 6, a bomb was dropped on Hiroshima, killing more than 100,000 people. On August 9, a second bomb was dropped on Nagasaki. The next day Japan surrendered.

WORDS TO NOTICE

reigned: ruled

luminosity: brightness

fleeting: brief

corona: small circle of surrounding light

doomsday: end of the world

millisecond: a thousandth of a second

supramundane: otherworldly

convulsively: violently

interval: time period between events

silhouettes: dark outlines

phenomena: remarkable forces

blockbusters: giant bombs

simultaneously: at the same time

reverberated: echoed

hitherto: earlier

evolutionary: gradually developing

telescoped: compressed, condensed in time

metamorphosed: changed

READ ON

1. What does the **headnote** say about the atomic bomb in the first month of its existence?

2. While reading this selection for the first time, jot down **margin notes** on your responses.

Suddenly, at 5.29.50, as we stood huddled around our radio, we heard a voice 1
ringing through the darkness, sounding as though it had come from above
the clouds: "Zero minus ten seconds!" A green flare flashed out through the
clouds, descended slowly, opened, grew dim, and vanished into the darkness.

The voice from the clouds boomed out again: "Zero minus three sec- 2
onds!" Another green flare came down. Silence reigned over the desert. We
kept moving in small groups in the direction of Zero. From the east came the
first faint signs of dawn.

And just at that instant there rose from the bowels of the earth a light not 3
of this world, the light of many suns in one. It was a sunrise such as the
world had never seen, a great green super-sun climbing in a fraction of a
second to a height of more than eight thousand feet, rising ever higher until
it touched the clouds, lighting up earth and sky all around with a dazzling
luminosity.

Up it went, a great ball of fire about a mile in diameter, changing colors 4
as it kept shooting upward, from deep purple to orange, expanding, growing
bigger, rising as it expanded, an elemental force freed from its bonds after
being chained for billions of years. For a fleeting instant the color was unearthly
green, such as one sees only in the corona of the sun during a total eclipse.
It was as though the earth had opened and the skies had split. One felt as
though one were present at the moment of creation when God said: "Let there
be light."

To another observer, Professor George B. Kistiakowsky of Harvard, the 5
spectacle was "the nearest thing to doomsday that one could possibly imagine. I am sure," he said, "that at the end of the world—in the last millisecond
of the earth's existence—the last man will see what we have just seen!"

A great cloud rose from the ground and followed the trail of the great 6
sun. At first it was a giant column, which soon took the shape of a supramundane mushroom. For a fleeting instant it took the form of the Statue of
Liberty magnified many times. Up it went, higher, higher, a giant mountain
born in a few seconds instead of millions of years, quivering convulsively. It
touched the multicolored clouds, pushed its summit through them, kept rising
until it reached a height of 41,000 feet, 12,000 feet higher than the earth's
highest mountain.

All through this very short but extremely long time-interval not a sound 7
was heard. I could see the silhouettes of human forms motionless in little
groups, like desert plants in the dark. The newborn mountain in the distance,
a giant among the pygmies of the Sierra Oscuro Range, stood leaning at an
angle against the clouds, a vibrant volcano spouting fire to the sky.

Then out of the great silence came a mighty thunder. For a brief interval 8
the phenomena we had seen as light repeated themselves in terms of sound.
It was the blast from thousands of blockbusters going off simultaneously at
one spot. The thunder reverberated all through the desert, bounced back and
forth from the Sierra Oscuro, echo upon echo. The ground trembled under
our feet as in an earthquake. A wave of hot wind was felt by many of us just
before the blast and warned us of its coming.

The big boom came about one hundred seconds after the great flash—   9
the first cry of a newborn world. It brought the silent, motionless silhouettes
to life, gave them a voice. A loud cry filled the air. The little groups that had
hitherto stood rooted to the earth like desert plants broke into a dance—the
rhythm of primitive man dancing at one of his fire festivals at the coming of
spring. They clapped their hands as they leaped from the ground—earthbound
man symbolizing the birth of a new force that for the first time gives man
means to free himself from the gravitational pull of the earth that holds him
down.

The dance of the primitive man lasted but a few seconds, during which   10
an evolutionary period of about 10,000 years had been telescoped. Primitive
man was metamorphosed into modern man—shaking hands, slapping his
fellow on the back, all laughing like happy children.

The sun was just rising above the horizon as our caravan started on its   11
way back to Albuquerque and Los Alamos. We looked at it through our dark
lenses to compare it with what we had seen.

"The sun can't hold a candle to it!" one of us remarked.   12

IN YOUR OWN VOICE

WHAT DOES IT SAY?

1. Which repeated signal overhead warns that the atomic explosion is about
   to occur?

2. To what is the light of the blast compared?

3. What are the shapes taken by the great cloud as it rises?

4. To what is the sound of the blast compared?

5. How do the observers react to the explosion?

WHAT DOES IT MEAN?

1. Why is the light "not of this world"?

2. Why does one observer think of doomsday?

3. Why is there silence when the blast is first seen?

4. Why does Laurence describe the blast as "the first cry of a newborn world"?

STYLE AND SENSE

This eyewitness account describes an event new in human history. To give the reader a vivid picture and understanding of this remarkable moment, Laurence blends the senses of sight and sound to convey the amazing reality of what he saw and heard.

1. How does the last word in each of the first four paragraphs emphasize the transition to a new age?

2. List details in paragraphs 5 through 12 that reinforce the contrast between light and dark.

3. How does the emphasis on the flow of colors in paragraph 4 make the reader see and understand the event?

4. How do the first sentences in paragraphs 7 through 9 emphasize the transition to a new age?

5. How does the statement "The sun can't hold a candle to it!" serve as a fitting conclusion to the description?

FROM THE TEXT

Read the following sentences:

> Another green flare came down. Silence reigned over the desert.

a. Combine the two sentences with a coordinating conjunction.

b. Combine the two sentences with a subordinating conjunction between the clauses.

c. Combine the two sentences with a subordinating conjunction as the first word.

See page 389 for more on preventing run-on sentences.

WRITE NOW

Do both of the following activities.

1. Choose one of the following Writing Suggestions. Narrow the subject matter by writing a paragraph that focuses on one detail or important idea.

2. **Revise** the paragraph—alone or with the help of another student.

WRITING SUGGESTIONS

1. For nearly fifty years, everyone on earth has been living in the atomic age. Discuss how you and your family's daily behavior and future plans have been or have not been affected by the possibility of a nuclear war or accident.

2. Describe what it would be like to be a survivor after a nuclear war.

3. Explain how the existence of nuclear bombs and other nuclear weapons has led to greater cooperation between nations with different political and economic beliefs.

FURTHER WRITING SUGGESTIONS

4. Discoveries in science, medicine, and technology occur constantly. Discuss one such discovery made in your lifetime that has caused reconsideration of traditional ethical and religious values.

5. Explain why you wish you had witnessed a specific historical event.

6. Discuss whether there should be limits placed on scientific research.

A FABLE FOR TOMORROW

By Rachel Carson

Rachel Carson (1907–1964) studied biology at Pennsylvania College for Women, Johns Hopkins University, and the Marine Biological Laboratory at Woods Hole, Massachusetts. Her first book, *The Sea Around Us,* won the National Book Award for nonfiction in 1951.

Her most influential work, *Silent Spring* (1962), was an urgent warning that the earth's environment and human and animal life faced destruction from the overuse and misuse of pesticides.

This selection is the opening chapter of *Silent Spring.*

WORDS TO NOTICE

fable: fictional narrative with a moral

backdrop: background

migrants: birds that travel seasonally

blight: destructive condition, disease

maladies: diseases

stricken: affected by disease, struck

moribund: in the process of dying

scores: a great number

brooded: sat on eggs

litters: groups of newborn animals

droned: hummed

withered: wasted away

anglers: people who fish

eaves: overhanging edges of roofs

counterparts: similar examples

grim specter: deadly ghost

stark: dark and bare

READ ON

1. While reading this fable for the first time, **star** the words and phrases dealing with unnatural and harmful effects on the environment.

2. While rereading, **find** the main idea.

There was once a town in the heart of America where all life seemed to live in harmony with its surroundings. The town lay in the midst of a checkerboard of prosperous farms, with fields of grain and hillsides of orchards where, in spring, white clouds of bloom drifted above the green fields. In autumn, oak and maple and birch set up a blaze of color that flamed and flickered across a backdrop of pines. Then foxes barked in the hills and deer silently crossed the fields, half hidden in the mists of the fall mornings. 1

Along the roads, laurel, viburnum and alder, great ferns and wildflowers delighted the traveler's eye through much of the year. Even in winter the roadsides were places of beauty, where countless birds came to feed on the berries and on the seed heads of the dried weeds rising above the snow. The countryside was, in fact, famous for the abundance and variety of its bird life, and when the flood of migrants was pouring through in spring and fall people traveled from great distances to observe them. Others came to fish the streams, which flowed clear and cold out of the hills and contained shady pools where trout lay. So it had been from the days many years ago when the first settlers raised their houses, sank their wells, and built their barns. 2

Then a strange blight crept over the area and everything began to change. Some evil spell had settled on the community: mysterious maladies swept the flocks of chickens; the cattle and sheep sickened and died. Everywhere was a shadow of death. The farmers spoke of much illness among their families. In the town the doctors had become more and more puzzled by new kinds of sickness appearing among their patients. There had been several sudden and unexplained deaths, not only among adults but even among children, who would be stricken suddenly while at play and die within a few hours. 3

There was a strange stillness. The birds, for example—where had they **4** gone? Many people spoke of them, puzzled and disturbed. The feeding stations in the backyards were deserted. The few birds seen anywhere were moribund; they trembled violently and could not fly. It was a spring without voices. On the mornings that had once throbbed with the dawn chorus of robins, catbirds, doves, jays, wrens, and scores of other bird voices there was now no sound; only silence lay over the fields and woods and marsh.

On the farms the hens brooded, but no chicks hatched. The farmers **5** complained that they were unable to raise any pigs—the litters were small and the young survived only a few days. The apple trees were coming into bloom but no bees droned among the blossoms, so there was no pollination and there would be no fruit.

The roadsides, once so attractive, were now lined with browned and **6** withered vegetation as though swept by fire. These, too, were silent, deserted by all living things. Even the streams were now lifeless. Anglers no longer visited them, for all the fish had died.

In the gutters under the eaves and between the shingles of the roofs, a **7** white granular powder still showed a few patches; some weeks before it had fallen like snow upon the roofs and the lawns, the fields and streams.

No witchcraft, no enemy action had silenced the rebirth of new life in **8** this stricken world. The people had done it themselves.

This town does not actually exist, but it might easily have a thousand **9** counterparts in America or elsewhere in the world. I know of no community that has experienced all the misfortunes I describe. Yet every one of these disasters has actually happened somewhere, and many real communities have already suffered a substantial number of them. A grim specter has crept upon us almost unnoticed, and this imagined tragedy may easily become a stark reality we all shall know.

What has already silenced the voices of spring in countless towns in **10** America? This book is an attempt to explain.

IN YOUR OWN VOICE

WHAT DOES IT SAY?

1. Why do people visit the countryside?

2. Why is it "a spring without voices"?

3. List three effects of the blight.

4. Who cause the blight?

5. How close is America to experiencing this "imagined tragedy"?

WHAT DOES IT MEAN?

1. Why are the town and its surroundings in harmony?

2. Why is there no warning before the blight comes?

3. How are the fates of human beings and animals related?

4. What is the white granular powder (paragraph 7)?

5. Why is there no mention of summer in this passage?

STYLE AND SENSE

A **fable** is a brief narrative that concludes with a **moral**, or lesson. The characters
are often animals that speak.

1. Which paragraphs tell the story of the life and death of the town?

2. Which paragraphs state the moral of the fable?

3. Which words in the opening sentence remind the reader of a fairy tale?

4. Which words in paragraphs 3 and 8 also recall the supernatural events of a
   fairy tale?

5. Which transitional word at the beginning of a paragraph signals the change from natural harmony to disease?

6. What moral is suggested by the question in the closing paragraph?

7. In paragraph 8, Carson writes of "the rebirth of new life." In what way does her fable bring to mind the opening chapter of Genesis?

FROM THE TEXT

Read the following sentence:

> The apple trees were coming into bloom but no bees droned among the blossoms, so there was no pollination and there would be no fruit.

a. Identify the four independent clauses.

b. Which coordinating conjunction joins the first two clauses?

c. Which coordinating conjunction joins the second and third?

d. Which coordinating conjunction joins the third and fourth?

e. Why is this sentence not a run-on or comma splice?

f. Rewrite Carson's one sentence as two sentences of your own.

See page 389 for more on preventing run-ons.

WRITE NOW

Do both of the following activities.

1. After doing any prewriting activity, write a **first draft** of an opening paragraph of an essay based on one of the following Writing Suggestions.

2. **Revise** the paragraph. Ask yourself these questions: Is the **topic sentence** stated clearly? Is there support for this sentence?

WRITING SUGGESTIONS

1. The fable starts at a time when "all life seemed to live in harmony with its surroundings." Discuss the possibility of such harmony in a specific place in today's world.

2. Discuss the most serious environmental or ecological problem facing the Americas. Describe the specific steps that need to be taken to solve this problem.

3. Children learn valuable lessons from their parents about ecology. Explain how daily household activities and habits show a family's concern or lack of concern for the environment.

FURTHER WRITING SUGGESTIONS

4. In the thirty years since "A Fable for Tomorrow" was written, the environment has improved in some respects and worsened in others. Compare and contrast today's environment with the state of the environment thirty years ago.

5. Describe a place where you experienced the beauty of nature. In your conclusion, comment on what the experience meant to you.

6. Write your own fable about a contemporary environmental problem. Be sure to include a moral in your conclusion.

FIRST ON THE MOON
By Neil Armstrong and others

President John F. Kennedy predicted in 1961 that the United States would land a man on the moon before the end of the decade. On July 20, 1969, three astronauts, Neil Armstrong, Michael Collins, and Edwin E. Aldrin, Jr., landed their module on the moon.

Armstrong (born 1930), commander of the Apollo 11 space flight, was the first one to set foot on the moon. Aldrin soon joined him.

This reading selection describes the actions and emotions of the astronauts' families as they waited anxiously for the historic moment.

WORDS TO NOTICE

hunched: bent over

descent: the spacecraft's downward path

banished: sent away

lunar module: small spacecraft designed for use on the moon

mantelpiece: shelf above a fireplace

digitalis: drug used to stimulate the heart

monitoring: paying careful attention to

dabbed: pressed lightly

out of detent: with its fastener released

muttering: speaking under his breath

hubbub: noise, uproar

touchdown: moment of landing

underwritten: supported

READ ON

1. While reading this selection for the first time, **jot down** what interests you most about the families' reactions to the mission.

2. While rereading, **find** the responses of friends, neighbors, and people the world over to the moon landing.

El Lago, Texas

Jan Armstrong had been hunched on her knees before a television set in   1
the bedroom, pencil in hand, studying the powered descent graph and check-
ing landmarks on a detailed map of the moon. "We're coming up on Dry
Gulch. Then Apollo Ridge. Twin Peaks. Off in the distance will be Smoky
Ridge." The dog Super wandered in, his tail wagging. He was banished under
the bed. At the 15,000-foot mark Jan sat up on her heels when she heard the
words "Go for landing," and said, "Come on, come on, Trolley!" (Armstrong
was flying the lunar module standing up, like an old-fashioned trolley driver.)
At 220 feet she put her arm around her son Ricky's shoulder and kept it there.

CAPCOM (Duke): Sixty seconds.   2

    Jan Armstrong leaned down, one hand over her mouth, her eyes a little   3
brighter than usual.

    At 3 P.M. Pat Collins was reading *Peanuts* and drinking a Coke. At 13,000   4
feet (four minutes to lunar landing) Pat shook her head and clenched a fist.
When Charlie Duke said everything was looking all right (she heard him, as
did the other crewmen's wives, over the "squawk box," a small loudspeaker
connected with central communications in Mission Control) she encouraged
him, "Charlie, you're a good boy, keep it up.' Then, 3,000 feet: "Oh God, I
can't stand it." At 2,000 feet she was biting her lip. Then, 1,600 feet: "Can I
bear it?" Down to 700 feet; now she was biting a finger.

    When the lunar module had come around the moon and reestablished   5
wireless communication, Joan Aldrin had crossed over to the fireplace and
bowed her head on her hands, resting on the mantelpiece. There was something very solitary about her, and everyone else in the room respected her
privacy, crisscrossing around her. She said, "Talk about killing time . . ."

    Nobody could find the ham sent by the ladies of the Webster Presbyterian   6
Church (it eventually turned up in the refrigerator); Joan was concerned about
Missy the dog getting her digitalis pill on time, and about the noise: "Girls,
will you *please* try to cut it down to a low roar?" Astronaut Rusty Schweickart
was monitoring the squawk box and making notes in the margins of the flight
plan. His wife Clare asked him, "Will you say 'That's bad' if anything's bad?"
Rusty said, "I will."

    The Aldrins' son Michael was suddenly not around. "Where's Mike?   7
Where's Mike?" asked Joan. Someone went upstairs and sent him down:
"What's the matter? I'm watching upstairs." Joan said, "I know you were,
dear. I know you were." She had a rather blank look on her face.

    She gripped a door and huddled against the frame. She put one hand on   8
the top of the lampshade. Nobody spoke. The lamp beneath her hand began
to shake; it was the only thing moving in the room. Her eyes were now large
with tears; she sniffed and dabbed at her nose with a tissue. *Sixty seconds
to go . . .*

ALDRIN: Lights on. Down 2½. Forward. Forward. Good. 40 feet, down 2½.   9
    Picking up some dust. 30 feet, 2½ down. Faint shadow. 4 forward. 4
    forward, drifting to the right a little. 6 . . . [*static*] . . . down a half.
CAPCOM (Duke): Thirty seconds.   10
ALDRIN: [*Static*] . . . forward. Drifting right . . . [*static*] . . . Contact light. Okay,   11
    engine stop, ACA out of detent.
ARMSTRONG: Got it.   12
ALDRIN: Mode controls, both auto, descent engine command override, off.   13
    Engine arm, off. 413 *is* in.
CAPCOM (Duke): We copy you down, Eagle.   14
ARMSTRONG: Houston, Tranquility Base here. The Eagle has landed.   15

CAPCOM (Duke): Roger, Tranquility. We copy you on the ground. You've got   16
    a bunch of guys about to turn blue. We're breathing again. Thanks a
    lot.
ALDRIN: Thank you.   17

Jan Armstrong hugged her son Ricky and smiled when she heard that they   18
had had only thirty seconds of fuel left when they landed. Jan's sister, Carolyn
Trude, leaned against a wall and said, "Thank you, God."

Pat Collins had her face screwed tight, head on her hands, when she   19
heard the words "contact light." Then she smiled. It was the first time anyone
had seen her smile in more than an hour. She said, "The Eagle has landed.
We're on the moon and they say, 'Thanks a lot.' Why aren't they cheering? I
guess that's why they don't send a woman to the moon—she would jump up
and down and yell and weep. . . . Oh, Mike didn't hear it!" Then she heard
Mike Collins's voice: "Yeah, I heard the whole thing." She said, "Oh, you did
hear it! Good, honey! Now all we gotta do is get them out of there." Her seven-
year-old daughter Ann cut in: "Tomorrow we're staying home from camp,
aren't we, Mommy?"

In Buzz Aldrin's home the words "Okay, engine stop" rang out with   20
surprising clarity. Everyone started clapping—everyone but Joan Aldrin, who
was still shaking, her head buried against the wall. Then she fell into the
arms of Uncle Bob—Robert Moon, the brother of Buzz Aldrin's mother. "Fantastic, fantastic," Rusty Schweickart was muttering through the hubbub. Joan
Aldrin walked straight out of Uncle Bob's arms into Buzz's study and into the
master bedroom without looking at anyone. Jan Aldrin, age eleven, was visibly
shaken. Michael Archer, Joan's father, took little Jan into his arms and gently
pushed open the study door for her to go to her mother. Later that night Joan
Aldrin recalled, "My mind couldn't take it all in. I blacked out. I couldn't see
anything. All I could see was a match cover on the floor. I wanted to bend
down and pick it up and I couldn't do it. I just kept looking at that match
cover."

Touchdown: it was 3:18 P.M. in Houston, where the event had the most   21
shattering personal impact; it was 4:18 P.M. in New York, where they stopped
a baseball game to announce the news and sixteen thousand people stood
in Yankee Stadium to sing, joyously, "The Star-Spangled Banner"; it was 6:18
A.M., July 21, at the Honeysuckle Creek tracking station in Australia, where a
staff of about one hundred was hanging onto the touchdown by radio circuits.
But the date that would live in the history books was July 20. That was the
calendar date in the United States, the nation which had underwritten the
incredible voyage with much of its treasure and a little bit of its blood. July
20: the aviator Alberto Santos-Dumont was born on that day in 1873; Guglielmo
Marconi, inventor of wireless communications, died on that day in 1937. But
as long as western civilization endured men would remember July 20 for
another reason: that was the day three American astronauts named Armstrong,
Collins and Aldrin put man on the moon.

IN YOUR OWN VOICE

WHAT DOES IT SAY?

1. Why does Jan Armstrong call her husband Trolley?

2. What is a "squawk box"?

3. What is the name of the spacecraft that lands on the moon?

4. After the landing, what is Joan Aldrin's reaction?

5. After the landing, what happened at Yankee Stadium?

6. Which date will live in the history books?

WHAT DOES IT MEAN?

1. Why is the map important to Jan Armstrong?

2. Why do the women of the Webster Presbyterian Church send a ham to the Aldrin household?

3. Why does Pat Collins think her reaction to the landing is different from that of a man's?

4. Which feelings unite people in Houston, New York, and Australia?

5. Why is teamwork essential to the mission's success?

STYLE AND SENSE

1. Why do the scenes shift from one wife to another?

2. Which details make this an "American" story?

3. How do numbers give a dramatic, but orderly sense of the gradual descent to the moon?

4. Why are specific clock times given in the closing paragraph?

5. Which words in the closing paragraph give the impression that the landing on the moon was a male achievement?

FROM THE TEXT

Semicolon: a punctuation mark generally used to separate two independent clauses; these clauses are connected in meaning.

Read the following sentences:

The lamp beneath her hand began to shake; it was the only thing moving in the room. Her eyes were now large with tears; she sniffed and dabbed at her nose with a tissue.

a. Identify the independent clauses in the first sentence.

b. Identify the two subjects and the two verbs.

c. Identify the independent clauses in the second sentence.

d. Identify the two subjects and the three verbs.

e. Which punctuation mark separates the related independent clauses?

f. Is the word after the punctuation mark capitalized?

g. Which punctuation mark separates the two sentences?

See page 389 for more on preventing run-on sentences.

WRITE NOW

Do both of the following activities.

1. Make a **cluster diagram** in response to one of the following Writing Suggestions.

2. Use the cluster diagram to write a **first draft** of your essay.

WRITING SUGGESTIONS

1. President Richard M. Nixon welcomed the astronauts on their return to earth. Discuss how and why the landing on the moon stirred the patriotism and pride of Americans.

2. Neil Armstrong's famous words as he became the first human being to set foot on another world were, "That's one small step for a man, one giant leap for mankind." Explain what he meant.

3. A U.S. government agency is accepting reservations for commuter trips to the moon. Tell whether or not you will be one of the travelers and why you are making this decision.

FURTHER WRITING SUGGESTIONS

4. The *Challenger 7* space disaster of January 28, 1986, cost the lives of seven Americans. The dead included astronaut Judith Resnick and New Hampshire school teacher Christa McAuliffe. Discuss whether women should risk their lives in the service of their country, either in the space program or in the military.

5. Discuss whether the money being spent on space research and programs should be reduced, eliminated, or increased.

6. Imagine that you are an astronaut from a different galaxy in a spaceship approaching the earth for the first time. Describe the sights and feelings you have as you descend gradually.

CHILDREN OF LATIN AMERICA AND THE CARIBBEAN

By Dr. Elsa M. Moreno, Dr. Nestor Suarez, and Dr. Ciro de Quadros

Children and adolescents, more than 200 million of them in the Americas, suffer from a disturbing number of health problems. Some of the highest rates of infant deaths are to be found in the Americas.

In the last decade, there has been some improvement in providing health care. However, much more needs to be done. Families and communities have begun to take more active roles in working with the World Health Organization (WHO) and similar medical and educational groups.

The three authors of this selection write from their firsthand experiences as key members of the Maternal and Child Health Program of WHO. The program's goal is summed up in its motto: Health for All by the Year 2000.

WORDS TO NOTICE

plunged: decreased greatly

excessive: greater than normal or necessary

mortality: death

annually: per year

acute respiratory: severe breathing

subject to: requiring

malnutrition: condition of not having enough food or nourishment

underlies: lies beneath, is the basis for

birth defects: imperfections at birth

morbidity: condition of being ill or unhealthy

unchecked: not stopped or not prevented

orientation: background, way of thinking or training

disciplines: fields of study or expert knowledge

classical: traditional, formal

popular mobilization: activities started by people or groups

decentralization: governmental organization based on local authority and participation

empowering: giving power to

leaven: influence, stimulator

priority: the most important

READ ON

1. While reading this selection for the first time, **underline** the statistics about infant mortality.

2. While rereading, **locate** the paragraph that begins the discussion of solutions to the infant mortality problem.

Childhood deaths in Latin America and the Caribbean have plunged over the last decade, but are still excessive in comparison to more advanced countries. Children's mortality rates vary considerably among countries. In 1984, for example, infant mortality ranged from 15 per thousand live births in Cuba to 117 per thousand in Haiti. Among one- to four-year-olds, Bolivia registered a mortality rate of 23 per thousand compared with only one per thousand in Costa Rica, Cuba, Panama, and Trinidad and Tobago, equivalent to the rate in the United States. These differences occur not only between countries, but also between different areas and localities of the same country.   1

If all the countries of the region could achieve, as some already have, infant mortality rates of 20 per thousand, then more than 500,000 children under one year of age could be saved annually. Although most countries have reached infant mortality rates below 50, more than 60 per cent of Latin American children live in geographic areas where mortality is higher than that.   2

Children of illiterate mothers face a risk of death five times that of children whose mothers have completed at least five years of formal education.   3

In most countries of Latin America and the Caribbean, the main causes   **4**
of deaths of young children are birth problems, diarrhea, acute respiratory
infection, and infectious diseases subject to vaccination. Malnutrition underlies many preventable deaths, although it is rarely recorded on death
certificates. Typically, countries with high rates of infant mortality, such as
Guatemala and Honduras, show diarrhea as the principal cause, while those
with low rates, such as Chile and Cuba, have birth defects in first place. This
change in the structure of morbidity/mortality seems to be a trend in most
countries and should be taken into account in any reorganization of services.

According to current estimates, some 60 million children lack access to   **5**
basic health services and, if this situation continues unchecked, these numbers could reach 100 million by the year 2000. This prospect indicates the
need for a fundamental change in health care delivery and in the orientation
of providers. Clear policy direction is needed to pull together efforts within
and between disciplines and to promote the active participation of families
and communities in the improvement of their own welfare.

Expanding coverage no longer means the classical solution of setting up   **6**
more physical plants to await the arrival of patients. Rather, the only acceptable avenue now is to recognize the community's key role and the impact
of popular mobilization as the last stage of a decentralization process empowering decision making and problem solving at the primary care level.
That is why, in the Americas, primary health care has become an action
strategy and the leaven for change throughout the health system as a whole.

The growing, developing young child always belongs to a given family   **7**
and a given nation. Improving health conditions for the children of the Americas depends on a process of identifying priority problems and searching for
solutions through the combined efforts of individuals, families, and neighborhood organizations.

IN YOUR OWN VOICE

WHAT DOES IT SAY?

1. Which country of the Americas has the highest infant mortality rate?

2. How many children under one year of age in the Americas can be saved if the infant mortality rate could be reduced to 20 per thousand?

3. What are the main causes of children's deaths?

4. How many children lack access to basic health services?

5. Which steps are necessary to bring about a positive change in the health care delivery system?

WHAT DOES IT MEAN?

1. Why does the infant mortality rate vary among the countries of the Americas?

2. Why are the years from infancy to age four the most dangerous for children?

3. Why does the length of a mother's formal education affect her child's chance to live?

4. How can an increased role for families and communities improve the quality of health care?

STYLE AND SENSE

This selection discusses both the perils to the health of children in the Americas and the promises of improved health care.

1. What is the main idea of the opening paragraph?

2. Why are statistics and factual details used in paragraphs 2 through 5?

3. How does the last sentence of paragraph 5 serve as a transition to paragraph 6?

4. What is the main idea of paragraphs 7 through 9?

5. How does the opening paragraph contrast with the closing paragraph?

FROM THE TEXT

Read the following sentence:

> In most countries of Latin America and the Caribbean, the main causes of deaths of young children are birth problems, diarrhea, acute respiratory infection, and infectious diseases subject to vaccination.

a. Why is there a comma after *Caribbean*?

b. Why are there three other commas later in the sentence?

c. Why is there no comma in the phrase "Latin America and the Caribbean"?

See page 465 for more on commas.

WRITE NOW

Do **both** of the following activities:

1. Make a **brainstorm** list for one of the following Writing Suggestions.

2. Using the brainstorm list, write a **topic sentence** for a paragraph in your essay.

WRITING SUGGESTIONS

1. If you were a doctor, nurse, scientist, or other health care worker, explain how you would use your skills and knowledge to keep the children of the Americas healthy and alive.

2. "The growing, developing young child always belongs to a given family and a given nation." Answer one of the following questions:

   a. Discuss how belonging to a given family affects a child's chances for life and health.

   or

   b. Discuss how being born in a given nation affects a child's chances for life and health.

3. Every year more than a million children under the age of five die in the Americas. Discuss why medical and scientific advances have not succeeded in lowering this number substantially.

FURTHER WRITING SUGGESTIONS

4. Discuss how the education of a mother can affect the survival of her children.

5. The children of the Americas have an immediate need for the best health care they can receive. Explain whether or not available money and resources should be used for primary health care today, or for research that may prevent death and disease in the future.

UNIT 9

THE IDEA OF DEMOCRACIES

This unit attempts to see democracy in the Americas from varied twentieth-century perspectives.

It begins with E. B. White's essay written during World War II hailing the ordinary joys and decencies of his America.

Eleanor Roosevelt's "Milestones" (1961) summarizes the view that the United States' role in the world can be enhanced by looking first at the suffering or hunger of the individual, then forming broader policies based on that awareness.

The Nobel Peace Prize address by Oscar Arias Sanchez, the former president of Costa Rica, expresses that leader's belief that each nation in the Americas, whether large or small, should determine its destiny in freedom and peace, without outside coercion or undue political or military pressure.

Concluding this section is Jamaica Kincaid's essay on freedom and slavery, the past and the future in Antigua.

BEFORE YOU READ

What is your idea of democracy?

What barriers to democracy still exist in the Western Hemisphere?

What role should the United States play in dealing with its American neighbors?

What role does geography play in the Americas? What role does language play?

What should smaller nations in the Americas do to secure the advancement of human freedom?

What ghosts or shadows of the past haunt present-day life in the Americas?

What blessings can the Americas count on in the future?

What safeguards to democracy do you think are most important?

How can you contribute to the growth of democracy in your community, nation, or area?

What is your definition of a good citizen?

Why do nondemocratic governments still exist in the Americas?

How can nations in the Americas resolve their problems nonviolently?

What makes a person really free?

Should some freedoms in a democracy be limited?

Can a democracy exist if people do not receive a good education?

Can democracy overcome poverty?

How will democracies change in the future?

THE MEANING OF DEMOCRACY*

By E. B. White

E. B. White (1899–1985) was best known as a writer and editor for the *New Yorker* magazine, and as the author of the classic children's books *Stuart Little* (1945) and *Charlotte's Web* (1952).

*Editors' title

The clarity of his writing style serves as a model for authors, teachers, and students. He edited and updated *The Elements of Style,* a guide to writing originally written by William Strunk, Jr.

In this *New Yorker* editorial, White gives his personal definition of democracy to Americans in the midst of World War II (1939–1945).

WORDS TO NOTICE

Writers' War Board: nongovernmental organization which aided the war effort by writing free of charge articles, slogans, stories, skits, and pamphlets

presumably: evidently, apparently

comply: go along, obey

stuffed shirt: (*slang*) pompous person

high hat: symbol of snobbery

recurrent: repeated

communion: spiritual unity

rationed: referring to the amount per person set by the government in wartime

READ ON

1. Before reading this selection, think about the word *democracy.*

2. While rereading, jot down comments on why images like "stuffed shirt" and expressions like "Don't shove" are included.

July 3, 1944

We received a letter from the Writers' War Board the other day asking for   1
a statement on 'The Meaning of Democracy.' It presumably is our duty to comply with such a request, and it is certainly our pleasure.

Surely the Board knows what democracy is. It is the line that forms on   2
the right. It is the don't in Don't Shove. It is the hole in the stuffed shirt through which the sawdust slowly trickles; it is the dent in the high hat. Democracy is the recurrent suspicion that more than half of the people are right more than half of the time. It is the feeling of privacy in the voting booths, the feeling of communion in the libraries, the feeling of vitality everywhere. Democracy is the score at the beginning of the ninth. It is an idea which hasn't

been disproved yet, a song the words of which have not gone bad. It's the mustard on the hot dog and the cream in the rationed coffee. Democracy is a request from a War Board, in the middle of a morning in the middle of a war, wanting to know what democracy is.

IN YOUR OWN VOICE

WHAT DOES IT SAY?

1. What does the Writers' War Board request?

2. What is similar about the "stuffed shirt" and the "high hat"?

3. How often are the people in a democracy right?

4. When does the Writers' War Board request come?

WHAT DOES IT MEAN?

1. Why is the date of this statement significant?

2. Why is writing this statement both a duty and a pleasure?

3. Why is democracy "the line that forms on the right"?

4. Why are voting booths and libraries part of "vitality everywhere"?

5. Why is democracy defined as "the score at the beginning of the ninth"?

STYLE AND SENSE

Definition: the meaning of a word or expression, either in its dictionary sense or in the meanings that are special to you; a dictionary defines *mother* as "female parent." To you, *mother* may have additional emotional qualities, such as warmth, concern, and love.

1. What words appear in both the opening and closing sentences?

2. What is the topic sentence of paragraph 2?

3. What two groups of words begin the definitions in paragraph 2?

4. What is the effect of beginning the definitions this way?

FROM THE TEXT

Clause: a group of words containing a subject and verb.

Phrase: a group of words, lacking a verb, which expresses one idea.

Read the following sentence:

We received a letter from the Writers' War Board the other day asking for a statement on 'The Meaning of Democracy.'

a. What is the independent clause?

b. To which noun does the present participle *asking* refer?

c. Are the words "asking for a statement on 'The Meaning of Democracy' " a clause or a phrase? Explain.

d. Can the words "asking for a statement on 'The Meaning of Democracy' " stand as a complete sentence?

See pages 382 and 383 for more on phrases and independent and dependent clauses.

WRITE NOW

Do both of the following activities.

1. Revise—alone or with another student—an essay written in response to one of the following Writing Suggestions.

2. Edit the essay, paying careful attention to sentence structure. Be sure there are no run-ons, comma splices, or sentence fragments.

WRITING SUGGESTIONS

1. Define *democracy*. Use examples and images to clarify your definition.

2. White is glad to contribute to the war effort by using his talent for writing. Describe how civilians are able to serve their country in wartime.

3. Discuss whether or not democratic ideals are appreciated more by those born in a democracy or by those who experience democracy later in life.

FURTHER WRITING SUGGESTIONS

4. White writes, "Democracy is a letter to the editor." Write a letter to your local newspaper on an issue of importance to you as a member of a community or cultural or ethnic group.

5. Discuss whether or not a classroom in any school at any level can be run on democratic principles.

6. According to White, one principle of democracy is "that more than half of the people are right more than half of the time." Discuss how an individual's sense of responsibility is affected by this principle.

MILESTONES

By Eleanor Roosevelt

Eleanor Roosevelt (1884–1962) was a world-renowned champion of the poor, the oppressed, and the hungry. She served as chairperson of the commission to draft the Universal Declaration of Human Rights, adopted by the United Nations in 1948.

The wife of Franklin Delano Roosevelt, president of the United States from 1933 to 1945, Eleanor Roosevelt became a political force in her own right. In her travels, writings, and lectures, she supported liberal causes. She herself admitted that her viewpoints brought upon her both great devotion and harsh criticism.

This selection from her autobiography sums up her personal philosophy on the need for individuals and nations to strive for a democratic, caring world.

WORDS TO NOTICE

stemmed from: originated, developed

abstract: theoretical

plight: terrible situation

overriding: primary

wreak havoc: cause destruction

impoverished: poor

apathy: indifference, lack of interest

Old World: Europe, Asia, and Africa

bolster: support

inevitably: always, unavoidably

peter out: diminish gradually and come to an end

moment: importance

on a par with: equal to

READ ON

1. While reading this selection for the first time, **underline** all of Roosevelt's recommendations for achieving a better world.

2. While rereading, **evaluate** the recommendations that interest you most.

On that seventy-fifth birthday I knew that I had long since become aware of my over-all objective in life. It stemmed from those early impressions I had gathered when I saw war-torn Europe after World War I. I wanted, with all my heart, a peaceful world. And I knew it could never be achieved on a lasting basis without greater understanding between peoples. It is to these ends that I have, in the main, devoted the past years. [1]

One curious thing is that I have always seen life personally; that is, my interest or sympathy or indignation is not aroused by an abstract cause but by the plight of a single person whom I have seen with my own eyes. It was the sight of a child dying of hunger that made the tragedy of hunger become of such overriding importance to me. Out of my response to an individual develops an awareness of a problem to the community, then to the country, and finally to the world. In each case my feeling of obligation to do something has stemmed from one individual and then widened and become applied to a broader area. [2]

More and more, I think, people are coming to realize that what affects an individual affects mankind. To take an extreme example, one neglected case of smallpox can infect a whole community. This is equally true of the maladjusted child, who may wreak havoc in his neighborhood; of the impoverished, who become either economic burdens or social burdens, and, in any case, are wasted as human beings. Abuses anywhere, however isolated they may appear, can end by becoming abuses everywhere. [3]

I learned, too, while I was groping for more and more effective ways of trying to cope with community and national and world problems, that you can accomplish a great deal more if you care deeply about what is happening to other people than if you say in apathy or discouragement, "Oh, what can I do? What use is one person? I might as well not bother." [4]

Actually I suppose the caring comes from being able to put yourself in the position of the other person. If you cannot imagine, "This might happen to me," you are able to say to yourself with indifference, "Who cares?" [5]

I think that one of the reasons it is so difficult for us, as a people, to understand other areas of the world is that we cannot put ourselves imagi- [6]

natively in their place. We have no famine. But if we were actually to see people dying of starvation we would care quite a bit. We would be able to think, "These could be my people."

Because of our rather extraordinary advantages, it is difficult for us to   **7**
understand the other peoples of the world. We started with tremendous national resources. Our very isolation, in those early years, forced us to develop them. Many of the people who settled here had escaped from poverty and want and oppression and lack of opportunity. They wanted to forget their background and they soon did, because the difficulty of travel made it hard for them to go back and refresh their memories. So we grew out of the past and away from it. Now it would be valuable for us to remember the conditions of that Old World. It would help us to understand what the poorer countries need and want today.

And this, I suppose, indicates what has happened to me in seventy-five   **8**
years. Though now as always it is through individuals that I see and understand human needs, I find that my over-all objectives go beyond individuals to the fate of mankind. It is within that larger framework that one must think today if mankind is to survive the threat that hangs, in a mushroom cloud, over it.

So I come to the larger objective, not mine, except as I am an American,   **9**
but America's. It seems to me that America's objective today should be to try to make herself the best possible mirror of democracy that she can. The people of the world can see what happens here. They watch us to see what we are going to do and how well we can do it. We are giving them the only possible picture of democracy that we can: the picture as it works in actual practice. This is the only way other peoples can see for themselves how it works; and can determine for themselves whether this thing is good in itself, whether it is better than what they have, better than what other political and economic systems offer them.

Now, while we are a generous nation, giving with a free hand and with   **10**
an open heart wherever there is need or suffering (that we can understand, at least), we have one weakness that, considering our political maturity as a nation, is rather immature. We continue to expect the world to be grateful to us and to love us. We are hurt and indignant when we do not receive gratitude and love.

Gratitude and love are not to be had for the asking; they are not to be   **11**
bought. We should not want to think that they are for sale. What we should seek, rather than gratitude or love, is the respect of the world. This we can earn by enlightened justice. But it is rather naïve of us to think that when we are helping people our action is entirely unselfish. It is not. It is not unselfish when we vaccinate the public against smallpox. It is a precautionary measure, but nonetheless good in itself.

Other nations are quite aware that when we try to bolster up their economy   **12**
and strengthen their governments and generally help them to succeed there is a certain amount of self-interest involved. They are inevitably going to be on the lookout to see what we want in return. Consciously we do not want

anything, but unconsciously almost anything we do, as a nation or through the United Nations, is intended to benefit us or our cause, directly or indirectly. So there is no reason for demanding either gratitude or love.

Our obligation to the world is, primarily, our obligation to our own future. **13** Obviously we cannot develop beyond a certain point unless the other nations develop too. When our natural resources peter out, we must seek them in other countries. We cannot have trade if we are the only solvent nation. We need not only areas from which to buy but areas to which we can sell, and we cannot have this in underdeveloped areas.

We must, as a nation, begin to realize that we are the leaders of the non- **14** Communist world, that our interests at some point all touch the interests of the world, and they must be examined in the context of the interests of the world. This is the price of leadership.

We cannot, indeed, continue to function in a narrow orbit or in a self- **15** enclosed system. We cannot weigh or evaluate even our domestic problems in their own context alone. We no longer have merely domestic issues. Perhaps the best illustration of this is the question I am asked everywhere in the world:

"We hear you Americans pay to keep land out of production because **16** there is too much to eat. Is there no better way to use your ability to produce food than to get rid of it?"

This is a home question; it is literally of vital moment to the millions of **17** starving in the world who look to us. I do not see how we can retain world leadership and yet continue to handle our problems as though they concerned us alone; they concern the world. We feel that a surplus of food is only an embarrassment. We solve it as though only we were concerned. But think of the hungry people and their bitterness as the food that could save their lives is plowed under. To say they think it highly unfair is to put it mildly.

We have never put our best brains to work on the ways we can produce **18** to the maximum, give our farmers a better income, and still employ our surpluses in a way to solve the pressing needs of the world, without upsetting our economy or that of friendly nations who might fear we were giving food to markets they are accustomed to selling to.

We have a great variety of climate, we can grow almost anything we want. **19** Canada can grow only wheat. There need be no clash of interests here.

How have we tried to "solve" matters up to now? We cut our acreage **20** and store the surplus or dump it; we pay our farmers too little to give them an income on a par with that of industrial workers, so we have a dwindling farm population. No one has ever sat down and said, "This is a problem you *must* work out."

It is in ways like these, using our intelligence and our good will and our **21** vast capacity to produce, that we can meet and overcome the Communist threat and prove that democracy has more to give the world.

IN YOUR OWN VOICE

WHAT DOES IT SAY?

1. What does Roosevelt wish for with all her heart?

2. Which examples teach Roosevelt that what affects one person affects all people?

3. Why is it difficult for the United States to understand other peoples and areas of the world?

4. What should be the objective of the United States?

5. Which question is Roosevelt asked all over the world?

WHAT DOES IT MEAN?

1. Why does Roosevelt place great value on personal experience?

2. Why does the solution to national or global problems begin with the individual?

3. Why should the United States help other nations?

4. Why is a food surplus "only an embarrassment" to the United States?

STYLE AND SENSE

A child dying of hunger ... Why must Roosevelt share this personal experience with the reader? Such a specific example serves as the **cause** that leads to an action or idea **(effect)**.

1. In paragraph 1, which idea stems from Roosevelt's seeing war-torn Europe after World War I?

2. In paragraph 2, which idea results from seeing a child dying of hunger?

3. In paragraph 3, which specific examples cause Roosevelt to realize that "what affects an individual affects mankind"?

4. In paragraph 9, what are some results of America's becoming "the best possible mirror of democracy"?

5. Find at least two other paragraphs that use a cause-and-effect approach.

FROM THE TEXT

Compound subject: Two or more subjects connected by a conjunction. If the conjunction is *and*, the compound subject usually is considered to be plural and therefore takes a plural verb.

Read the following sentence:

Gratitude and love are not to be had for the asking; they are not to be bought.

a. What is the subject of the first independent clause?

b. Is the subject singular or plural?

c. Which verb agrees with this subject?

d. Which pronoun in the second independent clause refers to the subject of the first clause?

e. Is the pronoun singular or plural?

See page 414 for more on the compound subject.

WRITE NOW

Do both of the following activities.

1. **Revise**—alone or with another student—an essay written in response to one of the following Writing Suggestions.

2. **Edit** the essay, paying careful attention to subject-verb agreement and the correct forms of the verbs. Be sure that your word endings are correct.

WRITING SUGGESTIONS

1. Roosevelt says that a peaceful world is possible only with "greater understanding between peoples." Discuss how this result can be achieved in the community, or in the nation, or in the world.

2. Roosevelt does not approve of those who say, "What use is one person? I might as well not bother." Explain how an individual can benefit from Roosevelt's caring, personal approach to life.

3. According to Roosevelt, the United States should help the less advanced countries in the world. Discuss the advantages and disadvantages to the countries accepting this aid.

FURTHER WRITING SUGGESTIONS

4. Describe how a government can better provide for the health and living standards of children.

5. It was said of Eleanor Roosevelt that "she would rather light candles than curse the darkness." Describe the personality and actions of a person who holds this belief.

6. Describe the threats facing democracy today.

ONLY PEACE CAN WRITE THE NEW HISTORY

By Oscar Arias Sanchez

Oscar Arias Sanchez (born 1941) became the president of Costa Rica in May 1986, when military and political turmoil threatened the stability of Central America.

To support his dream of democracy and self-determination for Central America, Arias, despite his strong opposition to Nicaragua's Sandinista government, resisted United States backing of the Contra forces seeking to overthrow the Nicaraguan government.

Instead, Arias met with the leaders of Guatemala, El Salvador, Honduras, and Nicaragua to bring about a peaceful solution to these nations' problems. He sought support for the Contadora peace treaty sponsored by Colombia, Panama, Mexico, and Venezuela.

Arias's plan, which he called "a risk for peace," was signed by representatives of five Central American nations in August 1987. Two months later, he was awarded the Nobel Peace Prize.

The following selection is the opening portion of Arias's Nobel acceptance speech on December 11, 1987.

WORDS TO NOTICE

Erasmus: Desiderius Erasmus (1466?–1536), Dutch philosopher and humanist

arrogance: exaggerated pride

presume: claim

humility: humbleness

exile: absence, usually as a punishment, from one's country

totalitarian regimes: governments that forbid opposing parties

prey to: victims of

apocalyptic prophets: those who predict great disasters

abound: are in great numbers or abundance

futility: hopelessness

subversive: traitorous

confronting: facing

dogmatism: absolute belief

utopian: ideal, perfect

prolong: continue in the ways of

isthmus: narrow strip of land between two bodies of water

unison: unity, unanimity

dispelled: scattered, driven away

fratricidal struggles: deadly fights pitting family members, neighbors, or citizens against one another

Pascal: Blaise Pascal (1623–1662), French philosopher, scientist, and author of *Pensées*, a collection of thoughts on the individual's role in the universe

sceptical: skeptical, uncertain of the truth

counter: opposite

READ ON

1. When reading this speech for the first time, make **margin notes** on the descriptions of Latin America.

2. When rereading, **summarize** the main idea.

Desiring peace

Peace consists, very largely, in the fact of desiring it with all one's soul. The inhabitants of my small country Costa Rica have realised those words by Erasmus. Mine is an unarmed people, whose children have never seen a fighter or a tank or a warship. One of my guests at this award, here with us today, is José Figueres Ferrer, the man with the vision to abolish my country's armed forces in 1948, and thus set our history on a new course.   1

I am a Latin American

I am not receiving this prize as Oscar Arias, any more than I am receiving it as the President of my country. While I have not the arrogance to presume to represent anyone, neither do I fear the humility which identifies me with everyone, and with their great causes.   2

I receive it as one of the 400 million Latin Americans who, in the return to liberty, in the exercise of democracy, are seeking the way to overcome so much misery and so much injustice. I come from that Latin America whose face is deeply marked with pain, the record of the exile, torture, imprisonment and death of many of its men and its women. I come from that Latin American region where totalitarian regimes still exist which put the whole of humanity to shame.   3

America's scars

The scars by which America is marked are deep. At this very time, America **4** is seeking to return to freedom, and it is only as it approaches democracy that it can see the dreadful trail of torture, banishment and death left by dictators. The problems America has to overcome are enormous. An inheritance from an unjust past has been aggravated by the fatal deeds of tyrants to produce foreign debts, social insensitivity, economic upheavals, corruption and the many other evils of our societies. The evils are manifest, naked to the view of anyone who cares to see them.

Seeing the size of the challenge, no wonder many are prey to discour- **5** agement; or that apocalyptic prophets abound, announcing the failures of the fight against poverty, proclaiming the immediate fall of the democracies, forecasting the futility of peace-making efforts.

I do not share this defeatism. I cannot accept to be realistic means to **6** tolerate misery, violence and hate. I do not believe that the hungry man should be treated as subversive for expressing his suffering. I shall never accept that the law can be used to justify tragedy, to keep things as they are, to make us abandon our ideas of a different world. Law is the path of liberty, and must as such open the way to progress for everyone.

Liberty performs miracles

Liberty performs miracles. To free men, everything is possible. A free and **7** democratic America can meet the challenges confronting it. When I assumed the Presidency of Costa Rica, I called for an alliance for freedom and democracy in the Americas. I said then, and I repeat today, that we should not be the allies, either politically or economically, of governments which oppress their peoples. Latin America has never known a single war between two democracies. That is sufficient reason for every man of good faith, every well-intentioned nation, to support efforts to put an end to tyranny.

America can not wait

America's freedom, the freedom of the whole of America, can not wait. I **8** come from a world with huge problems, which we shall overcome in freedom. I come from a world in a hurry, because hunger can not wait. When hope is forgotten, violence does not delay. Dogmatism is too impatient for dialogue. I come from a world where, if we are to make sure that there will be no turning back from our progress towards liberty, if we are to frustrate every oppressive intent, we have no time to lose. I come from a world which cannot wait for the guerilla and the soldier to hold their fire: young people are dying, brothers are dying, and tomorrow who can tell why. I come from a world which cannot wait to open prison gates not, as before, for free men to go in, but for those imprisoned to come out.

America's liberty and democracy have no time to lose, and we need the **9** whole world's understanding to win freedom from dictators, to win freedom from misery.

I come from Central America

I accept this prize as one of 27 million Central Americans. Behind the dem- **10** ocratic awakening in Central America lies over a century of merciless dictatorships and general injustice and poverty. The choice before my little America is whether to suffer another century of violence, or to achieve peace by overcoming the fear of liberty. Only peace can write the new history.

We in Central America will not lose faith. We shall set history right. How **11** sad that they would have us believe that peace is a dream, justice utopian, shared well-being impossible! How sad that there should be people in the world who cannot understand that in the former plantations of Central America, nations are asserting themselves and striving, with every right, for better destinies for their peoples! How sad that some cannot see that Central America does not want to prolong its past, but to create a new future, with hope for the young and dignity for the old!

Realising dreams

The Central American isthmus is a region of great contrasts, but also of **12** heartening unison. Millions of men and women share dreams of freedom and progress. In some countries, the dreams are dispelled by systematic violations of human rights; they are shattered by fratricidal struggles in town and country, and come up against the realities of poverty so extreme it stops the heart. Poets who are the pride of mankind know that millions upon millions cannot read them in their own countries, because so many of the men and women there are illiterate. There are on this narrow strip of land painters and sculptors whom we shall admire for ever, but also dictators whom we have no wish to remember because they offend most cherished human values.

Central America cannot go on dreaming, nor does it want to. History **13** demands that dreams turn into realities. Now, when there is no time to lose. Today, when we can take our destiny in our own hands. In this region, home alike to the oldest and strongest democracy in Latin America—that of Costa Rica—and to a history of the most merciless and cruel dictatorships, democratic awakening requires a special loyalty to freedom.

Seeing that the past dictatorships were only capable of creating misery **14** and crippling hope, how absurd to pretend to cure the evils of one extreme dictatorship by means of its opposite! No one in Central America has the right to fear freedom, no one is entitled to preach absolute truths. The evils of one dogma are the evils of any dogma. They are all the enemies of human creativity. As Pascal said: "We know a great deal to make us sceptical. We know very little to make us dogmatic".

History can only move towards liberty. History can only have justice at **15** its heart. To march in the opposite direction to history is to be on the road to shame, poverty and oppression. Without freedom, there is no revolution. All oppression runs counter to man's spirit.

IN YOUR OWN VOICE

WHAT DOES IT SAY?

1. On behalf of which groups does Arias accept the Nobel Peace Prize?

2. Which problems does America have to overcome?

3. What miracles can liberty perform?

4. Why does Arias say, "America's freedom, the freedom of the whole of America, cannot wait"?

5. In which direction does history march?

WHAT DOES IT MEAN?

1. Why does Costa Rica not have an army?

2. What does the word *America* mean to Arias?

3. Why are America's "scars" deep?

4. How can dialogue be an instrument for peace?

5. How does democracy cherish human values that dictatorships destroy?

STYLE AND SENSE

Comparison shows *similarities* between topics (persons, things, ideas, etc.).
Contrast shows *differences* between topics.
  Read paragraph 12.

1. Which two words in the opening sentence announce that differences and similarities exist in Central America?

2. How does sentence 3 contrast with sentence 2?

3. Which contrast is found in sentence 4?

4. Which contrast is found in sentence 5?

5. In the opening and closing sentences, what conjunction announces that a contrast follows?

FROM THE TEXT

Subject-verb agreement: the verb must agree with its subject, not with a prepositional phrase or with any other words that modify the subject.

Read the following sentence:

  The evils of one dogma are the evils of any dogma.

a. What is the subject?

b. Is it singular or plural?

c. What is the verb?

d. Is it singular or plural?

e. Identify the prepositional phrases.

See page 409 for more on subject-verb agreement with intervening words.

WRITE NOW

Do both of the following activities.

1. **Revise**—alone or with another student—an essay written in response to one of the following Writing Suggestions.

2. **Edit** the essay, paying careful attention to sentence structure, subject-verb agreement, and verb forms. Be sure that your spelling and punctuation are accurate.

WRITING SUGGESTIONS

1. Describe your plan for bringing peace to a war-torn country or region.

2. Arias writes, "I come from a world with huge problems, which we shall overcome in freedom." Discuss how freedom can overcome the severe problems facing the Americas.

3. The history of Latin America is filled with nondemocratic governments. Discuss how the absence of democracy affects the human spirit.

FURTHER WRITING SUGGESTIONS

4. Two of the Nobel Peace Prize recipients in this book are President Arias and Dr. Martin Luther King, Jr. Based on what you have read, compare the qualities of leadership and idealism shown by these men.

5. Discuss whether a small nation or region can control its own destiny in a world dominated by great powers.

6. Arias entitled his Nobel address "Only Peace Can Write the New History." Discuss the America that you would like your own children to be a part of.

ANTIGUA: A SMALL PLACE*

By Jamaica Kincaid

Born May 25, 1949, in St. John's on the eastern Caribbean island of Antigua, Jamaica Kincaid is now a citizen of the United States.

Her first book, *At the Bottom of the River* (1983), is a collection of short stories about daily life in Antigua. Kincaid's second book, *Annie John* (1985), contains related short stories about an Antiguan girl's maturation, relationship to her mother, and decision to become a nurse even if she must leave her home.

This selection is the last chapter of *A Small Place* (1988), a nonfiction portrait of Antigua and Antiguans.

WORDS TO NOTICE

strike: produce

dilapidated: faded, shabby

egrets: birds of the heron family

parched: completely dry

pauperedness: (*made-up word*) poverty

Industrial Revolution: early nineteenth-century growth of industry made possible by the use of machines

turbulence: disorder, disturbance

exalted: of high quality

stripe: kind, sort

yoke: harness, oppressive control

READ ON

1. What does the **headnote** suggest about Kincaid's feelings for Antigua?

2. When reading this selection for the first time, **underline** the words and phrases that are repeated more than once.

3. When rereading, look over the repeated words and phrases and **find** the main ideas of the selection.

---

*Editors' title

Antigua is beautiful. Antigua is too beautiful. Sometimes the beauty of it seems   1
unreal. Sometimes the beauty of it seems as if it were stage sets for a play,
for no real sunset could look like that; no real seawater could strike that many
shades of blue at once; no real sky could be that shade of blue—another
shade of blue, completely different from the shades of blue seen in the sea—
and no real cloud could be that white and float just that way in that blue sky;
no real day could be that sort of sunny and bright, making everything seem
transparent and shallow; and no real night could be that sort of black, making
everything seem thick and deep and bottomless. No real day and no real night
could be that evenly divided—twelve hours of one and twelve hours of the
other; no real day would begin that dramatically or end that dramatically
(there is no dawn in Antigua: one minute, you are in the complete darkness
of night; the next minute, the sun is overhead and it stays there until it sets
with an explosion of reds on the horizon, and then the darkness of night
comes again, and it is as if the open lid of a box you are inside suddenly
snaps into place). No real sand on any real shore is that fine or that white
(in some places) or that pink (in other places); no real flowers could be these
shades of red, purple, yellow, orange, blue, white; no real lily would bloom
only at night and perfume the air with a sweetness so thick it makes you
slightly sick; no real earth is that colour brown; no real grass is that particular
shade of dilapidated, run down green (not enough rain); no real cows look
that poorly as they feed on the unreal-looking grass in the unreal-looking
pasture, and no real cows look quite that miserable as some unreal-looking
white egrets sit on their backs eating insects; no real rain would fall with that
much force, so that it tears up the parched earth. No real village in any real
countryside would be named Table Hill Gordon, and no real village with such
a name would be so beautiful in its pauperedness, its simpleness, its one-
room houses painted in unreal shades of pink and yellow and green, a dog
asleep in the shade, some flies asleep in the corner of the dog's mouth. Or
the market on a Saturday morning, where the colours of the fruits and veg-
etables and the colours of the clothes people are wearing and the colour of
the day itself, and the colour of the nearby sea, and the colour of the sky,
which is just overhead and seems so close you might reach up and touch it,
and the way the people there speak English (they break it up) and the way
they might be angry with each other and the sound they make when they
laugh, all of this is so beautiful, all of this is not real like any other real thing
that there is. It is as if, then, the beauty—the beauty of the sea, the land, the
air, the trees, the market, the people, the sounds they make—were a prison,
and as if everything and everybody inside it were locked in and everything
and everybody that is not inside it were locked out. And what might it do to
ordinary people to live in this way every day? What might it do to them to
live in such heightened, intense surroundings day after day? They have nothing
to compare this incredible constant with, no big historical moment to compare
the way they are now to the way they used to be. No Industrial Revolution,
no revolution of any kind, no Age of Anything, no world wars, no decades of
turbulence balanced by decades of calm. Nothing, then, natural or unnatural,
to leave a mark on their character. It is just a little island. The unreal way in

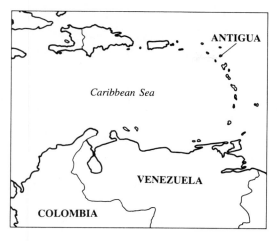

Antigua

which it is beautiful now is the unreal way in which it was always beautiful. The unreal way in which it is beautiful now that they are a free people is the unreal way in which it was beautiful when they were slaves.

Again, Antigua is a small place, a small island. It is nine miles wide by twelve miles long. It was discovered by Christopher Columbus in 1493. Not too long after, it was settled by human rubbish from Europe, who used enslaved but noble and exalted human beings from Africa (all masters of every stripe are rubbish, and all slaves of every stripe are noble and exalted; there can be no question about this) to satisfy their desire for wealth and power, to feel better about their own miserable existence, so that they could be less lonely and empty—a European disease. Eventually, the masters left, in a kind of way; eventually, the slaves were freed, in a kind of way. The people in Antigua now, the people who really think of themselves as Antiguans (and the people who would immediately come to your mind when you think about what Antiguans might be like; I mean, supposing you were to think about it), are the descendants of those noble and exalted people, the slaves. Of course, the whole thing is, once you cease to be a master, once you throw off your master's yoke, you are no longer human rubbish, you are just a human being, and all the things that adds up to. So, too, with the slaves. Once they are no longer slaves, once they are free, they are no longer noble and exalted; they are just human beings.

IN YOUR OWN VOICE

WHAT DOES IT SAY?

1. What makes the seawater seem unreal?

2. Why is there no dawn in Antigua?

3. Where is beauty found in the market?

4. Who first settled Antigua?

5. What change takes place in both master and slave when slavery is ended?

WHAT DOES IT MEAN?

1. Why is the beauty of Antigua like stage sets?

2. Why are the cows, grass, and parched earth included in the description of Antigua?

3. Why is Table Hill Gordon "so beautiful in its pauperedness"?

4. How does the unreal beauty of Antigua affect ordinary people in their daily lives?

5. Why are emptiness and loneliness "a European disease"?

STYLE AND SENSE

Repetition of key words reinforces and emphasizes major ideas. The beginning, middle, and end of a piece of writing are often unified by the use of **repetition**.

1. Identify five key words repeated in the first paragraph.

2. Why do the words *colour* and *colours* appear five times in the sentence beginning "Or the market on a Saturday . . ."?

3. Identify three key words repeated in paragraph 2.

4. How does the comparison of Antigua's beauty to a prison emphasize one major idea of this selection?

5. What contrasts occur in Antiguan life?

6. In what ways are contrasts lacking in Antiguan life?

FROM THE TEXT

Read the following sentence:

> Once they are no longer slaves, once they are free, they are no longer noble and exalted; they are just human beings.

a. Identify the two independent clauses.

b. Which mark of punctuation separates the two independent clauses?

c. Identify the two dependent clauses.

d. Which mark of punctuation separates the dependent clauses from the independent clause?

e. Is the sentence compound or complex?

See page 389 for more on preventing run-ons.

WRITE NOW

Do all of the following activities.

1. Write a **journal** on one of the following Writing Suggestions.

2. Use the journal to write a **first draft** of your essay.

3. **Revise** the draft—alone or with another student.

4. **Edit**, paying careful attention to sentence structure, verb forms, spelling, and punctuation.

WRITING SUGGESTIONS

1. Jamaica Kincaid has said, "What I really feel about America is that it's given me a place to be myself—but myself as I was formed somewhere else." Answer one of the following:

   a. Explain what a new land gives to immigrants.

   or

   b. Compare what is found in a new land with what is left behind in the homeland.

   or

   c. Explain what immigrants give to a new land.

2. Describe a place (town, area of a city, island, etc.) you lived in as a child and discuss how the place still influences you today.

FURTHER WRITING SUGGESTIONS

3. "Antigua is beautiful." The Americas are beautiful. Name one place in the Americas you would like to see or visit. Describe its beauty and explain why you want to go there.

4. Discuss how slavery causes both the slave and the master to lose their humanity.

5. Kincaid writes, "It is as if, then, the beauty ... were a prison." Discuss how living in a very beautiful place can imprison the human spirit.

QUOTATION BANK

The Quotation Bank is a collection of thoughts from many distinguished Americans—North, South, and Central. We encourage you to use it as a source of inspiration for your own writing.

You may find that these quotations help you to get started with writing a journal, freewriting, or developing an imaginary correspondence or conversation with a literary or historical figure. In addition, you may use them as topic sentences, supporting evidence, or as closing or summary sentences.

A city is in many respects a great business corporation, but in other respects it is enlarged housekeeping.

Jane Addams

*And I am a migrant, for if a migration is anything, it is a state of mind. . . .
And I am very much a migrant because I am still not quite at home in America.*

Jack Agueros, U.S. author

The forest! It is not a mystery, it is not a danger, a menace. It is a god!

Jorge Amado, Brazilian author

Men their rights and nothing more; women their rights and nothing less.

Susan B. Anthony, motto for suffragette magazine

So at last I was going to America! Really, really, going at last!

Mary Antin

I learned in New Jersey that to be a Negro meant, precisely, that one was never looked at but was simply at the mercy of the reflexes the color of one's skin caused in other people.

James Baldwin, U.S. author

I have fallen in love with American names. . . .

Stephen Vincent Benet, U.S. poet

Let us make the iron road, and make it from sea to sea.

Thomas Hart Benton, U.S. senator

God Bless America.

Irving Berlin, U.S. songwriter

For I am my mother's daughter, and the drums of Africa still beat in my heart. They will not let me rest while there is a single Negro boy or girl without a chance to prove his worth.

Mary McLeod Bethune, U.S. college president

I desire to see [all of] America fashioned into the greatest nation in the world, not so much by virtue of her area and wealth as by her freedom and glory.

Simón Bolívar

There is nothing that dies so hard and rallies so often as intolerance.

William E. Borah, U.S. senator

The immigrant's arrival in his new home is like a second birth to him.

Abraham Cahan, U.S. author and journalist

Under the philosophy that now seems to guide our destinies, nothing must get in the way of the man with the spray gun.

Rachel Carson

The business of America is business.

Calvin Coolidge, U.S. President

The American is a new man, who acts upon new principles; he must therefore entertain new ideas, and form new opinions.

J. H. St. John de Crèvecoeur, French-American author

The United States is grand and powerful.
Whenever it trembles, a profound shudder
runs down the enormous backbone of the Andes.

Rubén Dario, Nicaraguan poet

I believe that the school must represent present life—life as real and vital to
the child as that which he carries on in the home, in the neighborhood, or on
the play-ground.

John Dewey, U.S. educator and philosopher

I am not anti-American. But I am strongly pro-Canadian.

John Diefenbaker, Canadian prime minister

Power concedes nothing without a demand. It never did and it never will.

Frederick Douglass

America is a willingness of the heart.

F. Scott Fitzgerald

The general prosperity of the country, in spite of bad farm years, is in direct
proportion to the number of automobiles.

Henry Ford, founder of the Ford Motor Company

Human beings are not born once and for all on the day their mothers give
birth to them, but that life obliges them over and over again to give birth to
themselves.

Gabriel Garcia Marquez, Colombian author

I always wanted to be somebody. If I made it, it's half because I was game
enough to take a lot of punishment along the way and half because there
were a lot of people who cared enough to help me.

Althea Gibson, U.S. tennis champion

Show me the country in which there are no strikes and I'll show you that
country in which there is no liberty.

Samuel Gompers, U.S. labor leader

I only regret that I have but one life to lose for my country.

Nathan Hale, U.S. patriot before his execution as a spy

You must learn the American language if you want to understand the
American people.

T. C. Haliburton, Canadian legislator

Three hundred years ago we came, and we have remained.
Louis Hemon, French-Canadian author

Give me liberty, or give me death!
Patrick Henry, U.S. statesman

Someone is always at my elbow reminding me that I am the granddaughter of slaves. It fails to register depression with me. Slavery is sixty years in the past.
Zora Neale Hurston, U.S. author

Democracy does not necessarily result from majority rule, but rather from the forged compromise of the majority with the minority.
Daniel Inouye, U.S. senator

A chosen country with room enough for our descendants to the thousandth and thousandth generation.
Thomas Jefferson

I do not believe that any sex, class, or race can safely trust its protection in any hands but its own.
Helen Keller, U.S. author

I remember telling the Hawaiian teacher, "we Chinese can't sing 'land where our fathers died.'"
Maxine Hong Kingston, U.S. author

I am a subject of the British Crown, but whenever I have to choose between the interests of England and Canada it is manifest to me that the interests of my country are identical with those of the United States of America.
Sir Wilfred Laurier, Canadian prime minister

Give me your tired, your poor,
Your huddled masses yearning to breathe free, . . .
Emma Lazarus, "The New Colossus," poem appearing on the Statue of Liberty

My God, what have we done?
Captain Robert Lewis of the *Enola Gay,* after dropping the atomic bomb on Hiroshima, Japan, in 1945

With malice toward none; with charity for all; with firmness in the right, as God gives us to see the right.
Abraham Lincoln

We drew nearer the border, wondering aloud how we would know it.
Barry Lopez, U.S. author, on the Alaska-Canada border

When you say he is a man, you have said that he is the inheritor of every right.

José Martí, Cuban patriot and author

In the United States the striking characteristic is that each set of parents is different from each other set, that no two have exactly the same memories, that no families could be placed side by side.

Margaret Mead, U.S. anthropologist

I love the things I never had along with those I have no more.

Gabriela Mistral, Chilean poet

Once in his life a man ought to concentrate his mind upon the remembered earth.

N. Scott Momaday

Politics became part of my poetry and my life. In my poems I could not shut the door to the street, just as I could not shut the door to love, life, joy, or sadness in my young poet's heart.

Pablo Neruda, Chilean poet and political leader

The rights of citizens of the United States to vote shall not be denied or abridged by the United States or by any State on account of sex.

Nineteenth Amendment to the U.S. Constitution

Americans will do anything about Latin America except read about it.

James Reston, *New York Times* reporter and editor

It is not possible for a child, any child, ever to use his family's language in school.

Richard Rodriguez, U.S. author

With us it's: Nothing is too high! Get to the moon! We are just the guys that can run it, if we can reach it.

Will Rogers

For it is not enough to talk about peace. One must believe in it. And it is not enough to believe in it. One must work at it.

Eleanor Roosevelt

Let me assert my firm belief that the only thing we have to fear is fear itself.

Franklin D. Roosevelt, U.S. President

Science sometimes requires courage—at the very least the courage to question the conventional wisdom.

Carl Sagan, U.S. scientist and author

Equality of rights, embodied in general self-government, is the great moral element in modern democracy.

Carl Schurz, U.S. secretary of the interior

There is many a boy here today who looks on war as all glory, but boys, it is all hell!

William Tecumseh Sherman, U.S. Civil War general

Now he belongs to the ages.

Edwin M. Stanton, U.S. secretary of war, on the death of Lincoln

Suffering . . . comes from being shut out of paid and recognized work. Without it, we lose much of our self-respect and our ability to prove that we are alive by making some difference in the world.

Gloria Steinem, U.S. author

Sell [our] country! Why not sell the air, the clouds, and the great sea? Did not the Great Spirit make them all for the use of his children?

Tecumseh, chief of the Shawnee Indians

I had to reason it out in my mind. There was one of two things I had a right to, liberty or death. If I could not have the one, I would have the other, for no man should take me alive.

Harriet Tubman

The country is always stronger than we know in our most worried moments.

E. B. White

I have never wished to go back.

Narcissa Whitman, the first white woman to cross North America by covered wagon

The United States themselves are essentially the greatest poem.

Walt Whitman

GRAMMAR HANDBOOK

PARTS OF SPEECH

Every language has its own grammar or principles that govern the choice of words, as well as their order and functions.

In English, certain word groupings "feel" right, while others do not. For example, "The Civil War veteran quickly loaded his gun" communicates its meaning clearly. The expression "his gun the veteran Civil War loaded quickly," while containing the same words, lacks clarity because it does not follow any English word order pattern.

Parts of speech are the grammatical names given to words as they are used or arranged in sentences. The eight parts of speech are **nouns, pronouns, verbs, adjectives, adverbs, prepositions, conjunctions** and **interjections.**

Nouns are words that name persons, places, things, emotions, ideas, or qualities. Nouns may be subjects of their sentences or direct and indirect objects, or objects of prepositions.

In the following examples, the words in italics are nouns.

Ex. 1: Lincoln spoke movingly.

Ex. 2: Some *tribes* gave the *Pilgrims turkeys.*

Ex. 3: Pesticides are dangerous to the *environment.*

Pronouns are words that take the place of or substitute for nouns.

In the following examples, nouns appear first, followed by their pronouns. Both nouns and pronouns are in italics.

Ex. 1: The *horses* were exhausted; *they* had to rest.

Ex. 2: The *Depression* brought hard times to millions of Americans. *It* lasted for about a decade.

Exercise 1:   In the following sentences, underline each noun and circle each pronoun.

1. The Americas are the home of many democracies.

2. Jane Addams opened Hull House after she arrived in Chicago.

3. Before the Culebra Cut was finished, it was visited by many tourists.

4. The three ships were noticed as soon as they entered Cuban waters.

5. The preamble to the Constitution begins, "We the People."

Verbs are words that show action or provide a sense of being or becoming. Verbs may consist of more than one word, such as *could have* and *put up with*.
In the following examples, the words in italics are verbs.

Ex. 1: In Canada, Remembrance Day *commemorates* those who *died* during World War I.

Ex. 2: Columbus *appeared* happy at the sight of land.

Exercise 2:   In the following sentences, underline each verb.

1. Gatsby purchased an expensive mansion.

2. In 1814 Bolívar spoke before the Venezuelan Assembly.

3. Ten Bears, who was confident, demanded action.

4. As Holmes descended from her carriage, she could hear the sound of cannons.

5. Many towns will grow quiet unless people become aware of the danger to their environment.

Adjectives are words that describe, limit, modify, or give information about a noun or pronoun.
In the following examples, the words in italics are adjectives.

Ex. 1: The *small* town contained *old* buildings.

Ex. 2: Nick was *nervous* when he crossed the *wide* Mississippi.

Note 1: *A, an,* and *the* are called **articles.** They are also considered adjectives because they limit the nouns that follow them. (For correct use of *a* and *an,* see page 473.)

Note 2: Present and **past participles** are also considered adjectives when they modify nouns.

Note 3: Possessive words are adjectives if a noun follows: *Whitman's* poem, the imaginary *creature's* tail.

Adverbs are words that describe or give information about verbs, adjectives, or other adverbs.

In the following examples, the words in italics are adverbs.

Ex. 1: The Massachusetts colonists suffered *patiently* during their first winter.

Ex. 2: Canada is *extremely* beautiful.

Ex. 3: The Massachusetts colonists suffered *very patiently* during their first winter.

Exercise 3:   In the following sentences, underline the adjectives and circle the adverbs.

1. The young immigrant eagerly studied the life of George Washington.

2. Canadian prairies are flat and mostly without trees.

3. Cruel and hostile, the soldiers destroyed the native village entirely.

4. Despite numerous problems, Chrysler employees worked hard and sacrificed much to help their financially troubled company.

5. The famous photograph of the completed transcontinental railroad totally omits the Chinese workers.

Prepositions are words that give a sense of direction, place, or possession. They are part of groups of words called **prepositional phrases.** A prepositional phrase begins with a preposition and ends with a noun or pronoun. Prepositional phrases often answer the questions how, why, when, or where.

Note: No verb occurs in a prepositional phrase. In addition, a prepositional phrase is almost never the subject of a sentence.

In the following examples, the words in italics are prepositions.

to the ship

around the campfire

in the Constitution

by midnight

on the Mississippi

In the following examples, the words in italics are prepositional phrases.

> *Ex. 1:* The shots were fired *at Fort Sumter.*

> *Ex. 2:* The Wright brothers' machine slowly lifted *off the ground.*

Exercise 4:   In the following sentences, underline each prepositional phrase.

1. President Arias of Costa Rica won the Nobel Prize for his peace plan.

2. Sitting on a branch of a birch tree in her backyard, Vanessa waited for her parents to return from the Remembrance Day parade.

3. At dawn the atomic explosion rose through the clouds and over the desert.

4. Richard Hunter, by his own efforts and with considerable luck, was appointed to the job of head bookkeeper.

5. After the interview with Branch Rickey, Jackie Robinson promised to fight against bigotry by using self-control.

Conjunctions are words that join individual words, clauses, and phrases. Some common conjunctions are *and, or, but, since, because, if, when.*
In the following examples, the words in italics are conjunctions.

> *Ex. 1:* *When* Neil Armstrong *and* the other astronauts landed on the moon on July 20, 1969, they made history.

> *Ex. 2:* Chief Ten Bears spoke to keep his people free, *but* his words were not heeded.

> *Ex. 3:* To explore the west *and* to map the area were the tasks assigned to Lewis *and* Clark.

Interjections are usually single words expressing feelings or commanding one's attention.
In the following examples, the words in italics are *interjections.*

Ex. 1: Safe! Robinson had stolen home again.

Ex. 2: "*Wow!* That's an incredible sight," Antin said as she saw the Statue of Liberty.

Review Exercise: A word can function as more than one part of speech. In the space after each sentence, write the part of speech of the word *down.*

1. It was first *down* for Jackie Robinson and the other members of the UCLA

football team. _____

2. Do you think that UCLA will *down* USC today? _____

3. Even though the day was sunny, some fans wore *down* jackets to the

game. _____

4. Robinson looked *down* the field. _____

5. The quarterback yelled "*Down!*" as the ball whizzed by Robinson's helmet.

_____

6. After scoring, Robinson jumped up and *down.* _____

BASIC SENTENCES AND CLAUSES

A. A **sentence** is a group of words having at least three elements:

1. subject
2. verb
3. independent clause

B. The **subject** of the sentence is *who* or *what* does the action or *who* or *what* the sentence is about.

Ex. 1: Rachel Carson wrote books about the environment.

Rachel Carson (who) does the action (*wrote*).

Ex. 2: The Constitution belongs to the people.

The Constitution is *what* the sentence is about.

Ex. 3: Attacking the Spaniards brought success to Bolívar.

Attacking the Spaniards is *what* does the action (*brought*). (Bolívar is *not* the subject of the sentence.)

Exercise: Underline the subject in each sentence.

1. The rebellion occurred in Lares in 1868.

2. An Wang developed computer systems.

3. All last week, we hiked through the Laurentians in Canada.

4. Searching for summer's house kept the Kiowas busy.

5. Can peace and prosperity come to Central America?

C. The **verb** of the sentence has two functions:

1. It tells the action that the subject does.
2. It states something about the subject by linking it to words that identify (rename) it or describe it. (This type of verb, therefore, is sometimes called a **state of being** or **linking** verb.)

Ex. 1: The Panama Canal *connects* the Atlantic and Pacific oceans.

Connects is the action that the subject (*Panama Canal*) does.

Ex. 2: The Panama Canal *is* an engineering achievement.

The verb *is* links the subject (*Panama Canal*) to the words that identify it as *an engineering achievement.*

Ex. 3: The Panama Canal *looks* long and narrow.

The verb *looks* links the subject (*Panama Canal*) to the words that describe it as *long and narrow.*

Ex. 4: Many ships *have sailed* through the Panama Canal.

The verb sometimes consists of two or more words. *Have sailed* is the action that the subject (*ships*) does.

Note: In questions, the subject and verb are inverted (turned around) and often the two parts of the verb are separated by the subject, as in the following:

Ex. 5: Have many ships *sailed* through the Panama Canal?

The verb *have sailed* is separated by the subject (*ships*).

Exercise: In the spaces below each sentence, write (1) the verb and (2) whether it is an *action* or *linking* verb.

1. Oscar Arias received the Nobel Peace Prize in Oslo, Norway.

    1. _____   **2.** _____

2. In Rochester, New York, Frederick Douglass spoke.

1. _____   2. _____

3. A warm breeze would feel good to the weary Lewis and Clark.

1. _____   2. _____

4. In front of the saint's picture, her grandfather had recited the Spanish poem.

1. _____   2. _____

5. Every boy in a Horatio Alger story could have been a model of ethical behavior.

1. _____   2. _____

Review Exercise: In the spaces below each sentence, write (1) the subject and (2) the verb.

1. The Pony Express rider was practicing his skills in the corral.

1. _____   2. _____

2. Without a doubt, breaking baseball's color barrier will be Jackie Robinson's greatest claim to fame.

1. _____   2. _____

3. Is democracy the best system of government?

1. _____   2. _____

4. The atomic blast's mushroom-shaped cloud rose ominously over the desert.

1. _____   2. _____

5. In her diary Emma Holmes had recorded her observations and reactions to the U.S. Civil War.

1. _____   2. _____

D. A **clause** is a group of words containing a subject and a verb.

An **independent** (or **main**) **clause** is a clause that can stand alone as a sentence.

Ex. 1: Freedom guarantees individual rights.

Anytime a subject (*freedom*) and a verb (*guarantees*) are the first words of a clause, the clause is independent.

Note: The key to writing correct and complete sentences is the independent clause. If you have an independent clause, more information can be added to the basic sentence.

The independent clause is italicized in the following examples:

> *Ex. 2:* *Freedom guarantees individual rights* to each man, woman, and child.

> *Ex. 3:* According to the Declaration of Independence, *freedom guarantees individual rights* to each man, woman, and child.

> *Ex. 4:* According to the Declaration of Independence, which was written in 1776, *freedom guarantees individual rights* to each man, woman, and child, regardless of race, color, or creed.

The independent clause is a complete thought in itself, so information can be added before or after the clause.

E. A **subordinate** (or **dependent**) **clause** is a clause that cannot stand alone as a sentence. Usually, it begins with an introductory word that forces the clause to depend on or be attached to an independent clause to complete its meaning. Such introductory words include *if, since, because, when,* and *although.* (See page 393 for a list of **subordinating conjunctions.**)

> *Ex. 1:* Because freedom guarantees individual rights.

> *Ex. 2:* Although freedom guarantees individual rights.

> *Ex. 3:* Which guarantees individual rights.

These examples cannot stand alone as sentences. More information is needed. Subordinate clauses like these are known as **sentence fragments** when punctuated like a sentence—with a capital letter at the start and a period at the end. (See page 405.)

Exercise 1:   In the space next to each example, write *Ind* if it is an independent clause or *Sub* if it is a subordinate (dependent) clause.

1. As the tracks were joined at Promontory, Utah. _____

2. Harriet Tubman later returned to Maryland. _____

3. In the north woods, the *Teakettler* hid. _____

4. The Caribbean Sea which glistens in the sun. _____

5. Five hundred years ago, when Columbus reached land. _____

6. For many, Noah Webster's dictionary was a work of patriotism. _____

7. Ten Bears and the other tribal chiefs who met on the prairies. _____

8. Even though the Chrysler Corporation was going through difficult times.

_____

9. In 1889 the idea of Hull House captured the public's attention. _____

10. Because environmental problems have increased over the past two decades. _____

Exercise 2:   Each of the following paragraphs has three sentences. In the blank space after each sentence, write *Ind* if the sentence contains only an independent clause, or *I/S* if the sentence contains both an independent and a subordinate clause.

1. Antigua is Jamaica Kincaid's place of birth. _____ Her book describes the island's scenic wonders and people. _____ Because her descriptions are so vivid, Antigua seems like a fascinating place to visit. _____

2. During the flight to the moon, the astronauts had to concentrate on many tasks. _____ As their families back on earth listened intently to every detail, the astronauts described their final approach to the moon. _____ Feelings of relief swept over everyone when a safe landing was announced. _____

3. When Vanessa thought about not seeing the Remembrance Day parade, she became sad. _____ Her grandmother, who had lost a son in World War I, would be angry. _____ Therefore, Vanessa entered the house silently. _____

4. As a young man, An Wang studied electronics and engineering. _____ Soon after he left China in the late 1940s, he enrolled at the Massachusetts Institute of Technology. _____ Wang made his first discoveries about computers while he was there. _____

5. Nick Adams looked at the Mississippi, which seemed almost endless. _____ The river coiled under bridges and passed woods for as far as he could see. _____ Nick now understood the Native American name *Mississippi*, "Father of the Waters." _____

6. About a mile from the Charleston harborside was Fort Sumter, the U.S. military outpost. _____ As soon as she heard about the planned attack on the fort, Emma Holmes rode to join her friends. _____ They all excitedly watched the battle. _____

7. On the prairies whenever Chief Ten Bears wanted to make camp, he did it quickly. _____ The people of his tribe, who were very skillful, arranged the tents for protection and maximum security. _____ In no time at all, the chief and the tribe had established temporary dwellings. _____

8. Because Noah Webster took pride in his young country, he included many American words in his dictionary. _____ Native American words like *squash* and *opossum* were defined. _____ In the preface to this great work, Webster explained the purpose of the dictionary. _____

9. Up in the hills of Puerto Rico, before the sun rose, the rebels planned their raid. _____ Within an hour one squad advanced to the Spanish governors' stronghold. _____ Manolo el Leñero, who was just a young boy, waved the flag proudly until he fell in battle. _____

10. Before the slaves arrived in Barbados, they had been chained together and treated inhumanely on the ships. _____ Now they faced the humiliation of the slave market, which was the place set aside for their sale and purchase. _____ Nothing could have prepared them for their ordeal.

THREE TYPES OF SENTENCES

A. The **simple sentence** contains one independent clause.

Ex. 1: The Wrights flew the plane.

The simple sentence contains only one subject (*Wrights*) and one verb (*flew*).

Additional information can be added in the form of a prepositional phrase (*in North Carolina*), an adverb phrase of time (*on December 17, 1903*), an adverb modifying the verb (*daringly*), and an adjective modifying the direct object (*tiny*).

Ex. 2: In North Carolina on December 17, 1903, the Wrights daringly flew the tiny plane.

or

Ex. 2A: The Wrights daringly flew the tiny plane on December 17, 1903, in North Carolina.

Even with the additional information supplied, examples 2 and 2A are simple sentences because they each contain only one independent clause: *The Wrights flew the plane.*

B. The **compound sentence** contains two or more independent clauses. Usually, the clauses are joined by a coordinating conjunction.

Ex. 3: The Wrights flew the plane, and the age of aviation began.

The compound sentence contains two independent clauses, each of which can stand alone: (1) *The Wrights flew the plane* and (2) *The age of aviation began.*
The coordinating conjunction *and* shows that both independent clauses are equal in importance.
Note: A comma is used at the end of the independent clause *before* the coordinating conjunction. (See page 465.)
Additional information can be added to this type of sentence as long as two distinct independent clauses remain.

Ex. 4: The Wrights daringly flew the tiny plane on December 17, 1903, in North Carolina, and by this great achievement, the age of aviation truly began.

C. The **complex sentence** consists of one independent clause and at least one subordinate (or dependent) clause. The subordinate clause may be added before or after the independent clause.

Ex. 5: When the Wrights flew the plane, the age of aviation began.

or

Ex. 5A: The age of aviation began when the Wrights flew the plane.

The independent clause is *the age of aviation began;* the subordinate clause is *when the Wrights flew the plane.*
The subordinate clause cannot stand alone; it needs an independent clause to complete its meaning. The subordinating conjunction *when* indicates that this clause is subordinate and less important than the independent clause.

Note: If a subordinate clause comes *before* an independent clause, a comma is usually used to separate the two clauses. No comma is needed if the subordinate clause comes *after* the independent clause.

The length of a sentence does not determine whether it is simple, compound, or complex. The number and types of clauses determine this.

Exercise 1:   In the space next to each sentence, write *S* if it is simple, *Cp* if it is compound, and *Cx* if it is complex.

1. Harriet Tubman escaped from slavery. _____ She had personal freedom, but she wanted to help others escape. _____ After she made her plans, she returned secretly to Maryland. _____

2. With the help of Sacajawea, Lewis and Clark explored the western territory. _____ She used her knowledge of the land well, and the expedition never lost its way. _____ Lewis praised her efforts when he wrote to President Jefferson. _____

3. Because Canada is such a vast country, its people have developed many theories about True North. _____ To some, True North is a place on a map. _____ To others, it is a state of mind, for it affects their behavior. _____

4. The Depression of the 1930s was an economic disaster, and countless families lost their homes. _____ People who were forced to travel in search of jobs were known as Okies. _____ Many, obviously, had left Oklahoma's dust bowl. _____

5. At the beginning of this century, small towns seemed isolated from the big cities. _____ However, radio and television have turned the nation and world into a global community, and hardly anyone today is unaware of major events. _____ Also, superhighways, which came about because of the automobile, have brought city and town closer. _____

Review Exercise   Combine each pair of simple sentences into *either* a compound or a complex sentence. You may have to add or remove words, or change the word order.

The two sentences *Oscar Arias devised a peace plan. He received a Nobel Prize for his efforts.* may be changed into either:

Compound: Oscar Arias devised a peace plan, and he received a Nobel Prize for his efforts.

or

Complex: Because Oscar Arias devised a peace plan, he received a Nobel Prize for his efforts.

1. The birds were no longer there. Pesticides had driven them away.

   _____

   _____

2. Many ethnic groups lived near Hull House. Some of them did not take advantage of its services.

   _____

   _____

3. The Americas seemed like a paradise to Columbus. He recommended to the Spanish king and queen that colonies be established.

   _____

   _____

4. Bolívar at first rejected the offer of the presidency. The Venezuelan Assembly insisted he take the position.

   _____

   _____

5. Dangers of all kinds faced the Pony Express riders. They were mostly teen-agers.

   _____

   _____

RUN-ONS, COMMA SPLICES, AND SENTENCE FRAGMENTS

A. A **run-on sentence** occurs when two or more independent clauses are joined without a conjunction or the correct punctuation. A run-on is incorrect because two complete thoughts must be separated by a **period,** a **semicolon,** or a **conjunction.**

> *Ex. 1:* The weather looked bad some Pilgrims were worried.

> *Ex. 2:* The Kiowas rode through the woods they saw shadows against the moon.

In example 1, *the weather looked good* and *some Pilgrims were worried* are independent clauses. Without punctuation between these clauses, a run-on exists.

What are the independent clauses in example 2?

Note: It is helpful to read your written work aloud so that you can notice when one independent clause ends and the other begins. You may find that your voice drops naturally, and that you pause after the first independent clause.

B. A type of run-on not as easily recognized is the **comma splice.** The comma splice contains two independent clauses separated by a comma. The comma alone is not a strong enough punctuation mark to separate fully two independent clauses.

> *Ex. 3:* Eleanor Roosevelt spoke at the United Nations, she was the United States delegate.

Ex. 4: The soldiers began the massacre, in a few moments bodies lay all around the village square.

In example 3, *Eleanor Roosevelt spoke at the United Nations* and *she was the United States delegate* are independent clauses. With only a comma separating the two clauses, a comma splice exists.

What are the independent clauses in example 4?

Another way of looking at it: A run-on is two sentences punctuated as if they were one.

Note: The meaning of a run-on sentence may be unclear:

Ex. 5: Lee Iacocca managed to save the Chrysler Corporation after getting federal loan guarantees many celebrities also raised funds.

Who received the guarantees—Iacocca or the celebrities?

Exercise: For each of these run-ons and comma splices, underline the first independent clause and double underline the second independent clause.

1. In 1947 Jackie Robinson became a Brooklyn Dodger, the color barrier of major league baseball was broken.

2. Puerto Rican rebels attacked the Spanish stronghold within a few hours unfortunately they had to retreat.

3. Above the forty-ninth parallel to the north of the United States lies Canada it is a country with vast natural resources.

4. Any person can succeed in a business career without going to college he or she just needs to be in the right place at the right time.

5. The small villages that the people lived in had no strong defenses, they had no expectations of danger.

PREVENTING RUN-ONS AND COMMA SPLICES

A. A **period** between independent clauses prevents a run-on by creating two separate sentences.

Ex. 1: The weather looked bad. Some Pilgrims were worried.

Ex. 2: The Kiowas rode through the woods. They saw shadows against the
moon.

Exercise: Correct the following run-ons and comma splices by placing a
period between the independent clauses.

1. Out west a ferocious bear charged Meriwether Lewis, he was able to fight
   it off with a wooden club.

2. Frederick Douglass spoke out against slavery frequently before large audiences in some states his strongly worded remarks aroused controversy.

3. The astronauts landed on the moon in 1969 while watching the telecast
   their families were tense, excited, and proud.

4. The Declaration of Independence gained support for the new nation shortly
   afterwards this document inspired people in many countries.

5. When Chief Ten Bears spoke out against being confined to a reservation,
   Kiowas and Apaches joined the protest, the Indian Peace Commission insisted that Ten Bears sign the treaty and obey its terms.

6. None of the Pilgrims had ever sailed before few were sick on the voyage.

7. Aboard the ship, the young women thought of the future they spent hours
   wondering what their husbands-to-be looked like.

8. Arias hoped his peace plan would be a success, he wanted to end the
   conflicts among Central American nations.

9. The parade moved slowly along Main Street the veterans waved at the crowd
   lining the route.

10. Because people were suffering during the depression, Rogers wanted to
    speak out, his radio show reached millions.

B. Inserting a **comma** followed by a **coordinating conjunction** between independent clauses prevents a run-on. Adding a coordinating conjunction after
the comma prevents a comma splice.

Ex. 1: The weather looked bad, *so* some Pilgrims were worried.

Ex. 2: The Kiowas rode through the woods, *and* they saw shadows against
the moon.

A **conjunction** connects clauses, words, and phrases. **Coordinating** denotes that the connected parts have equal importance grammatically.

The most common **coordinating conjunctions** are

and	to introduce additional information
but	to introduce contrasting information
yet	to introduce contrasting information
for	to introduce a reason
so	to introduce a result
or	to introduce an alternative
nor	to introduce an alternative in a sentence with a negative word

Exercise: Correct the following run-ons and comma splices by punctuating correctly and by placing a coordinating conjunction between the independent clauses.

1. At dawn the scientists awaited the first atomic blast suddenly the skies were brighter than ever before.

2. Bolívar's troops may have camped in the valley, they may have stayed on the steep side of the mountain.

3. Most Pony Express journeys involved great risks, the riders had to go swiftly through rugged, uninhabited areas.

4. In the 1920s President Herbert Hoover promised the public "a chicken in every pot," his economic policies led to the Great Depression.

5. The Constitution is not a perfect document amendments are used to make improvements.

6. On the voyage from Africa to Barbados, the captain and crew treated the captives heartlessly nothing was worse than the years of slavery that awaited them.

7. Changing customs in the U.S. produced new words without much delay Webster decided to write a dictionary of the English language.

8. The wives of the Canadian pioneers worked in the fields alongside their husbands, survival depended on cooperation.

9. That town must stop the spraying of the crops, the farmers have to start growing them organically.

10. The creatures described by lumberjacks are imaginary no fossil traces of them will be found.

C. A **subordinating conjunction** between independent clauses prevents a run-on.

> *Ex. 1:* The weather looked good *although* some Pilgrims were worried.

> *Ex. 2:* The Kiowas rode through the woods *after* they saw shadows against the moon.

A **subordinating conjunction** begins a clause that is less important than its connecting clause. The **subordinate clause** cannot stand alone as a sentence.
   Note: No comma or other punctuation is needed before the subordinating conjunction.
   The most common **subordinating conjunctions** are

after	once	when	to introduce time
as	since	whenever	
before	until	while	
because	so that		to introduce cause
in order that	that		
since	whereas		
as if	unless		to introduce possibility
as though	whether		
if			
although			to introduce contrast
even though			
though			
than			to introduce comparisons

   Note: Words like *how, that, what, where, why* are used to introduce answers when they connect subordinate clauses to independent clauses.

Exercise: Correct the following run-ons and comma splices by using a subordinating conjunction and by punctuating correctly. Try to use a different subordinating conjunction for each example.

1. Bolívar warned his troops the upcoming battle would be dangerous.

2. On many occasions, Eleanor Roosevelt journeyed to distant places in each one she learned about other people's lives.

3. Traveling westward, Nick Adams looked forward to an adventurous life, earlier he had led a quiet existence.

4. One governor treated civil rights demonstrators badly they were criminals.

5. Harriet Tubman's life would be in danger, she escaped.

6. The rebels tried to overthrow the Spanish directors, it became clear that independence would not be granted.

7. To guarantee safety, the astronauts had to land the lunar module the surface leveled off.

8. Faced with disaster for his tribe, Chief Ten Bears signed the peace treaty, he had no other choice.

9. The King's Daughters did not know, their husbands-to-be would be waiting at the Canadian shore.

10. In the midst of the Great Depression, people sold apples as their livelihood, an improved economy made it possible for them to resume their careers.

Note: Because a subordinating conjunction introduces a dependent clause, a semicolon should not be used before it. Semicolons are placed between independent clauses.

D. A **subordinating conjunction** before the first of two independent clauses prevents a run-on.

Ex. 1: *Although* the weather looked good, some Pilgrims were worried.

Ex. 1A: *Although* some Pilgrims were worried, the weather looked good.

Ex. 2: *When* the Kiowas rode through the woods, they saw shadows against the moon.

Ex. 2A: *When* they saw shadows against the moon, the Kiowas rode through the woods.

Note: A comma is needed after the first clause.

Exercise: Correct the following run-ons and comma splices by using a subordinating conjunction at the start of each sentence and by punctuating correctly.

1. _____ The amount of the pollution increased, the songs of the birds fell silent.

2. _____ Canada lies north of the United States, its climate is colder.

3. _____ Riding through desolate country was not dangerous enough, a Pony Express horseman had to risk ambushes.

4. _____ There were many uncommon words in Webster's dictionary, they were easy to understand because of the clarity of the definitions.

5. _____ Columbus made an entry in his log, he recorded the date and the ship's location.

6. _____ At Kitty Hawk, the winds had not been brisk that day the Wright Brothers planned a flight later in the week.

7. _____ The Brooklyn Dodgers played in other National League cities, the center of attraction was Jackie Robinson.

8. _____ The aloe plant was located in Grandmother's house and garden everyone came to pick it.

9. _____ Richard Hunter remembered those who helped him rise from poverty to success, he became a very charitable businessman.

10. _____ The Constitution was ratified in 1789, the Bill of Rights was not added until 1791.

Note: Because a subordinating conjunction introduces a dependent clause, a semicolon should not be placed after this clause. Semicolons are placed between independent clauses.

E. A **semicolon** between independent clauses prevents a run-on.

> *Ex. 1:* The weather looked bad; some Pilgrims were worried.
>
> *Ex. 2:* The Kiowas rode through the woods; they saw shadows against the moon.

Note: A semicolon *must* be preceded and followed by an independent clause.

Exercise: Correct the following run-ons and comma splices by using a semicolon.

1. The Wrights' airplane shook in the blustery air the ground crew cheered as it took off.

2. Columbus kept a very detailed record of his voyage to establish proof of Spanish title was one of the log's purposes.

3. Standing before his Gettysburg audience, Lincoln seemed uneasy, to many there his brief speech would appear inadequate.

4. Civil rights workers were often arrested before segregation laws became illegal, in fact Martin Luther King, Jr., himself was jailed several times.

5. In treating an asthmatic patient, my grandmother applied medicinal herbs and plants soon his breathing would become more normal.

F. A **semicolon** followed by a **conjunctive adverb** and a **comma** between independent clauses prevents a run-on.

> *Ex. 1:* The weather looked bad**;** *consequently,* some Pilgrims were worried.

> *Ex. 2:* The Kiowas rode through the woods**;** *moreover,* they saw shadows against the moon.

A **conjunctive adverb** shows the relationship between independent clauses. *Note:* A **period** may replace the semicolon.

> *Ex. 3:* The weather looked bad**.** *Consequently,* some Pilgrims were worried.

The most common **conjunctive adverbs** are

therefore consequently thus hence	to introduce a result or conclusion
however nevertheless	to introduce contrasting information
furthermore moreover besides also	to introduce additional information
subsequently then	to introduce later events
otherwise	to introduce alternative information

Exercise 1:   Correct the following run-ons and comma splices by punctuating correctly and by using a conjunctive adverb. Try to use a different conjunctive adverb for each sentence.

1. Eleanor Roosevelt became famous for her humanitarian accomplishments, she won renown as an author and a lecturer.

2. With high hopes, the natives stole back to their village all their houses were destroyed.

3. After killing an overseer, Harriet Tubman escaped from Maryland it was no surprise that a reward was offered for her capture.

4. At first you drive north through the plains areas, the Canadian forests loom tall and magnificent before you.

5. The soldiers received dark goggles to shield their eyes from the flash of the atomic blast their vision could have been damaged severely.

   Note: If the conjunctive adverb is placed *within* the independent clause, the punctuation is different.

   Ex. 1: The weather looked bad; some Pilgrims were worried, *consequently.*

   Ex. 2: The Kiowas rode through the woods; they saw shadows, *moreover,* against the moon.

Exercise 2:   Correct the following run-ons and comma splices by inserting a conjunctive adverb wherever appropriate and by punctuating correctly.

1. A Canadian's sense of identity is tied to the land he or she therefore needs to understand "True North."

2. Frederick Douglass's words moved his audience deeply, many applauded and remained to talk to him.

3. Workers and executives made sacrifices during Chrysler's financial crisis, the company would have collapsed.

4. The blast shook the desert, the enormous cloud rose rapidly.

5. Writing the Declaration of Independence was not an easy task Thomas Jefferson produced a document of clarity and grace.

G. To prevent a run-on or a comma splice, a **relative pronoun** can be substituted for the subject of the second independent clause.

   Run-on: Bad weather bothered some Pilgrims they feared a harsh winter.

   Ex. 1: Bad weather bothered some Pilgrims *who* feared a harsh winter.

Comma Splice: The Kiowas stared at the moon, it was covered by strange shadows.

Ex. 2: The Kiowas stared at the moon, *which* was covered by strange shadows.

A relative pronoun relates (names or describes) a clause to a noun or another pronoun in the sentence. (See page 471 for more on the use of commas in restrictive and nonrestrictive clauses.)
The most common **relative pronouns** are

who, whoever, whom, whomever, whose	substitute for persons
which, whichever	substitute for things
that	substitutes for things

Exercise: Correct the following run-ons and comma splices by using a relative pronoun and by punctuating correctly. When using the relative pronoun, you may have to remove words in the example.

1. Sick persons often come to Grandmother, she treats them with medicinal herbs.

2. The lunar module descended slowly to the surface, it seemed solid enough.

3. Manolo el Leñero died during the 1868 revolt, the rebellion did not succeed.

4. Webster's dictionary contains many definitions all of them are accurate.

5. Crossing the Mississippi excited Nick he knew that his future would be brighter.

Note: The relative pronoun begins a **relative clause,** which is always dependent.

Review Exercise 1:   Correct the following run-ons and comma splices by using coordinating or subordinating conjunctions. In some examples, you may wish to reverse the positions of the clauses.

1. The Great Depression began in 1929, it lasted ten years.

2. Lewis and Clark explored the western territory they mapped their entire journey.

3. Walt Whitman has nothing but praise for the workers his poetry is democratic in spirit.

4. When Oscar Arias became president of Costa Rica, there was unrest in neighboring countries in his native land there was peace.

5. The town in Rachel Carson's fable was set on a beautiful hill by the river factories dominated the landscape.

6. Mary Antin's class in history became her favorite, she read a lot about George Washington.

7. Ships sail through the Panama Canal the former route was around Cape Horn at the tip of South America.

8. The tribes waited angrily, the commissioners argued about the words of the treaty.

9. The civil rights movement prospered, Dr. Martin Luther King, Jr., was a figure around whom people could rally.

10. All the tourists will want to return to Canada they get a glimpse of the scenic vistas.

Review Exercise 2:   Correct the following run-ons and comma splices by using periods, semicolons, commas, conjunctive adverbs, and relative pronouns. Use at least *two* of each.

1. Columbus held up the flag, the island now belonged to the king and queen of Spain.

2. Not a sound could be heard all living creatures seemed to have fled.

3. There are ten constitutional amendments in the Bill of Rights, freedom of speech is mentioned in the first.

4. Chrysler's recovery depended on cooperation between management and labor, they were unused to being allies.

5. During his first year in the major leagues, Jackie Robinson was often heckled his teammates, especially Pee Wee Reese, encouraged him.

6. Young Richard Hunter worked long hours for many weeks his boss did not notice.

7. After he had led armies for over twenty years, Simón Bolívar gained a taste for power he was reluctant to give up any of it.

8. Keeping open the route to California, the Pony Express carried the mail through storms and deserts the mail was delivered on a regular basis.

9. In the wilderness, the young couples lived in cabins, these homes were built with the brides' help.

10. Because Will Rogers had a humorous touch in talking about the Depression he could raise people's morale in many communities he was the sole bright spot in their lives.

As you saw in the above exercise, there are several ways to prevent run-ons and comma splices. In the following example, a semicolon and a period are used.

> Emma Holmes rode to the waterfront, she wanted to see the battle for Fort Sumter.

> *Semicolon:* Emma Holmes rode to the waterfront; she wanted to see the battle for Fort Sumter.

> *Period:* Emma Holmes rode to the waterfront. She wanted to see the battle for Fort Sumter.

Review Exercise 3:   Correct the following run-on sentences by using the specific method listed. You may change the order of the clauses.

> *Sentence 1:* There are more democratic governments now they give people hope for a better tomorrow.

1. coordinating conjunction: _____

    _____

2. conjunctive adverb: _____

    _____

3. subordinating conjunction at the beginning of sentence:

    _____

    _____

> *Sentence 2:* Abraham Lincoln spoke the crowd was silent.

1. coordinating conjunction: _____

    _____

2. subordinating conjunction at the beginning of sentence:

    _____

    _____

3. subordinating conjunction in the middle of sentence:

_____

_____

    Sentence 3: The road was almost impassable Martha Shaw and Johnny continued onward.

1. coordinating conjunction: _____

_____

2. conjunctive adverb: _____

_____

3. subordinating conjunction at the beginning of sentence:

_____

_____

    Sentence 4: The last tie was placed the transcontinental railroad was completed.

1. coordinating conjunction: _____

_____

2. subordinating conjunction at the beginning of sentence:

_____

_____

3. subordinating conjunction in the middle of sentence:

_____

_____

SENTENCE FRAGMENTS

A. A **sentence fragment** is an incomplete sentence because it lacks a subject, a verb, or both *and* because it does not express a complete thought.

    A sentence fragment, though incomplete, is punctuated like a complete sentence (with a capital letter at the beginning and a period at the end).

Ex. 1: Sparkled on the water.

Ex. 2: The sun on the water.

Ex. 3: Sparkling on the water.

Ex. 4: Which sparkled on the water.

Ex. 5: When the sun sparkled on the water.

These examples are punctuated like complete sentences, but they need additional words and information to become complete thoughts. They are sentence fragments.

Note: It is helpful to read your written work aloud so that you can notice whether each group of words can stand alone, without needing further information to complete its meaning.

Ex. 6: The crew cheered. When the ship left the harbor. Everyone had high hopes.

The sentence fragment *when the ship left the harbor* is not complete by itself. It must be attached to one of the other sentences here in order to complete its meaning:

Ex. 7: The crew cheered when the ship left the harbor.

or

Ex. 8: When the ship left the harbor, everyone had high hopes.

Exercise: Underline all of the sentence fragments in the following groups of words.

1. Harriet Tubman took the slaves out of Maryland. And waited for the signal to come out of hiding.

2. True North. A feeling as well as a place.

3. While his men applauded. Bolívar made new battle plans.

4. Lewis and Clark were guided by Sacajawea. Who was an American Indian woman.

5. Crossing the Mississippi by train. Nick thought of the World Series game won by the White Sox.

B. One type of sentence fragment omits the **subject.**

Ex. 1: Sailed at dawn.

Sailed at dawn is a fragment because it lacks a subject.

Complete Sentence: The ship sailed at dawn.

Exercise: Complete each of the following fragments by adding a subject to form a sentence. Choose from the list below.

Civil War soldiers

the young French woman

the astronauts

the Chinese laborers

Nick Adams

1. _____ worked hard to complete the transcontinental railroad.

2. _____ couldn't wait to cross the Mississippi.

3. Buried in the cemetery at Gettysburg are many _____ .

4. _____ reached their destination, the moon.

5. In Quebec _____ is marrying a farmer.

C. Another type of sentence fragment omits the **verb.**

Ex. 2: The ship at dawn.

The ship at dawn is a fragment because it lacks a verb.

Complete Sentence: The ship sailed at dawn.

Exercise: Complete each of the following fragments by adding a verb to form a sentence. You may place the verb wherever you wish and add other words, if needed.

1. The Pony Express riders late and tired.

2. Antigua, beautiful and complex.

3. Lumberjacks in the Wisconsin forests.

4. Men, women, and children on the slave ship.

5. The government of the people, by the people, and for the people.

D. A third type of sentence fragment consists of a **phrase** (prepositional, participial, infinitive, or gerund).

Ex. 3: The ship sailing at dawn.

The ship sailing at dawn is a fragment because the present participle *sailing* is not a verb and cannot stand alone without a helping verb or additional words to complete the thought.

Complete Sentence: The ship will be sailing at dawn.

or

The ship, sailing at dawn, reached port.

Exercise 1:   Complete each of the following fragments by adding a helping verb or other words to form a sentence.

1. Robinson breaking into major league baseball.

2. Immigrants to seek a land of freedom.

3. The automobiles on the assembly lines in the Detroit factories.

4. Forming the Wang Laboratories.

5. Hull House established by Jane Addams.

Exercise 2:   Complete each of the following fragments by inserting a subject and complete verb or by adding an independent clause to form a sentence.

1. Declaring its independence from England.

2. Exposed to radiation from the blast.

3. One of the best systems of government.

4. For many years to join the Atlantic and Pacific oceans.

5. Longing to become citizens.

E. A fourth type of sentence fragment consists of a **relative clause** only.

Ex. 4: That sailed at dawn.

That sailed at dawn is a fragment because the relative pronoun *that* cannot stand alone without being attached to a noun or pronoun that is part of an independent clause. *That* may also be changed to a subject pronoun.

Complete Sentence: The ship that sailed at dawn reached port.

The ship reached port is the independent clause.

or

It sailed at dawn.

The subject pronoun *it* replaces the relative pronoun *that.*

Exercise: Complete each of the following fragments by adding an independent clause or by changing the relative pronoun into a subject pronoun.

1. Who feared the dangers of misuse of pesticides.

2. Which began the atomic age.

3. That came to the new land.

4. Who spoke eloquently to the peace commissioners.

5. Whom the King's Daughters hoped to marry.

F. Perhaps the most common type of sentence fragment is one that occurs when a **subordinate** (or **dependent**) **clause** is punctuated with a period.
　　The subordinate clause may be recognized by its first or introductory word, called the **subordinating conjunction.** (For a list of common subordinating conjunctions, see page 393.)

Ex. 5: When the ship sailed at dawn.

When the ship sailed at dawn is a fragment because the subordinate clause cannot stand alone without being attached to an independent clause. The subordinate clause can appear before or after the independent clause to form a complete sentence.

Complete Sentence: When the ship sailed at dawn, the crew rejoiced.

or

The crew rejoiced when the ship sailed at dawn.

Note: A comma is needed when the dependent clause comes first. No comma is needed when the independent clause comes first.
　　Removal of the subordinating conjunction *when* will also produce a complete sentence.

Complete Sentence: The ship sailed at dawn.

Exercise: Complete each of the following fragments by adding an independent clause before or after the subordinate clause and by punctuating correctly.

1. After Dr. King delivered his "I Have a Dream" speech.

2. Because Lewis and Clark were sent on the expedition.

3. If the rebellion at Lares had been successful.

4. Although the Kiowas returned home.

5. Since the time when Arias became president of Costa Rica.

Review Exercise 1:   Correct each sentence fragment by any of these methods: adding a subject, adding or changing a verb, attaching the sentence fragment to an independent clause, or creating an independent clause wherever necessary.

1. If Columbus really wanted to cooperate with the islanders.

2. The colonies belonged to England. Until the Declaration of Independence proclaimed their freedom.

3. The United Nations delegates admired Eleanor Roosevelt. When she demanded that more attention be paid to children.

4. You will find the test site on the outskirts of the New Mexico desert. Just north of the sacred hunting area.

5. Especially when the first settlers arrived. There was a shortage of marriageable women in fact, women of any kind.

6. The true similarity between Arias and King being their belief in democracy and freedom.

7. Bolívar was a general whose writings were filled with hopes for independence. And to liberate his people from Spanish rule.

8. There was no better student than Mary Antin. Who studied about George Washington for hours.

9. The very spot where Las Casas saw the massacre.

10. Tip O'Neill elected to the House of Representatives by a large majority.

Review Exercise 2:   Each of the following paragraphs contains sentence fragments. Correct these errors in any way you wish.

1. As the astronauts prepared to land. Their wives and families watched them
   on television. In fact, the whole world watched and waited. For the historic
   first steps on the moon. Touching down on the moon's surface. The astronauts
   began a new era for the United States. And for the rest of the world as well.

2. The Pony Express riders. Mostly orphans took chances that more mature
   adults might not have taken. Fearful of ambush and unfamiliar terrain. They
   tried to carry the mail safely and on time. Because of their efforts. Communication to California was kept open. Their courage linking East and West.

3. To solve the Chrysler financial crisis. Many groups had to work together.
   Calling on union, management, the general public, and famous entertainers.
   Lee Iacocca worked day and night. To keep the automobile company solvent.
   After Congress guaranteed substantial loans. Which Chrysler would even-
   tually repay. The company was back. On the road to success.

4. Over the past twenty-five years. Concerns about the environment have mounted.
   Because there has been an overuse of pesticides. Not only cities and suburbs,
   but also in tropical forests and wilderness areas. Environmentalists and ordinary citizens trying to protect the world's natural resources. Have brought
   pressure upon their elected officials.

SUBJECT-VERB AGREEMENT

A. Subject-verb agreement means that a singular subject takes a singular verb, a plural subject takes a plural verb. In the **present tense,** the form of the verb is the same except in the **third person singular.**

	Singular	Plural
First person	I vote	We vote
Second person	You vote	You vote
Third person	He vote**s**	They vote
	She vote**s**	They vote
	It vote**s**	They vote

The third person singular subject may be one man (*Simón Bolívar*), one woman (*Eleanor Roosevelt*) or one thing (*canal*). The pronoun *he, she,* or *it* may be substituted for the appropriate third person singular subject.

The third person singular subject, whether it is a noun or a pronoun, agrees with the third person singular verb. In the present tense, the third person singular verb usually ends in *-s* or *-es.*

Ex. 1: The *astronaut* sets foot on the moon.

Ex. 2: *He* or *she* sets foot on the moon.

Ex. 3: The *astronaut* goes slowly on foot.

Note 1: There is *never* an *-s* or *-es* ending on a plural verb.

Note 2: The only past tense verb that may cause difficulty is *to be: I was, you were, he was, she was, it was; we were, you were, they were.*

Exercise 1:   Circle the subject or subjects in each sentence. Underline the present tense verb or verbs and add an *-s* or *-es* ending where needed.

1. Martin Luther King, Jr., quote from the Declaration of Independence that "all men are created equal."

2. Canal workers live under difficult and dangerous conditions.

3. The Gettysburg Address exist to this day as a stirring testimony to Lincoln's greatness.

4. Almost all Canadian cities have roads heading northward.

5. When today's student watch on videotape Neil Armstrong on the moon, he or she experience that moment with the same thrill millions did a generation ago.

Exercise 2:   Underline the subject and the correct present tense verb in parentheses.

1. My grandmother's house (remain, remains) vivid in my memory.

2. Historic airplanes (stand, stands) on permanent exhibit at the Smithsonian Institution in Washington, D.C.

3. The walls (is, are) constructed to hold back the pampas.

4. When a child (learn, learns) of Harriet Tubman's courage in freeing the slaves, he or she also (discover, discovers) human rights.

5. The market always (look, looks) attractive, especially after the Antiguans (display, displays) their wares.

B. Intervening words can come between the subject and verb. However, a verb agrees with its subject even when a word or a group of words comes between them.

Usually, the verb follows the subject directly:

Ex. 1: The *queen seeks* new lands.

Sometimes, additional information is placed between the subject and the verb.

Ex. 2: The queen *of the Spanish people* seeks new lands.

The prepositional phrase *of the Spanish people* describes the queen but is *not* the subject. It is the queen who seeks new lands, not the Spanish people. Therefore, the singular verb *seeks* agrees with the singular subject *queen.*

Ex. 3: The queen *who rules over Spain* seeks new lands.

The relative clause *who rules over Spain* describes the queen but is *not* the subject. The relative clause adds information, but the main idea of the sentence is *the queen seeks new lands.*
Note: The relative clause itself contains a subject (*who*) and a verb (*rules*). Since *who* refers to the singular subject *queen,* then *who* is singular and the singular verb *rules* agrees with it.

Ex. 4: The queen *eagerly* seeks new lands.

The adverb *eagerly* modifies the verb *seeks* by telling how or to what extent the queen seeks new lands. The noun *queen* remains the subject of the verb *seeks.*
In all of these examples, the subject and the verb remain the same. The intervening words have no effect on subject-verb agreement.

Exercise 1:   Circle the subject and verb in each sentence. Underline the intervening words. (Remember that sentences containing relative clauses will have more than one subject and verb.)

1. Democracy sometimes has a precarious existence.

2. The pages of Noah Webster's dictionary contain definitions of numerous American words.

3. A journey to the moon satisfies those with a sense of adventure.

4. The Native Americans who sign territorial treaties still try to retain their traditional way of life.

5. Lee Iacocca, operating his company, constantly makes important business decisions.

Exercise 2:   Underline the subject, then underline the correct verb in parentheses.

1. In the movie *Pony Express,* Charlton Heston, who carries the mail, (experience, experiences) many dangers.

2. In today's world, a leader of a country, with the consent of the people, (need, needs) to maintain a just and equal society.

3. King's "I Have a Dream" speech, which (express, expresses) the ideal of racial harmony, (live, lives) on.

4. The effects of pollution (seem, seems) to be everywhere today.

5. Arias's speech before the Nobel audience clearly (establish, establishes) the means to achieve lasting peace in Central America.

C. A **collective noun** identifies a group of people or things as one unit. When used as a subject, it is considered to be singular and therefore takes a singular verb.

> *Ex.:* The *army* awaits Bolívar's next order.

Here is a list of common **collective nouns:**

army	crowd	public
audience	family	society
class	government	team
committee	group	tribe
council	jury	troop

One way of recognizing that these words are singular is to remember that each of them forms its own plural. For example, *army/armies, family/families, team/teams.*

Note: See discussion on page 447 on agreement of pronouns and collective nouns.

Exercise 1:   Circle the subject in each sentence. Underline the present tense verb and add an *-s* or *-es* ending where needed.

1. The public hear of the Wright brothers' success.

2. In the book by Horatio Alger, one group of newsboys rises to fame and fortune.

3. The constitutional parade committee decide on the route through the streets.

4. The team of scientists measure the intensity of the nuclear blast.

5. Columbus's crew hails the sight of land.

Exercise 2:   Underline the subject and the correct verb in parentheses.

1. American society (recognize, recognizes) that cultural diversity (is, are) necessary to a democracy.

2. When the tribe (wish, wishes) to negotiate a treaty, the Canadian government (send, sends) its representative quickly.

3. After the unsuccessful uprising in Puerto Rico, a discouraged troop with few supplies (make, makes) its way to safety.

4. Dr. King's audience of civil rights marchers (number, numbers) over a quarter of a million.

5. As the grandfather's family (hear, hears) the traditional poem, a flock of falcons (fly, flies) over the ranch house.

D. An **indefinite pronoun** does not identify a specific person, place, or thing. It is usually considered to be singular. When it is used as a subject, it takes a singular verb.

> *Ex. 1:* If *nobody* sees the imaginary animal called the *Hidebehind,* it is not really there.

Here is a list of singular **indefinite pronouns:**

anybody	everyone	nothing
anyone	everything	one
anything	neither	somebody
either	nobody	someone
everybody	no one	something

In certain cases an indefinite pronoun may be *either* singular or plural, depending on the phrase that follows.

> *Ex. 2: Some* of the Constitution requires interpretation.

In this sentence, *some* refers to *Constitution.* Since the Constitution is one document, the word *some* is considered to be singular and takes the singular verb *requires.*

Ex. 3: Some of the amendments to the Constitution require interpretation.

In this sentence, *some* refers to *amendments*. Since there are twenty-six amendments, the word *some* is considered to be plural and takes the plural verb *require*.

Here is a list of indefinite pronouns that may be either singular or plural:

all	half	none
any	most	some

The following phrases involving indefinite pronouns are singular when used as subjects.

each of	every one of	one of
either of	neither of	

Note: See discussion on page 448 on agreement of pronouns and indefinite pronouns.

Exercise 1: Circle the subject in each sentence. Underline the present tense verb. If necessary, correct the verb by adding or removing an *-s* or *-es* ending.

1. Each of the immigrants takes English lessons at Hull House.

2. Everyone in today's cities face the reality of environmental problems.

3. All of the Antiguans love their island.

4. Somebody needs to replant Grandmother's herb garden.

5. One of the tourists want to canoe at the lake north of Toronto.

Exercise 2: Underline the subject and the correct present tense verb in parentheses.

1. In class, everybody (try, tries) to write about Lewis and Clark's expedition to the western territory.

2. Neither of the women who are standing at the Lincoln Memorial (has, have) a desire to rush away.

3. If anything (threaten, threatens) the success of the company, one of the executives (know, knows) exactly what to do.

4. Although all of the lumberjacks in the forest (work, works) hard, each (go, goes) at his or her own pace.

5. At the conference, someone (try, tries) to define democracy in just ten words, but nobody (accept, accepts) the definition.

E. A **compound subject** consists of two or more subjects connected by a conjunction. When the conjunction is the word *and,* the compound subject usually is considered to be plural and therefore takes a plural verb.

    Ex. 1: The *girl* and her *grandmother return* from the garden.

    The two nouns of the compound subject—*girl* and *grandmother*—share the plural verb *return.*
    When the compound subject is connected by *or* or *nor,* the verb agrees with the subject that is closer to it.

    Ex. 2: Either the *army* or the *rebels plan* to attack.

    The plural verb *plan* agrees with the plural noun *rebels,* the part of the compound subject that is **closer** to it.

    Ex. 3: Neither the *rebels* nor the *army plans* to attack.

    The singular verb *plans* agrees with the singular collective noun *army,* the part of the compound subject that is closer to it.
    Although example 3 is grammatically correct, the sentence may not sound or look right to you. If this is the case, place the plural part of the compound subject closer to the verb, as in example 2.
    In questions, the first part of the verb agrees with the subject.

    Ex. 4: Has the rebels *or the army* attacked?

    Ex. 4A: Have the army *or the rebels* attacked?

Exercise 1:   Circle the compound subject in each sentence, then underline the verb. In the blank space at the end of each sentence, indicate whether the verb is singular or plural.

1. The *Goofang* and the *Gillygaloo* appear in tall tales. _____

2. Neither Orville nor Wilbur Wright fears failure. _____

3. Does Nick Adams or any other passenger notice the width of the Mississippi? _____

4. In the campaigns to gain independence for the South American colonies, Simón Bolívar, Bernardo O'Higgins, and José de San Martín are honored above all others. _____

5. King's "I Have a Dream" speech or Douglass's Fourth of July address was to be selected for reading aloud. _____

Exercise 2: Underline the compound subject and the correct verb in parentheses.

1. Delaware and Rhode Island (were, was) two of the first states to ratify the Constitution.

2. (Do, Does) Richard Hunter and his coworkers achieve financial success?

3. Either Neil Armstrong or the other astronauts (has, have) decided to place a U.S. flag on the moon's surface.

4. Few people know for certain whether stagecoach drivers or a team of Pony Express riders (carry, carries) the mail more reliably.

5. Neither the poor morale of his men nor doubts about reaching land safely (discourage, discourages) Columbus on the voyage to the Americas.

F. Subject after verb: The verb agrees with its subject even in those sentences in which the subject follows the verb. This is most common in sentences starting with *there* or *here,* in questions, or in sentences beginning with phrases.

> *Ex. 1:* There *was* a strong *breeze* when the Wright brothers attempted their first flight.

The singular verb *was* agrees with the singular subject *breeze.* Note that the word *there* is not the subject because it is not a noun or pronoun.

> *Ex. 2:* Here *are* the *names* of those buried in Gettysburg National Cemetery.

The plural verb *are* agrees with the plural subject *names.* Note that the word *here* is not the subject because it is not a noun or pronoun.

> *Ex. 3:* Where *are* the *birds*?

In questions, the verb precedes the subject. The plural verb *are* agrees with the plural subject *birds.*

Ex. 4: Near Rainy Mountain *stands* the *village* of the Kiowas.

The singular verb *stands* agrees with the singular subject *village*. Note that the prepositional phrase *near Rainy Mountain* tells *where* the village is but does not tell *who* or *what* stands, and is therefore not the subject.
Note: In these examples, the words can be rearranged so that the subject precedes the verb.

Ex. 1A: A strong breeze was there when the Wright brothers attempted their first flight.

Ex. 2A: The names of those buried in Gettysburg National Cemetery are here.

Ex. 3A: The birds are where?

Ex. 4A: The village of the Kiowas stands near Rainy Mountain.

Exercise: Underline the subject and the correct verb in parentheses.

1. (Do, Does) Nick Adams remember whether the White Sox won the game?

2. There (are, is) hundreds of Americanisms in Noah Webster's dictionary.

3. By the light of a flickering candle (sit, sits) Richard Hunter studying his account books.

4. Here (come, comes) the heroes and heroines of Lares.

5. (Have, Has) the people of Canada more than one national language?

6. From the stands (echo, echoes) a cheer for Jackie Robinson.

7. In many western movies, there (seem, seems) to be an emphasis on the bravery of adventurous wanderers, including Pony Express riders.

8. (Was, Were) anyone aware of such creatures as the *Goofus Bird* or the *Upland Trout*?

9. Why (don't, doesn't) the canal workers finish the Culebra Cut quickly?

10. On the surface of the moon (remain, remains) the flag planted by the American astronauts.

G. A **compound verb** consists of two or more verbs connected by a conjunction. All the verbs have to agree with the subject.

Ex. 1: Noah Webster compiles, writes, and *alphabetizes* the entries for his dictionary.

The singular subject *Noah Webster* takes the three singular verbs *compiles, writes,* and *alphabetizes.*

Ex. 2: Borges's imaginary *creatures* of the Northwest *hide* behind trees or *swim* backward.

The plural subject *creatures* takes the two plural verbs *hide* and *swim.*

Exercise 1:   Circle the compound verb in each sentence, then underline the subject. In the blank space at the end of each sentence, indicate whether the subject is singular or plural.

1. The Gettysburg Address uses simple language but contains great wisdom.
   _____

2. Will Rogers's radio broadcasts either offer solutions to economic problems or poke fun at politicians. _____

3. Lewis and Clark map unknown territories, collect many regional plants, and keep a journal. _____

4. On their cross-country journeys, the young riders of the Pony Express carry mail, battle weather conditions, and risk their lives. _____

5. The Puerto Rican rebellion of 1868 stirs people's hearts and reminds them of the importance of independence. _____

Exercise 2:   Underline the subject and the correct verb in parentheses.

1. Don Cheo (speak, speaks) to a character on stage but (has, have) to be aware of the audience's reactions.

2. On the voyage to Canada, the French brides-to-be (imagine, imagines) their new lives and (look, looks) to the future.

3. For E. B. White, democracy (exist, exists) in many places and (surprise, surprises) people with its flexibility and stamina.

4. The warmth and comfort of my grandmother's house (is, are) still real to me, and (stay, stays) constantly in my memory.

5. Each of Walt Whitman's singers (try, tries) to work hard yet (leave, leaves) time for enjoying life.

Review Exercise 1: Correct errors in agreement between the subjects and the present tense verbs in these sentences.

1. The Bill of Rights contain ten amendments.

2. For their contributions to aviation, neither of the Wright brothers have been forgotten.

3. The team of astronauts practice long and hard for their mission.

4. Anyone who read the words of Simón Bolívar today find much to admire about his courage.

5. Independence for all the countries of the Americas exist as a praiseworthy ideal.

6. The veterans in the Remembrance Day parade marches along proudly.

7. Martin Luther King, Jr., quote from the Declaration of Independence and ask for equality among all people.

8. Among the strange creatures in the woods is the *Teakettler* and the *Goofang*.

9. The boys from the orphanage relies greatly on part-time jobs.

10. In his comments on the Depression, Will Rogers say that every business do not hire an extra worker.

Review Exercise 2: Fill in the blank with the correct word in parentheses.

1. Most of the district's residents _____ expected to vote for Tip
   (was, were)
   O'Neill.

2. From his research, Dr. Wang _____ a computer and
   (develop, develops)
   _____ its cost.
   (estimate, estimates)

3. Aimed directly at Fort Sumter for two weeks _____ been the
   (has, have)
   cannons on the Charleston waterfront.

4. Her grandmother and grandfather _____ simple and peaceful lives
   (lead, leads)
   on the Arizona border with Mexico.

5. _____ the young hunters of the Kiowa tribe _____ what
   (Don't, Doesn't)   *(realize, realizes)*
   the shadows on the moon really _____ ?
                                      (are, is)

6. The principles of the Declaration of Independence _____ impor-
                                                        (are, is)
   tant to all societies that _____ democracy.
                                 (cherish, cherishes)

7. Jackie Robinson and Pee Wee Reese _____ the double play better
                                        (complete, completes)
   than anyone else _____ .
                       (do, does)

8. In *The Cry of Lares,* Don Cheo _____ that the uprising of the
                                      (remark, remarks)
   rebels _____ to their love of freedom.
             (attest, attests)

9. One of the Pilgrims _____ that his family _____ to live
                          (decide, decides)   *(has, have)*
   near a running stream.

10. When someone _____ to learn about survival in a big city, Lewis
                    (want, wants)

    and Clark _____ the best guides.
                 (aren't, isn't)

PAST TENSE AND PAST PARTICIPLES

PAST TENSE VERBS WITH -ED OR -D ENDING

The *-ed* or *-d* ending on a verb is the usual sign of the **past tense.**

Ex. 1: Seventeenth-century Canadian settlers *wanted* marriage partners.

Ex. 2: The cemetery *overlooked* the deserted town.

Ex. 3: The Caribbean Indians *welcomed* and *honored* Spanish sailors.

Note 1: The *-ed* or *-d* ending is used on most past tense verbs, whether the subject is singular or plural.

Note 2: Spelling changes sometimes occur when the past tense is formed: *study/studied, cram/crammed.*

Exercise 1:   For each of the following sentences, add the past tense *-ed* or *-d* ending where it is missing. In some cases, you may have to make spelling changes.

1. Harriet Tubman escape to freedom in Canada.

2. In a poor Chicago neighborhood, Jane Addams establish Hull House.

3. A century ago, the Pony Express riders risk their lives to deliver the mail.

4. After running into the water, Lewis face the ferocious bear.

5. Bolívar address the Venezuelan Assembly in 1814.

6. Despite many obstacles, Columbus and his crew arrive in the Americas.

7. When eleven states ratify the Constitution, many people joyfully march in the streets.

8. Nick decide to cross the Mississippi River.

9. Grandmother MacLeod step into the room and grab Vanessa by the hand.

10. Because he possess faith in his own abilities, Dr. Wang move boldly to start a major company.

Exercise 2:   Fill in the blank with the past tense of the verb in parentheses.

1. President Arias of Costa Rica _____ the Nobel Peace Prize.
   (*receive*)

2. The astronauts' families _____ about the safety of the Apollo
   (*worry*)
   mission to the moon.

3. In the typical Horatio Alger story, a poor boy _____ for his
   (*plan*)
   success.

4. If you _____ the north woods, you truly _____ the
   (*visit*)   (*experience*)
   world of the lumberjack.

5. Soldiers at Fort Sumter _____ more ammunition.
   (*need*)

6. The young girl _____ her grandmother, who _____
   (*watch*)   (*apply*)
   herbs to the sick man's back.

7. In building the transcontinental railroad, the Chinese workers
   _____ hard and _____ little money.
   (*toil*)   (*earn*)

8. The auction at the slave market _____ high purchase bids.
    (*produce*)

9. When the Puerto Ricans _____ against the Spanish governors,
    (*rebel*)
    they _____ their defenses.
    (*fortify*)

10. The remoteness of the lumber town _____ to the sense of in-
    (*contribute*)

    dividualism that many Canadians _____ .
    (exemplify)

TWO SPECIAL CASES: USED TO, SUPPOSED TO

Before an **infinitive** (*to* and the dictionary or present tense form of the verb), the *-d* ending is required with the verbs *use* and *suppose*.

> *Ex. 1:* Dr. King *used to lead* civil rights demonstrations.

> *Ex. 2:* The Hull House settlement workers were *supposed to know* at least one foreign language.

A *-d* ending, of course, is required if *use* or *suppose* appears in the past tense, but there is no *-d* ending necessary in other tenses:

> *Ex. 3:* The Chinese transcontinental railroad workers *used* hand tools a century ago; now workers *use* more sophisticated equipment.

Exercise: Add a *-d* ending if necessary to *use* or *suppose* in each of these sentences.

1. Do you know if Lincoln is suppose to deliver a long speech?

2. Because Don Cheo supported the rebels, he use to supply them with weapons.

3. Iacocca use the services of celebrities to restore the Chrysler Corporation to financial stability.

4. The girl suppose that her grandmother's *savila* plants had magical powers.

5. The residents of the city near the pampas use to see the same faces every day.

PAST TENSE VERBS WITHOUT *-ED* OR *-D* ENDING

A. Many verbs form the past tense with an *internal* spelling change from their dictionary or present tense spelling. (The chart on pages 424–426 lists most of these common verbs.)

Present Tense	Past Tense
1. Antiguans *come* to the market.	Antiguans *came* to the market.
2. The Wrights' plane *flies* over the beach.	The Wrights' plane *flew* over the beach.
3. Mary Antin *is* a student.	Mary Antin *was* a student.

B. Some verbs form the past tense without any change in spelling.

Present Tense	Past Tense
1. Kiowas *cut* through the woods.	Kiowas *cut* through the woods.
2. You *beat* the competition.	You *beat* the competition.
3. Whitman *puts* faith in Americans.	Whitman *put* his faith in Americans.

C. Some verbs form the past tense by changing the final letter of the dictionary or present tense spelling.

Present Tense	Past Tense
1. The Pilgrims *build* cabins.	The Pilgrims *built* cabins.
2. Jackie Robinson *bends* over at bat.	Jackie Robinson *bent* over at bat.

Note: Remember that the *-ed* or *-d* ending is not needed for any of the past tense verbs described above.

Ex. 1: Tip O'Neill *left* Boston.	{not *lefted*}
Ex. 2: The battle *cost* many lives.	{not *costed*}

Below is an alphabetical chart of many common verbs that do not take an *-ed* or *-d* ending. When you are not sure how to form the past or past participle, check this list or your dictionary.

LIST OF VERB FORMS

Present	Past	Past Participle
arise	arose	arisen
be	was, were	been
bear	bore	borne, born
become	became	become
begin	began	begun
bet	bet	bet
bid	bid	bid
bite	bit	bitten
blow	blew	blown
break	broke	broken
bring	brought	brought
build	built	built
burst	burst	burst
buy	bought	bought
catch	caught	caught
choose	chose	chosen
cling	clung	clung
come	came	come
cost	cost	cost
cut	cut	cut
deal	dealt	dealt
dig	dug	dug
dive	dived, dove	dived
do	did	done
draw	drew	drawn
drink	drank	drunk
drive	drove	driven
eat	ate	eaten
fall	fell	fallen
feel	felt	felt
fight	fought	fought
find	found	found
flee	fled	fled
fling	flung	flung
fly	flew	flown
forbid	forbade	forbidden
forget	forgot	forgotten
forgive	forgave	forgiven
freeze	froze	frozen

Present	**Past**	**Past Participle**
get	got	got, gotten
give	gave	given
go	went	gone
grow	grew	grown
hang (a picture)	hung	hung
have	had	had
hear	heard	heard
hide	hid	hidden
hit	hit	hit
hold	held	held
hurt	hurt	hurt
keep	kept	kept
know	knew	known
lay (put down)	laid	laid
lead	led	led
leave	left	left
let	let	let
lie (recline)	lay	lain
lose	lost	lost
make	made	made
mean	meant	meant
meet	met	met
pay	paid	paid
prove	proved	proved, proven
put	put	put
quit	quit	quit
ride	rode	ridden
ring	rang	rung
rise	rose	risen
run	ran	run
say	said	said
see	saw	seen
seek	sought	sought
send	sent	sent
set	set	set
shake	shook	shaken
shine (the sun)	shone	shone
shoot	shot	shot

Present	Past	Past Participle
show	showed	showed, shown
shrink	shrank	shrunk
sing	sang	sung
sink	sank	sunk
sit	sat	sat
sleep	slept	slept
slide	slid	slid
speak	spoke	spoken
spend	spent	spent
spread	spread	spread
spring	sprang	sprung
stand	stood	stood
steal	stole	stolen
sting	stung	stung
strike	struck	struck
swear	swore	sworn
sweep	swept	swept
swim	swam	swum
swing	swung	swung
take	took	taken
teach	taught	taught
tear	tore	torn
tell	told	told
think	thought	thought
throw	threw	thrown
understand	understood	understood
wear	wore	worn
win	won	won
wring	wrung	wrung
write	wrote	written

Exercise 1:   Rewrite these sentences in the past tense. You may wish to consult the list of verb forms on pages 424–426.

1. E. B. White writes many definitions of democracy.

2. Because of air pollution, the sounds of birds become fainter.

3. As Harriet Tubman leads them to safety, the escaping slaves make their way along the Underground Railroad.

4. Do the lumberjacks really believe in those fantastic creatures?

5. At the battlefield in Gettysburg, a crowd stands as Lincoln speaks.

6. During the Depression, Will Rogers says, "I have money, so I buy food."

7. The Spaniards burst into the village.

8. Noah Webster knows that his dictionary keeps its emphasis on American words.

9. Chief Ten Bears brings his tribe to the meeting, but the U.S. Army breaks the treaty.

10. When Frederick Douglass begins his newspaper, there will be many articles that draw attention to racial injustice.

Exercise 2: Fill in the blank with the past tense of the verb in parentheses.

1. On many occasions, Eleanor Roosevelt _____ to visit miners,
   (choose)
   factory workers, and farmers.

2. Columbus _____ messages to his sailors, ordering them to treat
   (send)
   the islanders fairly.

3. The fans' insults and taunts _____ Jackie Robinson's pride.
   (hurt)

4. When Vanessa _____ about the Remembrance Day parade, she
   (think)
   _____ every detail in her mind.
   (see)

5. From the moment the King's Daughters _____ on board the ships,
   (be)

   they _____ that they _____ to marry in Canada.
      (understand)   (have)

6. Walt Whitman _____ the many voices of the people who
                     (hear)
   _____ as they _____ the United States.
      (sing)   (build)

7. An Wang _____ that starting a business _____ taking
               (find)   (mean)
   risks.

8. An early draft of the Declaration of Independence _____ slavery, (*forbid*)
   but Jefferson _____ the passage from the final version. (*cut*)

9. When construction of the Panama Canal _____ near, a great many (*grow*)
   West Indians _____ advantage of the job opportunities. (*take*)

10. Although   Gatsby   _____   a   mansion,   eventually   he (*buy*)

    _____ his society friends. (*lose*)

Review Exercise: Fill in the blanks with the correct past tense form of the verb in parentheses. You may wish to consult the list of verb forms on pages 424–426.

1. Columbus _____ from Palos, Spain, and _____ in the (*sail*)   (*land*)
   West Indies.

2. When   Walt   Whitman   _____   of   America,   his   verses (*write*)

   _____ voice to the common person. (*give*)

3. The birds _____ from the area as planes _____ pes- (*flee*)   (*spread*)
   ticides over the farmland.

4. The first modern democracy _____ the United States, whose (*be*)
   founders _____ human rights. (*guarantee*)

5. Vanessa _____ a   safe   hiding   place   until   the   parade (*seek*)

   _____ by. (*pass*)

6. Thoughts of life west of the Mississippi River _____ in Nick Ad- (*intensify*)
   ams's mind as the train _____ near. (*draw*)

7. The Kiowas _____ the shadows were ghost riders; therefore, they (*think*)
   _____ wonderful stories about them. (*tell*)

8. _____ the Barbados slave dealers care about those whom they (*Do*)

   _____ and those whom they _____ ? (*sell*)   (*buy*)

9. Lewis and Clark _____ ____ early, _____ quickly, and
   (rise)   (eat)
   _____ their goals for the day.
   (set)

10. In his speeches, Frederick Douglass _____ to challenge his au-
    (use)
    diences as he _____ emphasizing that they _____ not
    (keep)   (be)
    doing enough to end slavery.

PAST PARTICIPLES

A. The **past participle** is a verb form that is used with many verbs, especially with any form of *have*:

Ex. 1: The Pilgrims *have landed.*

Ex. 2: Modern democracy *has existed* for two hundred years.

Ex. 3: Bolívar *had moved* to Caracas.

OR with any form of *be*:

Ex. 4: President Arias *is respected.*

Ex. 5: The railroad *has been completed.*

Ex. 6: Many peace treaties *were signed.*

OR with any of these common verbs of being: *feel, become, seem, appear, get, look, taste:*

Ex. 7: Gatsby *felt honored* to be in their company.

Ex. 8: The Pony Express riders *became tired.*

Ex. 9: One imaginary creature *seemed confused.*

OR by itself as an adjective to modify nouns and pronouns:

Ex. 10: A *wounded* bear chased Lewis.

Ex. 11: The Constitution is an *amended* document.

Ex. 12: Dr. King spoke to the crowd *assembled* that day in Washington, D.C.

Note: The past participle in most cases has the same *-ed* or *-d* ending as the past tense verb. Check the chart on pages 424–426 for the past participles of verbs that do not have the *-ed* or *-d* ending.

PRESENT PERFECT TENSE

Have (or *has*) and the past participle of the main verb form the **present perfect tense.**
   This tense is used to indicate an action that continues to the present (*have* or *has* is the present tense verb) although it began in the past (*past participle*):

   Ex. 1: Mary Antin *has attended* Boston schools for three years.

   Antin began her schooling in Boston three years ago, and she is still going to classes.

   This tense is also used to indicate an action finished before another specified action or time.

   Ex. 2: Mary Antin *has attended* Boston schools, so she can qualify for the Massachusetts scholarship.

   Note the different meaning if the past tense is used:

   Ex. 2A: Mary Antin *attended* Boston schools for three years.

   Antin finished her schooling in Boston after three years, and she no longer goes to classes there.
   Note: The past tense uses *one* verb. The present perfect uses a set of *two* verbs.

Exercise 1:   Rewrite each of these sentences in the present perfect tense.

  1. The Northern troops at Fort Sumter try not to fire the first shot.

  2. In his dictionary, Webster defines many unusual words.

  3. Medicinal herbs help my grandmother to cure various ailments.

  4. Young Richard Hunter rescues Mr. Rockwell's son.

  5. Despite great obstacles, Frederick Douglass learns to read and write.

  6. Many social workers at Hull House work long hours.

  7. On many occasions, the Spaniards destroy local villages and kill the inhabitants.

  8. The marketplace in Antigua contains goods of all kinds.

9. When the birds stop singing, silence finally defeats life.

10. The United States signs a treaty to give Panama control over the Panama Canal in 1999.

Exercise 2:   Rewrite each of the following sentences in the present perfect tense. You may wish to consult the list of past participles on pages 424–426.

1. A Kiowa warrior takes many chances on the quest for summer's house.

2. On the wide prairies, William Least Heat Moon sleeps near the deserted Pony Express station.

3. In developing his business, Iacocca lays aside many doubts.

4. There will be several television programs about Eleanor Roosevelt.

5. The young girl stands in the kitchen of the small ranch house.

6. Because of the success of his plan, President Arias thinks of a lasting peace for Central America.

7. The horse in the Antiguan village throws the tourist to the ground and bites his arm.

8. When the mayor fights for a new environmental policy, she wins the loyalty of the townspeople.

9. The astronauts deal with the problems of landing on the moon, especially if their spacecraft sinks below the surface.

10. Although some workers quit their jobs, most keep them and dig through the frozen subsoil of the Canadian tundra.

PAST PERFECT TENSE

Had and the past participle of the main verb form the **past perfect tense.**
    This tense is used to indicate an action that took place before another past action.

> *Ex. 1:* Mary Antin *had attended* Russian schools until she moved to Boston.

    Antin finished her schooling in Russia before she moved to Boston. Notice that the past tense verb *moved* is used for the more recent past action.
    Note: The past perfect tense uses a set of *two* verbs.

Exercise 1: Two verbs are present in each sentence. Rewrite each sentence using a past perfect tense verb and a past tense verb.

1. Columbus visits King Ferdinand and Queen Isabella before he sails to the Americas.

2. By the time the astronauts land on the moon, many practice landings occur.

3. At the final ceremony, the supervisor asks whether the Chinese receive enough recognition for their contribution to the building of the transcontinental railway.

4. O'Neill, who confronts the bank president, achieves a change in anti-Irish employment policies.

5. On the trip north to Hudson Bay, the vacationers announce that they consider staying at a resort in southern Ontario.

Exercise 2: Two verbs are present in each sentence. Rewrite each sentence using a past perfect tense verb and a past tense verb. You may wish to consult the list of past participles on pages 424–426.

1. Lightning strikes the *Mayflower* after it sets sail.

2. Up to the moment they lose the battle, the Puerto Rican rebels think of victory.

3. Before Harriet Tubman steals back to Maryland, she holds meetings with abolitionists.

4. Whatever Richard Hunter does, his boss will forgive him.

5. The atomic bomb bursts over the New Mexico desert; then the scientists begin thinking of its effects.

PAST PARTICIPLES AS ADJECTIVES

The past participle is used as an adjective to describe nouns and pronouns.
    The past participle may appear in three places in the sentence:
    Before a noun:

Ex. 1: The *exhausted* troops surrendered at Fort Sumter.

or

Exhausted, the troops surrendered at Fort Sumter.

Ex. 2: Beware of the Spanish governors' *broken* promises.

In a phrase, before a noun or pronoun:

Ex. 3: Surprised by her grandmother, Vanessa had no excuse.

Ex. 4: Built over a ten-year period, the Panama Canal opened in 1914.

Note 1: For good sentence structure, the noun modified by the past participle should be the subject of the independent clause.

In a phrase, after a noun or pronoun:

Ex. 5: The Kiowas gazed at the coyote *caught* in the trap.

Ex. 6: Whitman thought highly of the workers *seated* at their benches.

Note 2: For good sentence structure, the past participle should be placed as close as possible to the noun that it modifies.

Note 3: With negative prefixes like *un-, dis-, mal-,* and *mis-,* past participles are used as adjectives: *uninterested, disenchanted, maladjusted, misinformed.*

Ex. 7: Columbus sailed into *unexplored* territory.

Ex. 8: Dissatisfied with the bank's policies, O'Neill warned that depositors would withdraw their savings.

Exercise 1:   Fill in the blank with the past participle of the verb in parentheses.

1. Webster's dictionary, _____ in 1828, was a runaway best-seller.
(*publish*)

2. _____ with resistance, Bolívar decided to make a formal address
(*Face*)
to the Venezuelan Assembly.

3. The _____ environment produced a silent spring.
(*pollute*)

4. _____ by her friends, Jane Addams opened Chicago's first settle-
(*Encourage*)
ment house.

5. Lumberjacks thought that they saw the *Hidebehind* _____ in the
(*crouch*)
tree's branches.

6. The _____ Harriet Tubman slipped back into Maryland.
(*disguise*)

7. Suddenly _____ by Gatsby, the once brightly _____
(*abandon*)   (*illuminate*)
mansion fell into disrepair.

8. Chief Ten Bears, _____ away from his _____ prairies,
(*force*)   (*treasure*)
spoke for the other tribal leaders.

9. The _____ Canadian lakes left the vacationers _____
(*unspoil*)   (*satisfy*)
and _____ .
(*delight*)

10. _____ from their _____ ones, the slaves suffered greatly.
(*Separate*)   (*love*)

Exercise 2:   Fill in the blank with the past participle of the verb in parentheses.
You may wish to consult the list of past participles on pages 424–426.

1. _____ for his homespun humor, Will Rogers also championed
(*Know*)
Native Americans' rights.

2. Automobiles were not common in Antin's Boston, a city not easily

_____ to accepting progress.
(*give*)

3. Many of the King's Daughters did not expect to see a _____
(*freeze*)
St. Lawrence River.

4. First _____ to the Montreal farm team, Jackie Robinson waited
(*send*)
to be called up to the Brooklyn Dodgers.

5. Looking through the train window, Nick saw the leaves _____
(*blow*)   to
the ground by the strong wind.

6. Antigua is noted for its colorful houses _____ all over the island.
(*find*)

7. _____ along by the winds and _____ by Orville Wright,
(*Bear*)   (*fly*)
the little plane soared into history.

8. The Gettysburg Address praises the _____ soldiers on both sides.
(*fall*)

9. Frederick Douglass's use of the _____ word impressed his listeners,
(*speak*)
_____ to the auditorium by his fame.
(*bring*)

10. _____ by his ambition, Columbus sailed to the long
           (*Drive*)

_____ -for island of Hispaniola, now _____ by the early
       (*seek*)   (*hide*)
morning fog.

WHEN THE *-ED* OR *-D* ENDING SHOULD *NOT* BE USED

The uses of the *-ed* or *-d* ending have been described earlier in this chapter. There are instances, however, when the *-ed* or *-d* ending should not be used.

A. Do not use the *-ed* or *-d* ending on any of the verbs that appear in the chart on pages 424–426.

Present Tense	**Past Tense**
Ex. 1: Poor people *come* to Hull House.	Poor people *came* to Hull House.
Ex. 2: Vanessa *swings* from the tree branch.	Vanessa *swung* from the tree branch.

Exercise: On the line below each present tense sentence, write the sentence in the past tense. You may wish to consult the list of past tense verbs on pages 424–426.

1. Harriet Tubman takes escaped slaves to freedom.

_____

2. Lumberjacks make up tall tales.

_____

3. Micky McGuire fights the pickpocket.

_____

4. At school, Mary Antin swears allegiance to the flag.

_____

5. The paraders stride along the avenue as the glee club sings patriotic songs.

_____

_____

B. When there is an **infinitive** (_to_ and the dictionary or present tense form of the verb), _do not use_ the _-ed_ or _-d_ ending:

> _Ex. 3:_ Iacocca wanted _to improve_ the Chrysler Corporation.

> _Ex. 4:_ The people of Charleston rushed _to see_ the battle.

> _Note 1:_ Sometimes the _to_ of the infinitive does not appear in the sentence after verbs like _hear, help, let, make, observe, see,_ and _watch._

> _Ex. 5:_ The atomic explosion's brightness made the scientists _hide_ their eyes.

> _Ex. 6:_ Many workers from Caribbean islands helped _build_ the Panama Canal.

> _Note 2:_ If the infinitive is _to_ and a set of two or more verbs, use the appropriate past participle ending.

> _Ex. 7:_ The people of Charleston rush _to be seen_ at the battle.

> _Ex. 8:_ Jackie Robinson never seemed _to get caught_ stealing home.

> _Ex. 9:_ The Pilgrims ought _to have been prepared_ for the winter's severity.

Exercise: In each sentence below, fill in the blank with the correct word in parentheses.

1. On their expedition, Lewis and Clark prepared to _____ out every
  (_map, mapped_)
route.

2. People saw no foxes _____ through the fields during the silent
  (_dash, dashed_)
spring.

3. Aboard the _Mayflower,_ forty-one male Pilgrims agreed to _____
  (_obey, obeyed_)
the terms of the compact.

4. The terms of the Mayflower Compact had to be _____ by the
  (_obey, obeyed_)
Pilgrims.

5. Oscar Arias says that other countries should let Central America

_____ out its own problems, and soon his region will be able to
(*work*, worked)

_____ democracy flourish.
(*watch*, watched)

C. *Do not use* the *-ed* or *-d* ending when the only helping verb is one of these:

can, could	must
do, does, did	shall, should
may, might	will, would

Ex. 10: President Arias and Martin Luther King, Jr., *did receive* the Nobel Peace Prize.

Ex. 11: Should poets *praise* the average worker?

Exercise 1: In each sentence below, fill in the blank with the correct word in parentheses.

1. My grandmother said that the *savila* plant should _____ many
(*cure*, cured)
health problems.

2. Visitors to Gettysburg National Cemetery will _____ Lincoln's
(*remember*, remembered)
words.

3. Must building the Panama Canal _____ such a great cost in workers'
(*have*, had)
lives?

4. The beauty of Antigua may _____ harsh realities.
(*disguise*, disguised)

5. For a short time, Wang himself could not _____ whether he should
(*decide*, decided)
_____ a new company.
(*start*, started)

Exercise 2: Fill in the blank with the correct word in parentheses. You may wish to consult the list of past tense verbs and past participles on pages 424–426.

1. The number of democracies throughout the Americas may

_____ in the near future.
(*increase*, increased)

2. Did you _____ them about the northern route through Ontario?
(*notify*, notified)

3. The Declaration of Independence promises to _____ life, liberty,
   (secure, secured)
   and the pursuit of happiness.

4. All during the night, Tubman watched the escaping slaves
   _____ to safety.
   (rush, rushed)

5. The Spaniards thought that the Indians had _____
   (be, been)
   _____ by the large ships.
   (impress, impressed)

6. To _____ healthy, the _Teakettler_ probably must _____
   (stay, stayed)   _(sun, sunned)_
   itself in the forest clearing.

7. Would the Chinese laborers _____ until they _____
   (work, worked)   _(drove, droved)_
   themselves to exhaustion?

8. Bolívar could not _____ until he was able to _____
   (stop, stopped)   _(defeat, defeated)_
   the Spanish troops.

9. Because Webster _____ to _____ American words,
   (choose, chose)   _(include, included)_
   his dictionary let the new nation _____ pride in its language.
                                     (take, took, taken)

10. To _____ by the extent of his success, Dr. Wang ought not to
    (judge, judged)

    _____ _____ _____ about starting a com-
    (have, had)   _(be, been)_   _(concern, concerned)_
    pany.

Review Exercise 1:   In each of the following sentences, write the correct past
participles. You may wish to consult the list of past participles on pages
424–426.

1. In order for the Panama Canal to be build, new engineering techniques were
   develop.

2. Dr. King, a distinguish orator, had never spoke before such a large assem-
   blage.

3. The earth's environment seems threaten by the pesticides release into the
   atmosphere and the ground.

4. Since Captain Narvaez is unimpress by Las Casas's pleas, he has not notify the Spaniards to stop their cruelties.

5. Not yet abolish in the Americas by the middle of the nineteenth century, slave auctions were hold in many areas.

6. Grandmother MacLeod, who remains distress by Vanessa's behavior, has went over to the parade.

7. Hurted by prickly thorns, Lewis had shoot at the bear and miss it.

8. Chief Ten Bears thought that the peace commissioners had misunderstand his plans, which were reach after much consideration.

9. After Nick had watch the river for a while, he knew he was suppose to travel westward.

10. Having become worry by conditions in Central America, President Arias has took steps to bring peace to the area.

Review Exercise 2: Fill in the blank with the correct form of the verb in parentheses. Some answers will require the *-ed* or *-d* ending; others will not. You may wish to consult the list of verbs on pages 424–426.

1. Must the King's Daughters _____, or should they stay
(*marry*)
_____ ?
(*unattach*)

2. One definition of democracy is to _____ your turn in line, not
(*wait*)
having to _____ ahead.
(*push*)

3. The doors of opportunity have _____ open for Mary Antin, so
(*swing*)
she can _____ her goals.
(*pursue*)

4. After Frederick Douglass had _____ the _____ slavery
(*criticize*)   (*continue*)

in the United States, the audience would _____ to
(*rise*)
_____ him.
(*applaud*)

5. Since the Wrights have _____ more and more _____
(*grow*)   (*accustom*)

to flying, they may _____ higher and higher.
(*fly*)

6. Bolívar did _____ democratic forms of government,
   (establish)
   _____ from the Spaniards' _____ rule.
   (free)   (despise)

7. Everyone should have been _____ by Lincoln's words, but the
                             (stir)
   speech seemed to _____ over before the audience could
                    (be)

   _____ to _____ .
   (begin)   (react)

8. _____ by the settlers, the Native Americans had _____
   (Harass)   (seek)

   justice, but often their pleas _____ on deaf ears.
                                  (fall)

9. The Pilgrims, who were _____ to have _____ the voy-
                          (ill-advise)   (undertake)

   age late in the year, barely managed to _____ that first
                                            (survive)

   _____ Massachusetts winter.
   (freeze)

10. Many Chinese railroad workers _____ their strength
                                  (find)

    _____ by the long hours, but they _____ hard to
    (sap)   (fight)

    _____ their spirits _____ .
    (keep)   (uplift)

PRONOUNS

A **pronoun** takes the place of a noun.

    Ex. 1: Bolívar commanded many soldiers. He led them into battle.

He is the pronoun replacing the noun *Bolívar*.
Them is the pronoun replacing the noun *soldiers*.
    The **antecedent** of a pronoun is the word or words to which a pronoun refers. The antecedent is usually a noun or pronoun.

    Ex. 2: Latin Americans honor Bolívar, for he led many countries to independence.

He is the pronoun referring to the antecedent *Bolívar*.
    Note: In most cases, the pronoun follows the noun.

Exercise 1:   Write (1) the pronoun and (2) its antecedent in the spaces below each sentence. You may wish to consult the list of pronouns on page 443.

1. Dr. An Wang began his business in 1951.

    1. _____   **2.** _____

2. Most Pony Express riders knew that danger awaited them.

    1. _____   **2.** _____

3. The Puerto Rican revolt was a brave venture, but it failed.

    1. _____   **2.** _____

4. A King's Daughter could wait a while before deciding on the man that she would marry.

    1. _____   **2.** _____

5. George Washington promised the Jewish people that their right to worship freely would be protected.

    1. _____   **2.** _____

Exercise 2: Each of the following sentences contains more than one pronoun. In the spaces below each sentence, write the pronouns in (1) and (3), and their antecedents in (2) and (4). You may wish to consult the list of pronouns on page 443.

There are many definitions of democracy, but all of them note the political power that it gives to the people.

    1. _____   **2.** _____
    3. _____   **4.** _____

2. Because Jamaica Kincaid grew up in Antigua, she is able to describe it in loving detail.

    1. _____   **2.** _____
    3. _____   **4.** _____

3. After negotiating with the army officers, Chief Ten Bears realized that he could not trust their promises.

    1. _____   **2.** _____
    3. _____   **4.** _____

4. Eleanor Roosevelt's achievements were not dependent on her husband's fame or his own accomplishments.

    1. _____   **2.** _____
    3. _____   **4.** _____

5. Martin Luther King, Jr., inspired many civil rights workers, and they have tried to fulfill his dream.

1. _____ 2. _____

3. _____ 4. _____

AGREEMENT OF PRONOUN AND ANTECEDENT

A pronoun and its antecedent must always agree in number.

A. A singular pronoun refers to a singular noun.

   Ex. 1: The *Constitution* with *its* Bill of Rights protects the individual.

   The singular pronoun *its* refers to the singular noun *Constitution.* (Note that a clue to the use of a singular pronoun is the presence of the singular verb *protects.*)

B. A plural pronoun refers to a plural noun.

   Ex. 2: The *residents* of Shaw's Kansas town knew that *they* would face changes in *their* way of life.

The plural pronouns *they* and *their* refer to the plural noun *residents.*
   Here is a list of **singular** and **plural pronouns:**

SINGULAR	PLURAL
I, me, mine, myself	we, us, ours, ourselves
you, yours, yourself	you, yours, yourselves
he, him, his, himself	they, them, theirs, themselves
she, her, hers, herself	they, them, theirs, themselves
it, its, itself	they, them, theirs, themselves

Exercise 1: In the spaces below each sentence, write (1) the pronoun, (2) its antecedent, and (3) whether it is singular or plural.

1. Grandmother MacLeod started to cry whenever she thought of Roderick's death.

   1. _____ 2. _____ 3. _____

2. The birds no longer sang; they had disappeared from the town.

   1. _____ 2. _____ 3. _____

3. The speech by Frederick Douglass aroused people because it criticized celebrating the Fourth of July while slavery continued.

   1. _____ 2. _____ 3. _____

4. Immigrants went to Hull House, knowing that the settlement workers would help them.

   1. _____ 2. _____ 3. _____

5. Is the Panama Canal outdated, or will it serve a purpose in the next century?

   1. _____ 2. _____ 3. _____

Exercise 2: Fill in the blank with the correct word in parentheses. Each pronoun must have an antecedent.

1. The constitutional parade made _____ way through the streets
   (its, their)
   of Philadelphia.

2. Pony Express advertisements were truthful because _____ em-
   (it, they)
   phasized the risks of the job.

3. Emma Holmes could hardly believe _____ eyes upon arriving at
   (her, his, its)
   the scene of the battle.

4. Read Oscar Arias's plan; _____ is an important step toward peace
   (he, it)
   in this hemisphere.

5. We the people believe that this land of _____ is the best.
   (ours, theirs, yours)

6. Riding _____ horses hard, the Kiowas searched for summer's
   (her, his, their)
   house.

7. Does dreaming of imaginary creatures make _____ seem less

frightening?
(it, them)

8. Gatsby's mansion was now abandoned, _____ windows broken.
(his, its, their)

9. As the Chinese and the Irish workers rushed to lay the railroad tracks, the

competition reached _____ maximum.
(his, its, their)

10. Holding the Puerto Rican flag by _____ corners, Manolo el Leñero
(his, its, their)

lost _____ life in the 1868 rebellion of Lares.
(his, its, their)

AGREEMENT OF PRONOUN AND COMPOUND SUBJECT

A. In most cases, a **compound subject** consists of two or more nouns or pronouns joined by _and._ The compound subject is usually plural, so use a plural pronoun to agree with it.

The plural pronouns are usually _they, them, their, theirs, themselves._

> _Ex. 1:_ _Orville and Wilbur Wright_ wanted to see if _their_ new invention would fly.

> _Ex. 2:_ When the _priest and the Spanish captain_ first came to Cuba, _they_ were overwhelmed by the island's beauty.

Note: If _and_ joins two subjects referring to the same person or thing, use a singular pronoun.

> _Ex. 3:_ Everyone knew of Eleanor Roosevelt; the famous _author and humanitarian_ served _her_ country well.

B. If the compound subject is joined by _or, nor, either . . . or, neither . . . nor,_ or _not only . . . but also,_ use the pronoun that agrees with the antecedent _closer_ to it.

> _Ex. 4:_ _Not only_ the overseer _but also_ the _slaves_ quickly learn that _their_ fates are intertwined.

The plural pronoun *their* agrees with the antecedent *slaves*. (Another clue to the choice of a plural pronoun is the presence of the plural verb *learn*.)

> *Ex. 5: Neither* his braves *nor Chief Ten Bears* wished to disclose *his* feelings about the treaty.

The singular pronoun *his* agrees with the antecedent *Chief Ten Bears*.

Exercise: Fill in the blank with the correct pronoun, one that agrees with its antecedent.

1. As Armstrong and Aldrin walked on the moon, _____ made careful scientific observations.

2. Neither the opposing representatives nor Tip O'Neill could hide _____ anger at the length of the debate.

3. Not only Bolívar but also his soldiers knew that victory was finally _____ when the Spanish forces retreated.

4. Will either Mary Antin or other members of _____ family know when _____ have to go to school?

5. Her grandfather and grandmother by _____ built _____ a house on the Arizona-Mexico border.

6. The minister and civil rights leader Dr. Martin Luther King, Jr., was known for _____ passionate speeches.

7. Either stagecoach drivers or a Pony Express rider could fulfill _____ promise to deliver the mail.

8. Lewis and Clark went _____ to examine the terrain that _____ would have to map out if _____ mission were to be successful.

9. Not only Jefferson but also fellow Virginians _____ voiced _____ belief that the United States should be free.

10. Do you believe that neither the supervisor nor the Chinese workers _____ received enough recognition for _____ contribution to building the railroad?

AGREEMENT OF PRONOUN AND COLLECTIVE NOUN

A. Singular pronouns are used with **collective nouns** that refer to a group as a unit. (See the list of collective nouns on page 441.)

The singular pronouns used are *it, its, itself.*

Ex. 1: Columbus's *crew* tried *its* best to avoid ocean storms.

Ex. 2: The Spanish *army* was disappointed that *it* did not capture Bolívar.

The collective noun, *crew* or *army,* is thought of as one unit, with each member sharing the same goals.

B. In some instances, plural pronouns substitute for collective nouns that emphasize the individuals of a group.

Ex. 3: The Kiowa *council* could not agree about the shadows *they* had seen.

Note 1: Many writers do not like to use collective nouns in the plural. Instead, they change the wording:

Ex. 3A: The *members* of the Kiowa council could not agree about the shadows *they* had seen.

Note 2: When using collective nouns, be sure that you do not write a plural verb and a singular pronoun.

[WRONG] Wilbur-Cruce's family *have* managed to retain *its* memories of life on the Arizona-Mexico border.

[CORRECT] Wilbur-Cruce's family *has* managed to retain *its* memories of life on the Arizona-Mexico border.

Note 3: When using collective nouns, write the singular pronoun even if the collective noun is followed by a prepositional phrase containing a plural noun.

Ex. 4: The *team* of business *experts* presented *its* report to Dr. Wang.

Exercise: Fill in the blank with the correct word in parentheses.

1. Chief Ten Bears' tribe swiftly established _____ camp on the
                                                          (its, their)
prairies.

2. When the school council met with Dr. King, he urged _____ to

(it, them)

desegregate.

3. The government of President Arias tried _____ best to bring

(its, their)

peace to Central America.

4. The scientists on the staff wondered if _____ had done the right

(it, they)

thing in creating the atomic bomb.

5. Wang Laboratories is a company that built _____ up from an

(itself, themselves)

initial investment of $600.

6. The class listened attentively as Mary Antin spoke to _____ about

(it, them)

George Washington.

7. Members of the class listened attentively as Mary Antin spoke to

_____ about George Washington.

(it, them)

8. Douglass's audience roared _____ approval as _____

(its, their)   *(it, they)*

rose in unison.

9. Eleanor Roosevelt said that society must help _____ members

(its, their)

live together in harmony.

10. Will Rogers wondered about the Great Depression's effect on the American

family, whether _____ would survive or not.

(it, they)

AGREEMENT OF PRONOUN AND INDEFINITE PRONOUN

A singular pronoun substitutes for one of these indefinite antecedents:

anybody	everybody	nobody	somebody	each	neither one
anyone	everyone	no one	someone	every	
anything	everything	nothing	something	either	

Ex. 1: Everybody on Columbus' ships knew what *his* job was.

Ex. 2: Each of the counselors at Hull House helped *his or her* clients to gain skills.

In the first example, since the crew members were male, the pronoun *his* is appropriate.

In the second example, since the counselors were of both sexes, the pronoun phrase *his or her* can be used. Until recently, in cases like the above, the male pronoun *his* was used. (For a fuller discussion, see the gender note on page 450.)

Some indefinite pronouns may be either singular or plural. (See the discussion on page 413.)

Ex. 3: Richard Hunter invested *some* of the money in real estate after *it* did not earn enough interest in the bank.

In this sentence, the word *some* refers to *money,* which is singular. The singular pronoun *it*, then, refers to *some.*

Ex. 4: Some of the Pilgrims carried *their* belongings with *them.*

In this sentence, the word *some* refers to *Pilgrims,* which is plural. The plural pronouns *their* and *them* refer to *some.*

The pronouns *both, few, many,* and *several* are plural. (See the discussion on page 413.)

Ex. 5: Both of the explorers wrote about the land *they* had journeyed across.

In this sentence, the word *both* refers to *explorers,* which is plural. The plural pronoun *they* refers to *both.*

Exercise: Fill in the blank with the correct pronoun in parentheses.

1. Anyone wanting to visit Antigua has to apply for _____ passport.
(his, his or her, their)

2. Emma Holmes would speak to everyone who had suffered a loss in _____ family.
(her, his, his or her, their)

3. Some of the pesticides stored in the warehouse were in _____ original containers.
(its, their)

4. Is there someone who does not remember the first time _____ read the Gettysburg Address?
(he, he or she, she, they)

5. Nobody wanted _____ children to view the parade more
(her, his, his or her, their)
than Mr. MacLeod did.

6. Each of the residents of Martha Shaw's western town was known for

_____ fiercely independent ways.
(her, his, his or her, their)

7. Walt Whitman sings the praises of all the workers who perform

_____ jobs with joy.
(her, his, his or her, their)

8. Is anybody aware that _____ can see *The Jackie Robinson*
(he, he or she, she, they)
Story on videotape?

9. Everyone in Mary Antin's class enjoyed _____ summer
(her, his, his or her, their)
vacation.

10. All the Puerto Rican rebels fought on, knowing _____
(hers, his, his or hers, theirs)
was a just cause.

GENDER NOTE: Male pronouns—*he, his, him,* and *himself*—traditionally have been used, even when the individual or group might be female. However, the use of male pronouns in cases where the gender is not known reinforces outmoded attitudes about women's roles and their actual and potential place in society.

Ex. 1: Each of the astronauts received *his* award from the President.

Obviously, such a choice of pronouns does not acknowledge the contributions of women as part of the space program.

One way of addressing this problem is to change to the pronoun phrase *his or her* or *her or his.*

Ex. 2: Each of the astronauts received *his or her* award from the President.

However, this phrase, if overused, can lead to awkward sentences:

Ex. 3: Each of the astronauts received *his or her* award from the President. *He or she* is proud of *his or her* role in the success of the space program.

Careful writers should consider other ways of phrasing this kind of sentence.

A. Use a plural antecedent and a plural pronoun:

> *Ex. 4:* All the *astronauts* received *their* awards from the President.

> Sexist language disappears with the use of the plural pronoun.

B. Eliminate the pronoun:

> *Ex. 5:* Each of the astronauts received *an* award from the President.

C. Use the passive voice:

> *Ex. 6:* An award was given by the President to each of the astronauts.

There are many other ways to eliminate the reliance on male pronouns.

SPECIAL CASES OF PRONOUN AGREEMENT

A. These words agree with singular pronouns:

each of	either of	every one of
neither of	one of	

> *Ex. 1: Every one of* the King's Daughters carries *her* belongings.

> *Ex. 2: Neither of* the Wright brothers doubted that *his* plane would fly that windy afternoon.

The singular pronoun is used because of the singular *every one of* and *neither of.* The plural noun in the intervening phrase does not influence the choice of pronoun.

B. These words agree with singular or plural pronouns:

all of	any of	half of
most of	some of	

> *Ex. 3: Some of* the *railroad* snakes *its* way through the mountains.

The singular pronoun is used because of the singular noun *railroad.*

Ex. 4: Some of the *trains* snake *their* way through the mountains.

The plural pronoun is used because of the plural noun *trains.* (Another clue to the choice of pronouns may be found in the verb; *snakes* in example 3 is singular, and *snake* in example 4 is plural.)

C. Some words ending in *-s* are singular nouns and agree with singular pronouns.

Ex. 5: Webster studied *linguistics,* finding *it* to be an interesting subject.

Ex. 6: Measles used to be widespread, but today *it* has nearly disappeared.

D. Some words ending in *-ing* are singular nouns called **gerunds** and agree with singular pronouns.

Ex. 7: Writing dime novels came easy to Horatio Alger, and *it* became his career.

Ex. 8: Jackie Robinson's baserunning was noted for *its* daring.

Exercise: Fill in the blank with an appropriate pronoun.

1. Only one of the Panama Canal dynamiters survived to pick up _____ paycheck.

2. News of Eleanor Roosevelt's humanitarian accomplishments spread far and wide; _____ was broadcast over foreign networks.

3. Were most of the children spared after _____ had asked Las Casas for help?

4. Did most of the village burn after _____ had asked Las Casas for help?

5. If either of the slaves escapes, the overseer will start searching for _____ .

6. Despite _____ dangers, dynamiting mountains was needed for the construction of the Panama Canal.

7. Each of the amendments in the Bill of Rights is important and _____ should be cherished by all citizens.

8. As a young man, Tip O'Neill became interested in politics and made a career of _____ .

9. Every one of the veterans marching on Remembrance Day looked awkward in _____ military uniform.

10. Because either of the two men, Lewis and Clark, stood out as a born leader, _____ could command the group's attention.

11. The Wright brothers loved flying planes, for _____ brought out their sense of adventure.

12. Are any of Gatsby's possessions still where _____ used to be stored?

PRONOUN AGREEMENT WITH RELATIVE PRONOUNS

A. Use a singular pronoun to agree with the singular relative pronoun.

> *Ex. 1:* The early Canadian settler was a *person who* relished the challenge of *his* or *her* new country.

Person is the singular antecedent of *who,* so the singular pronoun *his* or *her* is used.

B. Use a plural pronoun to agree with the plural relative pronoun.

> *Ex. 2:* Eleanor Roosevelt is one of those *women who* have left *their* mark on history.

Women is the plural antecedent of *who,* so the plural pronoun *their* is used.

Exercise: Fill in the blank with an appropriate pronoun.

1. Did you realize the *Hidebehind* is an imaginary creature that supposedly makes _____ home in the north woods?

2. Did you realize the *Hidebehind* is one of the imaginary creatures that supposedly make _____ home in the north woods?

3. The slave who intends to make _____ escape should plan carefully.

4. Most of the slaves who intend to make _____ escape should plan carefully.

5. Vanessa lives in one of those small towns that regard _____ as patriotic communities.

6. Vanessa lives in a small town that regards _____ as a patriotic community.

7. Chief Ten Bears, who was a cautious man, planned to make every word of _____ speech count.

8. Not one of the Pilgrims who built _____ log cabins along the shore knew how cold a Massachusetts winter could be.

9. Some of the early airplane flights, which had _____ share of danger, captured the public's imagination.

10. Horatio Alger wrote about the types of businesses that always reward _____ young employees.

SUBJECT, OBJECT, AND POSSESSIVE PRONOUNS

Because pronouns take the place of nouns, they can do the same jobs that nouns do in a sentence. They can be subjects and objects. They can also show possession.

SUBJECT PRONOUNS

	Singular	Plural
First person	I	we
Second person	you	you
Third person	he, she, it	they

1. As subject of a sentence (or independent clause):

   Ex. 1: *She* walked through Antigua's crowded markets.

2. As subject of a subordinate or dependent clause:

   Ex. 2: Las Casas tried to look after the native children because *they* were frightened.

3. As part of a compound subject:

   Ex. 3: "Wilbur and *I* have done what people have dreamed for centuries," Orville thought to himself.

4. As subject of an understood verb:

   Ex. 4: Lincoln is taller than *I*. (*am* is understood)

OBJECT PRONOUNS

	Singular	**Plural**
First person	me	us
Second person	you	you
Third person	him, her, it	them

1. As the direct object of the verb:

   Ex. 5: Thomas Jefferson wrote *it*.

2. As the indirect object of the verb:

   Ex. 6: The Pony Express rider brought *them* the mail.

3. As the object of a preposition:

   Ex. 7: Traveling north was a new experience for *her*.
   Ex. 8: Gatsby thought his secret was just between *him* and *me*.

4. As part of a compound object:

   Ex. 9: Sacajawea noticed Lewis and *him*.

5. As the object of an understood verb:

   Ex. 10: The woman respected Iacocca more than *them*. (*she respected* is understood)

POSSESSIVE PRONOUNS

Some possessive pronouns come before nouns.

	Singular	Plural
First person	my	our
Second person	your	your
Third person	his, her, its	their

1. Before a noun:

   Ex. 11: Her speech on human rights was received well.

2. Before a gerund:

   Ex. 12: Your speaking out on human rights abuses was a brave act.

Other possessive pronouns never come before nouns. They stand alone and act like nouns. They can be subjects and objects.

	Singular	Plural
First person	mine	ours
Second person	yours	yours
Third person	his, hers, its	theirs

Ex. 13: The King's Daughters knew that the decision whom to marry was *theirs* alone. (*theirs* stands for *their decision*)

Ex. 14: I had my opinion of the parade, and Vanessa had *hers.* (*hers* stands for *her opinion*)

Exercise: Fill in the blank with the correct pronoun in parentheses.

1. Columbus at times wondered if the crew would remain loyal to

   _____ .
   (he, him)

2. Tip O'Neill and _____ served in Congress.
   (I, me)

3. The Pony Express rider is not as old as _____ .
   (she, her)

4. Lewis and Clark knew that fame would be _____ when they
   (his, their, theirs)
   returned.

5. By working hard, a boy in an Alger novel knows that _____ will
(he, him)

win fame and fortune.

6. Gatsby and Daisy thought that the estate would be too large for

_____
(him, her, them).

7. Mary Antin and her sister said, "Public school education is a great help to

_____ immigrants."
_(we, us)_

8. Lincoln's beard is just like _____ .
(me, my, mine)

9. The race to finish the railroad was between _____ and
_(I, me)_

_____ .
(he, him)

10. Building airplanes enabled _____ to give up the Dayton, Ohio
(they, them)

bicycle store that was _____ .
(their, theirs)

Review Exercise 1:   Fill in the blank with the correct word in parentheses.

1. _____ grandfather is older than _____ .
(You, Your)   _(she, her)_

2. The settlement house _____ had as many clients as they could
(worker, workers)

handle.

3. A parent in a Cuban village realized that _____ had to be
(he, she, he or she, they)

cautious when the Spanish entered _____ living quarters.
(his, her, him or her, their)

4. E. B. White's definitions of democracy have _____ own sense of
(his, their)

logic.

5. As Armstrong and Aldrin stood on the moon, _____ could see
(he, they)

the earth as no one else had ever seen _____ .
(it, them)

6. No _____ at the atomic test fully understood the significance of
(scientist, scientists)
his or her research.

7. Had each of the state legislatures made known _____ views of
   (its, their)
   the Constitution?

8. Some of the Canadian forests have _____ share of wild animals,
   (its, their)
   but most of the wilderness is breathtaking in _____ splendor.
   (its, their)

9. If anyone wants to learn more about Eleanor Roosevelt, tell _____
   (him or her, them)
   to read her autobiography.

10. Several Kiowas spent _____ hours searching for summer and
    (his, her, their)
    _____ home.
    (his, her, its)

Review Exercise 2:   Fill in the blank with an appropriate pronoun.

1. Not one of the rebels made _____ way past the sentries.

2. Physics has _____ laws, a fact that atomic researchers must be
   aware of.

3. Harriet Tubman knew that success was _____ once _____
   and the others could escape _____ pursuers.

4. Making speeches had _____ benefits for Frederick Douglass,
   _____ mission was to deliver _____ antislavery message wherever _____ could.

5. Addressing the Venezuelan representatives, Bolívar spoke to _____
   of _____ reluctance to become _____ president.

6. Nobody had _____ reasons for believing that the Panama Canal
   and _____ locks would be completed quickly.

7. _____ principles make the Bill of Rights a model for other nations
   and _____ own constitutions.

8. Nick Adams thought that _____ dreams of success had _____
   basis in reality.

PRONOUNS 459

9. With _____ fame assured, the Pony Express stands as a monument to _____ riders and _____ resourcefulness and
   courage.

10. Because Antiguans enjoy _____ way of life, Kincaid writes that
    _____ occasionally lose sight of history and _____
    lessons.

APOSTROPHES

An **apostrophe** has two main functions.

A. An apostrophe is used to indicate a missing letter or letters in a contraction.

> *Ex. 1:* *Antigua's* a very beautiful island.

Antigua's is the contraction of *Antigua is.*

> *Ex. 2:* She'd been a citizen of Antigua.

She'd is the contraction of *she had.*

Note: As a rule, contractions are not used in formal college and business writing.

Exercise 1: Add apostrophes wherever they are needed. Next to each sentence, write out the contraction in full.

1. Wheres the Central American canal to be constructed? ＿＿＿＿＿＿＿＿ .

2. When he finishes his speech, well cheer. ＿＿＿＿＿＿＿

3. Its been more than two hundred years since the Constitution was ratified.

   ＿＿＿＿＿＿＿

4. "Those parading veterans arent very young," Vanessa thought. ＿＿＿＿＿＿

5. Chief Ten Bears was aware that the tribes mightve been deprived of their

   homelands. ＿＿＿＿＿＿＿

6. Do the rebels know that theyre losing the battle? _____

7. In spite of some doubts, Dr. Wang wont give in to fears. _____

8. Youd say that Arias knows theres an opportunity for peace. _____

9. Gatsby said, "Im now accepted by the rich and powerful." _____

10. That creatures imaginary—its just a folktale were told. _____

Exercise 2: In each of the following sentences, part of a contraction is missing. In the spaces below each, (1) write the correct contraction, then (2) write out the contraction in full.

1. They searching for Harriet Tubman.

    1. _____   **2.** _____

2. Here how Lee Iacocca plans to raise money.

    1. _____   **2.** _____

3. I am certain that I rather have sailed with the Pilgrims.

    1. _____   **2.** _____

4. Roosevelt knows that she been in the forefront of the struggle to end world hunger.

    1. _____   **2.** _____

5. Jackie Robinson had few doubts that he successfully break baseball's color barrier.

    1. _____   **2.** _____

B. An apostrophe is used to show possession.

    1. To form the possessive of a singular noun or indefinite pronoun, add apostrophe and *s* (*'s*):

       government's duty   Bolívar's speech   someone's beliefs

    2. To form the possessive of a plural noun that does not end in -*s*, add an apostrophe and *s* (*'s*):

       women's pioneer journals   men's jobs   children's books

3. To form the possessive of a plural noun that ends in -*s*, add an apostrophe only (*s'*):

horses' reins   Pilgrims' ship   tribes' lands

Note: Most singular nouns that end in -*s* form the possessive by adding apostrophe and *s* ('*s*). A few nouns, however, form the possessive with the apostrophe only so that the words are easier to pronounce:

boss's desk   Emma Holmes's diary

BUT

Las Casas' plea   Borges' tall tale

Note: An apostrophe is used with words of time.

Ex. 5: The railroaders gave up one *week's* salary.

Ex. 6: The three *months'* voyage was dangerous.

Exercise 1:   Add apostrophes or apostrophe *s* wherever they are needed.

1. My grandmothers healing powers were widely known.

2. Millions watched on their television sets as the astronauts spacecraft landed on the moon.

3. The attack on Fort Sumter aroused Emma Holmes curiosity.

4. Stores, vendors, and food shops make up Antiguas marketplaces.

5. The moon shone brightly on the Kiowas camp.

6. Much publicity was given to Douglass attacks on slavery.

7. After two years exploration, Lewis and Clarks expedition brought back valuable information.

8. Poor, orphaned boys good fortune is the theme of many of Horatio Algers novels.

9. Eleanor Roosevelts hope was to provide for everyones needs, especially the childrens.

10. Freedoms ideals are found in the Declaration of Independences words.

Exercise 2:   Add the possessive endings (*'s* or *'*) wherever they are needed.

1. Vanessa embarassment was noticeable as she thought about the parade.

2. The atomic explosion intensity amazed the onlookers.

3. The Nobel Peace Prize was awarded for Arias peace plan.

4. The Great Depression lasted until the decade close.

5. The escaping slaves morale improved as they made their way to Canada.

6. Anyone education can be improved by reading Webster dictionary.

7. Fantastic creatures are the products of Borges imagination.

8. The King Daughters arrival was celebrated in the streets of Quebec.

9. The crowds enthusiasm grew measurably during Dr. King speech.

10. After a few months hard work, the Chinese railroad workers efforts were still not recognized.

WHEN NOT TO USE APOSTROPHES

Do not use an apostrophe in these three cases:

1. Plural nouns ending in *-s* or *-es*:

   Ex. 1: Gatsby bought several expensive *cars.*
   Ex. 2: The *Holmeses* lived in South Carolina.

2. Present tense verbs that have *he, she, it,* or other third person singular subjects:

   Ex. 3: The Constitution *includes* the Bill of Rights.
   Ex. 4: Everyone *admires* the words of Chief Ten Bears.

3. Possessive pronouns: *hers, his, its, ours, theirs, whose, yours*

   Ex. 5: Rachel Carson believed that the world is *ours* to protect and enjoy.

Note: Do not use an apostrophe if two words are not contracted. Write *I am,* not *I'am.*

Exercise: Fill in the blank with the correct word in parentheses.

1. Danger faced the Pony Express _____ .
   (riders, riders', rider's)

2. Wondering if freedom was to be _____ , the slaves moved along silently.
   (their's, theirs', theirs)

3. The Panama Canal _____ Central America.
   (crosses', crosses, crosse's)

4. _____ success assured, Wang's company expanded.
   (It's, Its', Its,)

5. Environmental _____are of concern as the next century
   (issues, issues', issue's)

_____ .
(approaches, approaches', approache's)

Review Exercise: Add an apostrophe or apostrophe *s* wherever it is needed and remove an apostrophe wherever it is not needed.

1. The island of Puerto Ricos known for it's beauty.

2. Theres no doubt that pesticides mayve been misused.

3. Most tourists senses are dazzled by Canadas vast lakes.

4. That priests prayers weren't acknowledged by those Spaniards cruel leader.

5. The Remembrance Days celebration included veterans who's pride was apparent.

6. Its certain in an Alger novel that if a boy saved one weeks salary, hed soon be the boss favorite.

7. The Pilgrims childrens turkeys didnt take long to roast.

8. The Smiths and the Joneses of the United States owe a great debt to the early settlers democratic principles.

9. Wasnt it a dream of your's to memorize Lincolns speech?

10. No matter how long Bolívars soldiers sufferings lasted, the mens spirits stayed high.

COMMAS

The most important use of the comma is to separate words, clauses, and phrases so that the connection between the parts of the sentence, and the meaning of the entire sentence, are clear.

A. A comma is used with a **coordinating conjunction** to separate two independent clauses.

> *Ex. 1:* The astronauts landed on the moon, and their families watched the event on television.

The comma at the end of the first independent clause, followed by the coordinating conjunction *and,* separates the two clauses.

> *Ex. 2:* The weather for the constitutional parade was cloudy, but the sun appeared later in the day.

The two independent clauses are separated by a comma and the coordinating conjunction *but.*

The coordinating conjunctions are *and, but, so, yet, for, or, nor.*

Note: Do not use a comma alone to separate two independent clauses. This will create a **comma splice** (see page 389).

Exercise: Add commas and appropriate coordinating conjunctions to separate the independent clauses in the following sentences.

1. Eleanor Roosevelt traveled to all parts of the world she learned a great deal about people's problems.

2. The audience listened sympathetically they could not make Chief Ten Bears' dream come true.

3. The Kiowas were tired from their journey they set up camp for the night.

4. Environmental controls must be developed pesticides will poison the earth's atmosphere.

5. Columbus set sail for India his ships landed in the Americas.

B. A comma is used to separate an introductory **subordinate** (or **dependent**) **clause** from the independent clause that follows.

A subordinate clause is not complete by itself; it needs an independent clause to form a sentence and complete its meaning. A subordinate clause may be recognized by its use of such words as *because, since, when, although, if,* and other **subordinating conjunctions**. (For a complete list, see page 393.)

> *Ex. 1:* After Mary Antin came to the United States, she attended citizenship classes.

The introductory subordinate clause *After Mary Antin came to the United States* is followed by a comma.

> *Ex. 2:* If you want a good definition of democracy, you should read E. B. White's essay.

The introductory subordinate clause *if you want a good definition of democracy* is followed by a comma.

Note: There is no comma needed if the subordinate clause follows the independent clause.

> *Ex. 3:* You should read E. B. White's essay if you want a good definition of democracy.

Exercise: Add commas where needed to separate introductory subordinate clauses and independent clauses. In one sentence, no comma is needed.

1. When the slaves walked off the ship they all held their heads high.

2. After he cleared the campsite Lewis built a fire.

3. If you are interested in early American English spelling look in Webster's first dictionary.

4. Las Casas tried to stop the massacre of children because it was impossibly cruel.

5. While Gatsby flaunted his wealth there was a constant stream of socialites to his Long Island estate.

C. A comma is used after an introductory phrase of more than a few words to separate it from an independent clause.

> *Ex. 1:* After the constitutional parade, the crowd continued celebrating for hours.

A comma follows the introductory phrase *After the constitutional parade.*

> *Ex. 2:* Located in Chicago, Hull House became known all over the world.

A comma follows the introductory phrase *Located in Chicago.*

> *Ex. 3:* Counseling the immigrants, the settlement workers at Hull House provided much needed social services.

A comma follows the introductory phrase *Counseling the immigrants.*

> *Ex. 4:* To enter American life, Tip O'Neill's neighbors used political organization.

A comma follows the introductory phrase *To enter American life.*
Note: There is no comma needed if the phrase follows the independent clause.

> *Ex. 5:* Tip O'Neill's neighbors used political organization to enter American life.

Exercise: Add commas where needed to separate introductory phrases and independent clauses. In one sentence, no comma is needed.

1. Worried about the future Carson wrote "A Fable for Tomorrow."

2. After the Remembrance Day parade Vanessa came down from the tree.

3. To overcome prejudice Jackie Robinson had to discipline himself.

4. Addressing the Venezuelan Assembly Bolívar used his powers of persuasion.

5. Will Rogers spoke confidently of the common man in his radio talk.

D. A comma is used between words, clauses, and phrases that form a series of at least three items.

> *Ex. 1:* The children were suffering from rickets, pellagra, and malaria.

> *Ex. 2:* Martha Shaw traveled for days, showed great courage, and longed to see her new home.

Exercise: Use commas wherever necessary.

1. The names Armstrong Aldrin and Collins will forever remind people of the exploration of the moon.

2. City residents felt that they were oppressed by governmental decree by their own fears and by the walls that kept out the pampas.

3. Gatsby's mansion looked rundown seemed empty and was very isolated.

4. If Lewis and Clark had not drawn maps written diaries or come back with plant specimens, their expedition would not have been thought of as successful.

5. Wherever they go whatever they do and whomever they see, tourists enjoy being on Antigua.

6. Duniway advocated woman's suffrage property rights and equality of opportunity.

7. Just go to the north woods and you will sense the *Teakettler Hidebehind* or *Goofus*.

8. Attacking the Spanish positions raiding their arsenals and coming away with their weapons, Bolívar waged his successful military campaigns.

9. The staff at Hull House did not turn away any person who had no money who was suffering from disease or who did not speak English.

10. Jackie Robinson Larry Doby and Monte Irvin pioneered the breaking of major league baseball's color barrier.

E. Commas are used to mark an interruption in the flow of a sentence. Commas, in this case, are placed both before and after the intervening word or phrase.

> *Ex. 1:* Jane Addams, as a matter of fact, received the Nobel Peace Prize.

Commas appear before and after the phrase *as a matter of fact,* which separates the subject (*Jane Addams*) and the verb (*received*).

> *Ex. 2:* After the Great Depression began, however, the federal government developed public works programs for the first time.

Commas appear before and after the word *however,* which separates the subordinate clause (*After the Great Depression began*) and the independent clause.

F. Commas are used before and after an **appositive,** a word or phrase that renames a noun or pronoun.

> *Ex. 1:* Neil Armstrong, an engineer, was the first person to set foot on the moon.

Commas appear before and after the appositive (*an engineer*), which identifies the subject (*Neil Armstrong*).

> *Ex. 2:* Every sailor applauded the Panama Canal, a shortcut between two oceans.

In this sentence, a comma appears before the appositive (*a shortcut between two oceans*) and a period after, since the appositive ends the sentence.
Note: One-word appositives usually do not need commas.

> *Ex. 3:* Lewis and Clark's guide Sacajawea led them through unfamiliar territories.

The appositive *Sacajawea* is not set off by commas.

Exercise: Use commas where needed.

1. Imaginary creatures for example include the *Hidebehind* and the *Gillygaloo.*

2. Rachel Carson a marine biologist wrote *The Sea Around Us* and *Silent Spring.*

3. Learning English was difficult for some immigrants; Mary Antin on the other hand learned easily.

4. During the campaign, O'Neill by the way promised to lower taxes.

5. Thomas Jefferson the third president and the author of the Declaration of Independence was also an inventor and architect.

6. The sun always seems to shine on Antigua an island of great beauty.

7. Pony Express riders as a rule took the most direct routes.

8. Bolívar in fact liberated Colombia and four other South American nations.

9. The Pilgrims signed the Mayflower Compact a document in which they pledged to create a just community.

10. The orator Frederick Douglass spoke movingly about the evils of slavery.

G. Commas are used to separate the parts of a date.

> *Ex. 1:* On August 28, 1963, Martin Luther King, Jr. delivered his "I Have a Dream" speech.

Note: No comma is used with a prepositional phrase including a one-word date or the day of the month.

> *Ex. 2:* Dr. King spoke on Sunday.

> *Ex. 3:* Dr. King spoke on August 28.

H. Commas are used to separate the parts of a geographic location or address.

> *Ex. 1:* Mary Antin lived in Boston, Massachusetts, for most of her life.

Note: No comma is used with a prepositional phrase including a one-word location.

> *Ex. 2:* Mary Antin went to school in Boston.

Exercise: Use commas wherever necessary.

1. East Egg Long Island was the site of Gatsby's mansion.

2. O'Neill believed that Tuesday November 3 1960 would be the most important Election Day in his career.

3. Lewis and Clark set out westward from St. Louis on May 14 1804 and returned there in 1806.

4. Lincoln spoke on November 19 1863 in Gettysburg Pennsylvania.

5. The transcontinental railroad was completed on May 10 1869 near Promontory Utah.

I. Perhaps the most difficult aspect of whether or not to use a comma occurs with **relative clauses,** clauses that begin with *who, which, that, whom,* and *whose.*

Commas are used before and after a **nonrestrictive relative clause,** which can be taken out of a sentence without the sentence losing its essential meaning.

> *Ex. 1:* Chief Ten Bears, who was an old man, spoke on behalf of the assembled tribes.

Commas appear before and after the nonrestrictive relative clause (*who was an old man*), which is *not* necessary to the main idea of the sentence. The essence is that *Chief Ten Bears spoke on behalf of the assembled tribes.*

No commas are used with a **restrictive relative clause,** which is essential to the meaning of a sentence.

> *Ex. 2:* Most novels that Hemingway wrote are masterpieces.

No commas appear before and after the restrictive relative clause (*that Hemingway wrote*) because the clause is necessary to the main idea of the sentence. Take the clause out and the sentence reads *Most novels are masterpieces,* a sentence with a completely different meaning.

Note: In most cases, *which* begins a nonrestrictive relative clause and *that* begins a restrictive relative clause.

Exercise: Use commas with nonrestrictive relative clauses. Do not use commas with restrictive relative clauses.

1. The steam-powered locomotives that used to dominate the nation's railroads have almost disappeared.

2. Chicago which is the site of Hull House is the largest city in Illinois.

3. Bolívar who fought twenty years for independence became a much honored figure in his later years.

4. The lumberjacks talk of many strange and wondrous creatures that no one else has seen.

5. Arriving from France, the King's Daughters whom the settlers rushed to see were put under the care of nuns.

6. Las Casas and his guides traveled to many villages which were located near the island's coast.

7. Lee Iacocca whose company's problems mounted received help from many celebrities.

8. A Civil War battle that killed hundreds of black Union troops is reenacted in the movie *Glory*.

9. The bookkeeping course that Richard Hunter took enabled him to get a promotion.

10. Some Antiguan stores cater to those tourists who are looking for bargains.

COMMONLY CONFUSED WORDS

A/AN/AND

A is used before words starting with a consonant sound (even if the first letter is a vowel).

> *a* constitution, *a* soldier, *a* uniform (in this word, *u* sounds like the consonant *y*)

An is used before words starting with a vowel sound (even if the first letter is a silent *h*).

> *an* overseer, *an* immigrant, *an* honest person

And is a conjunction used to connect words, clauses, and phrases.

> Lewis *and* Clark; fame *and* fortune; of the people, by the people, *and* for the people

Exercise 1: Fill in the blank with the appropriate word: *a, an,* or *and*.

1. The right to liberty is _____ ideal mentioned in the Declaration of Independence.

2. Computers _____ electronic equipment were designed by Dr. An Wang.

473

3. Tip O'Neill became _____ candidate for Congress.

4. Mary Antin wanted to become _____ good citizen.

5. Knowing a person like Eleanor Roosevelt was _____ honor.

6. The Panama Canal is _____ huge engineering achievement.

ACCEPT/EXCEPT/EXPECT

Accept is a verb meaning "to receive" or "take gladly."

> Dr. King *accepted* the Nobel Peace Prize.

Except is usually a preposition meaning "not including" or "other than."

> All the Kiowas slept *except* the young hunter.

Expect is a verb meaning "to hope," "to wait," "to wish for."

> Nick Adams *expected* adventure on his train trip.

Exercise 2:   Fill in the blank with the appropriate word: *accept, except,* or *expect.*

1. Branch Rickey _____ Jackie Robinson to excel.

2. Nothing worried Lewis _____ the bear waiting on the shore.

3. All workers _____ the Chinese were included in the famous photograph of the completing of the transcontinental railroad.

4. Did Noah Webster _____ only American English words for his dictionary?

5. Will Rogers _____ the average worker's common sense to cure the Depression.

6. The King's Daughters would not _____ marriage proposals immediately.

AFFECT/EFFECT

Affect is usually a verb meaning "to influence" or "to produce a change in."

> Its losses will *affect* Chrysler's economic future.

Effect is usually a noun meaning "a result" or "an impression."

> Ten Bears' speech had little *effect* on the government.

Exercise 3:   Fill in the blank with the appropriate word: *affect* or *effect*.

1. Columbus's arrival _____ the culture of the island's inhabitants.

2. The environmental _____ of pesticide use has not been measured fully.

3. Douglass's speech on slavery _____ everyone deeply.

4. One _____ of the success of the Pony Express was the continued link with California.

5. Watching the moon landing on television had a powerful _____ on viewers all over the world.

6. Modern technology _____ workers and industries.

BEEN/BEING

Been is the past participle of *to be* and must follow all forms of *to have*.

> The atomic age has *been* a fact of life for forty-five years.

Being is the present participle of *to be*, or it is a noun meaning "something that has life" or "existence."

> *Being* free herself, Tubman wanted freedom for all enslaved human *beings*.

Exercise 4:   Fill in the blank with the appropriate word: *been* or *being*.

1. The green thistle, _____ an unusual sight, attracted many visitors.

2. Have you ever _____ to Antigua?

3. In Minnesota, there have _____ several reports of strange _____ like the *Teakettler* and the *Hidebehind*.

4. _____ back in her grandmother's house stirred many memories.

5. The Pilgrims placed their faith in a Supreme _____ .

6. Whitman's poetry has _____ called democratic in spirit.

CAPITAL/CAPITOL

Capital is a noun meaning "a city that is the center of government" or an adjective meaning "involving the death penalty."

San José is the *capital* of Costa Rica.

Capitol is a noun meaning "the building in which the legislature meets."

The *Capitol* in Washington, D.C., has a dome.

Exercise 5:   Fill in the blank with the appropriate word: *capital* or *capitol*.

1. The Wrights flew their plane over the _____ building.

2. Philadelphia was once the _____ of the United States.

3. The rebellion against Spanish rule was considered a _____ offense against authority.

4. Some state _____ , like those in Madison, Wisconsin, and Concord, New Hampshire, have gold ornamentation.

5. Ottawa, the _____ of Canada, is in the province of Ontario.

6. The Pony Express riders delivered the mail from one state _____ to another.

EMIGRATE, EMIGRANT/IMMIGRATE, IMMIGRANT

Emigrate is a verb meaning "to leave a country"; *emigrant* is a noun meaning, or an adjective referring to, "a person who leaves a country." *Emigrate* and *emigrant* are used when the emphasis is on the country left *behind*.

Mary Antin's family *emigrated* from Russia.

Immigrate is a verb meaning "to enter a country"; immigrant is a noun meaning, or an adjective referring to, "a person who enters a country." *Immigrate* and *immigrant* are used when the emphasis is on the *new* country.

Mary Antin's family *immigrated* to the United States.

Exercise 6:   Fill in the blank with the appropriate word: *emigrate, emigrant* or *immigrate, immigrant.*

1. The Pilgrims _____ from England.

2. _____ first to San Francisco, the Chinese later found employment on the railroad.

3. Lee Iacocca, the son of _____ parents, rose to head major corporations.

4. _____ from France, the King's Daughters looked forward to settling and marrying in Canada.

5. The settlement workers in Hull House worked long hours on behalf of the newly arrived _____ .

6. During the Great Depression, many people wondered why they had _____ from their homelands.

FORMALLY/FORMERLY

Formally is an adverb meaning "according to established customs or rules."

> Oscar Arias Sanchez was _formally_ inaugurated as the president of Costa Rica.

Formerly is an adverb meaning "in the past."

> The newspaper publisher Frederick Douglass was _formerly_ a slave.

Exercise 7:   Fill in the blank with the appropriate word: _formally_ or _formerly_.

1. _____ with the Kansas City Monarchs of the Negro League, Jackie Robinson joined the Montreal Royals of the International League.

2. Columbus _____ notified the king and queen that he had claimed the island in Spain's name.

3. The government officials greeted Chief Ten Bears _____ .

4. The United States built the Panama Canal, but the French had made similar plans _____ .

5. Puerto Rico _____ belonged to Spain; it is now a commonwealth of the United States.

6. To discuss the issues in his campaign for reelection, O'Neill _____ called a meeting of education, business, and political leaders.

IT'S/ITS

It's is the contraction of *it is* and *it has*.

> *It's* the parade celebrating a new nation!

Its is a possessive meaning "belonging to it."

> Grandmother's house had *its* own herb garden.

Exercise 8:   Fill in the blank with the appropriate word: *it's* or *its*.

1. The Bill of Rights has not lost _____ significance in two centuries.

2. _____ not simple for Canada to define _____ true north.

3. The Pony Express route had _____ scenic views and difficult mountain passes.

4. _____ hard to be certain if the strange creatures were really in the woods.

5. _____ not surprising that the Chrysler Corporation recovered _____ position under Lee Iacocca's management.

6. _____ been more than sixty years since the Great Depression started.

KNOW/NO/NOW

Know is a verb meaning "to recognize" or "to understand."

> The King's Daughters wanted to *know* more about Canada.

No is a negative answer or an adjective meaning "not any."

> "*No*, I see *no* signs of life here on the moon," Neil Armstrong said.

Now is an adverb meaning "at this time" or "immediately."

> Chicago's immigrants *now* rely on the services of Hull House.

Exercise 9:   Fill in the blank with the appropriate word: *know*, *no*, or *now*.

1. O'Neill soon learned that _____ election was certain until all the votes had been tallied.

2. Gatsby's mansion once bustled with activity, but _____ it stands dark and desolate.

3. Suddenly Vanessa cried to her grandmother, "I say _____ ! I won't go _____ or later! I _____ all there is to _____ about the parade already!"

4. Lewis and Clark saw _____ dangerous animals near their camp except every _____ and then.

5. Every citizen should _____ the effects of pesticides on the environment.

6. Did you _____ that _____ canal project of this magnitude had ever been undertaken?

PASSED/PAST

Passed is the past tense of the verb *to pass*.

> Traveling northward, the visitors *passed* Sudbury, Ontario.

Past is a noun or adjective meaning "time gone by," or a preposition meaning "beyond."

> From *past* experience, Las Casas knew that the soldiers had gone *past* the village.

Exercise 10:   Fill in the blank with the appropriate word: *passed* or *past*.

1. The Declaration of Independence lists King George's _____ injustices.

2. As the months _____ , it became evident that the Chinese and Irish workers were doing a superb job of building the railroad.

3. Chief Ten Bears was not comforted by his memories of a _____ when his people moved freely in their own territory.

4. When Richard Hunter _____ his bookkeeping course, he was immediately promoted.

5. Will Rogers told an anecdote about what had _____ between a banker and a family trying to hold on to its home.

6. Some of the evils done to the slaves are _____ imagining.

PERSONAL/PERSONNEL

Personal is an adjective meaning "private" or "of or relating to a person."

> Eleanor Roosevelt gave her *personal* attention to the problem of world famine.

Personnel is a noun meaning "staff, employees."

> The *personnel* at the Kennedy Space Center took pride in the successful moon landing.

Exercise 11:   Fill in the blank with the appropriate word: *personal* or *personnel*.

1. Wang Laboratories needed more _____ as it expanded.

2. The women went to the _____ office to apply for jobs in the steel mill.

3. Dr. King's "I Have a Dream" speech declares his _____ belief in equality for all.

4. The inclusion of many words of American English is Webster's _____ touch.

5. _____ pride inspired Mary Antin to become a fine student.

6. Major Anderson had to surrender Fort Sumter because he did not have sufficient _____ to combat the Confederate forces.

PRINCIPAL/PRINCIPLE

Principal is an adjective meaning "most important," or a noun meaning "person with chief authority" or "money on which interest is earned."

> The *principal* civil rights figure in the 1960s was Martin Luther King, Jr.

Principle is a noun meaning "a fundamental law or doctrine" or "a rule or code of conduct."

> Abigail Duniway believed in the *principle* of equality for all people.

Exercise 12:   Fill in the blank with the appropriate word: *principal* or *principle*.

1. The _____ of Mary Antin's public school instituted special language classes for newly arrived immigrants.

2. Bolívar was the _____ architect of Venezuelan independence.

3. What _____ of aerophysics did the Wright brothers rely on?

4. To Branch Rickey, Jackie Robinson's entry into baseball was a matter of

   _____ .

5. The basic _____ of cooperation helped to solve Chrysler's financial difficulties.

6. In the city on the pampas, the _____ character is the mayor.

QUIET/QUITE

Quiet is an adjective meaning "with little or no sound," or a noun meaning "the absence of sound."

   After dark, the Kiowas spent some *quiet* moments around the campfire.

Quite is an adverb meaning "completely" or "extremely" or "really."

   The Canadian north woods are *quite* peaceful.

Exercise 13:   Fill in the blank with the appropriate word: *quiet* or *quite*.

1. Grandmother enjoyed the peace and _____ of her garden.

2. Harriet Tubman's escape caused _____ a stir.

3. With _____ respect, the audience at Gettysburg listened to Lincoln's speech.

4. _____ early in the morning, the first floats were set up for the constitutional parade.

5. The lumberjacks looked _____ concerned about the unnatural

   _____ in the forest.

6. After the birds left, the woods were almost totally _____ .

SIGHT/SITE/CITE

Sight is a noun meaning "the ability to see" or "a place or thing seen," or a verb meaning "to look carefully."

> The ship's lookout hollered at the *sight* of land.

Site is a noun meaning "the land or place where a building stands or where an event occurs."

> The *site* of the massacre remained etched in the tribe's memory.

Cite is a verb meaning "to quote or mention in support of one's ideas" or "to recommend for an honor" or "to summon to court."

> Webster *cited* many authors in the definitions appearing in his dictionary.

Exercise 14:   Fill in the blank with the appropriate word: *sight, site,* or *cite.*

1. The _____ of speeches for the 1963 March on Washington was the Lincoln Memorial.

2. President Jefferson _____ Lewis and Clark for their courage upon their return from the western territories.

3. With a happy heart, Martha Shaw _____ her father in the distance.

4. Fort Sumter was the _____ of the first clash of the U.S. Civil War.

5. Despite the presence of leafy trees, Nick Adams _____ the Mississippi River from the train window.

6. The observers at the _____ of the atomic blast wore dark glasses; the brightness of the blast would have damaged their _____ .

STATIONARY/STATIONERY

Stationary is an adjective meaning "not moving."

> The train was *stationary* until the tracks were repaired.

Stationery is a noun meaning "writing materials." (You may find it useful to remember that the *-ery* ending means "lett*er*s" and "pap*er*s.")

> Many people are thrilled to receive letters written on presidential *stationery*.

Exercise 15:   Fill in the blank with the appropriate word: *stationary* or *stationery*.

1. The frightened coyote remained _____ until the Pony Express rider passed.

2. Wang was proud that his name appeared on the company's _____ .

3. In spite of their fears and tensions, the troops were _____ , awaiting Bolívar's orders.

4. Vanessa wrote a letter to her grandmother on personal _____ .

5. Lying at anchor, the _____ ship attracted the villagers' attention.

6. _____ supplies could be purchased in the mill town's general store.

THAN/THEN

Than is a conjunction used in comparisons.

> No one contributed more to the Declaration of Independence *than* Thomas Jefferson.

Then is an adverb meaning "next" or "at that time." (You may find it useful to remember that *then* is a word of time like *when.*)

> The slave ship sailed from Africa, *then* docked at Barbados.

Exercise 16:   Fill in the blank with the appropriate word: *than* or *then*.

1. Webster's dictionary contained more American English words _____ any previous work.

2. Faster _____ other groups of railroaders, the Union Pacific and Central Pacific crews moved through the mountains.

3. First the Kiowas searched for the home of summer, and _____ they rested.

4. The tiny plane increased its ground speed; _____ it gracefully rose into the North Carolina air.

5. On many occasions, Jackie Robinson stole second base, _____ third.

6. Democracy was less known _____ _____ it is now.

THEIR/THERE/THEY'RE

Their is the possessive meaning "belonging to them." (You may find it useful to remember that *their* and *heir* refer to possession.)

> The sailors returned to *their* ships.

There is an adverb meaning "at or in that place," or it is a word that may start a sentence or clause. (You may find it useful to remember that *there* is a word of direction like *where,* and a word of direction and introduction like *here.*)

> *Ex. 1:* The thistle was *there* in the middle of the city.

> *Ex. 2: There* was a need for a canal in Central America.

They're is the contraction of *they are.*

> The astronauts say *they're* confident about the space shuttle mission.

Exercise 17:   Fill in the blank with the appropriate word: *their, there,* or *they're.*

1. The U.S. commissioners were certain that Chief Ten Bears believed _____ promises.

2. When _____ examined, the children receive inoculations.

3. _____ experiments over, the scientists waited for the atomic test.

4. When _____ is a constitutional parade, it will take place over

_____ .

5. _____ are so many vividly painted houses in Antigua, it is no wonder the residents take pride in _____ neighborhoods.

6. _____ going to destroy the village, the priest thought as he ran

_____ in an effort to save the children sleeping in _____ beds.

THOUGH/THOUGHT/THROUGH

Though is the conjunction meaning "although" or "despite the fact that."

> It is true, *though* hard to understand, that there once was a color barrier in baseball.

Thought is the past tense of the verb *to think,* and a noun meaning "an idea" or "a way of thinking."

> Eleanor Roosevelt *thought* that international cooperation was needed to solve the world's problems.

Through is a preposition meaning "from one side to the other," "from beginning to end," or "by reason of," or an adverb meaning "finished" or "with a connection to."

> Once the parade was *through*, Vanessa walked *through* the yard to her house.

Exercise 18: Fill in the blank with the appropriate word: *though, thought,* or *through*.

1. _____ hard work, Richard Hunter rose from being a penniless orphan to a successful business executive.

2. The _____ of Jane Addams establishing the first settlement house in Chicago startled her well-to-do friends.

3. _____ the weather was not perfect that day, the Wright brothers scheduled a test flight.

4. No _____ of disaster went through the King's Daughters' minds even as their ship went _____ the worst of storms.

5. The Panama Canal workers were _____ with the blasting sooner than they _____ .

6. Dr. An Wang _____ he would start a company _____ many of his friends advised against it.

TO/TOO/TWO

To is a preposition meaning "toward, in the direction of," or a word followed by a verb to form the infinitive.

Mary Antin decided *to* walk slowly *to* school.

Too is an adverb meaning "also" or "overly, very."

Too much snow and cold weather gave some of the Pilgrims second thoughts about staying in Plymouth.

Two is the number 2.

In just *two* more minutes, the moon landing would occur.

Exercise 19:   Fill in the blank with the correct word: *to, too,* or *two.*

1. Tip O'Neill worked hard _____ ensure that his path _____ Congress would be smooth.

2. For _____ weeks, Columbus was not _____ worried about the amount of food supplies his ships carried.

3. _____ break free of Spanish rule, _____ of the Puerto Rican rebels planned a surprise raid.

4. Chief Ten Bears thought it was never _____ late or _____ difficult _____ hunt buffalo.

5. Did Walt Whitman plan _____ write poetry about the workers of America?

6. _____ get _____ California, the Pony Express riders had _____ face _____ many dangers _____ mention.

WEATHER/WHETHER

Weather is a noun or adjective meaning or referring to atmospheric conditions.

Hot and humid *weather* faced the Panama Canal workers.

Whether is a conjunction introducing an alternative choice.

E. B. White's definition suggests that democracy does not care *whether* a person is rich or poor.

Exercise 20: Fill in the blank with the appropriate word: *weather* or *whether*.

1. _____ permitting, the memorial baseball game for Jackie Robinson will take place later today.

2. _____ it's sunny or rainy, the memorial game for Jackie Robinson will take place today.

3. Some Canadians are uncertain _____ "True North" is a direction or a state of mind.

4. The Lewis and Clark expedition faced extremes of _____ .

5. The _____ vane on top of Rogers's house in Oklahoma spun crazily during the tornado.

6. Grandmother did not know _____ the herb would help to cure her patient's illness.

WERE/WE'RE/WHERE

Were is a past tense form of the verb *to be*.

The marchers in the Remembrance Day parade *were* tired.

We're is the contraction of *we are*.

"We're here to help the children," said the WHO doctors.

Where means "at, in, or to what place."

The Kiowas did not know *where* to find the home of summer.

Exercise 21: Fill in the blank with the appropriate word: *were, we're,* or *where*.

1. Holmes hurried to the harbor _____ the battle had begun.

2. _____ certain that Webster's dictionary had a great impact on literacy in the new nation.

3. _____ the Spanish troops willing to listen to the priest?

4. _____ _____ the escaped slaves going to hide?

5. The imaginary *Roperite* and *Gillygaloo* _____ thought to be _____ the woods _____ deepest.

6. If _____ to survive as a hemisphere, all the Americas must know _____ and when to confront prejudice.

WHO'S/WHOSE

Who's is the contraction of *who is* and *who has.*

> *Who's* speaking to the Venezuelan Assembly?

Whose is the possessive of the word *who.*

> *Whose* names appear on the Mayflower Compact?

Exercise 22:   Fill in the blank with the appropriate word: *who's* or *whose.*

1. During the 1980s, Lee Iacocca, _____ company was in jeopardy, went to Congress seeking loan guarantees.

2. _____ plan for the construction of the Panama Canal was finally approved?

3. O'Neill does not know _____ going to support him in the next election.

4. _____ marrying the Canadian settler _____ property is near the river?

5. The settlement house, _____ staff is on call twenty-four hours a day, does not care _____ been unable to receive help previously.

6. The leader _____ speaking on behalf of the tribe offers gifts _____ value could not be appreciated by the Spaniards.

WORSE/WORST

Worse is an adjective or adverb meaning "more difficult, bad, unpleasant," and is used in comparisons of two people or things.

> The economic depression was *worse* than anyone had predicted.

Worst is an adjective or adverb meaning "most difficult, bad, unpleasant," and is used in comparisons of three or more persons or things.

The Great Depression of the 1930s was the *worst* economic crisis in history.

Exercise 23: Fill in the blank with the appropriate word: *worse* or *worst*.

1. Nick Adams could not imagine a _____ job than the one he was leaving.

2. If working for Mr. Rockwell was the best experience possible, living in the orphanage had been the _____ for Richard Hunter.

3. _____ of all, Gatsby thought that he could return to Europe if he lost all his money.

4. _____ than the danger facing the Chinese railroad crews was the lack of respect shown them.

5. Her _____ moments came when Eleanor Roosevelt could not achieve her goals at the United Nations.

6. Many colonists realized that living under the rule of King George was _____ than risking their lives for independence.

YOUR/YOU'RE

Your is the possessive of *you.*

Is that *your* grandmother's garden?

You're is the contraction of *you are.*

You're an employee of Wang Laboratories, aren't you?

Exercise 24: Fill in the blank with the appropriate word: *your* or *you're.*

1. If _____ fond of folktales, read the stories of Jorge Luis Borges.

2. Are _____ relatives from Antigua?

3. _____ rights as a citizen are found in the Constitution.

4. Imagine that it's the year 1852 and _____ listening to a speech by Frederick Douglass.

5. Lewis and Clark told Sacajawea, " _____ our guide now and we trust _____ knowledge completely."

6. _____ the one responsible for preserving the earth for _____ children.

TITLES, QUOTATIONS, AND CAPITALS

A. You will notice in your reading that **titles** are treated in a special way to set them apart.

Generally, the titles of books, magazines, newspapers, plays, and poetry collections are set in *italics*. Titles of movies, television series, record albums, operas and other performances are also usually italicized.

To indicate italics, underline the words. (See page 495 on capitalizing words in titles.)

Ex. 1: *The Great Gatsby* was written by F. Scott Fitzgerald.

Ex. 2: Eleanor Roosevelt's picture appeared in *Life* magazine.

Ex. 3: Ernest Hemingway was a reporter for the *Toronto Star*.

Ex. 4: Did you ever see the play *The Cry of Lares*?

Italics are also used with unfamiliar foreign language words or phrases and with words or expressions when you define them.

Ex. 5: Grandmother placed salve from the *savila* plant on the wound.

Ex. 6: *Green* was a word unfamiliar to those who lived in the city near the pampas.

Exercise: Underline where needed.

1. On Tip O'Neill's desk lay day-old copies of the Boston Globe and Time magazine.

2. The Right Stuff, a movie based on Tom Wolfe's book, tells about the last great test pilots and the first astronauts.

3. In my grandparents' house were santos, pictures of their favorite saints.

4. The word freedom means many things to many people.

5. It is unfortunate that a play like Llorens Torres's El Grito de Lares has not been fully translated into English.

B. Quotation marks are used with titles of short stories, essays, newspaper and magazine articles, poems, and chapters of books.
   In addition, quotation marks are used for song titles and titles of television and radio programs.

> *Ex. 1:* "The Killers" is a famous short story by Ernest Hemingway.
>
> *Ex. 2:* Have you read E. B. White's essay "Democracy"?
>
> *Ex. 3:* "The Eagle Has Landed!" was the headline in the newspaper on July 20, 1969.
>
> *Ex. 4:* "A Cure for Depression" was broadcast over the radio in 1931.

Note: Be sure to place commas and periods inside quotation marks when appropriate.

> *Ex. 5:* We read Margaret Walker's poem "Harriet Tubman."
>
> *Ex. 6:* "A Fable for Tomorrow," the first chapter of Rachel Carson's *Silent Spring,* is included in this book.

Exercise 1:   Use quotation marks where needed.

1. Margaret Atwood's essay True North appeared in a special magazine issue devoted to Canada.

2. I Hear America Singing is written in free verse.

3. The Star-Spangled Banner was written during the War of 1812.

4. Did you see Culebra Cut, last week's episode of that new series about the Panama Canal?

5. If you want to get a quick insight into a girl's behavior, read A Bird in the House.

Exercise 2:   Underline and use quotation marks where appropriate.

1. Luisa Valenzuela's book Open Door contains a narrative called A Story About Greenery.

2. Both Robert Redford and Alan Ladd have played the title role in The Great Gatsby.

3. Because Latin words like ibidem and ab ovo were not commonly used, Webster defined them carefully in An American Dictionary of the English Language.

4. It surprises many people to learn that E. B. White wrote the children's classic Charlotte's Web as well as the essay Democracy, which first appeared in the New Yorker magazine.

5. A folktale, like Kiowa Summers, often has parallels in other cultures.

6. Originally a poem written in 1814 by Francis Scott Key, The Star-Spangled Banner did not officially become the national anthem of the United States until 1931.

7. President Arias's acceptance speech, Only Peace Can Write the New History, was eloquent.

8. In Rochester, New York, Frederick Douglass established The North Star, a newspaper that spoke out against slavery.

9. The story of the American Indian is told sympathetically in the movie Dances with Wolves.

10. I think The Great Railway Competition would be a fine title for a program in the How the West Was Won series.

C. Quotation marks are used for **direct quotations,** the exact words used by or between people in speech. They are also used when quoting material from a book, magazine, speech, or other publication.

Ex. 1: Dr. King said, "I have a dream today!"

Ex. 2: Lincoln stated, "Four score and seven years ago."

Ex. 3: The Declaration of Independence begins, "When in the course of human events."

Ex. 4: "You speak like a patriot," Don Cheo answered.

Ex. 5: Roberto told Maria, "I really liked learning about the moon landing."

Note 1: There are no quotation marks used when the exact words of a speaker are not given.

Ex. 6: Roberto told Maria that he enjoyed learning about the mission to the moon.

In example 6, the words *that he* indicate that Roberto's exact words are not being used. (Compare this to example 5.) This rewording of what someone has said is called a **paraphrase** or **indirect quotation.** It is often used in journalistic writing.

Note 2: A comma is used after the verb that introduces the quotation (see examples 1, 2, 3, and 5).

Note 3: If the quotation comes first, a comma is used inside the quotation mark after the last word (see example 4).

Note 4: The first word of the quotation is capitalized.

Exercise: Add quotation marks and commas where needed. Two sentences do not require quotation marks.

1. The mission commander said that the Eagle has landed.

2. Lewis's journal begins I decended the hill and directed my course to the bend of the Missouri.

3. The first line of Whitman's poem is I hear America singing, the varied carols I hear.

4. Arias's speech moved me with its simplicity and eloquence Teresa stated.

5. In Jamaica Kincaid's essay, she claims that Antigua is too beautiful.

6. Chief Ten Bears continued nor have we been made to cry once alone.

7. Benjamin Rush shouted at the end of the constitutional parade we have become a nation.

8. In *The Path Between the Seas,* David McCullough writes that the crossing at Panama would be one of life's memorable experiences.

9. I stole back to my Maryland to guide the slaves away declared Harriet Tubman.

10. Teachers, students, all people must strive to avoid a nuclear war concluded the professor.

D. Capitalized words fall into three main categories: the first words of sentences, proper nouns, and key words in titles.

1. Capitalize the first word of a sentence.

>   *Ex. 1:* When Nick Adams crossed the Mississippi, he had never been so far from home before.

>   *Note:* Do not use a capital for the first word following a semicolon.

>   *Ex. 2:* Yesterday Nick Adams crossed the Mississippi; he had never been so far from home before.

2. Capitalize proper nouns, names of specific people, places, and things.

>   *Ex. 3:* Rachel Carson was a marine biologist.

>   *Ex. 4:* E. B. White was a noted essayist.

>   *Ex. 5:* The Statue of Liberty greeted immigrants arriving in New York.

3. Capitalize such titles as *governor, doctor,* and *general* when they are used *with* the person's name or *in place of* the person's name. Also capitalize such titles when a person is spoken to. Do not capitalize titles that do not accompany the name of a specific person.

>   *Ex. 6:* Dr. Martin Luther King, Jr., believed in nonviolent protest.

>   *Ex. 7:* General George Washington led the troops at Valley Forge.

>   *Ex. 8:* "Hurry, Doctor, it's an emergency!" the WHO nurse said.

BUT

>   *Ex. 9:* The generals on both sides lost many troops during the battle at Gettysburg.

>   *Ex. 10:* The WHO doctor specializes in tropical diseases.

4. Capitalize the names of religions, nationalities, and languages—and the adjectives that are formed from these names.

>   *Ex. 11:* Columbus was Italian, but he sailed for the Spanish king and queen.

>   *Ex. 12:* The Chinese Exclusion Act was an insult to all Americans.

5. Capitalize the names of months and days, and the names of planets and other heavenly bodies. Do not capitalize *sun* or *moon*. Do not capitalize *earth* unless it is used with the names of other planets.

> *Ex. 13:* The Wright brothers' famous flight took place on Thursday, December 17, 1903.

> *Ex. 14:* Space probes have traveled not only to the moon, but also to Jupiter and Mars.

Note: Do not capitalize the names of the four seasons: *summer, spring, fall (autumn),* and *winter.*

6. Capitalize the names of specific courses, but do not capitalize school subjects (except for languages).

> *Ex. 15:* Mary Antin passed English 101 with honors, and she also did well in Spanish and mathematics.

7. Capitalize the names of important historical events and periods. Capitalize holidays.

> *Ex. 16:* Thanksgiving Day is celebrated in the United States and Canada.

> *Ex. 17:* The Civil War was an important period in American history.

8. Capitalize geographic regions, but do not capitalize compass directions unless they refer to a particular section of the country or the world.

> *Ex. 18:* Lewis and Clark traveled west of the Mississippi.

> *Ex. 19:* We live in the Western Hemisphere.

9. Capitalize all words in a title except for *a, an, the,* short prepositions, and short conjunctions (unless they are the first or last word).

> *Ex. 20:* Did you read Margaret Laurence's short story "A Bird in the House"?

> *Ex. 21: For Whom the Bell Tolls,* a novel by Ernest Hemingway, is set in the time of the Spanish Civil War.

Exercise: Capitalize where appropriate.

1. the antiguan marketplaces attracted canadian and american tourists.

2. echoing the stirring words of the declaration of independence, frederick douglass spoke to the crowd on the fourth of july.

3. in fact, i was there in oslo, norway, when president arias received the nobel peace prize.

4. on tuesday emma holmes wrote in her diary that the civil war between the north and the south had begun.

5. even with the sun shining down on main street, vanessa decided not to watch the royal canadian army veterans march in the remembrance day parade.

6. after jackie robinson's success, the major league teams began to scout for other players from the kansas city monarchs.

7. when doctor an wang spoke to students from the massachusetts institute of technology, he urged them to take physics 52 and other advanced science courses.

8. o'neill was greatly upset by the NINA ("no irish need apply") signs in the windows of stores along commonwealth avenue in downtown boston.

9. when the kiowas saw the shadows against the moon, they rested before crossing the arkansas river.

10. the history of the panama canal would not be complete without mention of the west indian workers, general goethals, and the doctors and nurses who treated yellow fever and malaria.

11. the title of e. b. white's essay is "the meaning of democracy."

12. the astronauts neil armstrong, buzz aldrin, and mike collins were congratulated by president nixon at the white house.

STRUCTURE:
PARAGRAPH
AND ESSAY

A basic structural design underlies every form of writing.

William Strunk and E. B. White, *The Elements of Style*

THE PARAGRAPH

Every piece of writing, whether a personal letter, an essay, or a report, has a pattern or structure. This pattern is called **organization.**

The most common type of organization is one with a starting point, a middle, and an end. This structure of writing may be seen in its most compact form: the **paragraph.**

The paragraph contains a sentence (usually the first) that states the main idea of the paragraph as a whole. This is called the **topic sentence.**

In addition to the topic sentence, the paragraph should contain examples, evidence, and specific details to support or illustrate the main idea.

The paragraph should end with a sentence that summarizes the main idea or that provides a bridge or **transition** to the next paragraph.

A paragraph with a topic sentence, supporting examples, and a summary or concluding sentence has unity.

A paragraph may be a complete unit by itself. In most cases, however, it is one of a series of paragraphs that make up the entire essay or piece of writing.

In the reading selections in this book, many paragraphs begin with a topic sentence that is then developed in the rest of the paragraph.

THE TOPIC SENTENCE

An example of a topic sentence at the beginning of a paragraph is found in Lee Iacocca's "Equality of Sacrifice" (see page 257). In this paragraph, the author describes the human cost in keeping the Chrysler Corporation alive after its financial difficulties:

> But the struggle had its dark side.

He continues the paragraph with details and examples that support the main idea stated in the topic sentence:

> To cut expenses, we had to fire a lot of people. It's like a war: we won, but my son didn't come back. There was a lot of agony. People were getting destroyed, taking their kids out of college, drinking, getting divorced.

Iacocca concludes the paragraph with a sentence that summarizes and restates the main idea of the opening or topic sentence:

> Overall we preserved the company, but only at enormous personal expense for a great many human beings.

This pattern of an opening topic sentence, details and examples in the middle sentences, and a concluding sentence summarizing the main point occurs in a paragraph from Rachel Carson's "Fable for Tomorrow" (see page 322). In this paragraph, the topic sentence is about the stillness caused by the disappearance of birds from a landscape destroyed by chemical pesticides:

> There was a strange stillness.

Examples and details follow in support of the opening sentence:

> The birds, for example—where had they gone? Many people spoke of them, puzzled and disturbed. The feeding stations in the backyards were deserted. The few birds seen anywhere were moribund; they trembled violently and could not fly. It was a spring without voices. On the mornings that had once throbbed with the dawn chorus of robins, catbirds, doves, wrens, and scores of other bird voices there was now no sound;

The paragraph concludes with a summary and restatement of the main idea of the topic sentence:

only silence lay over the fields and woods and marsh.

Exercise 1:   Read the following paragraph from "My Grandparents' House" by Eva Antonia Wilbur-Cruce and answer the questions.

The main feature of my grandparents' bedroom was the many prints of *santos* that covered all the walls. Sometimes a *santero,* a peddler of religious articles, would come by the ranch, and my Grandmother Vilducea would always buy the image of some saint from him that she did not yet have in her sacred collection. Room on the wall would somehow be made for it, usually by crowding the other images.

1. Identify the topic sentence.

2. Where does the topic sentence appear in the paragraph?

3. Which examples support or illustrate the topic sentence?

4. Identify another sentence that summarizes the paragraph's main idea.

Exercise 2:   For each of the topic sentences below, do the following:

A. Imagine how you might develop the rest of the paragraph. (You don't need to actually write out the entire paragraph; just jot down some ideas that you might include.)

B. Locate each topic sentence in the reading selection and compare your ideas for developing the topic sentence with those of the author.

1. We have also come to this hallowed spot to remind America of the fierce urgency of now. (King, paragraph 5, page 109)

2. Antigua is beautiful. Antigua is too beautiful. (Kincaid, paragraph 1, page 362)

3. My people have never first drawn a bow or fired a gun against the whites. (Ten Bears, paragraph 2, page 139)

4. When we got up, a wind of between 20 and 25 miles was blowing from the north. (Wright, paragraph 1, page 311)

5. Where is the north, exactly? (Atwood, paragraph 1, page 224)

6. Surely the Board knows what democracy is. (White, paragraph 2, page 343)

MORE ON THE TOPIC SENTENCE

In most cases, the topic sentence is the first sentence in the paragraph. However, the topic sentence may also appear at the end of the paragraph.

In "The Great Railway Competition" by Jack Chen (see page 144), the last sentence of the opening paragraph contains the main idea:

> On the plains, the Chinese worked in tandem with all the Indians Crocker could entice to work on the iron rails. They began to hear of the exploits of the Union Pacific's "Irish terriers" building from the east. One day, the Irish laid six miles of track, they were told. The Chinese of the Central Pacific topped this with seven. "No Chinaman is going to beat us," growled the Irish, and the next day, they laid seven and a half miles of track. They swore that they would outperform the competition no matter what it did.

In this case, Chen saves his main point until the end of the paragraph, using the earlier sentences to lead up to the topic sentence. This is done for emphasis and also to provide a transition or bridge to the paragraph or paragraphs that follow.

Exercise: Read the following paragraph from "I Never Had It Made" by Jackie Robinson and answer the questions.

> The next few minutes were tough. Branch Rickey had to make absolutely sure that I knew what I would face. Beanballs would be thrown at me. I would be called the kind of names which would hurt and infuriate any man. I would be physically attacked. Could I take all of this and control my temper, remain steadfastly loyal to our ultimate aim?

1. Identify the topic sentence.

2. Where does the topic sentence appear in the paragraph?

3. Which specific details lead to the topic sentence?

Some topic sentences appear in the second sentence or in the middle of the paragraph. This is done because the writer may wish to provide background information or create interest before presenting the topic sentence. Such a topic sentence appears in paragraph 4 of "The Promised Land" by Mary Antin (see page 283):

> So I was forced to revise my own estimate of myself. But the twin of my new-born humility, paradoxical as it may seem, was a sense of dignity I had never known before.

The remainder of this paragraph develops the idea of dignity, beginning with "For if I found that I was a person of small consequence, I discovered at the same time that I was more nobly related than I had ever supposed," and ending with the young immigrant girl stating that she must conduct herself "as befitted a Fellow Citizen."

THE ESSAY

Just as the paragraph has a beginning, a middle, and an end, so too does the essay. The essay, in fact, is made up of a series of paragraphs.

The essay often has three main sections: the **opening,** the **body** (or **development**), and the **conclusion.** The following chart shows these three main sections and what should be included in each.

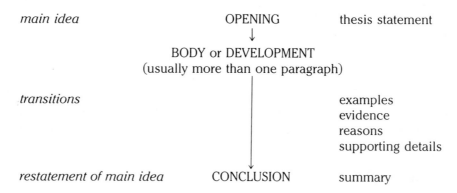

The opening introduces the main idea, the central topic to be discussed or the key question to be answered. Suspense, curiosity, or controversy may come from a good opening.

THESIS STATEMENT

The opening (usually one paragraph) contains the main idea of the entire essay in the **thesis statement.** The thesis statement not only states the essay's main idea, it also limits what will be discussed in the remainder of the essay. Therefore, the development paragraphs in the body will be able to stay on a clear, defined course.

In "Fauna of the United States" by Jorge Luis Borges (see page 194), for example, the thesis statement (which is also the essay's first paragraph) introduces the main idea (the unbelievable nature of tall tales) and establishes both a sense of place and a sense of wonder:

> The yarns and tall tales of the lumber camps of Wisconsin and Minnesota include some singular creatures, in which surely no one ever believed.

Exercise: Read the following openings and answer the questions.

A. Suddenly, at 5.29.50, as we stood huddled around our radio, we heard a voice ringing through the darkness, sounding as though it had come from above the clouds: "Zero minus ten seconds!" A green flare flashed out through the clouds, descended slowly, opened, grew dim, and vanished into the darkness. (W. Laurence, paragraph 1, page 318)

1. How does this opening begin in a suspenseful way?

2. Which words in the opening sentence create this feeling?

3. How does the second sentence develop the suspense and set the stage for the paragraphs that follow?

B. When we got up, a wind of between 20 and 25 miles was blowing from the north. We got the machine out early and put out the signal for the men at the station. Before we were quite ready, John T. Daniels, W. S. Dough, A. D. Etheridge, W. C. Brinkley of Manteo, and Johnny Moore of Nags Head arrived. After running the engine and the propellers a few minutes to get them in working order, I got on the machine at 10:35 for the first trial. (Wright, paragraph 1, pages 311–312)

1. Why is the first sentence an example of an effective way to begin?

2. Why are the men's names listed?

3. Why are the last sentence's final words a good way to end the paragraph?

BODY

The **body** (**development**) is the second section of the essay. It usually contains two or more paragraphs. These provide examples, reasons, and details to support the opening's thesis statement.

In "Fauna of the United States," Borges presents his first example of a "singular" creature:

> There is the *Hidebehind* which is always hiding behind something. No matter how many times or whichever way a man turns, it is always behind him, and that's why nobody has been able to describe it, even though it is credited with having killed and devoured many a lumberjack.

In the next paragraph, he presents another example:

> Then there is the *Roperite*. This animal is about the size of a pony. It has a ropelike beak which it uses to snare even the fleetest of rabbits.

Borges ends his list of examples by using the transition words *and finally*:

> And finally, there's the *Pinnacle Grouse,* which had a single wing. This enabled it to fly in one direction only, circling the top of a conical hill. The color of its plumage varied according to the season and according to the condition of the observer.

TRANSITION

The body (or development) paragraphs are connected to the opening and to each other by **transitions.**

Transitions are the links between sentences and paragraphs. These bridges in thought may be achieved by using synonyms, repetitions, or pronouns for nouns. Here are some examples of transitions:

Synonym (from Iacocca, "Equality of Sacrifice"):

> We were the underdog engaged in a heroic struggle, and *the public responded* accordingly. (paragraph 12)
> Many unknown *people wrote* to us, saying in a hundred different ways that they were with us, that Henry Ford's loss was Chrysler's gain. (paragraph 13)

Repetition (from King, "I Have a Dream"):

> I still have a *dream*. It is a *dream* deeply rooted in the American dream that one day this nation will rise up and live out the true meaning of its creed— we hold these truths to be self evident, that all men are created equal. (paragraph 18)

Pronoun for Noun (from W. Laurence, *Dawn Over Zero*):

> A great *cloud* arose from the ground and followed the trail of the great sun. At first *it* was a giant column, which soon took the shape of a supramundane mushroom. (paragraph 6)

Transitions also serve as introductions to paragraphs in the body of the essay or as a signal for the conclusion. Here is a list of some of the most frequently used expressions of this type:

To begin the development: first, first of all, in the first place, one example, one reason, to begin with, to start with

To continue the development: additionally, also, another, besides, furthermore, in addition, moreover, next, second, second of all

To contrast: however, nevertheless, nonetheless, on the one hand . . . on the other hand

To compare: in a similar way, in the same way, likewise, similarly

To close the development: as a last point, finally, lastly, to sum up

To present an example: for example, for instance

To indicate a result: as a result, consequently, therefore, thus

To indicate time sequence: after, afterward, before, beforehand, earlier, later, previously, subsequently, then

To conclude the essay: in conclusion, in ending, to sum up

Note: in almost every case, the transitional word or phrase is followed by a comma.

Exercise: Read the following sentence groups and choose the appropriate transition word from the list below. Use each word only once:

in addition	therefore
nevertheless	later
finally	first
next	

1. Some states opposed the formation of one United States of America. _____ , nine states did ratify the Constitution and a nation was born.

2. Frederick Douglass condemned the institution of slavery. _____ , he stated it was more evil than anything in the old world monarchies.

3. The Kiowas sought the home of summer, but _____ they decided to return to their home.

4. The Chinese immigrants helped to construct the transcontinental railroad. _____ , they found fellow Chinese excluded from the United States.

5. _____ Noah Webster compiled words and definitions used in the United States of his day. _____ , he began writing his ground-breaking dictionary.

6. Jane Addams believed that settlement houses could help the various groups new to Chicago. _____ , she, along with other women, established Hull House.

CONCLUSION

The last part of the essay is the **conclusion,** or summary. This brief section restates the main idea. Thus, the conclusion is a reminder of the opening of the essay.

The conclusion may also mention other questions still needing to be explored or discussed.

A conclusion of an essay, like a concluding sentence of a paragraph, brings the piece to a clear and fitting ending. The following is from "First on the Moon" by Neil Armstrong (see page 330):

> Touchdown: it was 3:18 P.M. in Houston, where the event had the most shattering personal impact; it was 4:18 P.M. in New York, where they stopped a baseball game to announce the news and sixteen thousand people stood in Yankee Stadium to sing, joyously, "The Star-Spangled Banner"; it was 6:18 A.M., July 21, at the Honeysuckle Creek tracking station in Australia, where a staff of about one hundred was hanging onto the touchdown by radio circuits. But the date that would live in the history books was July 20. That was the calendar date in the United States, the nation which had underwritten the incredible voyage with much of its treasure and a little bit of its blood. July 20: the aviator Alberto Santos-Dumont was born on that day in 1873; Guglielmo Marconi, inventor of wireless communications, died on that day in 1937. But as long as western civilization endured men would remember July 20 for another reason: that was the day three American astronauts named Armstrong, Collins and Aldrin put man on the moon.

Exercise: Read the following conclusions and answer the questions.

A. Today, thirty-five years after I founded the company, I continually hear people question whether Wang Laboratories can survive the competition with mighty IBM. My response is that the odds against Wang Laboratories surviving in 1951, and then growing to the size it has, were a lot worse than the odds of the company's successfully competing against IBM today. (Wang, paragraph 12, page 267)

   1. How does the first sentence suggest that this paragraph is the conclusion?

   2. Where does the paragraph seem to return to the essay's opening?

   3. In what way does the paragraph serve as a summary?

B. Hearken well to what I say. I have laid aside my lance, my bow, and my shield, and yet I feel safe in your presence. I have told you the truth. I have no little lies hid about me, but I don't know how it is with the commissioners; are they as clear as I am? A long time ago this land belonged to my fathers, but when I go up to the river I see a camp of soldiers, and they are cutting my wood down or killing my buffalo. I don't like that, and when I see it my heart feels like bursting with sorrow. I have spoken. (Ten Bears, paragraph 14, page 140)

   1. Which words in the paragraph clearly signal the end of the speech?

   2. Where else does Chief Ten Bears seem to be suggesting that he is ending his speech?

   3. Which details seem to summarize the main idea?

BRIEF
GLOSSARY

adjective: a word that modifies a noun or a pronoun.

  brave Bolívar   *some* rebels   *patriotic* ones

adverb: a word that modifies a verb, an adjective, or another adverb.

  King spoke *emphatically*; Columbus *slowly* walked *away*; the bomb is *very* dangerous; the astronauts moved *more* quickly.

antecedent: the word or words to which a pronoun refers.

  Martha Shaw kept her diary for forty years.

appositive: a word or phrase that renames a noun or pronoun.

  We visited Antigua, *an island in the Caribbean.*
  Neil Armstrong, *the first astronaut on the moon,* spoke to our class.

clause: a group of words containing a subject and a verb. A clause may be either **subordinate** or **independent.**

  The Pilgrims reached Plymouth, Massachusetts.

comma splice: see **run-on.**

conjunction: a word joining words or groups of words.

The railroaders worked hard *and* relaxed hard.

dependent clause: see **subordinate clause.**

fragment: see **sentence fragment.**

gerund: a word ending in *-ing* that acts as a noun.

independent clause: a clause that can stand alone as a sentence.

infinitive: the basic form of the verb, usually preceded by *to.*

Wang wants *to start* a company.
Ten Bears let the buffalo *go.*

main clause: see **independent clause.**

noun: a word that names a person, place, thing, idea, or quality. A *proper noun* names a specific person, place, or thing.

explorer   village   ship   democracy   bravery
Christopher Columbus   Mexico   the Lincoln Memorial

past participle: form of the verb (usually ending in *-d* or *-ed*) used with *have, be,* or a state of being verb. It can also function as an adjective.

the area was *polluted*; the immigrants looked *tired*; there are *unseen* animals in the forest.

person: the form of a pronoun or verb that indicates whether the subject is speaking (*first person*), is spoken to (*second person*), or is spoken about (*third person*).

First person	I walk We walk
Second person	You walk
Third person	He, she, it walks
	They walk

phrase: a group of related words without a subject or verb.

up the river   a young child   to sail across the sea

preposition: relates a noun or pronoun to another word in a sentence. A preposition with its object (the noun or pronoun and any modifiers) is called a *prepositional phrase*.

in the house   *near* the ocean   *between* the wall and the pampas

present participle: form of the verb ending in *-ing*. It can also function as an adjective.

the paraders are *marching*   you saw the *marching* band

pronoun: a word that takes the place of a noun. *Examples:*

I, you, me, my, mine, yours, yourself, who, which, what, that, this, someone, everybody, anything

run-on: incorrect sentence occurring when two or more independent clauses are punctuated as one sentence.

Tubman rescued slaves she took them northward.

A **comma splice** is a run-on that contains two independent clauses separated by a comma.

Tubman rescued slaves, she took them northward.

sentence: a group of words having at least three elements: a **subject**, a **verb**, and an **independent clause.** A sentence may be *simple* (containing one independent clause), *compound* (containing two or more independent clauses), or *complex* (containing one independent clause and at least one subordinate clause).

sentence fragment: incomplete sentence that lacks a subject, a verb, or both. It does not express a complete thought.

when Tubman rescued slaves
Tubman rescuing slaves
Tubman slaves northward

subordinate clause: a group of related words that contains a subject and a verb but that cannot stand alone as a complete sentence. It is introduced by a *subordinating conjunction*.

subject: a noun or pronoun that tells who or what the sentence is about.

Antigua is beautiful.
Words carry meaning.

verb: a word or group of words that shows the action or state of being of the subject.

Lewis and Clark *explored* the western areas.
Lincoln *was* a great President.

INDEX

Page numbers in **boldface** refer to the readings and to principal grammatical discussions.